THE PALE FOX

THE PALE FOX

Marcel Griaule and Germaine Dieterlen

Translated from the French
by
Stephen C. Infantino, Ph.D.

Originally published in French as *Le renard pâle*
by l'Institut d'Ethnologie, Paris, 1965

Afrikan World Books

THE PALE FOX

First English Edition

Originally published in French as *Le Renard Pâle* by l'Institut d'Ethnologie, Paris, 1965.

ISBN 978-1-60281-005-1

Manufactured in the United States of America

THE PALE FOX

TABLE OF CONTENTS

CHAPTER I — AMMA

CHAPTER II — OGO

3

LIST OF FIGURES

LIST OF PHOTOGRAPHS

INTRODUCTION TO THE ENGLISH TRANSLATION

Our attention was first drawn to the Dogon and their remarkable cosmology in 1972 when we received *Hamlet's Mill* by Giorgio de Santillana and Hertha von Dechend as a Christmas present. This fascinating work included several related diagrams and an excerpt from the introduction to *Conversations with Ogotemmêli (Dieu d'eau)*, an account of Dogon religious ideas imparted by one of the elders to the French ethnologist Marcel Griaule. Although our interest had been sparked, for various reasons we did not pursue the matter until several years later when we acquired a copy of the book. It left us eager for the elaborations published in a subsequent work co-authored by Marcel Griaule and Germaine Dieterlen, *Le renard pâle,* which had appeared in France in 1965. To our surprise we then learned that in the intervening years it had never been translated into English. We borrowed a copy of the French original from a university library in Southern California, and as we perused the text we became more and more convinced that a classic report of this caliber should definitely be available in the English language. Since it was evident no one had thought the enterprise worthwhile up to that time and, therefore, it was doubtful someone would in the future, we decided to explore the possibilities of producing an English rendition ourselves.

It must be said at the outset that our intentions might have remained unproductive without the help — moral, financial, and otherwise — of Hugh and Ruth Harrison, who have also continued to stand by through endless delays and setbacks. We wish here to express our deep gratitude to them both. It was at Hugh Harrison's suggestion that early in 1980 the Harrison-Moffett Publishing Group was formed by the Harrisons, my husband Blair Moffett, and myself for the purpose of publishing *The Pale Fox.* We sought a licensing agreement from Germaine Dieterlen, the heirs of Marcel Griaule, and the Institut d'Ethnologie in Paris, as joint holders of the rights to the original work. This contract was signed

in the fall. Toward the end of that year the Harrison-Moffett Publishing
Group was melded into the Continuum Foundation, a non-profit com-
munications enterprise. Translation work was begun by Stephen C.
Infantino in the summer of 1981.

It is beyond dispute that this translation of *Le renard pâle* will be of
value to those English-speaking scholars who are not sufficiently fluent
in French to make use of the original. However, we feel certain it will
not be consigned to oblivion in university libraries across the United
States, Great Britain, Canada, and elsewhere, but will appeal to many
among the general public who have a specific area of interest, such as
archaeoastronomy, Black studies, mythology, oral traditions, or comparative religion.

Additionally, *The Pale Fox* may find an even wider audience, for the
Dogon have been in the limelight a number of times during the 'seven-
ties, mainly in television programs. In part, these centered around the
"Sirius mystery," the puzzling fact that the Dogon, with no more aid
than the naked eye, have known of the existence of the two companions
of the star Sirius — a phenomenon that has generally been explained
away by attributing Dogon astronomical knowledge to outside, preferably recent sources.* Our translation is meant also for those individuals

---

*For those interested in the Sirius enigmas, we refer here to two statements by Griaule and
Dieterlen which, although rarely mentioned, are quite pertinent:
1. In 1931 they were shown a cave in Ibi in which the *kanaga* masks for that area were
stored. It is the Dogon custom to carve one of these masks for each Sigui ceremony held
every sixty years and related to Sirius and its companions. At that time, there were nine
masks, while the place of three more that had crumbled to dust could easily be recognized. This would date the ceremonies back to the thirteenth century. (*"Un Système
Soudanais de Sirius,"* Journal de la Société des Africanistes, Tome XX, Fascicule 1, 1950,
pp. 273-94.)
2. In a lecture given in 1970 (*"Les Cérémonies Soixantenaires du Sigui chez les Dogon,"*
Africa, Journal of the International African Institute, Vol. XLI, No. 1.) Germaine
Dieterlen referred to a very aged Dogon man who had participated in three Sigui
ceremonies: the most recent in 1969, the previous one that took place around 1909, and
once in 1849 or shortly thereafter, when he was still in his mother's womb, for even the
unborn are considerd to have attended if their birth takes place within nine months after
the event.
The first Western report about Sirius being a binary star came in 1844; the companion
was subsequently seen through a telescope by Alvan Clark in 1862.

who have been stimulated into further inquiries of their own, for it offers original source material (now in a form readable by all) which not only puts the question of the Sirius system into its proper setting and perspective, but, more important, presents the fullest recording to date of the cosmology of the Dogon — their spiritual heritage of many centuries. Furthermore, it confronts most occidental readers with a *Weltanschauung* fundamentally different from their own.

The subtleties of thought and consistency of development of the Dogon wisdom may lend credence to Professor Griaule's own opinion that it equals the traditions of the classical Mediterranean cultures. However, there is a crucial difference: the Dogon are a *living* society; their body of myths, instead of being the static lore of an extinct people, is the most active driving force of their existence. As is so amply illustrated in *The Pale Fox,* every aspect of individual life and of social institutions is modeled on their cosmogony in all its phases and permutations. In contrast to our own society which is almost wholly profane, the sacred being allotted a circumscribed and limited function, for the Dogon there is no schism between the sacred and the profane. As the universe is God Amma's creation, indeed, *is* Amma, it is sacred with all it contains from the infinitesimal to the infinite.

Thus, while to most of us the grains that make up our daily bread are merely the impersonal product of agrobusiness, to the Dogon they are lives endowed with a soul to be preserved between the harvest and the next seeding. Allied, moreover, to the "grains" that played a role in the creation process, they are both nourishment and sacrament. The stars and galaxies are viewed by few people in the West as more than accumulations of chemical compounds sweeping in their orbits through an empty space. To the Dogon they are inspirited components of a dynamic whole among which there is a constant exchange of energies; for like the ancient astronomers/astrologers, such as the Chaldeans, Chinese, Celts, Mayas, and other Amerindians, the Dogon are scientists and hierophants at the same time and thus concerned with both the physical and metaphysical realities of the universe.

Man, in the framework of Dogon belief, is the microcosm. As in many other cosmogonies, his body actually provides the imagery in which the intricate creative processes are expressed. The comparison of the human body as microcosm with the universe as macrocosm, is a classical method of teaching, because the human being is held to contain an expression of all the forces and energies of the solar system and the universe. If the Dogon speak more in sexual terms than do most traditions, it is because they regard the reproductive organs and functions as representative of the cosmic generative and creative forces.

Because it has taken much longer to produce this book than initially projected and costs have meanwhile risen appreciably, it has been necessary to take all polychrome drawings accompanying the text of the original and group them in one place in this English edition. Also, it proved to be technically and financially impossible for us to maintain the diacritical marks employed in transliteration of the Dogon language. Faced with the choice of omitting these or not being able to publish, we opted for the former. The small percentage of readers to whom they will be of interest are referred to the French original.

From the beginning it has been an important consideration with us that, through Marcel Griaule and his team of co-workers, a group of Dogon elders deliberately sought to make their systems of belief known to Western people; we feel this translation is a direct extension of their thrust.

Ida P. Moffett

ACKNOWLEDGEMENTS

Our special thanks go to John N. and Sarah B. Mitchell, Oscar Howard, Louis M. Moore, Robert Murray, Elizabeth Pegues, O. Donald Smith, Jr., and John Warder for their enthusiastic, sustained assistance. Under the able direction of John Mitchell, these leaders and members of the Black community in Minneapolis organized themselves as an ad hoc committee to seek funding for the production of *The Pale Fox,* since Continuum is not an endowed foundation.

Because of the committee's success we can here acknowledge significant fund grants from the Honeywell Foundation, the University of Minnesota Foundation, and the Jostens Foundation, all of Minneapolis; and from the Minnesota Historical Society of the twin city of St. Paul. In addition, besides their time and effort for the ad hoc committee, John and Sarah Mitchell, O. Donald and Helen Smith, Jr., and Louis M. and Harriett Moore made personal financial contributions toward our production costs.

Important help to the ad hoc committee and thus to this project has been given by Dr. Frank B. Wilderson, Jr., Vice-President for Student Affairs and Professor of Educational Psychology at the University of Minnesota in Minneapolis. Dr. Wilderson was instrumental in introducing to the committee Dr. Lansiné Kaba, from Guinea in West Africa, who is the Chairman of the Department of Afro-American and African Studies, and a distinguished Teacher-Award Professor of History, at the University of Minnesota. Drs. Wilderson and Kaba contributed informed guidance and counsel to the ad hoc committee.

At a time when obstacles to publication appeared formidable, we received much-needed encouragement and useful advice from Arthur M. Young, Director/Founder of the Institute for the Study of Consciousness, Berkeley, California. We wish to express our appreciation to Mr. Young for that and for continuing to be an interested friend of this project.

To all of the persons and institutions named here, Continuum Foundation extends warm gratitude not only for their material support but also for that extra dimension of value and meaning which their participation has imparted to this book.

FOREWORD

Intensive studies of the Dogon of the Bandiagara cliffs (Republic of Mali) have been conducted by expeditions under the direction of Marcel Griaule since 1931. Interrupted during the war, they were continued again in 1946. Since 1948, all have been funded by the Centre National de la Recherche Scientifique.

We wish to thank here all the organizations that have supported our efforts and made this publication possible:

— The Ministry of National Education
— The Centre National de la Recherche Scientifique
— The Museum National d'Histoire Naturelle
— The Musée de l'Homme
— The Institut d'Ethnologie
— The International African Institute
— The General Government of French West Africa: the High Commissioners, Governors, and Administrators for having graciously received us and for their support in the Sudan until the independence.
— The Institut Français d'Afrique Noire de Dakar
— The Centre IFAN de Bamako.

Since the independence, the government of the Republic of Mali has helped us to pursue our task. We thank them for their support:

— The President of the Republic of Mali and his government in particular:
— The Ministry of National Education and the Institut des Sciences Humaines of Mali.

—The Ministry of the Interior and the Ministry of Information and Tourism for facilitating our travels and sojourns and for backing us with their authority, as well as the Governor of the Mopti region and the Administrators of the Bandiagara region.

***

The investigations undertaken among the Dogon since 1931 by the members of the Griaule missions have been conducted principally in the villages in the Sanga region. Until 1939, the numerous visits at different times of the year have allowed exploration in nearly all locations in the plateau and cliff regions: almost every village or district chief was questioned.

Since the end of World War II, these investigations have been repeated regularly every year in the Sanga region; at different intervals in the communities of Iréli, Yougo, Arou, Orosongo, Nandouli, and Songo.

We herewith wish to thank all our Dogon interpreters, informants, and collaborators listed below, including those who passed away before the publication of this work.

A special mention must be made of our main interpreters:

Ambara Dolo, who has worked with us since 1931. He has not only translated the statements of the informants, but also supplied a great deal of information that revealed a profound knowledge of Dogon religious and social structures. He has produced and commented on very many of the ritual figures reproduced in this volume.

Amadigné Dolo, who has translated and collected a great deal of information and has participated in the collection of materials (plants, fabrics, pottery, etc.).

Koguem Dolo, presently a lieutenant in the Army of Mali, who has taken part especially in all the inquiries conducted by Marcel Griaule with Ogotemmêli.

All three men have, at times, accompanied us on our travels through Mali (in the regions of Lake Débo, Mopti, Diafarabé, Ségou, Bamako, Kangaba, etc.) and have taken part in parallel investigations among the neighboring populations — Bozo, Marka, Bambara, Peul, and Malinké — which have proven to be valuable to the knowledge of Dogon institutions.

We would like to add the names of those main informants who, since 1948, have supplied and commented on most of the information recorded in *The Pale Fox* with remarkable ability and untiring good will: Ogotemmêli, Ongnonlou, Yébéné, and Akoundyo Dolo of the Sanga region, the priest Manda of Orosongo.

We must also mention Douneyrou Dolo, now deceased, who was chief of the canton of Sanga, and his sons Laya and Ogobara, who have always helped us under all circumstances.

We also thank Apourali — who takes care of the safekeeping of our material in Sanga — Mégnou, Ana, and Denla Dolo, who devotedly served our cause during our stays.

For their patience, perseverance, good will, and zeal to instruct us, all of our Dogon collaborators are held in our highest esteem and gratitude. Let them find here the expression of our loyal attachment to a country and to a people with whom many close ties have been made, all in the course of long, fruitful investigations and during extended and repeated visits.

We thank here all of the Dogon people, the chiefs of the cantons and villages who, after the death of Professor Griaule had two solemn ceremonies performed in his honor in 1956, a funeral and "end of mourning" (*dama*), with the participation of all the inhabitants of the Sanga region and its closest neighboring groups.

The names of our Dogon collaborators are listed below in alphabetical order. The names of the tribe or caste to which they belong are shown as well as the area where they live:

SANGA REGION: those of this region bear the emblem and the name of Dolo.

AROU TRIBE:

Apourali	Lower Ogol, Sangabinou quarter
Barou Kommo†	Lower Ogol, Sangabinou quarter
Koguem	Lower Ogol, Doziou Orey quarter
Kenné	Go
Ongnonlou, patriarch of Sanga-binou	Go

Innékouzou,† a woman diviner, born in Dini, married in Doziou Orey.

Syémon or Yasiyemmé, daughter of Innékouzou, born in Lower Ogol, Doziou Orey quarter.

Yanindyou,† Koguem's mother, born in Diamini, Na.

Yadommo,† friend of Koguem's mother, born in Enguélé, married in Lower Ogol, Tabda quarter.

DYON TRIBE:

Amadigné	Upper Ogol, Pamyon quarter
Ambara	Lower Ogol, Amtaba quarter
Andyé,† *yapilu* priest	Bara
Akoundyo, † *yapilu* priest, son of Andyé	Bara
Antandou†	Lower Ogol, Tabda quarter
Apama†	Lower Ogol, Amtaba quarter
Denla	Upper Ogol, Pamyon quarter
Dogollé†	Lower Ogol, Doziou Orey quarter
Dogonno†	Upper Ogol, Do quarter
Dougodyé, chief of the goatherds until 1962	Bara
Douneyrou† and his sons Ogobara and Laya	Lower Ogol, Tabda quarter
Dényé,† Hogon of Sanga	Upper Ogol, Sodamma quarter
Goummoyana, totemic priest	Upper Ogol, Sodamma quarter
Iréko	Lower Ogol, Guinna quarter
Mégnou	Upper Ogol, Guendoumman quarter

Nyamanou†	Upper Ogol, Sodamma quarter
Nyamanou, healer and soothsayer	Lower Ogol, Tabda quarter
Ogotemmêli,† healer	Lower Ogol, Tabda quarter
Songouno, † Hogon of Sanga	Lower Ogol, Tabda quarter
Tabéma†	Lower Ogol, Guinna quarter
Yébéné, † son of Andyé, totemic priest	Bara

OTHER REGIONS:

Apégné†	Yougo
Dousso Wologyem†	Bandiagara
Manda, totemic priest	Orosongo
Nommo, totemic priest	Nandouli

SMITHS:

| Akoundyo† | Lower Ogol (Sanga region) |
| Baysembé | Dini (Sanga region) |

GENEALOGICAL GRIOTS:

| Ammadaga, griot of the Hogon of Arou | Iréli |

LEATHERWORKERS:

| Ambibé Badadyi† | Sanghi (Sanga region) |

* * *

The inspection of thousands of descriptive ethnographical index cards, the classification of collections (objects, insects, plants, etc.), and the publication of this book would not have been possible without the help of those collaborators and colleagues to whom we address here our sincere thanks:

— Madame Jeanne Ferrand, who read, classified, and prepared a great many documents for their insertion into chapters in progress.

— Madame G. Calame-Griaule, who reviewed all phonetic transcriptions and all translations of the texts in the Dogon language.

— Monsieur P. Martory, Mesdames A. LeRoy, D. Garde, O. Ducret, and Mlle. M. Hugon, all of whom have helped us on the material level (classification, stenography, correction of proofs, etc.).

— Madame Jean-Charles and Monsieur R. Sillans, who reproduced the figures created by our Dogon informants.

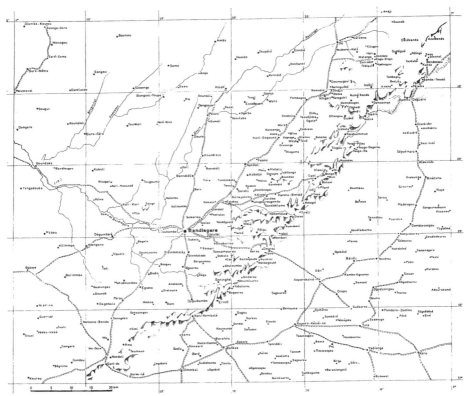

MAP No I — The Regions of Bandiagara, Sanga, Kassa (according to the I:200,00 scale map of the National Geographic Institute).

INTRODUCTION[1]

The Dogon occupy a territory situated at the border between Mali and Upper Volta, which is part of the vast primary peneplain at the bend in the Niger (between 14° and 15°5 north latitude and 1°5 and 4° west longitude). Dogon country is comprised of three regions: cliffs, plateau, and plain. Of these, the cliffs form the most typical and the most populated part.

There is no permanently running stream, but during the rainy season there are numerous torrents, which are soon dried up. The Dogon land, situated in the climatically transitional fringe between equatorial Africa and the Sahara, has a Sahelian climate, that is to say, four months of rain (from mid-June to mid-October) followed by a long dry season. The Dogon have made an effort to resolve the water problem by maintaining natural reservoirs, ponds, and watering holes, and by digging wells reaching depths of 80 meters into the plain.

The region suffers from an increasing aridity, made evident by the gradual disappearance of big trees and carnivores.

The principal tree species of the plateau are: *oro*, baobab (Adamsonia digitata), *ommolu*, tamarind (Tamarindus indica), *pelu*, cailcidrate (Kahya senegalensis), *yullo*, flamboyant (Parkia biglobosa), *sa* (Lannea acida),

---

1. *Note* — We have taken, either entirely or in part, the general facts making up this introduction from those principal published studies on the Dogon (*Masques Dogon, Organisation sociale des Dogon, Les Ames des Dogon, Les Devises des Dogon, La langue secrète des Dogon de Sanga, Les Dogon*) adding to them the findings of investigations conducted after their publication. These works are listed in the bibliography at the end of this book.

minu, karité (Achras parkii), *onugo*, jujube tree, *sene* (Acacia (Faidherbia) albida) . . . Trees play an important role in the life of the Dogon, from a practical as well as a religious point of view. They are used for construction and heating, many bear edible fruit, the leaves serve as fodder, etc.

The wild fauna includes hyenas, panthers, foxes, monkeys, crocodiles, reptiles, snakes, etc. Game is comprised of birds, pigeons, partridges, ducks, etc., leporidae, and antelopes. The ponds or watering holes supply some fish during the dry season, especially siluridae.

The sparse natural resources, animal and vegetable, are not sufficient to sustain the inhabitants.

The subsoil contains iron and copper, once mined by local industry, and black marble used for making bracelets.

Despite inexact census taking, due to emigration to large cities and to worsening conditions, one may estimate that nearly 250,000 Dogon inhabit Mali and Upper Volta. They constitute demographic agglomerations of widely varying importance, forming villages and small towns. Some groups of villages are connected and placed under the authority of a religious chief (Hogon).

In the plain, the Dogon — who then occupy a neighborhood — sometimes live in symbiosis with the Mossi and Kouroumba, each group occupying a neighborhood of the same village. There are two similar situations in other regions with the Bambara or the Songhai. The Dogon, who are farmers, maintain special relations with the Bozo, fishermen of the Niger, which the Dogon call *sorogon;* they are united through a cathartic relationship or "joking kinship," which implies the observance of a certain number of prohibitions and also mutual aid, both rigorously defined.

HISTORY.

Historically, the first inhabitants of the region seem to have been the Kouroumba, whom the Dogon call Tellem. They left many pise structures (dwellings, granaries, sanctuaries), particularly in the steep and most inaccessible walls of the cliffs; cemeteries, and also religious material, especially wooden statuettes of a remarkable esthetic quality.

Like the Kouroumba whom they supplanted on the cliffs, the Dogon claim to have come from Mandé. This region, extending to the west of Bamako, is the site of the ancient Mandingo empire of Keita, also called Mali, which dominated a great part of West Africa in the thirteenth century.

Now, simultaneously with studies conducted among the Dogon and Kouroumba, research on the neighboring populations, among the Mandingo, Bambara, Bozo, Samogo, Marka, and Fulbe in particular, has revealed the existence of an organization of these peoples that may be considered as international, and which may have been codified at the time of Sundiata.

The social structure of these different populations, who are united by kinship or marriage and, in some cases, by common origin, is based upon analogous principles and is strengthened by an identical cosmogonic myth. The ritual manifestations, though apparently different, reveal the same beliefs and originate from a comparable mental structure. In addition, within this system opposite social forms are conceived as being complementary and deliberately established — this complementarity being regarded as necessary to the functioning of the whole. This system is well known by the initiates in societies that have preserved their traditional religion as well as in those which have converted to Islam.

The principles of the unity of West African societies on a very large scale — a scale exceeding the one described in the preceding paragraph — are expressed during a septennial ceremony we attended in April of 1954. It brings the Keita and their kin together in Kaba (Kangaba on the map), a village situated on the Niger 100 kilometers up-river from Bamako, for the rebuilding of a sanctuary, called the "hall of Mandé." In the course of this five-day ceremony, Dyabaté genealogists of Kéla, traditionally the *griots** of the Keita, enter the sanctuary before the roof is put on and recite, each in his turn, the myth of creation of the world by the "word" of a unique God, the mythical and then historical genealogies of the Masaré or Keita and of the "families" related to them through alliances or kinship. These families developed, multiplied and, nowadays, constitute "populations." Related to these "families" (thirty in number) are not only all the groups of the Mandingo tongue, Malinke, Bambara, Dyoula or Kassonkhé, but also the majority of the populations of Senegal, the Sudan, the Ivory Coast, Togo, Ghana, etc.

"In addition, one of the geographic axes associated with the representation of this system is the course of the Niger from its source at Lake Débo. Its course is marked by settlements which, for the users of the route, delineate the stages of mythical, proto-historic, and historic events related to the development of the "families" mentioned above and to their territorial expansion. In each community, several places by the riverside are the subject of important rituals."[2]

Such is also the case with a certain number of other geographic locations or settlements, where sanctuaries and materials are to be found that are directly associated on the mythical, ritual, economical, and political levels with the representations we have just summarized: at Dya, among the Malinke and the Bozo, founders of the city; at Accra among the Gah and Fanté fishermen; at Koumassi and at Lake Bosumtwi for the smiths, who constitute a separate group, which is endogamous and of international standing.

Before their migration, the Dogon in Mandé represented a branch of

---

*The *griot* is the tribal oral historian. Trsl.

2. G. DIETERLEN, *Résultats des Missions Griaule*, p. 141. We give the list of the 30 families as well as the inexhaustible list of the population descendant from them or associated with this organization in *Mythe et organisation sociale au Soudan français*, p. 40-41.

the Masaré or the Keita; were they to return to that region, they would have the right to bear that patronym. They may have been natives of a village — perhaps present-day Dogoro — located in the Kouroula mountains which stretch between Sibi and Nyagassola, and the "descendants of Keita ancestors named Mansa Kourou and Mansa Kanda."[3]

Regarding their origin and history, the Dogon say that before occupying Mandé, the Keita lived in a vast region located on the same river bank as present-day Timbuktu, a region they call Dyigou. From there they traveled by river to live in Mandé. The Dogon of the Hombori region, currently called Dyomborou ("Dyon of Hombori"), may not have migrated westward, but rather gone directly to their present habitat.[4]

The departure from Mandé by the groups who were to form the Dogon people was caused by their refusal to convert to Islam: this took place between the tenth and thirteenth century. Their migration seems to have extended over a rather long period of time.

Generally speaking, and by taking different routes, they came towards the cliffs, which they approached from the southeast and where they first founded Lébéré Kan or Kani Na — now no longer in existence — situated near what is now Kani Kombolé. From there they swarmed in groups to their present habitat, after having shared with the members of other tribes the earth of their main altar, the altar to Lébé, brought from Mandé during their migration. They came up against the Kouroumba, who were occupying the cliffs and had come before them from Mandé,

---

3. *Mythe et organisation sociale au Soudan français,* p. 42, n. 1. This information was gathered at Kangaba and Bamako through our Malinke informants. This investigation must be continued at these locations and in the Kri region.

4. This recent information may explain the fact that certain Dogon and Kouroumba situate their places of origin to the east of their present home and not to the west (G. DIETERLEN, *Les Ames des Dogon,* p. 5, n. 3).

ONGNONLOU.

INNEKOUZOU.

AMBARA.

PL. I

YÉBÉNÉ.

MANDA OF OROSONGO.

NOMMO OF NANDOULI.

AMADIGNÉ.

DOUGODYÉ.

PL. II

APOURALI.

where they were called Kourouma.[5] The Dogon, who supplanted some groups of Kouroumba, nonetheless, lived for a certain time in symbiosis with others. The Kouroumba — some of whom had already left the cliffs by the time the Dogon arrived[6] — permanently abandoned the place to inhabit the plain.

An important segment of the Dogon first occupied North Yatenga (presently in Upper Volta). The Dogon of Sanga, belonging to the Dyon tribe, claim to have lived in Bousanga, a village located between Ouahigouya and Ouagadougou, inhabited by the Mossi.[7]

Whatever may have been the peregrinations of the various divisions of the Dogon during their migration, they already formed — according to their statements — four large tribes: Dyon, Arou, Ono, Domno. They traveled separately at first: respectively, the Arou beginning at Kan along the cliffs, the Dyon on the plateau, the Ono and Domno in the plain.[8] The Dogon still maintain very close ties with one of those tribes, even though they are presently mixed together in one area. For the members of the tribes are not grouped territorially: now a village or

---

5. G. DIETERLEN, *Mythe et organisation sociale au Soudan français*, p. 41.

6. In the Sanga region, the Tellem or Kouroumba had left before the settlement of members of the Arou tribe — the first Dogon inhabitants of the area. Caves put into use on the plateau — especially in the I and Tonloÿ valleys — were explored by members of the Griaule missions. Series of pottery and shards were collected as well as pieces of fabric. More than fifty skulls and numerous bones, collected from the Tonloÿ Tellem cemetery in 1952, have been placed with IFAN of Dakar, together with other bones uncovered at Bara, where they were the subject of studies conducted by Madame J. LESCHI, who has published her findings in two articles:

— *Premières données craniométriques concernant des Noirs dogon de la boucle du Niger, Soudan français. Variations des indices craniens*, pp. 160-168.

— *Quelques mesures concernant la tête osseuse des Noirs dogon de la boucle du Niger (Falaises de Bandiagara)*, pp. 185-195.

The series of bones from the second group mentioned in these articles, namely those found at Tonloÿ, concerns the Tellem (or Kouroumba), and not the Dogon.

According to repeated information, some Kouroumba of the plain would come by night to offer sacrifices at certain places in the cliffs where their sanctuaries used to be, especially near Yaye).

7. The long-term occupation had given the Dogon religious rights over the land; before the war in 1914, Mossi delegates came to ask the Hogon of Sanga, named Dyougodyem, for the right to settle in an area previously occupied by Dogon of the region. (G. DIETERLEN, *Les Ames des Dogon*, p.7).

8. G. DIETERLEN. *Les Ames des Dogon*, p. 23 and ff.

group of villages may contain families of different kinship.

Since their settlement, the Dogon, in turn, have had to submit to the authority of more powerful neighboring peoples: The Songhai of Gao, the Bambara of Ségou, the Fulbe of Macina and the Tukulor. French occupation put an end to the age-old struggles between the Dogon and their neighbors and promoted the settlement of the Dogon in the plain.

*
* *

LANGUAGE.

The Dogon speak *Dogo so,* "Dogon word-language," which borrows from Mande and Gjur, but has not yet been classified for certain. It comprises several dialects that sometimes differ considerably in vocabulary and morphology. Some of these are further divided into subdialects.[9] The most archaic are *Dyamsay,* spoken in the Seno Gondo plain, *Tombo,* spoken in different areas of the plateau: mottos, traditional prayers, ritual chants are most often pronounced in *Dyamsay.*

The instruction of the young children takes place early, because the Dogon, conscious of their linguistic diversity, "attach great importance to the purity of the language which, for them, is on a par with knowledge."[10]

There exists a ritual language, *Sigi so,* or "language of the Sigui," which is taught to the dignitaries of the Society of the Masks, *awa,* at the time when they take office during the ceremony of the Sigui, held every sixty years. *Sigi so* is a poor language containing about a quarter of the vocabulary of *Dogo so*; its words seem to stem from Gjur and Niger-Congo languages. The very marked contrast between long and short syllables accentuates the rhythmic character of the language, which thus lends itself to recitation. The Sigui dignitaries, the *olubaru,* are skilled in declaiming in the Sigui language the story of the creation of

---

9. G. CALAME-GRIAULE, *Les Dialectes dogon,* p. 68. See in this article the map showing the distribution of dialects, p. 64.

10. G. CALAME-GRIAULE, idem, pp. 70-71.

the universe, of human life, and of the advent of death on Earth, during funeral ceremonies and the rites of the "end of mourning," *dama*.

* * *

MATERIAL LIFE.

On the plateau, the Dogon groups have established their settlements on the rocks, so as not to occupy any of the arable soil so vital to their needs.

On the cliffs, a village is often backed against the walls of a fault or in the scree; access is sometimes difficult. On the plain, however, where arable land is not lacking, the village has been able to spread out.

The village includes the public domain, granaries for common use, *toguna* or "shelters of men," where the tribesmen meet, huts for menstruating women at the edge of the village, altars of public cults, wells, and watering holes. They are generally composed of neighborhoods whose inhabitants are grouped around one or more family "houses" *(ginna)*. Each family has its own granaries. Members of castes, smiths and shoemakers, live either close to the village in isolated houses or, like the others, grouped together in neighborhoods.

Living quarters, granaries, and sanctuaries are made of clay bricks mixed with straw and dried in the sun; the walls are coated and smoothed over with clay. A house is generally rectangular, sometimes flanked by semicircular rooms with a terrace on top. The rooms have small dimensions and are often poorly lighted: a hole in the ceiling allows the smoke to escape. One climbs to the upper floors by a ladder made of a large carved forked branch. The granaries are identifiable by their circular or square base; one enters through a small opening, placed up high, reached by a ladder; a wooden shutter closes it. The interior is divided up to the third of its height into a variable number of compartments. Placed above the intersection of the walls is a clay pot containing seeds and objects of value.

The main house is surrounded by annexes — women's quarters, granaries, stables, and storehouses — which together form a closed courtyard, entered through a passage opening onto the street.

The Dogon are farmers, and agriculture is the basis of their economy. In the plain, the problem of parceling out arable land is non-existent, as it stretches as far as the user desires. But on the cliffs and the plateau, "practically all that is not rock is used, even at a great distance from the villages. The smallest amount of surface is utilized. To bring their gardens closer to the water, gardeners erect entire artificial terraces with the aid of low stone walls, which often enclose extremely small spaces. Elsewhere, by means of ladders, access is gained to miniscule fields set up on isolated rocks. The worker is not deterred by any incline, and certain hills and rocky mountainsides are utilized from top to bottom. In the stream beds, one observes some plots of less than twenty square meters. Sometimes a hollow containing a bit of soil affords the growth of five or six millet shoots."[11] The many different methods of soil cultivation established by the Dogon are admired by everyone who visits the region, for this has permitted this industrious and brave people to maintain their internal economy to this day.

The agricultural cycle regulates the calendar. The year begins toward mid-October with the millet harvest, celebrated with a feast. The year includes twelve moons of thirty days divided into five-day weeks. There are four seasons: *bago* (beginning of the dry-season), *nay banu* (full dry-season), *bado* (month of May, last moon before the rains), *dine* (rainy season).

During the rainy season, the entire able population works in the fields; the men do the heavy labor, the women and children help by keeping away animals that are harmful to the crops.

---

11. M. GRIAULE, *Masques dogon,* p. 10.

Millet and sorghum are sown in mid-June. Using hoes, the men dig shallow holes; the women and children drop in the seeds and level the soil. Weeding takes place twice during the growing season, with the help of the entire family. The harvest takes place in October. The men cut the stalks, which the women and children bundle and bring back to the village.

Rice is sown one month after the millet and harvested one month earlier. The seeds are sown broadcast. Men, women, and children quickly turn the soil with their hoes to bury the seeds in the ground. The field is flooded, and the rains will keep it so until the harvest. The stems are cut with a sickle, left to dry, and later flailed in mid-air.

The cultivation of the *po (Digitaria exilis)** is easy and not time-consuming as it requires little care. The seeds are sown broadcast into a millet field, which has been left fallow. Weeding is done after the sprouting of the first shoots, which are tiny and fall quickly. Therefore, they must be flailed immediately after the harvest. The cultivation of the *po* is the subject of special events in the life of the Dogon, made evident by the reversal of social situations and a great freedom of language. The entire neighborhood takes part in the reaping of the field of every family head, the elders harvesting before the young. In addition, the flailing of the *po* takes place at night and all the young people of both sexes must participate under penalty of a fine.

Onions are cultivated on large surfaces and intended for export. They are crushed, packed into balls, sun-dried, and sold by peddlers in the regional markets, or sent to Mopti for exportation.

Certain fields near water sources are used for market gardening, for condiments (tomatoes and red peppers), and also for tobacco. The produce of each field is the personal property of the person who has looked after it.

Arboriculture is highly developed: species that can be used as food for people and domestic animals, for building, and as tools are planted at the edge of the village which they protect by their shade. The Dogon raise domestic animals. Mules serve as transportation; poultry, goats,

---

*fonio

sheep, and cattle are raised for food. Meat is rarely consumed, except on market days when a steer or some sheep are slaughtered. Some domestic animals are also killed during sacrificial ceremonies.

Hunting, much reduced due to the progressively worsening drought and the scarcity of game, is done by the men during the dry season and supplies the inhabitants with only a passing bit of nourishment. Fishing, generally collective, also takes place in the dry season. All the inhabitants of the area participate and receive in exchange a part of the catch, the most important share going to the owners of the pond. The fish is dried, smoked, and kept for use in making sauces.

In addition, fruits are gathered from cultivated and wild trees, honey is collected, and vegetable oils are prepared: sesame oil, karité oil, etc.

Food preparation is the work of the women and girls: they make porridges from all sorts of grain, they prepare cooked vegetables, grilled meats, bean-fritters, sauces made with a great many condiments, and millet beer.[12]

Besides agriculture and herding, the Dogon dedicate themselves to several other activities, performed according to a rigorous division by sex.

Pottery is essentially a feminine activity. Some women make an industry of it. Theirs is a modeling technique. They form a truncated cone from clay and drop a heavy roller in the middle. With the help of the roller, they beat and press the clay so as to fashion it. The outside is usually decorated with relief designs. The pottery, placed to dry in the shade, must bake for twelve consecutive hours.

The women pick, card, and spin cotton in their homes. The spinner works seated on the ground; she twists the fiber by rotating a bobbin held in her right hand, and holding the mass of fiber from which the thread comes in her left.

Dyeing is a technique often practiced by women. The usual colors are white, red, yellow, and black. Dyeing in indigo is the specialty of the wives of shoemakers. They dye the skins or fabrics. In order to dye, a

---

12. Cf. G. DIETERLEN and G. CALAME-GRIAULE, *l'Alimentation Dogon*.

ditch is dug in the ground and sealed with water in which some *yullo* bark had softened. It is filled with water, and an indigo cake is thrown in. After three days the dye is ready. The fabric is soaked for several days and dried. The cloths may be decorated in batik, that is, by covering certain parts so they cannot be touched by the dye.

Weaving and basketry are masculine activities. Weavers, who belong to all classes of society, work sometimes in wool, but especially in cotton. The looms are usually set up in the middle of the village or at crossroads.

Metalwork, woodwork, and leatherwork are performed by members of castes. The smiths, *iru,* often inhabit special sections at the edge of the village, where they live separately from the rest of the population. As artisans, they do not cultivate the earth, but manufacture all tools necessary for agriculture, as well as arms for hunting or fishing. A great number of ritual objects (in wood or metal) must be manufactured exclusively by the smith. In the past they were paid in kind for their labor. The smith occupies a separate, yet prominent place in society. Considered as the civilizing mythical hero, he plays an important role in initiation.

Leatherwork is practiced by the caste of shoemakers *(dam)*, who also live at the fringes of Dogon society. They buy sheepskins and goatskins for tanning or sometimes for dyeing, and make them into satchels, belts, sandals, saddles, bracelets, etc.

In the neighboring regions of Sanga, commercial trading takes place at the market held every day (the Dogon week is five days long) in the different settlements: the first four days of the week each bearing the name of the village where the market is held, the final day being *dambay* "forbidden day" (which means: "for the working of the ritual fields").

Each sells his own products: the women sell grains and other plant-foods, wood, indigo cakes; the men sell meat; the Fulani women bring the products of their herds.

At the market, regional merchants or traders sell manufactured import items, sugar, salt, and dried fish from Mopti. They buy local products for resale to the Bozo of Mopti, who transport them by dug-out canoe to more distant markets. The exportation of packed dried onions constitutes an important economic resource of the Dogon: merchants transport them by truck as far as the Ivory Coast and Ghana.

SOCIETY.

Dogon society, complex at first glance, is in fact rigorously divided into numerous opposite and complementary social groups; the masculine domain is opposite the feminine, the initiates are opposite the non-initiates, the different classes of age separate and distinct, etc. Thus it forms a complex system of different types of social relations, through which the respective statutes of its members are lived and expressed.

On a larger scale, the Dogon, as farmers, are opposite the caste members (artisans, griots), with regard to whom they maintain a strict exogamy, but with whom they live in symbiosis from a viewpoint of technical, economic, and religious complementarity.

Meanwhile, among the Dogon, as elsewhere, the social, political, and economic organizations are interdependent with the system of beliefs, this being in function of a general apprehension in their social life, of the supernatural world, the world of the living, and that of the ancestors.

The establishment of a settlement, the land regulations and everything that is connected with it are, of course, included in this unitary system: one can neither buy nor sell land where an ancestor of the tribe, clan, or lineage has settled. Each one, according to his rank in the social hierarchy, has the right to develop a parcel of land of which he has temporary possession or usufruct, and the allocation of which adheres to strict rules within the lineage at the time when its chief succeeds his deceased "brother" or father.

CULTS.

The principal cults are devoted to:

1) the supreme god Amma, creator of the universe;

2) the first living and moving creatures created by Amma, i.e., Nommo Monitors, "ancestors" of man, to whom Amma entrusted a part of the management of the universe, specifically to the first three, the Nommo *die,* the Nommo *titiyayne,* and *o* Nommo. The first two reside with

Amma in the empyreal sky. The third is the "father" of man. He was sacrificed to heaven to atone for the misdeeds of his twin, the fourth Nommo, shaper of the Earth, who had fallen and been transformed into the Fox; later resurrected, he has ever since resided in the water, his domain;

3) the "ancestors" of the four lineages, the "sons" of the sacrificed and resurrected Nommo, respectively Amma Sérou, Lébé Sérou, Binou Sérou, Dyongou Sérou, and their female twins; together they are symbolically considered as the apical "eight ancestors" of the four Dogon tribes.

By strict division, these mythical beings are, under "Amma's eye," responsible for the working of the world. They are the guardians of life, holders and protectors of the spiritual principles of man and of grain, the basis of human sustenance. The agents of the principal cults are their witnesses: they symbolically represent some of these personages and, at the same time, are ministers of the cults consecrated to them.

All cults, regardless of their specific character, address themselves first to God Amma, then to his three deputies, celestial and terrestrial; and this pertains to all levels of territorial and social organization: lineage, clan, village, or region. As for the three Monitors, they are distinguished according to the status or role of the mythical personality in question and to the size and character of the group. For example: the lineage and clan worship the sacrificed Nommo as the holder and protector of the spiritual principle of man and grain; the whole village worships him as the reorganizer of the universe that was disturbed by the misdeeds of the Fox, and as the protector of all its inhabited territory.

This being said, the extremely complex Binou cult is devoted to the sacrificed Nommo, but on the level of the totemic clan; each clan corresponds to one of the parts of the dismembered body, while all the clans together represent the entire resurrected body.

The Lébé cult is devoted to the ancestor Lébé Sérou who, in the beginning, was responsible for the integrity of the cultivated land, and was sacrificed on Earth for reasons similar to those which necessitated the sacrifice of the Nommo in Heaven: in this case worship is rendered on a territorial basis (groups of villages, regions).

The Society of Masks, which includes all circumcised men, worships, through its dignitaries, the ancestor Dyongou Sérou, hunter and healer, who died following the violation of a prohibition. As a result of this event, death appeared in the terrestrial and human world. This cult includes the inhabitants of only certain regions of the plateau and cliffs.

A cult is devoted to the ancestors of every lineage in the house that was the first to be built and is the main one in the quarter where the group in question lives and where the altars that have been raised are the responsibility of the patriarch who occupies the dwelling.

4) the Fox, witness of the "ancestor" who formed the Earth, cast down by Amma for having introduced disorder and impurity at the time of the creation of the universe. By his traces left in the sand of the divination tables, he reveals to men their destiny. In every village the diviners, who form a society of their own, are the ministers of this cult.

TRIBES.

Social organization is based primarily on a four-part system, not unique to the Dogon, who consist of four principal tribes, as do other peoples.[13]

The four great Dogon tribes are called Dyon, Arou, Ono, and Domno. Theoretically, they are considered to be the replica of the four mythical lineages of humanity's four male "ancestors," respectively Amma Sérou, Lébé Sérou, Binou Sérou, Dyongou Sérou. The word *seru* means "witness"; the term symbolically relates to the functions of those in charge of the present main Dogon cults.

LINEAGE, GINNA, *AND THE CULT OF THE ANCESTORS.*

The heart of Dogon society is the extended family, *togu* or *ginna,* both patrilinear and patrilocal.

Each village is composed of a certain number of exogamous extended lineages grouped in neighborhoods; each lineage has collective rights to cultivation areas.

"The *togu* originally referred to the four 'ancestors' and their wives, descended from the same 'father' and inhabiting the same house, *ginna*

---

13. Cf. G. DIETERLEN, *Mythe et organisation sociale au Soudan français,* p. 41; A.H. BA and G. DIETERLEN, *Koumen, Texte initiatique des Pasteurs Peul,* p. 10.

(contraction for *ginu na* 'big house'). As a result of this common origin, the Dogon claim to be all descended from the 'same *togu*' *(togu tumoy)*, the 'only *togu*' *(togu turu)*; the term, in its strictest sense, presently applies to all individuals belonging to a common exogamous family and related to the same *ginna*. Because of the development of its branches, a *ginna* may be subdivided into several small families *(tire togu)* spatially grouped in dwellings around the 'big house' and dependent upon it."[14]

The term *ginna* designates the members of a lineage as well as the dwelling of its founder and the land that is the common property of the group. By extension, the term also designates the "neighborhood," that is to say, the group of dwellings built around the founder's house, which thus assigns a common residence to the lineage. Thus, each village is composed of a certain number of exogamous extended lineages, grouped in neighborhoods; each lineage claims collective rights to cultivation areas.

The administration of the *ginna* is the duty of the *ginna bana,* patriarch of the lineage, the oldest man of the oldest generation of the common ancestor's descendants. In his decisions and actions, the *ginna bana* must keep in mind the opinion of the members of the lineage; nevertheless, his authority is incontestable.

At the time he takes office, he makes a redistribution of property: he takes possession of the *ginna,* leaving his old house to the one who comes after him. Then he redistributes the lands according to age, down to the youngest, because the property is inalienable and is passed on within the familial group.

He must reside in the founder's house, which contains the altars consecrated to God the creator, Amma, to the sacrificed Nommo, "father of man," and to the ancestors of the lineage *(vageu)*. He manages the material and spiritual well-being of the group and ensures the worship of the community of which he is the priest. He gives the newborn their names, is responsible for the consecration of the pottery of the dead in the altar of the ancestors, for the regular performance of sacrifices to their souls, and for the rituals during the agricultural year: purification before seeding, offerings of the first fruits, and closing of the harvest ceremonies (winter solstice).

---

14. G. DIETERLEN, *Parenté et mariage chez les Dogon,* p. 113 and 114.

Within his lineage, an individual is always situated in relation to four ascendent and four descendent generations. Similarly when offering sacrifices, a given individual calls his ancestors by name only until the fifth generation, saying after the sixth: "May all those who have passed on come and drink." This structure corresponds to the Dogon establishment of a system of kinship and marriage extending over five generations for the four mythical lineages.

As for marriage, the Dogon presently practice a general exchange among the four original tribes. Exogamy is the rule within the parental group, the *ginna;* the ideal mate is the daughter of a maternal uncle. This and other customs are indicative of the presence of a system of kinship through the women in which the maternal uncle plays an important role.

"Marriage is called *ya di,* literally 'taking wife.' The polygamous Dogon call their first wife, chosen by the parents at childhood, *yabiru* (work wife). The term alludes to the payment the fiancé must make to his parents-in-law *(igebiru).* Women married afterwards are called *yakezu* (separate wife), because they are either engaged, or have been divorced from their first husband. No payment is to be made to his parents-in-law by the husband of a *yakezu* who is called *anakezu.*"[15]

"The settlement of the family group on the land and the sharing of the soil is associated with the sharing of wives. Although a married woman remains a member of her clan and of her father's *ginna* and enjoys a certain autonomy during her entire life, the Dogon marriage is nevertheless solidly established: the wife, at her first pregnancy, is introduced into her husband's *ginna* so as to ensure the legitimacy of the child she bears."[16]

"In the past, a young woman remained in her father's home until the birth of her third child. She then left her family to go and live with her husband, leaving her first-born with her father. Presently, this rule is no longer strictly observed, and the woman comes to live with her husband much sooner."[17]

Upon the death of one of the spouses, the widow or widower may

---

15. G. DIETERLEN, *Parenté et mariage chez les Dogon,* p. 115.

16. *Idem,* p. 137.

17. *Idem,* p. 142.

remarry after the last funeral rites *(dama)* have been performed. The Dogon practice the levirate, called *ke ya di* "marriage of inheritance;" its purpose is to ensure continuity of the extended family by maintaining the wife and children of the deceased in the latter's *ginna*. The widow, however, is free to refuse this marriage and marry the man of her choice, even if he is of another lineage, but the children remain members of their father's own lineage.

THE CLAN AND THE INSTITUTION OF THE BINU.

The Dogon claim to be equally united by a more extensive kinship than the preceding one, which applies to members belonging to one *binu,* i.e., a group that may include several *ginna.*

"The institution called *binu* (literally: left and returned) presents the characteristics of totemism: a clan, a name, a prohibition, etc.

a) Related to the same totem[18] may be either the members of a large common patrilinear or patrilocal *ginna* (literally: big house) or the members of several *ginna.*

For example: in Sanga (the double village of Ogol), the descendants of the four *ginna,* Pamyon, Do, Guinna, and Tabda, who occupy four sectors, have Tiré as their totem.

Only the *ginna* is exogamous: a man of the Do *ginna* may marry a Tabda woman of the same clan as himself, but belonging to a different *ginna.*

b) All members of both sexes of the same *binu* observe the same prohibition.

c) Married women are introduced, on a certain level, into their husband's *ginna* during their first pregnancy so as to ensure the legitimacy of the child they bear; but they remain members of their own lineage and maintain their relation to the paternal clan.

d) The priest is the only one who bears the name of the totem. He is

---

18. The term totem is meant to designate the institution of the *binu,* with the limitations implied by its use here. One of the functions of this extremely complex institution is to manifest and promote the existence of categories and correspondences, classifications in every way comparable to those analyzed by C. LEVI-STRAUSS in his final works on totemism *(Le Totétisme aujourd'hui* and *La Pensée sauvage).*

responsible for the sanctuary, a small building containing altars and cult objects and generally placed in the courtyard of the particular *ginna*. By virtue of his office he has the use of a field, connected with the sanctuary, but he must also set aside from the harvest those grains needed for the performance of rites (sacrificial porridges, communal beer, first fruits, etc.). He is skilled in performing rites involving particular individuals of the clan (pregnancies, assigning a name to a newborn child, purifications, etc.) as well as those of collective interest (plantings, successive ceremonies for the desacralization of the harvest, etc.). He observes the prohibition of the collectivity as well as seven other ones connected with his office (the same for all totemic priests).

At the death of the priest, the family head of the *ginna* that contains the sanctuary (which remains closed) takes care of the performance of the indispensable rites during the entire interim, until another member of the group proves himself qualified to take office.

e) The *binu* are male or female. Their characteristics as well as certain of their roles within and outside of the clan vary in accordance with these representations.

Example: the priests of the male totems, but never those of the female totems, would intervene in wartime.

f) A totem may be 'shared' when the members of a village have become too numerous and one group decides to leave and found a new *ginna*. At that time, the ritual objects within the sanctuary are divided; the part that is removed constitutes the material of the sanctuary built in the courtyard of the new *ginna*. Such a case is rare at present, but occurred rather frequently in the past during the settlement and migrations of the Dogon on the cliffs. The new *binu* may: either keep the name and prohibitions of the original *binu*, or separate itself completely in appearance (in the event of a misunderstanding), by adopting a different name and different prohibitions. But the members will always know the origin of their *binu*."[19]

From both the mythical and the religious point of view, the institution of *binu* represents the worship of the collectivity of man's mythical ancestor *o nommo*, who was sacrificed and resurrected, because all *binu* stem from the first one, which was overseen by one of the epony-

---

19. G. DIETERLEN, *Note sur le totémisme dogon*, p. 106-107.

mous ancestors, Binou Sérou, "witness of the Binou." This first *binu* was divided among the twenty-two males of the fifth mythical generation, thus resulting in twenty-two basic Binou of which we have the nomenclature, with the list of corresponding prohibitions and with the distribution within the present four great tribes of the Dogon. It is in the image of this first mythical "partition" — a replica of the twenty-two principles or "articulations" recognized in the resurrected body by the Dogon — that the division of a clan takes place at the present time, such as we have just described above.

The prohibition of a *binu* (animal, plant, or object) — which was revealed to the clan through the intermediary of a distant, quasi-legendary ancestor — "is considered as 'evidence' of the cosmobiological corre-spondences that exist between the parts of the resurrected body, the stellar system, the animal kingdom, the plant kingdom, etc. It is a summary of these relationships."[20]

THE TRIBE, THE INSTITUTION OF THE LEBE, AND THE HOGON.

Formerly, the mouthpiece of government in Dogon society was the council of patriarchs, placed under the authority of the Hogon who, as the political head, also administered justice and maintained order through the intermediary of his delegates, who were especially responsible for policing the markets: price surveillance, proper course of transactions, etc. Fines were the sanction and, for more serious crimes, exile, or slavery. In the event of murder, the culprit was permanently excluded from the group, considered dead, and his belongings were divided among his heirs. Among the Dogon theft is severely punished. In the past, a thief caught in the act could be killed or led before the Hogon, who would impose a heavy fine upon him. If the fine was not paid, the thief could be sold into slavery.

The Hogon has remained the religious head and, by virtue of this, has great authority: he is priest of the *lebe,* which is to say, he is responsible for the worship rendered by all the Dogon to the mythical ancestor Lébé Sérou, sacrificed because he had violated a prohibition, so that the stain that had been transmitted to the cultivated earth might be purified.

---

20. G. DIETERLEN, *idem,* p. 108.

"From the standpoint of social organization, the four mythical lineages are the symbol of the four present Dogon tribes. Amma Sérou, Lébé Sérou, Binou Sérou, and Dyongou Sérou are the 'apical' ancestors of the Dyon, the Arou, the Ono, and the Domno, respectively.

"The Arou tribe, representing the lineage of Lébé Sérou, appoints one Hogon, priest of Lébé who represents this mythical ancestor. He holds his seat in the village of Arou-near-Ibi, and his authority is felt in particular by all the members of that tribe, no matter what their place of residence. This dignitary is generally considered the political and religious leader of all the Dogon.

"The Dyon, Ono, and Domno tribes appoint several Hogon, whose authority extends over different parts of the territory of the particular tribe. For example, the Hogon of Sanga is the leader of all the Dyon of the many villages that make up the region.[21]

"The positions of Hogon of Dyon (Amma Sérou) and of Ono (Binou Sérou) are held by the eldest man of the territorial group in question; the Hogon of Arou (Lébé Sérou) and of Domno (Dyongou Sérou) are elected among the younger members of a particular territorial group. Thus, Dyon and Arou on the one hand, Ono and Domno on the other, together constitute two complementary and parallel groups with regard to the choice of the tribe's principal leaders.

"Each Hogon is assisted by a council, which meets for all decisions of common interest and for community ceremonies. The way in which the council is made up is related to social organization and varies according to the tribe: among the Dyon and the Arou, these dignitaries, seven in number, are the eldest men of the region under the Hogon's authority . . . The Hogon of the Ono and Domno are assisted respectively by three or four notables . . ."[22]

The Hogon ranking highest in the sacerdotal hierarchy is considered God Amma's representative on earth and, of course, representative of the celestial supernatural forces which assist him. He is called *amma seru,* "Amma's witness." He is at the same time the priest of Lébé. This cult, whose sacrificer is its principal officiator, is devoted both to the sacrificed and resurrected Nommo and to the ancestor Lébé Sérou.

---

21. We should mention that the Arou of Sanga, a minority in the region, recognize the authority of the Hogon of Dyon for certain ceremonies regarding the territorial collectivity.

22. G. DIETERLEN, *Parenté et mariage chez les Dogon,* p. 132.

PL. III   1) Upper Ogol, Sanga.

2) Tellem granaries and dwellings (locality of *dama ommoro*).

1) Yougo Dogourou.

2) Songo. *(Photography J. Rouch).*

An altar of the *lebe* is erected in the residence of the Hogon, who may no longer leave the sanctuary after his ordination. Corresponding to this, another such altar is situated in the main square of the village on a platform, which is the image of the "sky" where the primordial sacrifice took place, by way of testimony to the supernatural powers that hold the spiritual essence of the seeds. The Hogon is the safekeeper of the purity of the cultivated land, *izubay minne,* "earth of the day of the fish," and of the seeds; he must also observe a great many prohibitions. He is assisted by the priest of the region's principal totem, who is his sacrificer and who officiates in his name during agrarian ceremonies.

OTHER SOCIAL GROUPS.

We have seen that each individual descends from a lineage, *togu,* from a *ginna,* and from a totemic clan, *binu.* He also belongs to other social groups, established by village and region, themselves placed under the authority of a religious leader, the Hogon.

As is the case with the system of kinship, the system of age classes and the Society of Masks give the Dogon their structural framework.

Each individual is admitted or introduced ritually into these associations after circumcision, which forms one of the fundamental steps in life: the operation and succeeding rites bring about the permanent fixing of the spiritual principles of body and sex of the adolescent. His person is stabilized: he will, when the time comes, be fit for procreation. At the same time, during the retreat he receives the beginning of an education that will later permit him to play his role and fulfill his functions in the heart of his society.

AGE CLASSES.

Each group of graduated, circumcised men composes an age class, *tonno.* The members of a *tonno* must help each other for the rest of their lives. From an economic point of view, they are a sort of non-remunerated work group, that tills the fields, repairs houses, etc., for individuals or for the community. They are thanked with offers of drink and meals.

The members of the *tonno* sometimes maintain a dwelling, *dunu,* built in each neighborhood, where they meet after those work hours to which their elders are entitled. They may spend the night there and also receive their friends and the young girls of the village. The latter, too, are grouped in age classes in accordance with the time when they were excised.

Theoretically, each Dogon group is divided into seven age classes, the entirety of which is represented by the Hogon, who is beyond all classes, so to speak. These eight strata of men are the symbol of the eight ancestors. But these, in turn, have eight elders as their substitutes in each village, who must possess the knowledge in its entirety and who act as a body in the course of the different ceremonies. This means that if the whole group is represented by its leader, the seven groups and their leaders, in turn, have a chapter of eight notables as their deputy who, to a certain degree and under particular circumstances, act on behalf of the whole.

THE SOCIETY OF MASKS, AVA.

In certain regions of the cliffs and plateau, each circumcised man becomes a member of the *ava* or Society of Masks. He must carve (or have carved for him) and wear the mask of his choosing in order to dance during the funeral rites.

The *ava* is a male association charged, among other things, with the worship rendered to the first dead — the mythical ancestor Dyongou Sérou — represented by the "great mask" *imina na,* which is the collective property of the village.

The presiding dignitaries of the *ava* are the *olubaru,* recruited from among the *inneu puru* of each lineage in turn at the time of the sixty-year ceremony of the Sigui. For three months these dignitaries go into retreat and receive instruction: they live in the bush in the cave that has been assigned to the newly carved mask where they are taught by the elders. They memorize especially the incantations and texts in the "Sigui tongue," *sigi so,* which tell, in a very abbreviated manner, the story of the creation of the world and of the appearance of death on Earth and in the human world. Until the performance of the rites of the Sigui sixty years later, it will be their duty to worship the ancestor Dyongou Sérou through the intermediary of the great mask, keeper of his spiritual principles.

Next to the *olubaru,* in charge of the cult for the first dead, all men qualified to wear a mask perform a similar service for each man who has died. Rites performed during the funeral and the *dama* (end of mourning), during which the masks dance, honor the spiritual principles of the dead which must be accompanied, led, or directed all the way until the depositing of the funeral earthenware in the family altar, thus consecrating his passage into the rank of ancestor.

Women are excluded from anything touching on the activities involving the masks which, in their association with death, harm the fertility, a major preoccupation of every traditional African society and of the Dogon in particular.

They are, however, represented in the *ava* by a dignitary, the *yasigine,* "woman of Sigui," consecrated at the time of the sixty-year ceremony. On the religious plane, the *yasigine* represents *yasigui,* the twin of one of the beings first created by God, a causer of disorder, cast asunder and transformed into the Fox. However, the *yasigine,* who attends the funeral ceremonies where she plays the role of the mythical ancestor, may neither enter into the place where the masks are kept nor learn the *sigi so.*

All men qualified to wear the mask must dance at the funerals and especially during the "end of mourning" rites, or *dama.* Thus they participate in the rites relative to the spiritual principles of the dead.

VARIOUS ASSOCIATIONS.

We should point out the existence of certain institutions into which an individual may be introduced by virtue of his practical skills, for example, those including goatherds (for children), cattleherds, hunters, healers, or diviners (for adult men). Each group has its special altar upon which they collectively offer sacrifices to the supernatural powers or the ancestors supposed to further that particular activity: the sacrificed Nommo for the cowherds, the ancestor Dyongou Sérou for the healers and hunters, the Fox for the diviners, etc.

WOMAN'S PLACE IN DOGON SOCIETY.

The Dogon woman has an unobtrusive role in the social organization as concerns the village and, of course, in political life. It is the men and the councils and associations that they establish who make the important decisions. She is in charge of the upkeep of the home which she alone manages: this is her main role. She is essentially the "mother": she feeds her children, she also takes care of the food for her husband and the entire household. In addition, she 'devotes herself to agricultural labor: the products of her harvest or the cotton she has spun she sells for her own profit.

The woman participates in the entire religious life, except for anything involving the Society of Masks. She receives a training and an initiation similar to that of the men, but administered exclusively by women. This instruction, of which we know very little, is still an object of further in-depth study.

The woman also enjoys a relatively great measure of freedom, and she has control over her personal goods. She is held in esteem and respect by all.

**

THE PERSON.

The notion of "person," *dime,* is very elaborate. A man is constituted by: a) a body *(gozu);* b) four "body souls": one couple of twin souls of opposite sex, *kikinu say,* "intelligent souls"; and its reflection made up of a comparable couple, *kikinu bummone,* "errant souls";[23] c) four "sex souls" grouped like the preceding ones; d) a composite vital force *(nyama),* characterized as a fluid circulating conjointly with the blood in the veins. An important part of this force comes from the *nani* of the particular individual, which is to say, from the patrilinear ascendant who, following his death, appeared before the Nommo to ask that he be granted his souls;[24] e) the symbol of the basic foods placed in the clavicles, compared to two granaries, each containing four seeds.[25]

---

23. The individual's spiritual twinness is projected in the symbolism of numbers: the number 7, which represents the person, is the sum of 3 (the male sex — penis and testicles) and 4 (the feminine sex — the four labia), which also represent the two *kikinu* of opposite sex. A man repeats the ritual gestures three times, a woman four times.

24. The word *nani* designates the ascendent as well as the descendent to inherit the life force; for the purposes of this presentation, we will designate the first one by *nani* (ancestor) and the second by *nani* (descendant).

25. The notion of the clavicles as containers of the symbols of food is not uniquely Dogon, but is widespread over a great number of other Sudanese peoples. The content varies according to their essential function: hence, the Bozo fishermen have the symbol of eight fishes in the clavicles; cf. M. GRIAULE and G. DIETERLEN, *L'Agriculture rituelle des Bozo.*

For the Dogon, the formation of the child in the womb begins with the skull and clavicles. The formed being is at first comparable to the silurus *anagonno (Clarias senegalensis);* several months before birth, he leaves the fish form to take on the human form.[26]

The clavicles are considered as the support of the skeleton to which they are not definitely attached until the human being is completely formed, that is, theoretically for the Dogon towards the age of twenty-two. These various qualities make them the seat of the symbols of the essential food of the Dogon, which is the seeds of the cultivated food plants. The eight symbolic seeds stand for the organization of the world within the body of man conceived as a microcosm: they represent the four elements (air, earth, water, and fire) and the four cardinal points, like the eight ancestors whose role is institutional. Their arrangement, which varies according to sex, function, and caste, locates the individual both in the universe and in society. The children have in their clavicles the same seeds as their parents; those of the father are in a dominant position for a boy and those of the mother for a girl; eight in number and of different "sex," the boy first inherits the "masculine seeds" from his father, which are the same as those of his agnatic* ancestors, and the daughter the "feminine seeds" of her mother, which are the same as those of her uterine ancestors. Thus, in a symbolism of a biological nature the presence of a double filiation is delineated.

A person is socially established, "seated" (in Dogon terminology), by being given his first names and being granted the mottos which are rightfully his.[27] The successive bestowals of first names are the fundamental acts which confer upon the newborn child both its spiritual and social status. Most often, a Dogon has four given names (the last being a sort of nickname), which are associated with his body souls. If it is a

---

*Ancestors who are related or akin through males or on the father's side.

26. See M. GRIAULE. *Rôle du silure Clarias senegalensis dans la procréation au Soudan français.* For the analogy between the human clavicle and the pectoral fin of the silurus cf. *infra.* p. 163, 164, n. 201.

27. The rites of the giving of names have been described by D. PAULME. *Organisation sociale des Dogon.* p. 443 and ff.; G. DIETERLEN, *Les Ames des Dogon,* p. 155 and ff.; D. LIFCHITZ and D. PAULME. *Les Noms individuels chez les Dogon,* p. 311 and ff. On the mottos, cf. S. de GANAY. *Les Devises des Dogon* and D. LIFCHITZ. *Les Formules propitiatoires chez les Dogon.*

boy, the "forbidden name," *boy dama,* first given by the totemic priest, confers on him the *kikinu say ya,* which resides with Nommo, but at this time brings to the newborn child the "seeds of the clavicles."

The name he will use in daily life, *boy toy,* "seed name," given by the patriarch of the joint family, confers on the newborn the *kikinu say ana,* which gives him life.

The "mother's name," *na boy,* given by the patriarch of the mother's paternal family, confers the *kikinu bummone ya* on him; this soul, giving life to the bearer when he lives in his own region, leaves him and remains in the totemic sanctuary during all of his journeys away from the familial center.

The *kikinu bummone ana* resides with the forbidden totemic animal *(babinu dama);* it is related to the nickname, *tonno boy* or *anuge boy,* a name of friendship given to the child by his friends in his age group *(tonno).*

It is the same for a girl, the sexes of the souls in question being reversed: thus the *boy dama* bestows upon her the *kikinu say ana* of her body.

Besides his given names, a Dogon has the right to bear several mottos: those of his people, his tribe, his region, his village, and his quarter. Finally, he inherits the personal motto of his *nani* (ancestor). All of these mottos are related to his life force, *nyama.*

The body souls, placed under the protection of the mythical and ancestral personalities which are the relatives of the bearer, are associated with the collective family altars; they are, in part, beneficiaries of the rites of which they are the object, especially at the time of the consumption of sacrificial victims. The two *kikinu say* of sex are permanently "fixed" after male and female circumcision and before marriage. They take part in worship rendered on the individual altars, *kutogolo* and *dabie,* consecrated at that time by the fathers of the respective betrothed.

The life force, *nyama,* benefits from all the contributions due to these different sacrifices, offerings, and consummations.

Thus the constituent elements of a person (souls, body, life force, clavicular content) are in constant relationship; the movements of the life force and of the seeds of the clavicles, which are able to leave and reintegrate their bearer, are associated with the movements of the souls;

their very complex study extends beyond the framework of this account. For example, we have seen that, during life, one of the body souls *(kikinu say)* of the same sex as its bearer gives life to him, whereas the other remains in the power of the Nommo; thus the Nommo protects the man at the same time he directs and controls his actions. He does, however, send back this soul during certain rituals marking the passage from one condition to another, especially during male or female circumcision, marriage, and ordination into some social or religious office (chiefdom or priesthood).

The simultaneously physical and spiritual constitution of a person, such as has just been described, applies to the majority of men called *inneu omo,* "living men." Certain individuals, charged with defined religious and social functions by virtue of their status, are called *inneu puru,* "impure men." The *inne puru* is incomplete; he has seven seeds in his clavicles instead of eight; his *kikinu bummone ya* of the body resides permanently in the totemic sanctuary and does not accompany him on certain occasions, as is the case with the *inne omo.* This condition is not due to biological conditions of birth, but rather inherited from the *nani* (ancestor) of the particular individual.[28]

The concept of the person is the basis for the representations and rites which accompany and follow the individual's death. Their purpose and effect is to first regroup certain elements which have left the body, then to accompany them, each of them remaining afterwards in a particular place.

As a matter of fact, "upon death, the constituent elements of personality separate. The *nyama* escapes from the body and becomes an active force which is to be directed by funerary ritual; it will be transmitted according to the rules to descendants born in the extended paternal family of the deceased, who will become their *nani* (ancestor). The souls too leave the body: under the Nommo's control, they will serve to advance those of the children who will be the *nani* (descendants) of the deceased and who will receive his life force."[29]

The ancestors' cult directs itself in a precise manner to certain elements of the being's spiritual principles — the *kikinu say* of sex — which

---

28. G. DIETERLEN, *Parenté et mariage,* pp. 111-113.

29. *Idem,* p. 113.

will be "called" during rituals performed on one of the family altars, the *vageu,* consecrated in the principal dwelling of the lineage. And it is through their intermediary that the life force which animated the deceased will be progressively transmitted to certain descendants. "Reincarnation" is strictly limited to this transmission — which ensures continuity of the blood and lineage — each individual preserving in his person, until death, all of his spiritual principles *per se.*

* *
*

DOGON THOUGHT.

Like other African societies, the Dogon know and have analyzed all the facts, beings, and things which surround them; like others, they have attempted to make a synthesis of these. Having observed and studied everything within range of their perception, "they have constructed an indigenous explanation of the manifestations of nature (anthropology, botany, zoology, geology, astronomy, anatomy, and physiology) as well as social facts (social structures, religious and political structures, crafts, arts, economy, etc.)."[30] The Dogon possess "systems of signs or ideographs including several thousands, an astronomy and calendars, a numerical system, extensive physiological and anatomical knowledge, genetics, and a systematic pharmacopoeia."[31] This knowledge encompasses the smallest twig and the tiniest animal; the spider, the worm and the dragonfly are considered of the same importance as the lion. All the conditions of life to which man is subject are inscribed therein; refuse and debris have their place in it. Man has, of course, a privileged place in this universe, but the Dogon adopt the words of the Fulani initiate: "Knowledge lies in knowing man, but also all that which is not man, for it has been given to him to know that which is not himself."[32] The world is conceived as a whole, this whole having been thought, realized, and

---

30. G. DIETERLEN, *Tendances de l'ethnologie française,* p. 24.
31. G. DIETERLEN, *Les résultats des Missions Griaule au Soudan français,* p. 139.
32. A.H. BA and G. DIETERLEN, *Koumen,* p. 93.

organized by one creator God in a complete system which includes disorder.

The originality of this thought lies in the fact that it postulates a series of correspondences between all these elements, grouped in categories that can be broken up and linked together.

"The principles at the base of Dogon social organization are especially expressed in the classifications, which include all natural manifestations as well as those of their own invention. These classifications constitute a system in which, for example, plants, insects, fabrics, games, and rituals are divided into decomposable categories, numerically expressed and related to each other. In addition, the religious and political authority of the chiefs and also the family and juridical structures (particularly systems of kinship and marriage) are established upon the same principles; all activities of daily life of the individuals depend on these."[33]

The development of Dogon thought, and hence the elaboration of concepts, proceeds by analogy and has constant recourse to the symbol. An expression opens and closes a sentence when the Dogon wish to underscore the presence of a symbol: *aduno so,* "the (spoken) word of the world" is used by them in the same way we say "symbolically" . . . On the other hand, the Dogon term expresses the function of the symbol itself integrated into a system which simultaneously describes and comprises everything contained by "the universe," *aduno.*

Because the principles establish the categories and the relationships between them, that is to say, the correspondences, the symbol fully capsulizes an entire series of concepts. For it is "a flexible model. It may exist only in a small quantity, be replaced by a being or object which is similar or declared as such, or be evoked verbally, without losing any of its efficacy: one grain of 'female' sorghum in a plate of rice gives to it the qualities of that plant; the many sorts of beers used both in ceremonies and in daily life are most often brewed with the sorghum or millet on hand, but the introduction of a single seed of those cereal grains that are required bestows upon the rest of them the desired value. In the same way, a thumb-size piece of the appropriate fabric helps the wearer to overcome a certain illness or trial, to get him out of a problem or serious situation. Better still, a simple thread of suitable color tacked

---

33. G. DIETERLEN, *Les résultats des Missions Griaule au Soudan français,* p. 139.

on to the bottom of a robe suffices to put oneself in a favorable atmosphere."[34]

Thus, the symbol plays the role "of conveyor of knowledge. It will have led man to collect materials and actions in his memory, but it will have familiarized him with the games of abstraction. The succession of symbols will have led him from the prepuce, symbol of the female soul, to the lizard, symbol of the prepuce, to the shawl, *ya nunu,* symbol of the lizard, to the drawn sign of the shawl, symbol of the shawl itself, and finally to those figures traced haphazardly in the center of the family field before seeding, which symbolize all known signs including, among others, that of the shawl. Thus he will have learned that with the help of a line, drawn carelessly but purposefully, a long series of ideas or actions is evoked."[35]

A typical example of the usage of symbols is found in "the immense system of drawn signs expressing the sum of Dogon knowledge. Composed of twenty-two categories of twelve elements (264 total), each of which is at the head of a list of twenty-two pairs, this construction of 11,616 signs expresses all possible beings and situations as seen by the males. That of the women, just as important, corresponds to it . . ." The Dogon, without any lasting records, has taken the use of the symbol to its extreme and has tried, so to speak, to codify it.

"By means of drawn signs, classified and grouped into a hierarchy, the most intellectualized production of the symbol, the Dogon expresses that between Sirius and sacrifice, marriage and eggplant, there are closely felt, efficacious ties, and that the distinctions we make between facts of religion, crafts, or germination, or between the motions of the stars and structural changes within certain animals are useless."[36]

The value and efficacy of the symbol are such in this system, that the Dogon declare that it is not the thing itself, but "the symbol alone which is essential."[37]

Thus ". . . the thought of the Black world is oriented towards a

---

34. M. GRIAULE, *Réflexions sur des symboles soudanais,* pp. 24-25.

35. *Idem,* p. 26.

36. *Idem,* p. 7 and p. 28.

37. *no duma so tuma kugo von.* Literally, "that 'word of the world' alone is the head (the main thing)." (Wazouba dialect).

knowledge which may sometimes be confused with an adequate understanding, but which is most often a *'sophy.'* This thought makes of the universe an orderly whole, where the notion of law is less present than that of pre-established harmony, incessantly troubled and continually reordered. Each part of this entirety epitomizes the whole. There is neither subject nor object, only things linked in one domain. As a result of the preceding principle, the Black mind establishes a network of equivalences between all things by means of a system of symbols which, by harmonious interplay and imperceptible shifts, leads from the harp to the craft of weaving, from the garment to the creative word, from the demiurge to refuse. For it involves a sort of practical and theoretical metaphysics which, on the one hand, explains the universe, thus responding to the innate need to understand, and, on the other hand, forms the spiritual framework of men's lives."[38]

Indeed, another feature of the way of thinking and expression of the Dogon must be pointed out here. Because of the postulate establishing categories and the relationships between them, everything is significant, everything is a sign, in the reality of daily life and even in dreams. Leaving no room for what we call chance, every element or event is charged with meaning in relation to and in interaction with others, simultaneously in space and in the present and future time. Actually, it is not a matter here of an analysis of static facts, but rather a general understanding of something alive, viewed from a biological standpoint. The entire universe is moving; man on earth is in motion, and life, even inside the smallest seed of grain, is in motion.

In the religious domain, this system is linked together by the existence of elaborate myths dealing with the fundamental notion of God, the history of the creation of the world, of the establishment of order and the appearance of disorder, of a sacrifice of reparation, and of man's life in a populated and reorganized universe. "The myth, *so tanie,* 'astonishing word' which the Dogon consider to be 'real' history . . . constitutes here the whole of coherent themes of creation";[39] this is why, by virtue of their coherence and their order of succession, they make up a "history of the universe," *aduno so tanie.*

---

38. M. GRIAULE, *La connaissance de l'homme noir,* pp. 13-14.
39. G. CALAME-GRIAULE, *Esotérisme et fabulation au Soudan,* p. 308.

By no means, here, ". . . should the word myth be understood in its ordinary sense, as a childlike or fantastic, somewhat absurd poetic form. The myth is, for the Blacks, only a means by which to explain something; it is a consciously composed lore of master ideas which may not be placed within reach of just anyone at any time. Certainly it constitutes a form of 'slight knowledge' — a Bambara expression — sometimes available to the average man. It conceals clear statements and coherent systems reserved for initiates, who alone have access to the 'deep knowledge.' The myths present themselves in layers, like the shells of a seed, and one of their reasons for being is precisely to cover and conceal from the profane a precious seed which appears to belong rightly to a universal, valid body of knowledge."[40]

God holds a primordial place in this mythology and cosmology; he alone is considered to be unique and perfect: he created the world, he can destroy it and make another, in which there may or may not be a place for the supernatural powers upon whom he bestowed his Word and who presently direct the universe under his authority. He alone is outside of everything else; it is to him, the supreme head, that all men pray.

The network of categories, classifications, and correspondences constitutes a structure comparable to the framework of a house, or the articulated bone structure of the body. That which gives them life — their own physiology — is, for the Dogon, their relationship with God and with the order of the world he created, that is, the manner in which the universe has been organized and functions today.

The whole is illuminated by the myth. Structures in it appear progressively in time, the one superimposed on the next, each having its own meaning, each also displaying close correlation with the others. This is what gives meaning to these successions of categories and levels of classification, themselves evidence of the nature of the relationships established between man and all in the universe which is not man.

Only the dimension and transcendence of the creator surpass the whole: the Dogon do not incessantly repeat "Amma-God is great," but their beliefs and all of their institutions demonstrate it.

Thus, the system we have just summed up and introduced contains

---

40. M. GRIAULE, *La connaissance de l'homme noir,* p. 14.

mythical themes. This system, underlying all Dogon activities, is expressed through them, in the social, family, technical, juridical, and religious organization of these people. And this at all levels: ". . . not only in individual or collective deeds and ritual gestures, but also in special materials (rock paintings, raised stones, altars, figures, pictures, etc.), in the texts of prayers or invocations, in stories or mottos, understandable only through the accompanying commentary, as well as in the form of objects or utensils, even those of everyday usage."[41]

A. In their social structure, the Dogon have deliberately constructed a system of kinship and marriage based on four lineages and five generations. "This system, known by the family head patriarchs, *ginna bana,* and, in a more general way, by initiates of both sexes, presents a synopsis of the following elements:

1) The make-up of the four mythical lineages corresponding to a cosmogonic division (elements, cardinal points); to the division and ownership of the cultivated soil; to the four main present tribes of the Dogon.

2) The development of these four lineages over five generations. At present, an individual is always situated in relation to four generations before and after his own.

3) The chronology of marriages in terms of: biological conditions of each party's birth (twin, single birth, etc.) and the order of their successions, the parental proximity of the partners, the position of the partners with regard to the usufruct of the cultivated soil.

4) The chronology of births (twin, single, abnormal) within different sorts of marriages, in relation to the respective positions of the parents in the different generations; the bestowal of first names as determined by these births.

5) The determination of social and religious functions, individual and collective, in relation to the mythical events marking the succession of the first five generations.

The genealogical table covers almost all types of marriages contracted by the Dogon; each of them has one or several names, according to biological status, rank of birth, and social status or function of those

---

41. G. DIETERLEN, *Tendances de l'ethnologie française,* p. 24.

involved. It also includes the free unions *(dimu),* contracted out of wedlock, and the levirate.

We find in this complete and chronologically established table, not counting the prohibition of incest, a great many classic marriages recognized in Africa (marriages between cross-cousins, or with the daughter of a maternal uncle, arranged marriages, levirate marriages, etc.). The functioning of this system of marriages results in a generalized exchange by the fifth generation.

It is to these data that the Dogon refer when an event of community interest presents itself: in the case of almost any kind of marriage being represented, a present-day union is always prefigured by a mythical one, which determines the name or names given to that union, the sacrifices offered, and sometimes even a prediction of the number and qualities of the possible resulting births."[42]

B. In those representations associated with crafts, and especially in the basic crafts of the Dogon. The present world is conceived as having come out of a first seed formed by God, this being *Digitaria exilis,* the fonio. It contains the essence of creation, including the four basic "elements" (air, earth, water, and fire) and the "word" of the creator, that is to say, life manifesting itself within, in the form of eight segments, animated by a motion that is both vibratory and spiraling. It is also endowed with eight basic spiritual principles — four of "body" and four of "sex" — which ensure its dependence with regard to the creator, but also its immortality: the plant dies and is reborn the following year from the seed it has formed. In like manner, man — even already in the fetal state where he is fish-like — will be animated by spiritual principles of the same essence. This explains the identical structures of the fish egg and the grain. Man is consubstantial with the grains, the symbol of which he bears in his clavicles.[43]

All farm labor, from seeding to garnering, and the accompanying

---

42. G. DIETERLEN, *Parenté et mariage chez les Dogon,* p. 108 and p. 115.

43. "Man is a combination of seeds, symbols of the life forces. He is also a supplier of forces: in the act of cultivation, he puts the germs of his clavicles in the soil . . . Sower of himself, the peasant reaps his own life and symbolically stores it within his person for future germinations. He is a living field and an animate granary for the coming and going of the harvest and the sowing"; M. GRIAULE, *Connaissance de l'homme noir,* p. 21.

rituals are in keeping with this conception and this "mythology of the grain."

It is the same with the forge; the implements symbolically represent certain organs and articulations of the resurrected Nommo, humanity's ancestor, considered a twin of the mythical artisan. The forge is a sanctuary, the tools are the altars to the group offering sacrifices to the ancestor to propitiate the work performed with them.

The weaver has consecrated a personal altar to God the creator, for the band of cotton he weaves is the image of the divine "word" in that, at the same time, it contains the "word" transmitted to man by the resurrected ancestor and "woven" by him in the water, his domain on Earth.

These examples, of which there are many more, are evidence of the amplitude of representations connected with the various crafts and with their implications in Dogon social and religious life.

C. In the entirety of profane or religious material (architecture, everyday objects, ritual objects) by form, decoration, and use.

For the Dogon, as for other societies of West Africa, "the least ordinary object reveals in its forms and designs the conscious expression of a complex cosmogony . . . Thus, a checkered Sudanese blanket is a text in which woven designs constitute signs intentionally displayed by its users and understood by the initiates; a basket intended for carrying things represents, when turned upside-down, the ark on which humanity descended from heaven to earth, the square bottom of the object representing space and the cardinal points."[44]

It is, of course, the same for religious material *per se*. The plan and proportions of certain dwellings, family houses, sanctuaries, etc., are symbolic. The form, the distribution of altars in the house, in the village, and in the fields, demonstrate, as we shall see, the desire to represent the different stages of the myth on the soil, to inscribe it on the very earth where man lives and walks.

For example, in the village the shape of objects placed in the totemic sanctuary and the ornaments and insignia of the priests are all based on the same principles. They are charged with the same symbolic functions,

---

44. G. DIETERLEN, *Les résultats des Missions Griaule au Soudan français* (1931-1956), p. 139.

for they connote the elements and stages of the sacrifice that reorganized the universe, with totemic worship being rendered to the resurrected victim.

In the bush, for identical representations, and for reasons of ritual and initiation, raised stones or stacked boulders have been put up, generally oriented in relation to each other: they are located near water supply points or on steep slopes, sometimes at considerable distance from one another. Numerous caves have been arranged as well as pise structures.

So, whether of daily or religious use, "these almost innumerable materials constitute the established 'archives' of this people — as well as evidence of that knowledge. They constitute also, for the learned men, a mnemotechnic aid."[45]

D. In religious life, both individual and collective. The rituals cadence the important moments of the community's life: they perform a crystallizing function in that they are almost always reactualizations of mythical events.

The rite is projected into the myth which bears a chronological account of all the institutions. The structure of the myth is always viewed by the initiates in relation to the rites and altars or groups of altars which are its bases. More precisely, the people's belief rests upon the yearly (or seven- or sixty-year) performance of the successive rites as well as on the proceedings within a particular rite (preparation — opening — execution — closing).

The celebration of the sowing — a spectacular event involving the entire population of the region — has been noted and described, but has not been clarified. In fact, it can only be understood in relation to the successive rites of desacralization of the harvest. These numerous rituals, performed by different groups according to social context, are related to each of the seed's spiritual principles — it has eight "souls," as does man. The purpose of the rites is to liberate these, that is to say, to render the harvest edible, by placing each of the grain's spiritual principles under the protection of the supernatural powers. The following year during the celebration of the sowing, these same powers are asked to send back the "souls" of the seeds. Thus the "millet cycle" ends and

---

45. G. DIETERLEN, *Tendances de l'ethnologie française*, p. 24.

begins anew.

The design and the parallel sequences of the myth must be linked to the same concepts.

One repeats the corresponding rite when officiating in function of an episode of the myth which is parallel to a preceding one. An infinitely slight difference within the ritual (the use of a different grain for brewing the beer, for example) alone will reveal the heart of the matter, namely, the resurrection invoked and represented by the fermentation and the cult — as well as to which of the myth's personages the rite is addressed: the whole thing is conveyed by and to the officiants and beneficiaries of the rite, who represent the very first ones.

It also happens that a superposition is produced: thus the ceremonies of the Sigui, the primary commemoration of the revelation of the "word," also commemorate, by adjunction with another sequence, the appearance of death in the human world.

In the course of these rites, established texts, prayers, invocations, or the recitation and chanting of songs are introduced. Most of them present episodes of the myth in a very synthetic or deliberately obscure manner, relating one or two of its sequences: all require a gnostic knowledge to be understood in their deepest sense, i.e., the meaning by which such invocations and chants "act" intrinsically in the ritual. For example, the prayer called *amma boy,* "the name of God," recited at the time of the second weeding of the Hogon's field, constitutes an initiation text and is intelligible only if accompanied by commentaries.[46]

Gesture is an integral part of the rites: the steps of the participants, the gestures of the performers, constitute the recalling of mythical events; the spiral outlined by the dancing of the entire social community around Lébé's altar on the day of the sowing celebration recalls the internal spiral of the elements of the "word," that is to say, of life inside the first seed.

The center or axis of the rites, in almost every case, is the blood sacrifice. Now, for all initiated men, no matter what the place, purpose, means, officiants, or subject, every sacrifice repeats the mythical sacrifice of the reorganization of the universe, the subject of the main

46. G. DIETERLEN, *Textes sacrés d'Afrique Noire,* p. 32 and ff.

chapter of this book. All sacrifice is, like the prototype, simultaneously cathartic and reorganizing: it frees the life forces of the victim to purify whatever or whoever is weakened and therefore threatened by mistakes, errors, and the violation of prohibitions. It brings about the revivification of the whole, the resurrection, that is to say, a total renewal, life in all its plentitude.

The fundamental role of ritual figures drawn by the Dogon should be mentioned here: a theory of the function of graphic drawings is explained in the first chapter of this book;[47] for each being or object, the Dogon produce four successive figures.

They are placed at different stages in the most diverse places: on the ground, when sanctuaries and dwellings are established and when an altar is erected; on the sanctuary walls and on the façades of certain altars during the performance of rites (annual or occasional); on the walls of caves or rock shelters set up for initiations and ritual purposes. There, the rock paintings are witnesses: in abstract or realistic form they relate mythical, protohistorical, even historical events; likewise, they are associated with the rites performed in those places, relative to the events and personages evoked in those rites. The position of the figures indicates systematically whether they have to do with mythical events having taken place in the "sky" (drawn on the ceiling), or those having taken place on Earth (drawn on the wall or floor).

Thus, for lack of a current system of writing, the Dogon have multiplied the uses of drawing and paintings, and with these figures have inscribed their entire cosmogony in a durable fashion.

* * *

INITIATION.

How is this knowledge taught to man? In different ways, depending on the people, but which stem everywhere from what one calls initiation. It may be collective as among the Bambara, by the individual's progressive admission into different associations or societies, male or female according to the individual's sex, to which he gains entry by successive degrees; or it may be individual, as among the Fulani. Among the Dogon this knowledge is acquired in successive stages or "words more and

---

47. *Infra,* p. 117 and ff. See also G. DIETERLEN, *Blasons et emblèmes totémiques des Dogon,* p. 40.

more both explicit and complete."[48] For the boys, this begins after
circumcision, first collectively during the retreat following the operation.
At that time, the boy is introduced to the existence of a system, but in a
superficial way; he is rarely told more. After his return, the circumcised
boy is introduced into the community life of men. He will be able to see
and hear many things, to participate in activities from which he had thus
far been excluded. From then on, he will receive from the elders of his
lineage or clan — usually beginning with his father — certain teachings
to which he must listen and which he must absorb.

This knowledge, "is also acquired through the individual's personal
experiences and through the functions he performs in the heart of
society." The exercise of family authority or of the priesthood, the
degrees he attains in the associations of which he is a part (hunters,
diviners, "ritual thieves," the Society of Masks, etc.), work together so as
to permit the integration of these traditions. The individual's penetration into one or another of these groups or associations is accompanied
by teachings and explanations given by the group's responsible leaders:
there are established texts which are commented upon, materials and
regular collective ceremonies, the symbolism of which is explained. In
this way the apprentice diviner will learn from his elders the deeper
meaning of the gestures he performs: an entire series of the myth's
sequences will be illustrated by a series of figures, deemed "instructional,"
drawn upon the divination tables.

Moreover, collective rites and the commentaries to which they give
rise, progressively place a higher level of knowledge within the reach of
everyone. Actually, they are often the occasion of recited prayers or
regular invocations, the deeper meaning of which may be revealed to
anyone wishing to learn. In addition, the part of the myth (the "story of
the world") having to do with any particular ceremony is commented
upon during subsequent meetings or in conversations held in the shelter
of men *(toguna)*. Thus the story is told, bit by bit and always in fragments.
One of the personal tasks of the initiate is to make the connections and
final synthesis on his own.

Actually, this "story" is much too long, its meanderings and different
implications are much too rich to be recounted in one sitting, or even
divided into periods.

---

48. G. DIETERLEN, *Tendances de l'ethnologie française*, p. 24.

Besides, the instruction demands a permanent effort of anyone wishing to be initiated. If he is to learn what will be told or communicated to him spontaneously, he must want to educate himself and to understand; he himself must question his father — or his mother — his maternal uncle, and finally the learned elders of the group who, if he proves himself worthy and manifests the necessary patience and perseverance, will answer all his questions. The answers themselves give rise to other questions necessary for a complete understanding. If the candidate does not actively participate in the exchange, it is because:

— either he has understood what he was previously told, but does not perceive the continuation of the problem;

— or he is not yet mature enough to understand it in its symbolic sense.

In both cases, the instructor is required to remain silent. He must wait for the other to come back at his own initiative — perhaps pursuant to another problem — to the subject in question; he will then give an answer. His good will is not at all diminished: he is there, present, untiring, but in a somewhat passive way; he doesn't give a lesson, but rather directs and guides a sort of investigation.

However, even during instruction and if the student has understood that a system does exist, he is not given the key to it; it is up to the candidate himself to find it. Likewise, when he has eventually received and assimilated this knowledge, understood a certain number of sacred texts, realized the meaning of ritual gestures, etc., he himself must make the connections between the different fragments or points of view, and produce the synthesis of the "story of the world."

The Dogon, who have classified everything, have established a hierarchy by degrees of instruction of the initiates. Their knowledge spans four degrees which are, from least to most important, the *giri so,* the *benne so,* the *bolo so,* and the *so dayi.*

"The *giri so,* 'fore-word,' is a first source of knowledge with simple explanations in which mythical personages are often disguised, their adventures simplified or fantasized, all this in seemingly unrelated parts. It deals with visible things and deeds, with rituals and modern materials.

"The *benne so,* 'side-word,' includes the 'words which were in the *giri so'* and the deeper explanation of certain parts of the rites and representations. Its coordination appears only within the greater divisions of knowledge, which remain partly unrevealed.

"The *bolo so,* 'back-word,' completes the preceding knowledge on the one hand, and furnishes syntheses applicable to greater parts of the whole on the other hand. It does not, however, contain the very secret parts.

"The *so dayi,* 'clear-word,' concerns itself with the edifice of knowledge in its ordered complexity."[49]

But initiation is not only an accumulation of knowledge, nor even a philosophy, a manner of thinking. It is of an educational nature, for it forms or models the individual at the same time he is assimilating the knowledge it offers. But it is still more than this through its vital character; by making the structures of the universe understood, it progressively leads the initiate to a way of life as conscious and complete as possible in nature and within his society, in the world as it was conceived and organized by God.

We feel that another aspect of the effects of the instruction should be considered: it stems from a psychology of a particular nature.

The Dogon myth does not relate facts merely involving adventures, rivalries between the gods, or the effects of love and hate — love of God, wickedness of the evil one — such as they are presented by other religions. Nor does it lead to a great detachment, this ideal being proposed to man as a final end, and in view of death or of the melting into a "great whole."

Rather it shows evidence of a serious examination of the very conditions of life and death; hence, its precise biological aspect. Certainly, the universe is treated as a whole, but also as a living body, articulated, ordered — to the extent that even disorder has its place — functional, with interlocking parts dependent upon each other. The myth presents a construction of the universe — from that of the stellar system down to that of the smallest grain, with man in between, himself a microcosmic image of this world. It is from this perspective also that the psychological element comes into play: hence the personalities and manner of conduct of the principal agents of the myth. The emphasis is placed upon the personage of the Fox, *semper peccatus semper justus.*

---

49. M. GRIAULE, *Le savoir des Dogon,* p. 27.

Independent but dissatisfied to be so; active, inventive, and destructive at the same time; bold yet timid; restless, sly, yet indifferent, he is the incarnation of the contradictions inherent in the human condition.

In this scheme of things, it is of course important to know and understand the structure of the universe; but it is also a matter of living it, in the fullest sense of the word, in body as well as in spirit.

When the learned members of a *ginna* drink (together) the ritual beer of a particular type of sorghum, at a particular time, for a particular ceremony, they know to which sequence of the myth and to which greater set of connections the act itself corresponds. But, if they know it on the intellectual level, they do not dissociate their knowledge of it from another form of indispensable understanding, such as their blood and organs acquire through this communal consumption. The nourishment is then complete — of the body and the spirit — and the social relations are biologically maintained.

Thus is introduced into the life of the Dogon this "fourth dimension," characteristic of myth and symbolism, as necessary to their existence as drinking and eating, in which they move with ease and flexibility, but also with the profound feeling of the immanent presence of the invisible which they evoke.

It is fitting to tell how the investigations which made this book possible took place on location.

The Dogon had, since 1931, answered questions and commented on the observations made during the successive expeditions from the perspective of factual interpretation which they call "the fore-word," *giri so,* that is to say, the first one they give to those wishing to learn: the publications preceding the investigations of 1947 all stem from this first interpretation.

In view of the perseverance manifested by Marcel Griaule and his team; in view of the abundance of questions which became more and more difficult to answer without penetrating into another level; in view, also, of the desire to understand what motivated us (which remained far from satisfied by previous discussions); in view of the fact that obviously this desire was more important to us than any other concern; and in view of the interest constantly shown by Marcel Griaule for Dogon daily life, observing their efforts to cultivate a difficult terrain where water was often lacking in between seasons; in view of personal relations which were not limited to the investigation, but rather became more and more confidential and friendly, the Dogon made a decision.

We discovered this only later. They themselves told us about it. The patriarchs of the lineages of the double Ogol village and the principal totemic priests of the Sanga region held council and decided to instruct Marcel Griaule. For the preliminary work, they designated one of their most qualified elders — Ogotemmêli — who, as is told in the introduction to *Dieu d'eau*,[50] solicited the first meeting. The investigation lasted exactly the number of days specified in *Dieu d'eau*, in which the rambling stream of information was faithfully recounted. And each day — unbeknown to us — a report was made to the council on the progress of instruction.

The task was all the more worthy in that the Dogon knew perfectly well that in doing this they were opening the door not just to thirty-three days of information, but to months and years of intensive work. They never deviated from this position and we express here all our gratitude; after Ogotemmêli passed away, other initiates took his place; after Marcel Griaule's death they persevered with the same patience and desire to perfect the job undertaken.

The narrative we transcribed here stems from the interpretation of facts seen from the point of view of the "clear word," *so dayi*, also called "good word," *so ezu*, the fourth word. For the initiate, it constitutes "the final state of knowledge (which) is only acquired through long years of application and perseverance." But this narration does not constitute the entirety of this word, because "the possession of very secret general principles and processes of calculation is not enough to say of someone that he holds the 'clear word;' he must materially know all the details involved. Thus the system of graphic signs, which includes thousands, must be theoretically possessed in its entirety and not simply known in its structure and its functioning."[51]

---

50. M. GRIAULE, *Dieu d'eau*, p. 7.
51. M. GRIAULE, *Le savoir des Dogon*, p. 29.

It contains, nevertheless, the essence of the broad outline of Dogon initiate knowledge.

There is no text of this myth in the Dogon language.

Certain sequences of the story it relates are the subject of invocations in the "Sigui tongue," *Sigi so;* others of certain prayers in Dogon tongue which are called *amma boy,* "the name of God"; in both cases it is a question of extremely condensed versions or of texts containing only allusions. The texts in the Sigui tongue, with the exception of the first three, deal with mythical events which will be the subject of the next installment. In the appendix to this second volume we shall give the correspondences between the myth as it is transcribed in this book and the texts in *Sigi so* already published, as well as some examples of prayers accompanied by their indispensable commentary.

It has, therefore, been necessary to follow the information in order to retell the myth. This difficult procedure offered the advantage of having to carefully match the thought processes of the informants with those of the Dogon in general.

Also, the wording as it is presented reveals the manner in which the learned men remember in relation to the plenitude of information before them; it also shows the way in which the myth is integrally lived by the population, from the representations related to the presence of an insect in the granary to those related to the performance of the most complex collective rites. For the informants the points of reference are composed of: almost all the material in Dogon use in every form and all the crafts from which each category stems; the rites (chants, prayers, dance, gestures, etc.); the figures drawn on sanctuaries and altars; individual and collective behavior.

To these points of reference — whose presence or role often relates to daily life — the commentaries are added.

From this perspective we make some comments which, by themselves, constitute glosses of certain parts of the myth. They also describe or reveal certain aspects of the rites. Being integral to the myth, they may tend to weight the text, but they demonstrate how much the Dogon are given to speculation on the history of creation, and to what extent their spirit has developed and concretely realized the consequences of this system. Strictly speaking, they do not comprise variants; these are given in the text under such a heading. But they follow the indigenous development of thought based upon mythical facts.

In the same vein, we give the indigenous etymologies, most often spontaneously offered by the informant; they may have no value from a strictly linguistic point of view, but they do reveal the Dogon mode of thought.

There follows a necessary intertwining of the narrative *per se* and all the different aspects of Dogon traditional life.

From the investigator's point of view, the commentaries on signs and drawings are indispensable to the elaboration of a text, such as the one we are presenting. So necessary these were and so natural their execution appeared to the Dogon during the investigation, that they themselves (like the Bambara) illustrated their words with ritualistic figures, without ever being asked to do so. The majority of the drawings were done on the ground or on notebooks in charcoal or pencil; the informant always worked by orienting himself to his drawing, thus underscoring the importance of that orientation.

The rapid evolution of West African societies leads us to believe that the Dogon, who had, up to now, kept their traditions, will adapt themselves, as have other populations, to a different type of life, established on other social, religious and economic bases. Political life, economic evolution, and the increasing number of conversions — especially to Islam — bring profound changes. The conditions of education, necessary for the evolution towards modern ways of life, will no longer leave the young people enough time to enter into initiation in its traditional aspects. But the knowledge of the traditions of Black African societies is of great value to the history of civilization. Therefore it becomes more necessary with each passing day that they be recorded and published, in order to be preserved, taught, and written down in the heritage of the people who have lived them.

The myths of the Dogon are presented in the first volume of *The Pale Fox;* the story of the creation of the world by Amma, God, is related in the first segment, in the second segment is related the story of the first sixty-six years of the life of man on Earth.

The reflections that have formed the subject of this introduction, concerning the social organization, Dogon thought, initiation, and the roles played by myth and cosmogony in the life of these people, far from resolve all the problems posed to the observer.

In this first volume, a certain number of themes have been brought up for examination that have already drawn the attention of sociologists and historians of religion, especially with regard to the value and function of sacrifice, the structure of totemism, and ideas concerning the existence of a supreme God and creator, etc. Other fields require other studies; for example, the important role of astronomy and, with regard to the representations, the existence of territorial constructions (raised stones and rock paintings), which concern prehistory and protohistory.

At present, it is not a question of explaining the entire theoretical structure of the system, but rather of presenting it as it appeared to us, that is to say, simultaneously thought and lived by the Dogon people.

At the end of the second installment we plan to provide the reader with some analyses and commentaries on various problems. Volume II will be devoted to the graphic initiation signs of the Dogon.

G. Dieterlen

Paris, 1963.

Note. Since 1963, expeditions led jointly by the Institut des Sciences Humaines du Mali and Mr. H. Haan, archaeologist, are conducting a systematic inventory of the settlements of the Tellem of the Cliffs, particularly in the Pegua region. This research has brought to light important material, which is at present under study (Mission Tellem Hollando-Malienne).

Paris, 1965

ILLUSTRATIONS

The map of the region inhabited by the Dogon was made from the map drawn up by the Service Geographique National at the scale of 1/200,000. The map of the Sanga region, where we have indicated the altars and sanctuaries mentioned in this work, is based on the land-apportioned layout of the Ogols, published on a large scale in 1936 by S. de Ganay. All maps have been produced by the Service de Muséologie du Musée de l'Homme, Paris.

The ritual figures illustrating this work have all been produced by our Dogon informants. Except for those specifically mentioned, the photographs were taken by M. Griaule, G. Dieterlen, or other members of the Griaule mission. The objects were photographed either by the Service de Photographie du Musée de l'Homme, or by the photographic service of the Musée National du Mali and the Musée Royal de l'Afrique Centrale (Tervueren).

MAP NO. II — Sanga Region.

The region is divided into two parts occupied by two groups of settlements: Upper Sanga and Lower Sanga, the first on the plateau, the second on a ledge at the edge of the cliff overlooking the four Banani villages established among the boulders. This territory is inhabited by the Dyon and the Arou.

Upper Sanga includes 11 villages:

— Upper Ogol, which has four quarters: Sodamma, Guendoumman, Pamyon and Do (Dyon).

— Lower Ogol, which has four quarters: Amtaba, Guinna, Tabda (Dyon) and Doziou (Arou), itself divided into two: Doziou Orey and Doziou Sangabinou.

— Go (Arou), former village of the Sangabinou family, reconstructed and inhabited by members of that family (for more than ten years).

— Upper Sanghi and Lower Sanghi (Dyon).

— Upper Ennguel and Lower Ennguel (Dyon).

— Dini (Dyon).

— Barna and Barkou (Arou); this twin settlement has the name of Barou.

— A small village inhabited by the shoemakers.

— Lower Sanga includes five villages all belonging to the Arou tribe: Gogoli, Bongo, Kangadaga, Dyamini Kouradondo and Dyamini Na, which has three quarters: Kommo, Guinna, and Somna.

The Arou, who came from Kani Kombolé along the cliffs, were the first to settle in the region where they founded Penne, now abandoned, then Gogoli and Bongo. There they found the remains of Tellem settlements, dwellings, granaries, cemeteries — particularly at Dama, Tonloÿ, I, Bara, Dalé, Amakogno, Piedonno, Dogodonno, etc., where at present bones, bricks, pottery, or potsherds are still being found. The Tellem had, in fact, left the plateau to settle in the faults and crevices of the cliffs.

The Dyon, who, like the Arou, came from Kani Kombolé, scaled the cliffs and settled on the plateau at Yaïrem Kommo; then, not far from there, they founded Kani Gogouna. One lineage left the area and migrated to the Sanga region, where they constructed dwellings and annexes in the vast rock shelter of Kéké Kommo, where one can still see the remains of former homes, granaries, sanctuaries, and altars (Map II, B). From there, the same group founded Upper Ogol, then other settlements in proportion to the development of the families.[1]

The Arou were the first to delimit the fields; they prepared caves for purposes of rituals and initiation — particularly in the valleys of Tonloÿ, Kelousommo, and Iguili. The Dyon also did the same and for the same purpose, continuing to erect sheltered constructions, rock paintings, raised stones, etc. throughout the territory.

The Arou originate from the Hogon of Arou-near-Ibi. The Hogon of Sanga is, by succession, the eldest of the Dyon patriarchs in both Ogols; he must live in Upper Ogol during his entire tenure. The altar of Lébé, the object of a collective cult, surrounded by several altars consecrated to the main *binu,* is situated on raised ground south of the village.

Legend — A, *amma doy;* B, cave *keke kommo;* C, cave of the *imina na* of Upper Ogol; D, cave *dyemme togolu* of Barna; E, *lebe dala;* F, cave of the Sigui of Lower Ogol; G, cave *toy nama kommo donu;* H, cave *toy namma kommo da;* I, *tenu amma;* J, *pegu* of Kangadaga; K, *pegu* of Dina ; L, *pegu* of la Gona; M, *polyo kommo;* N, pond of Dona; O, triple *mono* of Upper Ogol; P, *yapunu dya tolo* of the market.

---

1. For the occupation of the region, cf. G. DIETERLEN, *Les ames des Dogon,* p. 49-52 and notes.

MAP No II – Sanga Region

CHAPTER I
AMMA

I. AMMA

Creation and morphology of the signs. Classification and multiplication of the signs. From the sign to the drawing. Representations. The role of the signs.

In the beginning, before all things, was Amma, God, and he rested upon nothing. "Amma's egg in a ball"[1] was closed, but made of four parts called "clavicles," themselves ovoid and attached, as if welded together. Amma is four joined clavicles; he is only these four clavicles. It is said: "Amma's four joined (stuck together) clavicles form (are) a ball"; and one adds: "After that, there is nothing,"[2] which is to say, aside from that, nothing existed.

This egg, in its entirety, is compared to a termite hill, the base of which fans out into several cones;[3] it simultaneously evokes unity and multiplicity, for it is also said: "Amma's clavicles were stuck together; Amma's four clavicles were like four eggs."[4]

In their original sense, the four clavicles are also the prefiguration of the four elements, *kize nay,* "things four:" water (*di*), air (*ono*), fire (*yau*), earth (*minne*); likewise, the ideal bisectors which separate them will mark the collateral directions, *sibe nay,* "angles four," that is to say, space. Thus, all the fundamental elements and future space were present in the morphology of the primordial "egg."

Finally, the clavicles, in another manner, by their union, recall the form

---

1. *amma talu gunnu.*

2. *amma ani guyo vomo dania gunnu-go vo; voy la ley sele.*

3. The termite hill, *tu penu*, has several outgrowths. Very small in size, it is the work of the termite called *tu penu* or *tu tuluku.*

4. *ani guyo nay dana; amma ani guyo nay talu yege vo.*

of cereal, particularly the *yu* grain, a form described by the figure that represents it, called: "figure of the clavicles of Amma"[5] (fig. 1). It is said: "Amma's clavicle resembles the form of the *yu,* "[6] for "Amma holds life, therefore millet"; it is white, for "Amma is all white" (*amma pili vo*).

FIG. 1: *tonu of "Amma's clavicles."*

The word *amma* means: to hold firmly, to embrace strongly and keep in the same place. "One calls Amma's name all day long, one calls him when the day begins; he is Hogon (chief) of the scheme, Hogon of wasters; Amma arranges the scheme of things after he had wasted. Amma one is space fourteen (-fold). To pronounce the name of Amma is to preserve all space. The name of Amma is preservation and safe keeping of all things."[7]

---

5. *amma ani guyo tonu.* Made with porridge of *yu pilu* and *ara geu* under the altar of Amma called *tenu amma*, at the time its foundation is laid. Regarding this altar, cf. *infra,* p. 357.

This figure is also drawn every year in *yu pilu* porridge at the sowing feast, on the west side of the altar to Amma called *ka amma* (cf. also p. 354). This altar, located in Upper Ogol, belongs to the Dyon of the Sanga region; to this group, it represents the altar to Amma consecrated for the entire Dogon people in Kani Kombolé when they arrived in this region from Mandé (cf. *supra,* p. 29).

Altars consecrated to Amma (altars of the *ginna, binu,* weavers, roads, etc.) are composed of a vertically placed stone, wrapped in a mass of clay which is given an ovoid form. The stone and earth are collected at the edge of a pond. The clay contains certain elements related to the attribution of the altar: hence, the clay of the *amma* of the *ginna* contains all varieties of cereal grains (Pl V and VI).

6. *yu yege vomo amma ani guyo munu.*

7. This text is recited during the "thanksgiving to Amma" pronounced during most rites: *amma boy bononu denu, bononu ba(y) yay, kene ogone, yonone ogone; yonone beze amma kenene kene. amma vo turu, ganna pelu nay sige vo. amma vo boy vomo bone. ganna amma gele amma boy kize pu amma gele.* For "space fourteen (-fold)" cf. *infra,* p. 194.

CREATION AND MORPHOLOGY OF THE SIGNS.

Amma preserved the whole, for he had traced within himself the design of the world and of its extension. For Amma had designed the universe before creating it. The material for the design was water with

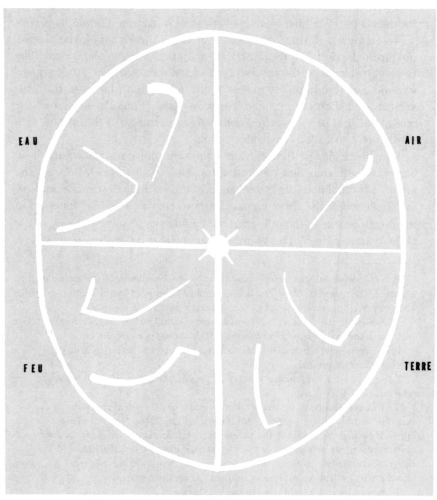

FIG. 2: *"Womb of all World Signs"* or *"Picture of Amma."*

which he traced figures in space.

Amma's egg is represented in the form of an oblong picture covered with signs, called "womb of all world signs"[8] (fig. 2), the center of which is the umbilicus. From the meeting point of the two axes extended two intersecting signs, forming bisectors marking the four cardinal directions. Each of the four sectors thus formed contained originally eight drawings, each of which, in turn, produced eight more. Thus, the oval contained 8 x 8 x 4, that is 256 outlines, to which were added 8 (2 per semi-axis) and 2 for the center. The total was then 266 "signs of Amma" (*amma bummo*).[9]

An element is attributed to each sector. Counter-clockwise, beginning from the right lower sector, they are: earth, fire, water, and air. The two central signs at the intersection of the axes are the "guide-signs," *bummo giri* (literally, "eye signs"); the four pairs placed in the four sectors are called *bummo ogo,* "master-signs";[10] the 256 signs are "the complete signs of the world" (*aduno liga bummo*). All these signs as a whole are also called "invisible Amma."

This hierarchy of figures that composes the central picture is in harmony with the "descent and extension" of the world. It bears the name of "articulated (organized) signs of the world in descent,"[11] indicating that each of the three categories performs a particular function in the development of the universe: the "guide-signs" show the way to the eight master-signs.[12] The expression may also be understood to say:

---

8. *aduno tonu fu bere.* Figure drawn during the foundation of the altar called *ka amma,* in white porridge of *ara geu. aduno* is not an Arab word for the Dogon, but rather comes from *a,* "to catch," "to seek." It is "to catch things with the mind."

9. *bummo,* literally "trace," will be translated as sign. The term implies the abstraction with which the Dogon regard the *bummo* (with reservation expressed *infra,* p. 97).

Again, the *bummo* is indeed drawn as a "trace," much like that left by a snake or insect moving across the ground.

10. *ogone* (plural *ogo*) means "chief, rich" (man); the *ogone* (Hogon) is the supreme religious and civil leader.

11. This expression alludes to the different stages of the myth in which the descents of "arks" from the sky upon the Earth will take place. Cf. p. 204 and p. 447. In Dogon tongue, *minne* connotes the element, the substance, and the planet. In order to distinguish between them, we will use earth to designate the element or substance and Earth to designate the planet. Likewise, sky, in this volume, designates the empyreal sky, called *amma alagala,* where Amma resides, and not the sky-atmosphere.

12. *bummo giru vo bummo ogo gagara ozu tagaze.*

"The guide-signs show (make known) the series[13] of the eight master-signs." This is to say that they govern and classify the following signs. As for the "eight master-signs, they give soul and life force to everything."[14] In addition, these "ten signs determine whether (a thing) is great or small in volume."[15] Finally, "the complete signs of the world give all things color, form, substance."[16] Thus do they allow an understanding of the creation, for "one knows the root (the principle or essence) of things by their form, their substance, their color."[17] This amounts to saying that signs, manifestations of creative thought, existed before the things that they determined. "In the Dogon word (idea), all things are manifested by thought; they are not known by (i.e., do not exist in) themselves."[18]

In the graphic depiction, the mechanism of creation thus contains ten fixed signs (two "guides" and eight "masters"), which give life to the mobile ("complete") signs, which then bring things into existence.

a) The first of the two "guides" is called *burigia goy,* "the springing forth of conception"[19] (fig. 3, to the right). The essential part, air, is formed in the center by a sort of "S" (from *b* to *c*); the air blows on the water, the bent segment (*b* to *d*), recalling the winding of the torrents, making it spurt into droplets, which form beings. It acts in like manner on the earth, indicated by the lightly curved extension of the "S" (from *d* to the end). It erodes the earth and projects it into dust, which forms beings. Fire, lower part of the "S" (*a* to *b*), is as if separated from the other elements; in its meandering are seen the wood of the hearths (break on the left) and the rising flame (break on the right). Air blows upon the fire, which throws off sparks and forms beings. Mixing together the whole and creating from his own substance a fourth type of beings,

---

13. The word *ozu,* "way," also means "continuation, series, alignment."

14. *gagara ogo bummo be nyama-le kikinu-le obonu.*

15. *bummo pelu-go bari-go daga-le die-le kolo biedo-go vogoy.* The term *kolo* means "belly" and, by extension, "interior, volume."

16. *aduno liga bummo be gozu-le yege-le digu-le obonu.*

17. *kize du dugomo-de yege vomo-le bana vomo-le gozu vomo-le. gozu,* "body," also means "color or appearance."

18. *dogo so-ne kize fu azubu-le taganu, kugo dugomole.* The term *so* may be translated as "word, meaning, or idea."

19. *burigia* means "combination of ideas, design, or views."

Amma causes in each of the particles an explosion that is at the origin of existence.

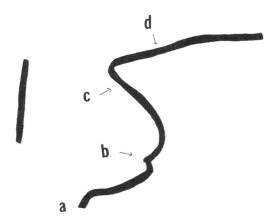

FIG. 3: The two "guide-signs."

b) The second of the two "guides" is called "sign of the envelope" (*kogo bummo*). It is made with a simple vertical line representing the envelope (*kogo*)[20] of beings (fig. 3, to the left). Its role is to bring over to the "master signs," repositories of souls and forces, the exuviae of the "four elements" used in the mixture determined by the first guide.

The exuviae are the testimony of existing things; they remain inside of Amma and recall that in the beginning Amma first created his own twin, that is, the universe itself. Just as the universe is the replica of Amma and contains him, this universe was — and will remain — contained by Amma in the form of signs.

c) The pairs of "master-signs" assigned to each sector (fig. 4) relate to the corresponding elements of which they represent two principal states.

— In A, we see an obliquely laid arc with a straight segment on the bottom forming a hook. This is the sign of the earth in its incompleteness (because the segment is to be broken by the Fox who will steal the

---

20. *kogo* is said especially of the skin of an exuviable animal. The Bambara see in the being's covering or exuvia (*mana* or *folo*), not only a residual form, or shadow of what it was, but also a deposit which may be donned again by a new life. Cf. G. DIETERLEN, *Essai sur la religion bambara,* p. 4, n. 1.

end of it).[21] In *a,* a sign vaguely repeating A, the bottom part forming a hook, is the piece stolen by the Fox, who descends along the vertical axis. The stolen part is represented by a thinner line, minimizing the felonious act.

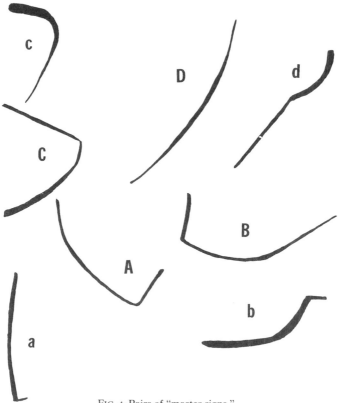

FIG. 4: Pairs of "master-signs."

—In B, a hooked curve with a straight end recalls the crooked stick of the ritual thief with which he stole the celestial fire, that was later used by the blacksmith. In *b*, the forge oven and firewood are represented by a thick curved line raised on the right, ended by a thinner appendage, the flame.

---

21. Cf. *infra,* p. 208.

— In C, an arc, with its concavity directed to the left, is attached to a tilted straight segment, symbolizing the opening of the sky giving passage to water. At the juncture of the two segments, the thinner line of the arc's extremity represents the source from which issue forth two flows of water. In *c,* this opening has grown larger to permit the descent of the "ark of the world"; the line of *c*, which widens from bottom to top, represents a widening flow of water.

— In D, a long, thin, wide-open crescent moon is the air spread across all the regions; thick in the center, it is rarer in the heights and depths of space. *d* is a sort of thick scythe, wide open with a thin handle. It symbolizes strong, warm air, the handle being the air of cool climates.

The role of the "master-signs" is to receive, one by one, the signs ejected by the first guide before they are thrown into space to manifest things.

d) The development of "complete signs," the third sort of sign, from creation to the realization of the thing, is shown here below, taking as an example that of the house.

The sign of the house (fig. 5) in Amma's body, before any manifestation, is made of a point *a,* called "courtyard of the house," *ginu gonno,* which belongs to the earth sector. The courtyard, where all those living in the house must pass through, is the meeting place of souls and forces, the place of words and ideas. "In this point is the idea for the future design

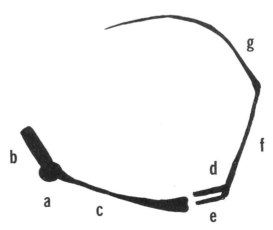

FIG. 5: Sign of the house.

of the house,"[22], that is to say, the idea of the four signs articulated into one, which form that of the house, and which are:

— Line *b,* thick, forming an obtuse angle at *a,* up and to the left, and called "form of the house" (*ginu yege*); it is in the domain of the earth.

— The very wide are *c* "post of the house" (*ginu dey*), from *a* to the right; it is somewhat widened at its end to recall the irregularity of the house which grows in every direction. It is in the domain of fire, for wood is at the source of man's fire.

— After *c* and its extension, a thin line, *e,* is the "life force of the house" (*ginu nyama*). Line *d,* somewhat thicker than *e* and parallel to it, is the "soul of the house" (*ginu kikinu).*[23]

— Finally, the open arc *f,* to which are attached *d* and *e,* is the "wind of the house," which has brought the soul. It is in the domain of air. Arc *g,* which extends it by bending back toward *b,* is the "water of the house" (*ginu di*), which brought the force, *nyama.* It ends in a point, the source. It belongs to the domain of water.

In the form of point *a,* the sign first passes through the "master-signs" corresponding to it in the earth sector, where it receives the souls and force, *nyama,* of the house, which gives it form *b.* Then it comes into contact with the "master-signs" of the fire sector, where it takes on *c.* In the "master-signs" of the air sector it takes on *f,* which gives form to the soul, until then attached to the *nyama.* In the water sector it takes on *g.* Souls and *nyama* are definitively separated; thus, each sign contains one principal element and, less importantly, the three others.

Continuing to turn, the sign is ejected from the picture and describes a spiral plane, in the course of which the four parts separate to each take on a new appearance. (cf. fig. 6):

---

22. *gunnu-go-ne ginu tonu vede-go azubu kolo-go-ne to.*

23. *kikinu* in Sanga, in Tombo *so kindu kindu,* this word comes from *kinu,* "breath , life" and, by extension, "nose." The living beings will be animated by four pairs of souls or *kikinu,* two of body (*gozu kikinu*), two of sex (*du kikinu*). Each pair includes a male element (*ana*) and a female element (*ya*); in each of the two groups, one of the pairs is called "intelligent" (*say*); the other, considered as a double or reflection of the first, is called "trace," *bummo* or "fool," *bommo.* Therefore, it is compared to the "shadow" borne by a body and may have been confused with it at the beginning of the investigations.

—*b,* the form, becomes *b',* earth, because it is the earth which gives
the house its form. Arc-shaped, the sign shows one thick end, the first
earth and first world, and a tapered one, the second earth and second
world.

— On *c',* an arch with the right end raised, the left break symbolizes
the hearth where the wood burns that is used in construction.

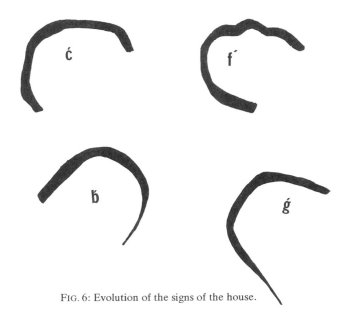

FIG. 6: Evolution of the signs of the house.

— *f* becomes *f',* the form of which is similar to that of *c',* and it shows a
meandering downstroke to recall the vibration of the air.

— *g'* corresponding to *g,* shows a tapered extension of its lower
branch, the flowing of water.

But the forms and the volumes were not abruptly acquired. In the
course of these transformations, which proceed in a continuous movement,
like a series of explosions each element of the decomposition was
formed through seven stages, respectively marked by the sign corresponding to each of the seven increasingly larger volumes.

Thus, the part of the sign of the "tomato" *kelie,* which has the meaning
of fire and is made of a long vertical line with a horizontal hook, develops

according to the diagram of fig. 7, C: the final drawing, the eighth (fig. 7, B), keeps the same form on a larger scale.

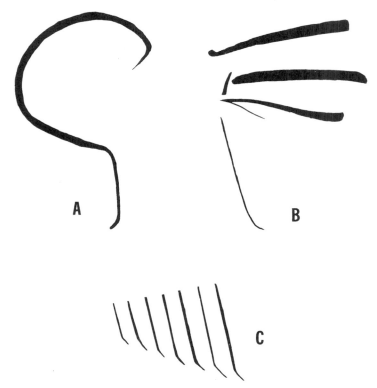

FIG. 7: Sign of the Nommo's tomato. A. Sign of the tomato.
B. Decomposition of the sign. C. Example of the progression of the bottom line of B.

Theoretically, each of these seven signs possesses a "soul," which is eventually mixed in with the others and with the whole; hence, the name of *kikinu say* (euphemism for *kikinu soy,* "souls seven") given to the spiritual principles, which are the consciousness and intelligence of every being.

When each part is formed according to the process described above, the sign, in its four-part situation, manifests the thing created, brings it into existence: "Amma's signs, which he sent into the world, went, entered into things which (at that moment) became."[24]

But if the sign precedes the thing signified, it is dependent upon the conscious and active mind. It is said, "Amma, in beginning things, chose the *bummo* with thought. The first design, it is through (the work of) thought that it was divided (into four). It is (also by) this that the final design (in four parts) was made."[25] It is the mind which conceived and produced the initial design and which perfected it by dividing it, so as to specify the essence of things. In its first state, the sign is an articulated whole, then divided into four parts, permitting the recognition of the basic elements which give rise to the thing. But a thing, in turn, is a rearticulation of the parts forming a complete and unique whole, which is the thing itself: "The sign of Amma is one (whole). (Amma) broke it down (into) distinct (parts), he presented the image of the four elements, (the thing) existed (by forming) a whole."[26]

And having sprung into existence, the thing becomes conscious of itself, "comprehends itself,"[27] as indicated by the presence of the *kikinu say,* "intelligent soul," in the sign. It does all the more so in that the purpose of the decomposition was to go into the details of a definition, more explicitly by the separate elements than by the total sign they finally form.

All of the "complete signs" undergo the transformations and elaborations presented above. They are the development of a family comparable to that of man and mythical ancestors: the initial pair at the center is the pair of great Nommo. The eight masters are the eight ancestors; the others are descendants of the first ten, and they form a set of *nani,* that is, of relays supporting the spiritual principles of the first.

Moreover, in the formation itself of the abstract signs that prefigure the world the very essence is manifest of this creation that is about to be

---

24. *amma tonu aduno-ne vo ti-go ya, kize-ne yoa, voy bi.* The last term literally means "have become."

25. *amma tolo-vo-ze kize azubu-le bummo bozi. tonu la-go vogo azubu-go gammala dagu. vogo-de-go tonu-go doga via yegi.*

26. *amma tonu koturu, vo dede bozo-go kize nay tana, tana vomo-le monu-go bie gay. koturu* means "one, unique, unity." It is said of two things of which one wishes to express the identity, like one would say "it's all the same thing." *mono* means "whole, all, coming-together"; it is a question of a unity composed of several parts.

27. *ku vomo-le dana.*

sexualized. The being created will possess male principles, *ana,* and female principles, *ya.* Of this it is said: "Amma, when he created a living thing, puts the *kikinu say ya* in the designs of the placenta. The *kikinu say ana* is placed in the womb itself. In each articulation of the sign there are the different designs of the *kikinu say ya.* The different articulations all drawn together are like a person."[28]

With regard to social structure, "the 266 mother-signs belong to the four families as a whole."[29] As such, they will be schematically represented either on the walls and doors of dwellings and on the main family sanctuaries, or in the sacred fields.

Moreover, Amma's 266 *bummo,* of which we have seen the basic division into 8 (cf. p. 84), are also classified in the following manner: 6, then 20, then 4 times 60. During the sowing celebration, when the sacrifice is offered on the altar called *manna amma,* "Amma of the sky," the Arou priest says: "Amma's number is 266; it begins with 6 *bummo* to which are added 20; 4 times 60 more; Amma made 6 *bummo* of things in the beginning; he added 20 (then) placed 4 times 60 more (*bummo*)."[30]

These two ways denote a division in base 8, female, and a division in base 6, male. This expresses that the *bummo,* symbol of Amma's creative thought, contains in essence — by the specific value of the number, another fundamental expression of the groundwork of creation — sexual twinness, male and female, which will be at the base of the realization in matter of divine thought.[31]

CLASSIFICATION AND MULTIPLICATION OF SIGNS.

The 266 signs of Amma, called "mother-signs," *bummo na,* are classified into categories which sum up the essence of his thought.

---

28. *amma kize omo vo mani, me tonu-ne kikinu say ya kunni. kikinu say ana valu-ne to. kikinu say ya tonu dede digu tuturu to. digu dede mona tumogo inne anay.*

29. *tonu sunu tanu pelley kuloy sige vogo togu nay fu vey.*

30. *amma lugu sunu tanu pelley kuloy sige oboze. tologo kuloy bummo pelley bara. pelu kuloy kule nay sigiri. amma kize polo bummo kuloy pelley bara. pelu kuloy kule nay sigera dagi.*

31. Cf. p. 142. This division of signs is also reflected in the social structure. The female number is attributed to the Dyon and represented by the figure drawn under their main altar. The male number is mentioned during the ceremony performed by the Arou and in relation to their main altar.

This distribution defines itself as follows:

— The two "guide-signs" by virtue of their essence "belong" to Amma alone, and because of this they are set apart;

— the 264 following signs are classified into 22 categories, called "twenty-two families of king-things" (*kize ogo pelley ley sige togu*); they each bear a name that characterizes their content; they are, in order:

amma	"Amma," God
vageu	"ancestors"
lebe	"Lebe"
binu	"Binou," totem
so	"(spoken) word"
goru	ceremony of the winter solstice, the Dogon new year
mono	"meeting"
bado	"father come" spring (sowing)
dine	"winter-time" rainy season
bago	"father gone" autumn (harvest)
nay banu	"red sun," dry, hot season
volu	"cultivation"
gelu	"harvest"
iru	"forge"
soyti	"weaving"
toro may	"pottery work"
yau	"fire"
di	"water"
ono	"air"
minne	"earth"
dogo	"grass"
di bana	"master of water," Nommo

Each of these categories includes twelve signs.

But the abstract signs are not limited to the first series. Just as the universe will expand, as the beings created by Amma will multiply, as the worlds formed by him will be innumerable, so too the signs must multiply. Each of them, in the beginning, is considered as having to form, in its turn, a series of 266 signs. It is said: "Two hundred sixty-six (signs) emerge from the inside (foundation) of each sign."[32] Also, the signs will proliferate in order to produce in the abstract all of the things which must make up the universe.

FROM SIGN TO DRAWING.

The development of the beings and things of the universe is prefigured not only by the 266 *bummo* and their multiplication, but also by the modification and progression of the form of the sign that will lead to the realization of the thing or being.

Because after the first series, that of abstract signs or "trace" *bummo,* will come the second series, that of the *yala* "mark" or "image," executed in dotted lines (fig. 8). "The *yala* of a thing is like the beginning of the thing."[33] Therefore, when one builds a house, one delineates the foundation with stones placed at the corners: these stones are the *yala,* the "marks," of the future dwelling. The term *yala* also has the meaning of "reflection," which expresses the future form of the thing represented.

The third series of signs is that of the *tonu,* "figure," "diagram," or

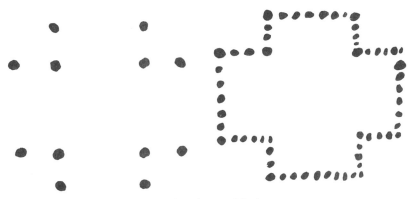

FIG. 8: *yala* and *tonu* of the house.

sometimes "periphery," of things. The *tonu* is a schematic outline of generally separated graphic elements; it is the sketch, the rough draft of the

---

32. *tonu sunu tanu pelley kuloy sige tonu tuturu-ne vogo doy goy.* The complete study of the theory of signs and the great many *bummo* which have been brought to light, classified, and commented upon will be the subject of volume II.

33. *kize yala kize tolo anay.*

thing or being represented. The word *tonu* comes from *tono*, "to portray," which also means "to begin," but in the dynamic sense of the word.[34] It is said that Amma "began things," *amma kize tono,* to demonstrate the initial impetus he gave to creation. This idea of impulsion is not expressed in *amma kize mana,* "Amma created things," which denotes the action undertaken and finished by Amma. The *tonu* of the house connotes the pebbles that have been placed between the corner-stones to delimit the walls (fig. 8).

The fourth series consists of the "drawings," *toymu* (or *toy*), as realistically representative of the thing as possible. It is also the thing itself. When one has finished the building of a house, it is as if one had made a complete drawing, *toymu,* of the house.

In speaking of the *toy* and of Amma, one says: "To make the drawing is to make the thing that he (Amma) has in mind."[35] It is, therefore, to represent the thing created in its reality.

The successive appearance of the spiritual principles is also stressed by the progressions of the figures: in the *bummo* are the four *kikinu* of body, which are the four elements created by Amma from them. In the *yala* and the *tonu* is placed the life force, *nyama.* Thus, the *nyama* of earth is in the stones at the corners of houses which are said to possess "the *nyama* of the corners of the house."[36] It is said of the *tonu* of the house (that is, the elements placed between the stones at the corners defining the wall boundaries), that it possesses "the *nyama* of the four sides of the house."[37] In the *toymu,* the living being is animated and his spiritual principles are gathered together. The *toymu* of the house is like the house itself containing the four elements. And as the house is an inanimate being, its "souls," *kikinu,* remain in the initial *bummo* in the hands of Amma: their evidence will be the incorruptible bulb called *nono*[38] (a word meaning "immortal"), which is placed deep in the

34. *tono* is different from *tolo,* which means "beginning" or "first" and is used in the preceding sentence.

35. *kize yiru vomo-ne to kani.* One also says *kize bere vomo-ne to kani.* "It is to make the thing he has in his womb."

36. *ginu sibe nyama.*

37. *ginu benne nay nyama.*

38. Cf. G. DIETERLEN, *Classification des végétaux chez les Dogon,* p. 153.

ground at one of the corners of the house.

With regard to living beings, the process of coming into being is the same. The semen that penetrates the woman is called *i yala illi* "blood-mark of the child." It is transformed into the fetus which is the *tonu;* the child itself, when it has been completely formed, is a *toy*: "The four (body) *kikinu* of man are the *yala* (images) of the four elements together; man's four *kikinu* are (like) *tonu;* a man by himself is a *toy.* "[39] When the mother's belly stirs, it is said: "The woman's belly has drawn the child."[40]

In like manner, the succession of figures is representative of the growth of grain. "Drawing the *bummo* is like (drawing) the life of the grain; drawing the *yala* is like the seeding; drawing the *tonu* like the germination; drawing the *toy* like the growth of the stem."[41] And one adds: "Carving is like the forming of the ear."[42]

The difference that exists between these various representations expresses the stages of creation. (That is why we give the pertinent explanations here.)

In the *bummo* lies a prefiguration of the being, not in its physical form, but insofar as a material form may be interpreted into the image of the ideas and functions related to the being that is represented.

— The *bummo* of the *po* prefigure its spiral movement. The image does not connote a seed, but the internal life of that seed.

— The *bummo* of the house made of associated elements connotes the "family circle" around the dwelling's central courtyard.

— The *bummo* of the *nommo anagonno,* symbol of the fetus, is the image of its future multiplication and of the number of its spiritual principles.[43]

Thus, the abstraction we attribute to the *bummo,* which is a real one with respect to the material realization of the being it designates, is only a pseudo-abstraction: the symbolism encompasses characters, ideas, functions, and designs.

---

39. *inne kikinu nay kize monu yalay; inne kikinu nay toni; inne voturu toyi.*

40. *yana bere i tonati.*

41. *toy bummo dene kinu anay; toy yala dene i anay; toy tonu dene tele anay; toy toymu dene kinu timmu-ne anay.*

42. *lobolo dene puru anay.*

43. For these different *bummo,* cf. *infra,* p. 136, fig .21 and p. 166, fig. 35.

The *yala*, on the contrary, brings into play two complementary yet different elements:

1. By a dotted line - drawing it connotes the theoretical design of the being represented, this theory also defining function, here associated with form.

2. The dotted line is number, and this number corresponds to the fundamental numerical classification of the universal elements. In this way, the dotted line classifies the thing:

— The *yala* of the house indicates the corners of the future dwelling, the supports for the structure. It is made of twelve dots, the number attributed to uncultivated land and to the Fox.

— The *yala* of Amma's "egg" features within it a spiral indicating the form of the development of life inside the "egg." It is made of 266 dots, standing for the 266 fundamental signs.[44]

The *tonu* is a diagram which connotes the being in the process of formation, focusing upon the organs or elements essential to that being:

The *tonu* of the *nommo anagonno* connotes:

a) its internal organs at the rough draft stage,

b) the "putting into place" of these elements.[45]

The *toy* is a drawing which attains maximum realism. *"toymu* (drawing) and *tonu* (figure) are not alike. The drawing resembles the thing (represented) and the figure is the diagram of the image (symbol) of the thing."[46]

The independence and autonomy of the sign in relation to the drawing representing the formed being are also emphasized: "The sign is and walks about in the mind and the head. The words of the drawing are in the body. The word (of) that which is painted is in the joints. The sign is the drawing that walks about."[47] And again: "The sign of the Dogon (spoken) word represents things. The sign is things that move about in the world. The sign is the thing of all men. Commerce makes things go around in the world. The sign and commerce are one thing, just one word."[48]

---

44. Cf. *infra*, p. 121.

45. Cf. *infra*, p. 169, fig. 37.

46. *tonu-le toymu-le tumoy la. toymu kize vogo-le munu, tonu kize vogo-le yalay.*

47. *tonu ku bonnu-ne to yayala. toy so gozu-ne to. so digu-ne to toymu. toy tonu yalay.*

48. *tonu dogo so koro kize tanaze. tonu aduno-ne kize yalay. tonu inneu voy kizey. tonu aduno-ne kize vilemeze. tonu tonu-le keke, boy tumoy.*

Moreover, as we have seen, first the sign and then the diagrams are evidence of the genesis of the thing they represent; whereas the drawing realizes it and therefore leads it to its end. It is said: "The sign which one writes (is) the good to come. The drawing that one draws is, after the good, the bad (which) follows (literally: ends)."[49] This expression is commented upon as follows: "In Amma's body were the signs. Amma made the world through the addition of signs (that is, by accumulating signs). The signs went into each thing, transformed themselves into drawings, drew the departure toward the end (that is, marked the beginning of the transition). The sign is (a) good thing (always) there; the drawing is a thing that has an end."[50] To draw is to make (something) begin to be, thus marking the first step toward destruction.

But if the sign and the drawing are the history of the past, they are also a means of acting upon the future. The ritual execution of successive graphic designs is effectual and active: it promotes the existence of the thing represented, "re-edits" it by having it pass through its successive stages of formation (particularly on the inside and on the façade of sanctuaries).

The material used for the figures has a value in itself; hence, the use of this or that variety of cereal grain in the preparation of the porridges intended for their production, and the use of red earth, *bana,* of charcoal, etc., for figures in color. Added to the symbolism of the figure itself is the symbolism of the color used. Polychrome paintings, so-called *toy lelemu,* "variegated drawings," attain a maximum of expression and effectiveness (Plate VII).

We have seen that the morphology of the *bummo* is associated with the presence of the four elements (*kize nay*), which remains implicit in the series of figures that follow it. But all must show evidence of the complementary presence of the four directions of space (*sibe nay*), which will locate the thing represented: thus all figures will always be oriented.

The *bummo,* symbol of Amma's work, accomplished in the confines of his "bosom," is ritually executed — and generally only once — under

---

49. *tonu ezu vedo tononu. toymu ezu onune monu dogoydo toymonu.*

50. *amma gozu-ne tonu tobe. amma tonu-go-le bara ganna ginne gala. tonu kize dede-ne yoa, toymu tana, ya-ye dogoydo toymonu. tonu kize ezi-vo, toymu kize dogoydo.*

the altars at the time of their founding, or inside the sanctuaries where none except the priest responsible may penetrate. On the other hand, the *toy* drawings representing the realized thing (which has) "emerged from the bosom," are made on the façades of dwellings or sanctuaries and may be seen by all. In addition, the drawing is washed by the rain, which "carries along (to the outside)" its form and force to "give it to man" and to promote that which it represents into reality.

Example: the first year of the construction of a totemic sanctuary, the priest himself draws the *po* with the porridge of *po pilu* inside the building. The second year, the *po* is drawn on the outside by the sacrificer; the rain water "carries down the drawing to the fields," where it promotes growth.

This idea of the specific action of the sign or drawing in the future also applies to the lines traced on the ground for divination on the tables of the Fox. It is said: "The things which one draws, one draws the drawings in order to know the things which will come tomorrow (that is, in the future)."[51]

Finally, the graphic designs contain a teaching: the abstract sign, executed in a profane manner, but in secret (in the image of the "secret" of God's bosom where it was formed), is done for the initiate; the actual drawing, which all may see, is for the neophyte. For they form a system of archives. "The signs of things of the past teach the children; the signs of things of the past, that is the road one follows; it is so that the children will take again (re-make) the signs of the old things (customs) that one draws them."[52]

The more signs a man possesses the more learned he is; the knowledge of the elements of creation consists not only of the knowledge of the sign, but of the elements that compose it. Yet no one would know how to invent a *bummo,* nor how to modify the traditional set of *bummo.* To trace a new sign would be to create a new thing, thus to go "further" than Amma.

One would say of a person acting this way: "He has surpassed (lacked respect for) Amma," *amma galay.*[53]

---

51. *kize tononu, yogo kize vedo dugo tonu toni.*

52. *ya kize pey tonu unu taguru. ya kize pey tonu ozu dimmi. unu ya kize pey tonu dey dey voy toni. dey "to learn."*

53. One may insult another person by saying to him: "Amma drew (designed) you badly," *amma uy toni ezila.*

Plate V: 1) The altar to Amma in the *ginna* of Doziou-Orey (Lower Ogol).

2) Shelter of men, *toguna,* and altar to Amma at Iréli.

3) The altar to Amma in the *ginna* of Amtaba (Lower Ogol).

1) *amma doy*.
In the background, the last constructions
to the north of Lower Ogol.

Plate VI:

2) Altar to Amma and totemic
sanctuary of Kèkè Kommo.

3) Kèkè Kommo cave (south part) first dwelling of the Dyon of Sanga.

Upon executing the figures, the priest says: "May the mind of Amma pass into me; may Amma place me before men, may he add more life to me."[54]

REPRESENTATIONS.

This conception of creation is recalled by a figure of the 266 primordal signs schematically drawn under a raised stone at the time when it is erected in a certain area representing, in the territory of Sanga, the "seat of Amma," *amma doy* (cf. Map II, A and Plate VI: 1). This place is theoretically both the "picture of signs" and the "center of Amma's egg," his first manifestation after the picture itself (fig. 9). It is said of this figure of 266 signs: "The *bummo,* which are Amma himself, are the 266 things that he began."[55]

It reflects the series of signs which repeat the successive stages of all things: the *bummo* (are shown) by zigzagging dashes (this formation testifying to the "life" of the *bummo*); the *yala* by dashed lines; the *tonu* shown on a circle divided into four segments: their appearance, which is that of form, is also that of space, for they stand for the four collateral directions or "angles four," *sibe nay.* Finally, the central *toy* where the signs are linked in a zigzagging line, thus evincing both their final stage and their animation.[56]

In this system of representation, the succession of figures also signifies the presence of the four elements, the *bummo* being air, the *yala* fire, the *tonu* water, and the *toy* earth. An analogous figure is drawn under the altar to Amma in the first Arou *ginna,* located at Arou-near-Ibi, but the four segments of *tonu,* also oriented, present the cardinal directions, *benne nay,* "sides four," in relation to terrestrial space, whereas those in the preceding figure are positioned according to a celestial orientation (*sibe nay* "angles four").[57]

---

54. *amma ku bonnu mane; tana inne mo-ne ma giru kunno, kinu tamu sige mane bara.*

55. *bummo amma ku vomo-le kize sunu tanu pelley kuloy sige vo tolo.*

56. The outside circle was made by scratching the soil with the bark of *pelu* to obtain the "traces," the dotted line with a stalk of *yayaga* grass, the four *tonu* with a stalk of *sana,* the *toy* with bark of *kilena.* For the reasons for the use of these plants (which are agents of purification), cf. *infra,* p. 330. For the "mythical" revelation of the 266 *bummo* to man and the determination of the site of the *amma doy,* cf. volume I (2nd installment, first year).

57. Drawn as follows: the *bummo* in crushed *pelu* bark mixed with water (water); the *yala* in *kilena* bark prepared in the same way (air); the *tonu* in *yu* porridge (fire); the *toy* in

The role of the signs is recalled by the prayer accompanying the sacrifice offered on this altar at the time of the *goru* ceremony (performed at the winter solstice).

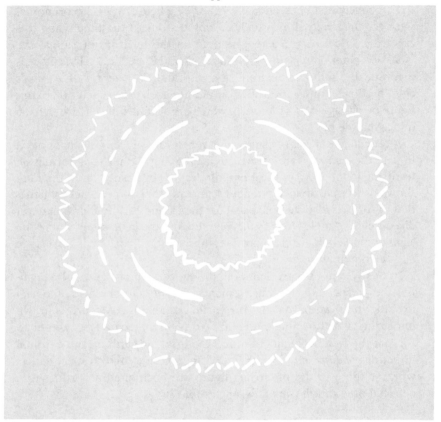

FIG. 9: Figure of signs drawn under the "seat of Amma," *amma doy.*

The patriarch who convenes the whole family in the *ginna* says: "Amma of the *ginna*, who emerged from the body of Amma the creator, may Amma give us persons (to be born), from his body there came forth 266 things;

porridge of *ara geu* (earth). The four substances produce four colors also associated with these representations.

give us marriage, give us children to be born; have us bear (upon our shoulder) the casting stick *(donnolo);* give us the eight grains and the calabash as the ninth; take and drink (the sacrifice); drink not the blood of man but that of fowl, of beasts; make that the 'coming (out) of the father' (the harvest) finds us (in the same place)."[58] Then he orders the sacrificer to make the offering by saying: "pour" *(suro).*

The autonomy of the sign *(bummo)* and its character of primordial essence of the thing it designates, by a sort of manipulation of the four elements, are also emphasized by the fact that only the three circles *yala, tonu* and *toy* are drawn under the altar called *anakazu dummo,* "stone of the worthy," consecrated to Amma and placed in the central square *(tay)* of each village at the time of its founding; for if the *amma doy* represents "Amma in the sky," the *anakazu dummo* represents him on Earth among mankind. The stone is carved into a slight point (in the form of an egg); it is quadrangular, the corners marking the cardinal directions of the future "opening of Amma's egg."[59]

Moreover, the entire set of signs, in all their forms (*bummo, yala, toy,* and *tonu),* is drawn on the inside and on the façade of the principal totemic sanctuaries over a period of sixty years, sixty being the "number of the placenta" *(me lugu).* In their totality they are called: "drawings of all the years which come" or "drawings of all of the sixty years."[60] "On the sanctuary, one draws some things, (that) goes (i.e., leaves) and will happen (up until) sixty years."[61]

Now, for every sanctuary the series of figures drawn each year is different. "Each year, the drawings change for every different sanctuary."[62]

---

58. *ginna amma, amma manu gozu-ne goy, amma inneu emmi solu solo, gozu uone kize si sunu tanu pelley kuloy sige goy, yadi emmi obo, i nonu emmi obo donnolo emmi gogoro, dene gagara gaba kozu-le tuo emmi obo, yabu no, inneu illi nono, ene illi no, belu illi no, ba go-ye emmi temmemo.*

59. The *anakazu dummo* will be built with a stone picked in the field of the *ginna* during the sacrifice and resurrection (in the form of a snake) of the ancestor Dyongou Sérou (vol. II, third year).

According to rule, it is built in the public square of every village, preferably to the north, and not far from the "shelter of men" *togu-na.*

60. *anakuzu vedo voy tonu* or *anakazu pelu kuloy tonu.*

61. *binu ginu-ne kize dede tononu. yaye anakuzu pelu kuloy doze.*

62. *anakuzu turu binu ginu-ne tonu dede toni.*

The entire set of drawings of all the sanctuaries drawn in a single year represents, in mythical time, "Amma's work of one day." "In one year the different drawings on the sanctuary, this is Amma's work of one day. The different drawings that one draws on the sanctuary each year, when one arrives at sixty years, (their) entirety is the number of Amma who creates the world."[63]

So, for all the totems of the Dogon people, all of Amma's signs that formed the world are repeated over a period of time, which connotes the time or duration of Amma's creation. This repetition, considered active and effectual, has as its function to perpetuate the being or the thing represented.[64]

The 266 primordial signs are executed on the platform of the Hogon of Arou during the ordination ceremonies of that dignitary. The figure consisting of a circle (made with the porridge of *yu* and *ara geu*), in the center of which are placed 266 dots, is drawn by the patriarch of the oldest family of the tribe which founded the village; he then has the new Hogon sit upon the signs.

In the past the whole set of signs was carved on the entrance door of the Arou chief;[65] this was the collective work of the oldest smiths, chosen from among the *demmene*.[66] It was made of two panels that were joined

---

63. *anakuzu voy tonu binu ginu dede dilleze, amma bay turu bire vomoy. binu ginu-ne tonu anakuzu dede tononu anakuzu pelu kuloy doze mona amma aduno manu lugi.*

64. The figures constitute the "totemic emblems" of the Dogon. The signs corresponding to one of the categories are drawn on the respective façades of the different totemic sanctuaries; in Sanga, the signs of the category *amma* are drawn upon the sanctuary of the Yébéné totem; those of the category *inne,* on the sanctuary of the Ogoiné totem; those of the category *dine,* on the sanctuary of the Tiré totem; those of the category *di,* on the sanctuary of the Goummoyana totem; those of the category *nay banu,* on the sanctuary of the Sangabilou totem, etc. There are eight permanent signs or drawings for each totem and permutations of the other figures. In practice, keeping in mind the duration of the act of drawing, which most often exceeds the length of the priest's administration, the application of this theory cannot be very strict; however, in the eyes of its users, it retains all its value and effectiveness. Cf. G. DIETERLEN, *Blasons et emblèmes totémiques des Dogon,* p. 4. For the totem and its function within the clan, cf. *infra,* p. 338.

65. Ongnonlou saw this door in its place in the village of Arou-near-Ibi around 1900. Around 1948, he saw some pieces of it kept in one of the chief's granaries.

66. The *demmene* are considered to be the only true smiths. The *iru,* however, who are spread throughout the plateau, share their skills and privileges.

together, each showing eleven columns of twelve elements, a total of 264 (fig. 10, A).[67] The whole set was surrounded, or rather connected, by a sort of network formed by the twenty-two signs of series 11 of the *di bana* category (fig. 10, B), which, carved according to numerical order, marked the angles of a broken spiral, starting at the center and unwinding toward the periphery, closing upon itself again.

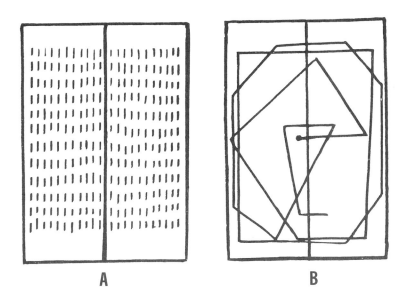

A　　　　　　　　　　　　　B

FIG. 10: Theoretical diagrams of the carved panels of the door of the Hogon of Arou; A. The 266 primordial signs; B. the twenty-two signs of the *di bana* category engraved upon A.

The eight doors of the various dwellings and annexes of a large family formerly used to be covered with signs reserved for the tribe. The most important one, *ogo ta,* "chief door," placed at the entrance of the dwelling, showed half of the signs; together the following seven showed the other half.

---

67. In reality, Arou is considered as owning only half the signs, the other half belonging to the Dyon. The construction of the *ginna* will be described in the second installment, first year.

The creation and the picture of the signs are also commemorated annually before sowing (*bado*) by the following ritual. Early in the morning the head of the family goes to the "field of the ancestors," *vageu minne,* and clears a neat area at the center for making the signs. On this spot he then places a *tazu* basket upside down to draw a circle, which will bear the same name as the altar of the field: then he makes a pile of stones, *sogo.*[68] Facing the east, he first draws on the ground a small circle about 12 cm. in diameter inside the first circle, with a dot in the center. In the course of that day, he makes a zigzag line around the

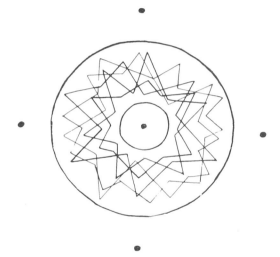

FIG. 11: Theoretical diagram of the 266 signs drawn on the ground of the "field of ancestors," *vageu minne.*

inner circle, repeating this twenty-two times, so as to fill the outer circle with an intricate tangle of lines representing all possible signs (fig. 11). One says of this gesture: "The 266 (signs) are drawn in the center of the field of the ancestors."[69] While he is drawing them, the patriarch says: "Amma, give rain, give ripe millet, may the millet re-enter by the East."[70]

---

68. For the *sogo,* cf. *infra,* p. 164, note 201, and p. 492.

69. *sunu tanu pelley kuloy . . . sige-go vageu minne-ne logorogo-ne tononu.*

70. *amma ana di dele, yu ille dele, yu du yo.* The rain comes from the east in the cliff region. The patriarch can also draw a 23rd zigzag for the signs corresponding to his personal activity, those of weaving or of divination, for example.

The area of the field on which the signs are made remains clear of grain, but one places a bit of manure outside at the four cardinal points and plants a seed, which is covered with a mound of earth.

The central circle, not covered by signs, is the sky; around it are the heavenly bodies. To each sign corresponds a heavenly body. The four seeds are the four cardinal points. The drawing also connotes all the grains which are thus represented in the *yu* field, even though they are not actually sown. The field is then seeded by the family; in the wintertime, one can recognize in the empty center the spot where the signs were made.

ROLE OF THE SIGNS.

Thus, by signs, the direct expression of his thought, Amma will begin his creation, the creation of the "world" *aduno.* "The *bummo,* which are Amma himself, are the 266 beginning things (i.e., that he began)."[71]

One says of Amma that he "began things," *amma kize tono;* this last term in its dynamic sense indicating the initial impetus he gave to creation, as well as his intention to create. "When Amma began *(tono)* things, he had his thought in his mind. The thought he had written *(tono)* in his mind. His thought, it is the first figure *(tonu).* "[72]

But one also emphasizes the identity of "signs" and of "words," the verbal expression of thought. Thus, it is said that "in the clavicles of Amma in a ball, all the things he had were signs."[73] But, "if the signs existed before the words, words and signs of Amma's clavicle are one."[74]

One emphasizes this identity in affirming that "the roots (bases) of the entire Dogon tongue are numerous like the number of signs."[75]

The egg with signs is called "egg of Amma guardian of the world."[76] When creation will be terminated and then destroyed, one will say of it "the empty egg of Amma who destroyed the life of the world,"[77] because

---

71. *bummo amma ku vomo-le kize sunu tanu pelley kuloy sige vo tolo.*

72. *amma kize tonoy-go ku bonnu vomo-ne azubu vomo sebe. azubu vomo ku bonnu vomo-ne tonu. azubu vomo tonu polo voy.*

73. *amma ani guyo gunnu-go kize fu bummo vo.*

74. *tonu-go so giru-ne tobe. amma ani guyo-ne tonu-le so-le tumoy.*

75. *dogo so fu du-go tonu-go vo-gin, yi segi.*

76. *amma aduno domu talu.*

77. *amma aduno kinu vo yammalu talu kolo.*

just as Amma began the world by the sign, it is by destroying the signs that he will annihilate it.

2. FIRST GENESIS

Creation of the *sene.* Creation of the "first world." Destruction of the "first world."

CREATION OF THE SENE.

Having thought and then designed the world he wished to create, Amma tried as an experiment to superpose a bit of every kind of substance that formed a "flesh" originating from his own person, a "dross" to which he added his saliva. Softly kneading it with his hands, he molded it into the form of a seed, *i,* (one also says "of a child" *i*); the parts that ran out between his fingers formed "roots." The result of this first labor was the seed of the tree *sene na*, the first of all plants. The work is remembered by one of the names given to the creator, "Amma kneader" (*amma manane*). The oval-shaped seed, comparable to a "chicken's egg" (*ene talu*), had to contain four elements and the principle of all beings. It was larger than the other seeds would later be, particularly those of the cereals.

It is said that in order to create the *sene na,* Amma "cleared his throat," which made earth; his saliva became water; he breathed when he returned to the sky, this being fire; he blew hard, this being wind. He did not mix the elements, but superposed them: he put down earth, then water, then fire, then air. "Amma, to create the *sene na,* superposed things separated into four."[78] It is also said that the four elements of the *sene* are "the four 'nails' of Amma's thumb and fingers." A figure, called "seat of the *sene* in four (elements) put on top of each other when one builds the *lebe* altar of the Fox,"[79] represents the seed (the circle) and the four elements, deliberately placed off-center (fig. 12).

---

78. *amma sene na vo mani kize bullogu nay timmi.*

79. *sene na doy timmu nay yurugu lebe dananu.* Made with porridge of *ara pilu* and *yu* under the altar of the Fox, *yurugu lebe,* at its foundation, and for the creation of a new divination table.

N

FIG. 12: *tonu* of the "seat of the *sene.*"

The work performed inside "Amma's oval egg in a ball" and by the superposition of the elements is compared to the creation of a nest, *senu;* hence the name given to the seed, *sene i.*[80] This action is also associated with the etymology of the word that designates the tree in general, *timmu,* which comes from *timme,* "to superpose."

Recalling both the formation of the primordial *bummo* and of the *sene,*

---

80. According to another popular etymology, *sene* comes from *sige,* "addition." Amma wanted to make a first trial with the tree whose seed will somehow be "in addition" to the other seeds created afterwards.

it is said: "Water is the food, the *sene* represents the first thing created by Amma."[81]

CREATION OF THE "FIRST WORLD."

Beginning with the seed of the *sene na* and the tree, which are said to be "the created things of the first world,"[82] Amma formed a first universe. Of this creation, carried out secretly in "Amma's clavicles," little is known, for it was destroyed; only its rough outline can be told. He began by planting a seed of *Acacia Faidherbia (sene i),* which had the shape of the thorn of the present tree, also compared to the hand bell *ganana,*[83] which ends in a tapered point. On the tip of this upward pointed thorn, he placed, upside down, a small cap of the same wood by way of a cover; it had a mushroom-like bulge at its pole that served as a handle. This cap was inverted in order to receive everything that was in the "sky," and then to spill it out over the "earth." On the circumference and on the inside were the signs. He steadied it with the help of another thorn pointing downward and forming, together with the first one, an axis on which spun the cap, a symbol of space. The parts of the cap have the following meaning: the bulge is "the ball of the world," *aduno gunnu,* containing the germs of beings and things. The cap itself, which flares out from the top bulge, represents the "extension of the world" *(aduno ginnay)* (fig. 13, A). The whole thing is called "hand of the Fox,"[84] because the germs, in order to be projected into the world, are drawn out as if by a "hand," which is in itself a passage; one also says that "the germs were projected by a hand." It is also said that Amma first put the things of the *sene* one on top of the other and in the second place the "hand" itself (fig. 13, B).

This entire device represents the world standing on one foot, turning on itself, and filled with germs that are fertilized by the contact between the two thorns; the upper thorn is the male "sky," the lower one is the female "earth." Its bell shape, a symbol of the widening inherent in multiplication, allowed things to descend by their own weight, in order

---

81. *di kayle-go vo, sene amma kize polo manu tozo-go vo.*

82. *ganna polo kize vo manu.*

83. The *ganana* is a small iron bell which is struck with a wand.

84. *yurugu numo.* This cap is represented by the smoothing tool called "hand," used to smooth the sand of the divination tables of the Fox (cf. *infra,* p. 294).

to pass back into the *gunnu* (the "ball" containing the germs), so as to be like filtered, clarified, and purified.

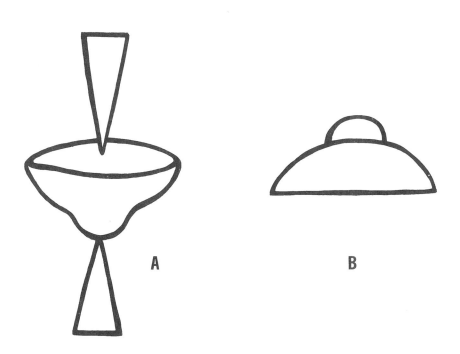

FIG. 13: Amma's work with the *sene* (explanatory figure).

The cap turned slowly between the two thorns (a top made of *ponnu* fruit recalls this).[85] When speed had increased, the device exploded and all the germs were scattered. After the germs had developed inside the cap, Amma took it and turned it right-side up. This was like a birth process of germs, poured out over the "earth," where they spread out because of their own weight and subsequently developed on their own,

---

85. When playing tops with the *ponnu* fruit, if one spins it point down (regular spinning), one says it is "the creative dance of Amma"; if it is spun upside down (irregular spinning), one says it is "the dance of the Fox." For the games of tops and whirligigs, cf. M. GRIAULE, *Jeux dogon,* pp. 68-70.

while the two points were rejoined.

This is how the world first functioned, which is described as follows: "Amma placed 'the Fox's hand' between the upper point and the lower one, and things began in that. Amma made 'the Fox's hand,' which was in the middle, spin, scattering what was inside; all sorts of things came out of it. The hand of the Fox, which was with the palm up, contained all sorts of things belonging to the world; in turning it upside down, (everything) was scattered. When Amma stopped the spinning of the hand, which was between the upper and lower thorns, and drew it back, the two (thorns) which remained were like a man and a woman who lie down and unite (literally; to enter into). These two thorns (represent) the union of the sky and the earth."[86]

When the germs were scattered, it is said that the empty hand "thinned down" and took the flattened form of the hand of the Fox as it is at present.

DESTRUCTION OF THE "FIRST WORLD."

But Amma had put too many things into the first creation. Moreover, their superposition was not effective; it failed. In fact, during the spinning the basic element "water" left the whole. Therefore, when emphasizing that this scattering of the elements contained in the grain had been the cause of disorder, one says that "the *sene* seed is neither dead nor alive," "that it is neither plant nor tree nor anyone, and represents Amma's failure."[87]

Amma was not satisfied with the creation of this world by the *sene,* which constituted a first failed attempt, a first exercise. He abandoned and destroyed it, keeping of this roughly drafted creation with the *sene* only the seed itself and the four elements as well as certain germs of wild seeds, which were to develop later.

These events are represented by a figure drawn under the altar to the

---

86. *amma keu da-mogo-le donu-mogo-le logoro-ne yurugu numo kunna, kize vogo kologo-ne toli. amma yurugu numo logoru-ne tobe-go ginne gilay. kize voy togu goy. yurugu numo bere-go da-go be-go-ne aduno kize si tobe-go binema donu goy. didi damogo-le donu-mogo-le logorogo-ne amma numo-go ginnegilia vo ya. ley vazu-go yana-le ayne-le unu yoy vogo ley-go alagala-le minne-le moni.*

87. *sene i yimi-la omoy-la.* One also says that it is a *bibile,* an "image," a "transformation" of the first world.

Fox (*yurugu lebe*) at its foundation. It associates the "hand of the Fox," *yurugu numo,* and the four elements contained in the *sene,* preserved by Amma. These consist of four *yala,* called *sene i yala,* placed at the center in a line oriented east-west which separates two inverted hands (of the Fox) respectively pointing to the north and to the south (cf. fig. 14).[88]

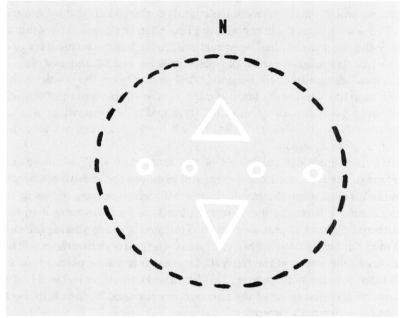

FIG. 14: Figure executed under the altar to the Fox: the *yala* of the *sene* and the "hands" of the Fox.

Amma decided to resume his work, to create another universe that would have man as its foundation. This new world — already included in, and prefigured by, the *bummo* of the "womb of the world" (see fig. 3, Ch. I) and depending upon the progression represented by the series of

---

88. Drawn with porridge of *yu* and *ara geu.* The "hands" represent, respectively, the stone "hands," used for the instruction of neophytes, and the wooden "hand" of *sene,* used by the diviners; it is also the hind paw of the animal. In their entirety the six figures are related to the six compartments of the divination tables (cf. p. 295).

signs denoting different stages — will be formed according to another technique in which the elements will not be superposed, but rather mixed and blended in a continuous movement, the condition for their perfect integration.

It is said of the *sene* kept by Amma, and which will find its place in the second universe: "The *sene* is the present witness of the former creation,"[89] which is called "world which has passed before."[90] It will transmit to the "second world" the fundamental elements conferred upon it by Amma.

The *sene* was, and will remain, the first plant life created by Amma; since the "first world" had been realized through the intermediary of a plant, in the second world the plant will be considered just like a "person." A sacrifice will be performed annually on the trunk of the *sene na* in the "field of the family house," *ginna minne,* and this sacrifice will hold good for all vegetation. It is said: "The sacrifice offered (sacrificed) to the *sene* is (valid) for all trees; the trees are like the Nommo, like a person."[91]

When animals eat the leaves of the *sene,* they will assimilate the *nyama* of the tree; their excrement will promote the growth of cereals and of all vegetation. Men will absorb this force by eating the seeds of fruits and the leaves of the different plants, and will transmit it to the earth and the rocks by moving about. The aged who are nearing the end of their days will sleep on a board of *sene.* The gutter of dwellings will be made of *sene* wood; at the funeral of its owner it will be placed next to his blanket in the main square. This ritual will unite the witnesses of the former world and those of the new one, represented by the cloth, both symbols of Amma's "word."

---

89. *sene aduno girune gali sere.* Sentence recited during the ceremony annually performed by the diviners, which includes a sacrifice to the altar to the Fox, *yurugu lebe.*

90. *aduno girune gali.*

91. *sene-ne numpugu pugonu-go vogo timmu pu-moy; timmu nommo tozoy, inne tozoy.*

3. AMMA'S EGG

Second genesis; first *yala* of "Amma's egg." Opening of "Amma's eyes";
second *yala* of "Amma's egg." Representations.

SECOND GENESIS.

So Amma began his work anew and proceeded with a second genesis. First of all, he decided to form new seeds, that is to say, new "germs" with which he would produce a second world. These seeds would be those of cereals, *dene,* and of food plants: the first and most important — but also the smallest — was to be the *po* seed (*Digitaria exilis*).

Starting from the primordial "traces," *bummo,* Amma first drew the "marks," *yala,* of a new universe inside his "womb" or his "egg." This formation took place in two stages, the succession of which shows the internal movements impressed, from the beginning, upon the fundamental elements used for the creation of all things, animate and inanimate, which were to make up this universe. Amma's drawings for the elaboration of this second genesis are represented by two successive figures.

FIRST YALA *OF AMMA'S "EGG."*

The first figure is called: *yala* of Amma's egg" (*amma talu yala*) or *"yala* of Amma's egg with 266 (signs),"[92] and denotes the original thought of the creator (fig. 15). It is composed of dots that are undifferentiated, yet of an exact number, corresponding, one to one, with the *bummo* traced in his womb at the beginning, emphasizing the intrinsic value of number in the realization of the universe. For it is said: "The thing that Amma created, that he sent into the world, that is what one has counted."[93]

---

92. *amma talu sunu tanu pelley kuloy sige to timmelu yala.*

93. *amma kize mana aduno-ne ti-le vogo-le lugu lugi.* This sentence is pronounced (at the *bulu*) during the sacrifice offered on the altar called *ka amma,* "Amma of Kan."

N

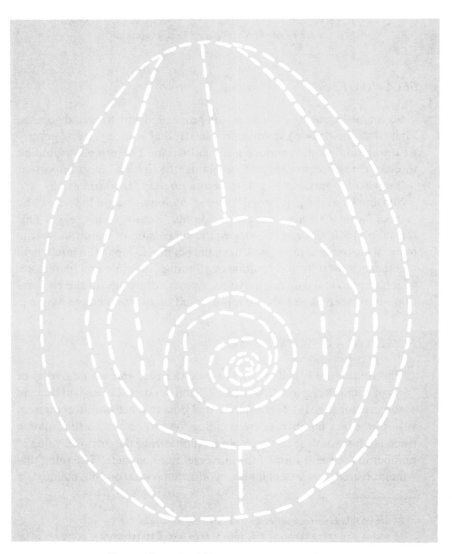

FIG. 15: First *yala* of "Amma's egg," *amma talu.*

1) House of the Hogon of Arou-near-Ibi. Trichromatic paintings executed at the time of the *bulu*. The Hogon is seated on his platform.

(Photograph by Mme R. Guilbaud).

PL. VII

2) Totemic sanctuary of Manda at Orosongo. Trichromatic paintings and bas-reliefs produced at the time of the *agu*. At the center is a series of *bummo,* done vertically in black.

1) Cave *tete kommo:* the four boulders placed before the opening
represent the four "clavicles of Amma";

2) Cave *tete kommo:* white paint representing
"the *po* coming out of Amma's clavicles."

In this figure, the "egg of the world," still closed, is divided into four sectors, prefiguring the four divine "clavicles" which will open when the world is cast out of Amma's bosom. Indeed, the clavicles form the suspension system of the body as a whole: "The clavicles are the equipment for the body's suspension."[94] God will open himself up into two twin pairs of "clavicles," thus emphasizing the essential value of these supports for the human being; they will contain the symbols of the seeds of cereal grains, that is, of the basic elements of the second world.

"The number in Amma's egg is 266."[95] The outline of the drawing encompasses the picture of the signs; the spiraled center plays a role on the inside comparable to that of the yolk in an egg. These 266 *yala* are positioned in the following manner (from the center to the periphery):

— 66 for the *po*, the other cereal grain seeds, and the *sene*

— 4 for the *gaba* seeds and 4 for the *anu* seeds

— 128 for the circumference of the central circle or *gaba gunnu* "ball of the calabash" or *amma kolo doy* "seat of the inside of Amma"

—64 for the egg itself, which will later open into four "clavicles."[96]

a) The sixty-six *yala* of the central spiral break down as follows: twenty-two at the center for the *po*, then forty for eight seeds, at the ratio of five per seed, and finally four for the *sene* at the tip of the spiral.

The *po*, in the body of which Amma will build the world, is here understood to be the principle and prefiguration of the seed. Therefore, one says that the *po*, symbol of the smallest thing in the world, is "the greatest of the cereals." It has twenty-two *yala*.

At the center of the spiral of the twenty-two *yala* of the *po*, first six *yala* are counted (as were the first six *bummo* in the breakdown of the picture

---

94. *ani guyo gozu delle gogie vo.*

95. This is said at the time of construction of a totemic sanctuary: *amma ene talu sunu tanu pelley kuloy sige.*

96. This figure was drawn with porridge of *ara geu* and *yu pilu* during the foundation of the first altar to Amma by the Dogon at Kani Kombolé at the time of their arrival from Mandé. This altar is called: "first (altar to) Amma placed below (i.e., 'upon earth')" (*amma polo donune dani*). It was also drawn with porridge of *po pilu* on the rocky surface which constitutes the ceiling of a small enclosure built inside the cave *kukulu kommo,* a construction which, for initiates, represents the first totemic sanctuary constructed by man (vol. I, 2nd installment, 2nd year).

of the signs). These six *yala* are the "sex of the *po*"; their number connotes the initial masculinity of the *po's* sex, for three will represent, in man, the penis and the two testicles. The repetition of the number 3 underscores another fundamental aspect of Amma's second genesis: twinness. In essence, the *po,* the first living germ, will be twin (3+3). When it will come into being, the seed of the male *po pilu* will be doubled by a female seed. Moreover, Amma will confer a double role upon the *po pilu:* as a male, it will give its impetus to the universe; as a female, at a precise moment of the development of this universe, it will play a role nearly comparable to that of Amma himself.

The *po* will be twin because everything in this universe will have to be able to reproduce itself. The repetition of these two numbers in itself also connotes this essential duality: Amma, who created; the world which he created. For Amma will remain present in this universe by his creative word, of which one says: "The word came out of the first *yala* of the *po.* "[97]

The six *yala* of the "sex of the *po*" are considered as the *yala* of the "sex" of the universe; they will also be the image of the sex of the first animate being formed in Amma's womb, the *nommo anagonno,* symbol of the human fetus.

With regard to the cereal seeds, the six *yala* prefigured the six varieties of *po.* The sixteen *yala* which follow are the "body of the *po,* " *po gozu,* that is, the seed itself and the plant that will sprout from it germ.

The spiral formation of the *yala* makes it clear that the *po* will be "alive," for it is prefigured in movement. It denotes the formation of the *po* seed, symbol of "the smallest thing," as well as of the vital force that will give it an internal movement, life. In addition, the number of *yala* assigned to the future seed recalls the basic number of categories classifying the sum of primordial signs. In essence, through number, the *po* will contain the entire universe conceived in thought by Amma.

At the time of the *dineu kono,* "beer of the twins," a ceremony which begins the offering of the first fruits, the patriarch says: "God has given

---

97. *yala polo-go-ne so goy* (or *tobe*). At the *pagu* of the Hogon this sentence is addressed to the altar called *de lebe "lebe* of the inside," situated to the left of the door when one enters the room (*kana*) which is reserved exclusively for this purpose within the dignitary's dwelling. The clay covers a red egg-shaped stone which was brought from Mandé. This stone represents *po tolo,* the star of the *po.* (cf. *infra,* p. 415). For *de lebe,* cf. vol. I, installment 2.

us *bago,* the most ancient of cereals is the *po,* its number is twenty-two, Amma, here is your water." He then pours the porridge on the altar and adds: "We have had some harvest, may Amma have us finish it in the hole of the tooth: may he allow the cereals to be good, may Amma let us find the next year."[98]

Next come forty other *yala* assigned to eight cereal grain seeds, five for each of them, in the following order: *emme ya, emme pilu, emme di giru, emme na kolo, yu, ara, nu, namu.* "The number in the eight seeds is five, together they are forty."[99] The numbers eight and five, into which the *yala* break down, refer to the "eight ancestors" of humanity, the "families," *lato sensu,* which were later to develop on the Earth, and the five first generations that were to succeed each other within each lineage.[100]

The four final *yala* are assigned to the *sene,* here called "testimony of the former world" (*aduno pey sere*) and of the first genesis. Their number emphasizes the presence in the new universe of the four elements, preserved by Amma with the *sene,* in the following order: water, fire, earth, and air, the last being located at the tip of the spiral. For Amma, in order to insert the four elements that he had kept after he had destroyed the first world formed with the seed of the *sene,* picked them up again and incorporated them into the seed of *po* from which the new universe was to emerge. It is said: "Amma who had brought the four 'kinds' of thing to the world which had passed before, modeled this (present) world with the four divided things and put them into the body of the *po.* "[101]

The fundamental value of these sixty-six spiraling signs — which convey Amma's dynamism — is recalled during the foundation of a totemic sanctuary with a sentence uttered by the priest: "At the beginning (of the founding) of the sanctuary of the *binu,* the sixty-six *yala* of Amma's body are all drawn together."[102]

---

98. *ba gonu; dene die poy; lugu vomo pelley ley sige; amma di uo uvo. gayle emme-go, amma inu komu-ne yalamo, dene pelu bozo, amma bago temmemo.*

99. *dene gagara lugu ebe numono, mona pennay.* This sentence is pronounced by the farmer during the sowing.

100. For the "eight ancestors" and the "five generations" cf. *infra,* p. 338.

101. *amma ya girune aduno gali kize si* (or *togu) nay delebe ie aduno mana si nay gammala pu oba po gozu-ne kunni.*

102. *binu ginu tolo-ye amma yala pelu kuloy sige yala, bey voy bo kana* (literally: "he made them companions").

b) The internal spiral of the egg is flanked on each side by two series of four *yala*, vertically positioned, which support it. Each of these four points is assigned to the *anu* seeds on the left, and to the *gaba* seeds on the right. As a sign, they respectively prefigure the male and female "souls," *kikinu*, which will animate the *po* and the other seeds when they are formed. Therefore, when later a field of *po* will be sown on Earth, it will be mixed with the seeds of the *anu*, and the *gaba* will be sown on a hill, both of these being "guardians of the souls of the *po*" and, therefore, of all cereal grains.[103] Everywhere the millet fields are also surrounded by *anu* plants; all these seeds are put into a calabash for the sowing time.[104]

When sowing *gaba* (to the northeast and southeast of the field, since rain comes from the east), one says: *"gaba,* your number is four, enter into the field."[105] When sowing *anu: "anu,* your number is four, surround the field at the four cardinal points."[106]

The vertical position of the *yala* of the *gaba* and *anu* — fixed in relation to the spiral of the *po* — also stands for the future "descent" of the universe out of Amma's womb.

c) This set of three figures is enclosed in a circle, made of 128 *yala,* that prefigures the shape of the calabash, *gaba,* at the state of maturity and represents "the seat (or the womb) of Amma's inside," *amma kolo doy.* These 128 points comprise primarily 120 *yala,* that is to say, 2 x 60, sixty being called *me lugi,* "number of the placenta," connoting the future formation in that place of a double placenta where the first animate beings created by Amma, the *nommo anagonno,* will develop later. The eight remaining *yala,* placed in the bottom of the circle, are "Amma's eyes," *amma giru,* and they prefigure the formation of the four collateral directions of future space, called "angles four," *sibe nay.*

d) The sixty-four *yala,* which outline the egg and Amma's closed clavicles enclosing "Amma's seat," are the representations of the develop-

---

103. This method of sowing the fields of *po* is currently used, especially in the regions of Wazouba, Mendeli or Kamma.

104. They will be brought to Earth by the Fox in the calabash of the smallest variety, called *sesege* (cf. *infra,* p. 224).

105. *gaba lugu uo nay, minne-ne yo.*

106. *anu lugu uo nay, minne sibe nay gonno.*

ment and future organization of society within a territorial group of several extended families. For the extension of the universe will take place at the opening of Amma's clavicles; this extension is also manifested by human societies. In the course of the ritual performed during the feast of the sowing around the altar of Lébé, the priest says: "The men of Amma and of the *vageu* who have come, their number is thirty because of their name; the men of the *lebe* and the *binu*, their number is thirty-four; let men be born unto them. When they are gathered together, their number is sixty-four." And then, addressing those present, he adds: "Do not take the wives of your friends; do not give the women of this village to another man; he who wishes to give them away, Amma sees him, the ancestors see him, the *lebe* sees him, the *binu* sees him. May Amma give us the next day";[107] for the sixty-four *yala* of the egg were "the promise of the world."

OPENING OF AMMA'S "EYES": SECOND YALA OF AMMA'S EGG."

Amma, having thus positioned the *yala* for the prefiguration of the universe, acted upon them. He "opened his eyes." This act provoked the emergence of the *yala* from the spiral which, turning in the other direction, will prefigure, inside the egg, the future expansion of the universe.[108]

Because of this, it is said that Amma "pushed aside the *yala* of the *gaba* and of the

FIG. 16: Opening of "Amma's eyes."

anu," in order that the spiral turning on its axis might be able to reverse itself. Thus Amma had pierced the envelope of his own womb, and his

---

107. *amma-le vageu-le anau ebe viey, lugu ebe peran boy-le ko voy; lebe-le binu-le anau ebe viey, lugu ebe peran nay sige boy-le ko voy; i nonu beme naniemo ko voy mona pelu kuloy nay sige lugi; tumone yana deno; anna-go yana are inne vaza oboylo-oobodo bana amma ieze, vageu ieze, binu ieze, amma bay tolo obo.*

108. The rotations of the palmyra leaf weather vane are compared to the movements of Amma forming the *yala* inside the "egg." One says that "it turns like Amma when he began the *yala.*"

"eye," as it burst forth from the hole, had become a light that illuminated the universe and revealed the existence of all things in their formation.

This stage of Amma's acts is represented by a parallel figure, called *amma talu yala leye,* "second *yala* of Amma's egg," and also *"yala* of Amma's removed egg with 266 (signs)"[109] (fig. 17). At the bottom of the central circle eight *yala,* so-called "Amma's eyes," *amma giru,* formed a star pattern and, having become *tonu,* prefigured the "four angles" (*sibe nay)* or the four collateral directions of future space (fig. 17). "Amma's eyes are on (are watching) the world."[110] The drawing of these *tonu* also symbolized the future opening of the four "clavicles" that are still closed; and, at the same time — as a part of the *gaba* containing the seeds — the four chambers of a granary. The clavicle is indeed called "granary of *anu" (anu guyo).* It is also said that "Amma's eyes (are) like the inside of a granary."[111] In this figure of the second stage of the egg's *yala,* the spiral turns in the opposite direction from the spiral in the preceding drawing and seeks a "way out" through Amma's open "eyes." So, the first *yala* shown at the exit are those of the *sene,* i.e., the four elements in the following order: air, earth, fire, and water. The *yala* of the cereal seeds follow in order, those of the *po* — created the first — having to leave last.

The number of lines is the same as in the preceding figure; this expresses the duality of "Amma's egg" and of the universe in formation — both are 266 — for it is said that, while unfolding themselves, the spinning *yala* became twins.[112]

The emergence of the *yala* from the spiral crossing the signs of the collateral directions of space prefigured the future creation of all the heavenly bodies: as they come out they will become *tonu.* However,

---

109. *amma talu sunu tanu pelley kuloy sige to gommu yala.* This figure was drawn next to the first one under the altar to Amma at Kani Kombolé, and with the same uncooked pulp. Morever, in a manner much like that of the drawing of the first figure inside the cave of Kukulu Kommo, it was drawn on the rock set up to represent the ark of the Nommo which *descended on earth, polyo kommo* (for *polyo kommo* cf. infra, p. 490), in porridge made of four cereal grains, *ara geu, yu, emme ya,* and *emme nakolo.*

110. *amma giru aduno-ne vo.*

111. *amma giru guyo kolo anay.*

112. In like manner, certain seeds will split themselves, undergoing a metamorphosis (bibile) in the course of their formation inside Amma's womb.

N

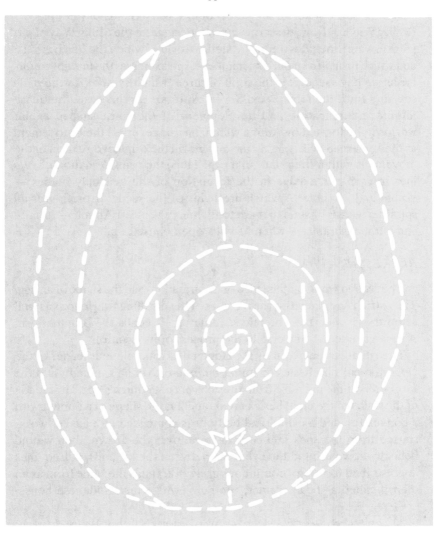

FIG. 17: Second *yala* of "Amma's egg."

reversing their movement a second time, they will once again spin in the direction of the spiral inside the egg. Thus animated, they will be called "diagram of the space of the *po* become seven 'bounds of (the) place'" (Milky Way).[113] Now, the term *yalu ulo,* designates the Milky Way of our galaxy, which includes the entire stellar world of which the Earth is part, and which turns in a spiral. The number seven expresses the multiplication, for as we have seen, it is the total of three, which symbolizes the male sex, and four, the female sex. Seven expresses, in this case, the quasi-infinite multiplication and development of the spiral-shaped stellar worlds to be formed by Amma which, having reversed their movement as they emerged, will spin, on the outside, in the original direction of the movement within the primordial egg. Thus, the transformation of *yala* into *tonu* marks a stage in the formation of the heavenly bodies — visible and invisible — which are twins of the seeds. It prefigures all spiraling worlds of stars that are to fill the universe of Amma — infinite and yet measurable — when he will "open himself up."[114]

REPRESENTATIONS.

The second world, at this stage of its formation, had the shape of an egg. The ostrich egg placed on the terraces of the dwellings of Hogons as well as on those of certain totemic sanctuaries[115] recalls the original form Amma gave to the universe in the process of its creation.

The ritual bonnet worn by the Hogon of Arou, religious leader of the Dogon, recalls both the 266 initial *bummo* of Amma's thought and the formation of the universe from the 266 *yala* of "Amma's egg." It is made of the stalks of the eight basic cereals and has the shape of a bonnet with a convex top and a cylindrical body. It is composed of a basket work, started from the apex in a conical spiral over the crown, then wound helically down around the cylinder. Between the six coils, paired lines are inscribed forming a continuous grillwork. It has the same form as an utensil called a "bean bonnet," *nu goro,* with which Sudanese house-

---

113. *po ganna yal(u) ulo tani tonu* (or *"tonu* of the spinning of the world by the *po* become *yal(u) ulo").*

114. The stars will be the "counterparts" of the seeds, the evidence of their existence in Amma's hands in the sky.

115. On the sanctuaries of the Déwa and Nembé totems.

wives separate beans from the sand in which they are stored.

Made in this way, the head-dress represents a theoretical diagram of the 266 signs placed in six rows. These six rows recall the six *yala* in the center of the spiral in the "egg." The helix turns in the direction of the development of the universe, that is, in the direction of the spiral after the opening of "Amma's eyes." One also says of this head-dress: "The number of the Hogon's bonnet is sixty; the number of the Hogon's men is sixty."[116] These expressions also point to the 120 *yala* forming the center of the "egg" or "Amma's seat," which will become the womb, the "placenta" where all beings are to be formed.[117]

The bonnet, therefore, symbolizes the world and its formation as well as the very essence of the thought and deeds of the Creator. Its importance is emphasized by the rites accompanying its making or its use, the purport of which we will explain below.

The head-dress of the Hogon of Arou is braided by eight Hogon who meet at the village of Arou-near-Ibi. This meeting, called "the world has arrived," *aduno viay,* is held inside the house or, if attendance is great, outside. The chief of Arou, seated on his platform, faces the door, i.e., the east. His colleagues, seated in a circle before him, face the center, after having reached their seats by completing a circle from left to right. Between them and the master of the house, four totemic priests are positioned, substitutes for the four cardinal points. Each works with the stalk of one of the primordial plants — white millet, white sorghum, bean, rice, sesame, hibiscus, female sorghum, and "road" sorghum — after the Hogon, Amma's substitute, has taken the first one to begin the spiral.

The eight plants that are used recall the first dispensation of edible seeds to man: the different colors of the stalks are those of the rainbow.

The head-dress is never exposed to anyone's view, with the exception of the totemic priests, who help the Hogon, or other dignitaries. When the Hogan wears it for public ceremonies, it is completely enveloped in a turban or covered with a sort of tarboosh.

---

116. *ogo goro lugu pelu kuloy; ogone turu anau pelu kuloy.*

117. The "number of the placenta" is 60 (called *me lugu*); the number of *yala* (120) connotes the formation of two twin placentas (cf. *infra,* p. 153).

In the event of serious problems or a calamity, a ceremony, also called "the world has arrived," *aduno viay,* brings all the chiefs together around the Hogon's head-dress to invoke Amma. The Hogon, seated on his platform in the main room of his residence, faces the door opening to the east; the other leaders sit in a semicircle opposite him, their gaze directed at the center embodied by the head-dress, this time having entered by turning from right to left. Four priests are placed, two by two, on each side of the platform and in front; they represent the four cardinal points. The Hogon implores Amma and speaks with his eyes fixed on the bonnet placed in the middle, top down, like a "world turned upside down," *aduno bileniay.*

4. CREATION OF THE *PO*

Creation of the *po.* Creation of the eight seeds. *Gaba* and *anu.* Fermentation.

CREATION OF THE PO.

Thus, inside the egg Amma himself was like a spiraling motion, called "accelerated ball," *ogoru gunnu;* then the oval *po* seed was created, which placed itself invisibly at the center.

It is said: "When Amma broke the egg of the world and came out, a whirlwind rose. The *po,* which is the smallest (thing), was made, invisible, at the center; the wind is Amma himself. It is the *po* which Amma let come out first."[118] Amma's creative will was located in the *po,* the smallest of things. Like a central air bubble, it spun and scattered the particles of matter in a sonorous and luminous motion which, however, remained inaudible and invisible. It was less a word than a thought.[119]

As the *sene* might have been in the first creation (with which Amma was dissatisfied), in the second one the *po* is the image of the origin of matter. Therefore, it will later be forbidden for different categories of men to eat it or speak about it; because "the beginning of things is Amma's greatest secret." Moreover, the *po* is also the image of the creator. "Amma, the creator, was not himself great (big), but of that it is forbidden to speak; in his place (i.e., in order to replace himself) he

---

118. *aduno talu amma doga goygo, ono simu goa digile. po i vo gayle digo iemele kanu. ono simu amma ku vomoy. po amma kize la vogonu.*

119. The informant declares "that a man can sometimes hear it deep down inside."

transformed the *po* into wind and left it that way. Amma, from the moment when he created all things, each was like the *po;* they grew larger whereas the *po* did not; the seed was formed like wind and it is forbidden to talk about it."[120]

The seed is in this fashion a "living testimony of the air," that is, the proof of Amma himself who, at the beginning, was comparable to the whirlwinds, today's visible elements. It is called *po,* a word considered to have the same root as *polo,* "beginning."

Indeed, due to its smallness, it is the image of the beginning of all things. "All the things that Amma created begin like the little (seed of) *po.*"[121] And, beginning with this infinitely small thing, the things created by Amma will form themselves by the continuous addition of identical elements: "Amma makes things begin (by creating them as) small (as the) *po;* he continues to add (to the things created) little by little, that thing (i.e., the element as infinitesimal as the *po*). As Amma adds that (i.e., elements the size of the seed), the thing becomes large."[122]

While molding the *po,* Amma placed the signs in it that were in his hand; this is represented by a figure called "drawing of Amma as a person making the body of the *po,"* or again "Amma making the world in the body of the *po.* "[123] Amma is presented there in anthropomorphic form, because of the "hands" with which he creates matter. The drawing placed under Amma represents the initial *po* at the moment of its formation. The three central figures are the penis (the circle) and the testicles (the two filled-in figures), and the dotted line surrounding them in a spirial is the semen (or seed). Thus, the fact is emphasized that the creation of the seed began by the creation of sex, the very source of

---

120. *ambanam vole dego beli yem sogo gadunga vogo pada kize udigo votogogo yem padi odogoro bileɲa. ambanam kize kem varu vo manu-le kem pogin bie vadungo be solya vo yaga solieli vogo odorogo yen tona sosogo gadenga ko tonga yem padiya* (Wazouba dialect). The most scrupulous priests never call the seed *po;* they designate it by saying "the small(est) thing," *kize uzi.*

121. *amma kize vo manaze fu po uzi vo-gin toloze.*

122. *amma kize dagi vo tolo dogo fu kize vogon dagi dagi baran yaze. amma vogo degedege baranu kize die-go bieze.*

123. *po gozu-ne amma inne mana kunni toy;* or *po gozu-ne amma aduno kunna toy.* This drawing is drawn on a great altar to Amma (on *ka amma,* for example) with porridge of *yu pilu,* at the *bulu,* once every sixty years.

FIG. 18: Amma making the world in the body of the *po pilu.*

transmission of life. The figure is the *toy* of the first six *yala* of the spiral within the egg which de-

noted, at the beginning of the progressive realization of matter, "the sex of the *po.*"[124] The last dot has two lines coming off it: it thus represents the future germ of the seed piercing the two "skins" of the envelope that will open at the time of germination.

And as germination is comparable to the birth of a new being — the plant in this case — the figure conveys that "Amma created the *po* as twin,"[125] that is to say, male and female. In addition, it underlines the fact that the *po* will produce six varieties on earth: the ini-

FIG. 19: Diagram of the four elements of the *sene* seed in the four corners of the sanctuary.

tial *po pilu, po na, po banu, po yayuguzu, po sizu,* and *tenu po;* these varieties will be considered as twins, two by two, the last two having appeared belatedly during cultivation.

In this infinitely small thing Amma then placed the four elements which thus far had contained the four *tonu* of the *sene.*[126]

---

124. Cf. *supra*, p. 122. Just as this explanation is among the most secret, the figure showing the creation of matter by beginning with the sex is part of the most profound initiation and may only be revealed at a later time. This primacy of the sex in the creation of the *po* is recalled by the texts of chants that accompany the threshing of the fonio (cf. D. PAULME, *Organisation sociale des Dogon*, p. 161).

125. *amma po mani dine.*

126. Cf. *supra*, p. 114.

Amma's acts are represented by a series of figures. The first, called "diagram of the *sene* seed placed high up inside the four corners of the sanctuary,"[127] shows in the four corners of a square the four elements contained by the *sene* in the form of *tonu* (fig. 19). It evinces the role of the *sene* in the second genesis, and also connotes the superposition of the four elements in the formation of the seed.

In accordance with Amma's will, each of them extended its "germ" to touch its neighbor, from east to north, from north to west, etc. This "crossing of the germs" is compared to the intertwining of twigs forming a "nest," *senu*.[128] These germs then gathered at the center, where they mixed together and were transformed at the very site of the *po*, which was still invisible. Then, surrounding the seed, they made it visible.

This second stage is represented by an analogous figure, called *"tonu* of the four elements of the *sene* passing into the *po* (drawn) on the sanctuary platform"[129] (fig. 20). It shows the extension of the "germs" from one to the other inside Amma's egg and the extension of his four "clavicles" around the central "seat" where the *po* is to be formed. "Amma took the four things of the world which had passed before, he modeled the world of today with the four separate things to put all of them into the body of the *po.*"[130]

Thus the first *po* seed was created. In this infinitely small element resided an even smaller principle. It is said: "Inside the *po*, which is (the symbol) of the smallest, is an even smaller thing which is life."[131] Life developed at the same time as its (means of) support made of the

---

127. *sene i binu ginu-ne kolo dane da sibe nay tonu.*

Drawn in *ara banu* inside the sanctuary, at the building's four corners and under the terrace, at the time of the *pagu* of all the priests of *binu na*. The morphology of the drawing connotes the form of the rectangular wooden case called *imizi koro,* "box of dry earth," used to transport earth for the construction of dwellings. The rectangles represent the rectangular boxes used to mold the bricks. The whole thing recalls "the building of the world."

128. Even the name of the acacia, *sene,* is related to the word *senu* which designates the nest of interwoven branches built by storks or crows.

129. *sene kize si nay po-ne yoy binuginu dummu donune tonu.*

Drawn with *ara geu* on the stand bearing the ritual objects inside the totemic sanctuary, during the *duguru* of all the priests of the *binu na*.

130. *amma ya girune aduno gali kize si nay gelebe ie aduno mana si nay gammala pu oba po gozu-ne kunni.* This sentence is recited during the building of a new totemic sanctuary.

131. *po vo dagi-vo-gin vogo kolone kize vo-de dagi, vogo kini.*

blended elements: this development worked on the principle of a motion turning in a conical spiral. It is said: "When life increases, it increases by whirling,"[132] which is a repetition of Amma's first act, because "that imitates how Amma came out of the egg of the world."[133]

FIG. 20: *tonu* of the four elements of the *sene* seed passing into the *po pilu.*

The *bummo* of the *po* provide a first view of the internal movement of the seed (fig. 21, a,b,c). The first prefigures its spiraling motion; in the second, the curve twists as if rolling itself up in continuation of the spiral; and in the third (fig. 21, c), called "trace of the image of the ending of the creation of the world by the *po,* "[134] this same curve no longer bends

132. *kinu varu barie-vo-ze-le digili gala barieze.*

133. *amma talu-go-ne go-vo-ze-go vogo yala yalanu.*

134. *po ganna mana dogonu bummo.*

when it emerges, but rather extends itself more, prefiguring the "complete opening of the created world."

FIG. 21: The *bummo* of the *po pilu.*

This spiraling motion is evidence of Amma's intentions. On the one hand, to avoid what happened with the *sene* seed made of the superposed elements (one of which, water, had detached itself), Amma blended and mixed these same elements in the *po* seed. "Except for trees (which are all of the same essence as the *sene,* Amma created things by mixing together the four separate things."[135] On the other hand, this mixing caused vibrations inside the seed. These vibrations were evidence of the action of the "word" of Amma — a "word" which, at this stage, formed the life of the seed.

---

135. *timmu tolo-go, amma kize manu bullogu ganama mani.*

The development of life inside the seed is represented by a series of figures called "drawings of the multiplication of the word of the *po*,"[136] which suggests the successive appearance of seven vibrations developing in star-shaped fashion around a central nucleus.

FIG. 22: Drawing of the multiplication of the "word" of the *po pilu*.

The first contains a central spiral, which recalls the form of the *bummo* and the formation from it of the first vibration of the "word"; the vertical bar placed below symbolizes the presence of the spiritual principles of the future seed (fig. 22, at right). The following figures show the development of the vibrations in segments of increasing size, ending with the seventh (at left), called *"tonu* seven," *tonu soy.*

In this figure, which evinces the fundamental action of Amma's "word," the seven branches must be interpreted as the sum of three, the male number, and four, the female number, indicating a creation of the seed in both masculinity and femininity.

Thus, an important turning point occurs in the labors of creation: while the seven segments marking the seven first internal movements have the

---

136. *so nani po tonu.* These figures are drawn during the foundation of a *ginna* with *yu* flour, mixed with *sa* drink (*sa di),* by a delegate of the head of the family of the first *ginna* built in the village (if it concerns a new neighborhood) or in the region (if it concerns a new village). The first seven figures are made on the ground at the place of the four corners of the dwelling whose plan they underline. The eighth is placed where the entrance door to the courtyard will be (cf. *infra,* p. 373). They are also called: *"tonu* of the *po* of the foundation of the *ginna"(ginna tey po tonu).* These figures also represent the multiplication of fonio seeds on earth. They will be drawn on the soil in the dust when the fonio granary of the family house is built, set apart in the courtyard, before the first stones are laid of the foundation of the building, that contains four compartments (vol. I, 2nd installment, first year).

nucleus as their point of departure, their extremities are at a progressively greater distance from the center. As a result, these extremities are on a spiral comparable to that of the *yala* of the *po*. The development of the seed can take place only on the outside after the seventh segment had gone through the "wall" of the egg; because of this, it split up to form an eighth element. Thus, the seventh vibration reached the wall, pierced it and, its extremity passing to the outside, made itself into an eighth segment. The eighth figure shows the appearance of this segment, which is compared to a "birth." In this way, the eighth articulation of the "word" within the seed will also have the privilege of being the germ of the first in a new being.

This procedure is called "expansion of the creation of man,"[137] an expression used to designate the initial spiral. For it is repeated in human reproduction, where the semen develops in the same way to form the placenta, which bursts and brings forth a new being, who repeats the begetter. It is comparable to the development of the millet grain, whose husk bursts under the pressure of the seed of the future stalk.

With regard to the formation of seeds, such as it was prefigured by the *yala* of the central spiral in Amma's egg, the seventh figure must be read as follows: in the center of the oval, a point represents the germ of the *po,* the smallest of all cultivated grains. Around it are seven rays of increasing length, in the form of a star, marking the seven hypostases of "Amma's word," seven vibrations which are, in order, the principal seeds: *yu, emme, nakolo, emme digiru, nu, namu, ara, emme ya* (fig. 23, A). The last figure, in which the eighth segment has appeared, detached from the seventh, is the image of their germination and of the future reproduction of the cereal grains.

This figure is also called Amma's *tonu* (fig. 23, B), one of the images of the creator, for "Amma is (like a couple of) original twins,"[138] which is expressed by the sum $3 + 4 = 7$, as indicated by the reproduced figure if read according to its own duality, i.e., by separating the four upper vibrations (2-3-4-5) from the three lower ones (1-7-6). The two top rays (3 and 4) form the head; the two below (2 and 5) the arms; the bottom two

137. *inneu tonu vannu.*

138. *amma dineu pologo voy.*

(1 and 6) the legs; and the last (7) the sex. This last ray divides itself into two, ejecting an eighth segment. It is the illustration of one phase of the creation when Amma divided himself into two parts, the first (the central point and seven vibrations) being his word and himself, the second being the eighth segment, representing in itself the total of the first, that is to say, the whole creation in formation, i.e., the *po* seed. It is said: "The *po* came out of Amma like a *bibile* (a mutation or metamorphosis)."[139]

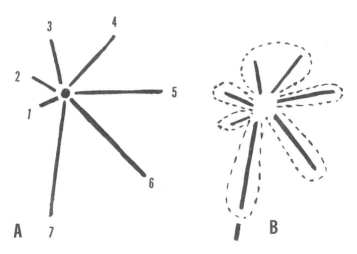

FIG. 23: A. The seven vibrations inside the *po pilu;*
B. Amma's *tonu.*

In such an anthropomorphic form , it is also the prefiguration of the formation of the eight first animate beings (the *nommo anagonno*), which Amma will create after the production of the seeds, and who will be his workers, whose duty it is to perfect his creation.[140] Now, the realization of this group of nine will entail the presence of both perfec-

---

139. *po amma gozu-ne goy bibile bilay.*

140. They will receive the "word" in the life-giving form it had taken on in the *po* seed, symbolized by the eight seeds of the contents of the clavicles (cf. *infra,* p. 394 and ff.).

tion and imperfection in the universe. From this perspective, the figure called "sign of the Nommo's head"[141] must be read as follows: the first seven segments will first form an androgynous whole, each containing twice the four elements (water, earth, air, and fire); they will thus be made up of eight substances. Upon the creation of the eighth, each of the seven will give up a bit of its substances towards its formation, the whole of these contributions being equivalent to one part, so that the eighth will receive seven parts or seven substances. It will be less complete than the others, which possess eight. The missing substance is water; the new being, formed in this way, will become the Fox.

Amma had deliberately acted in this manner. The eighth had to be incomplete so that everything would be contained in nature, perfection as well as imperfection. Just as later, at a more evolved stage of creation, there had to be dryness and moisture, fertility and sterility, life and death, and also at the beginning of the world there had to be the dry *po* seed and the oval drop of the water element, the twinness of which is simultaneously antithetical and complementary.

The number of vibrations also bears evidence of a quasi-genetic link associating the "word," *so*, with "seven," *soy*. Indeed, *soy* literally means "this is the word." Amma placed his "word" in the *po* where it progressively took on the form of seven vibrations: "The first thing that Amma did was to put the seven words into the *po*."[142] The seven words, as we have already seen, constituted a couple of opposite sexes. The eighth word will be like the birth of a new being, begotten of the original couple; it prefigures the birth of Amma's second universe, which will emerge from the *po*.

The spiraling motion attributed to the "word" inside the seed is connoted by the name it has been given: the word *po* comes from a root meaning "to roll up" (into a turban).

Finally, the *po*, having reached a maximum of internal dynamism caused by the development of life, burst. And, imitating what had happened in Amma's egg, the inner spiral then turned in the other direction. The figures denoting the formation of the seed recall these final stages. The *yala* of the seed is made of twenty-two *yala* in a spiral (twenty-two being in the "egg" the total number of the sex (six) and body (sixteen) of the *po*). The spiral turns in the direction imposed upon it by

141. *nommo ku tonu.*
142. *amma kize polo vo mani so soy po gozu-ne kunni.*

the opening of "Amma's eyes" (fig. 24, A). The *tonu* is made of seven rays around a dot, recalling the presence and action of Amma's "word" (fig. 24, B). In the completed seed this burst of rays causes the spiral to spin in the other direction, as is shown by the *toy* of the seed.[143] It represents the rolling up of the "word" — thus of life — in the mature seed (fig. 24, C).

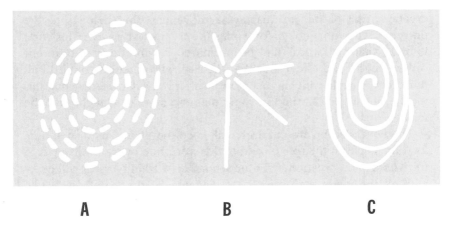

A   **B**   **C**

FIG. 24: A. *yala* of the *po pilu;* B. *tonu;* C. *toy.*

At this stage of creation, the "seat" or womb of Amma — represented in the "egg" by the *yala* of the *gaba gunnu* — contained the *po* seed like a spring, rolled up on itself. Inside, having spun in the direction imposed on the *yala* of the internal spiral of the "egg" after the opening of "Amma's eyes," Amma's "word," the seed's life, once again spun in the original direction of that same creative spiral.

---

143. The *yala* was drawn under the altar to Amma of the first *ginna* of the Ono (*ono togu die amma*), located at Gué Oulou, when it was founded; the *tonu,* under the altar to Amma of the Domno, called *domno soy* located at Domno; the *toy* under the altar of the Arou at Arou-near-Ibi. The *bummo* having been drawn under the Kan Amma altar of the Dyon (cf. fig. 21, p. 136), the four stages of the formation of the first seed were represented under the four first altars to Amma of the four Dogon tribes (by figures made with the porridge of *po pilu).*

In like manner, the figures drawn on the wall inside the sanctuaries of the *binu ana* when they are founded are in *yu* and *ara* porridge.

The internal movement of germination was prefigured by this spiral movement in two directions, which is the movement of the *po*. It is said: "The seed grows by turning."[144] Inside, while germinating, it first spins in one direction, then, after bursting, that is, after the emergence of the germ, it spins in the other direction, in order to produce its root and stalk. In addition, the explosion and release of the spiral in the opposite direction produced — in the image of the "word" which it contained — the fundamental twinness of the *po,* as provided for by Amma. It is said: "The *po,* spinning as it came out, became twins."[145] Thus this second creation, that of the *po,* displays a movement that belongs to the universe. It was not enough for Amma the creator, who was a whirlwind himself, that his "word" had been emitted in vibrations of different order, length, and effect, nor that their spiral formation could fill all things of the world with internal movement: it was still necessary that this moving whole be churned in some manner, so that it might later be fertile.

The *po,* coiled up around itself, will keep the "word" until such time as Amma gives it the role of setting this word free by transmitting it to the whole of his creation.[146] In the second created universe it will be — with all the seeds born after it — evidence of the "vital" aspect of Amma's "word."

CREATION OF THE EIGHT SEEDS.

Continuing his work, Amma then created the other grains, *dene,*[147] beginning with the eight seeds prefigured by the forty internal *yala* of the spiral. Like the *po,* they will be twins, male and female. And the movement imposed upon their creation will allow some of them to form mutations (*bibile*) within the womb and produce other varieties (the *emme ya,* for example, producing other varieties of sorghum, the *ara geu* producing other varieties of rice, etc.).

He began with the *emme ya,* "female sorghum," the most important of

---

144. *yu digilie te.*

145. *po digilie goze dine bi.*

146. Cf. *infra,* p. 415 and ff.

147. *dene* means "to seek," because "on Earth one seeks the cereals necessary to the life of man."

the cereal grains after the *po pilu,* a seed which will have a status and role similar to that of the *po* (fig. 25).

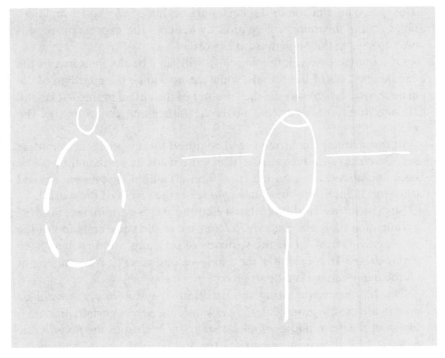

FIG. 25: *yala* and *tonu* of the *emme ya* seed.

It is said that the *emme ya* seed, which Amma held between his fingernails, was the most tiring to make because it does not stand well on its ear.[148] The grain's pod represents "Amma's fingernails" that still hold it in place. For unlike the *po pilu,* which will come under many avatars in the course of the events that will take place on Earth, the *emme ya* will always remain intact. One says of it that "it is the purest of the cereal grains."[149]

---

148. In the ear it easily falls off, as it is attached by a tiny stem.

149. *emme ya dene pu omo voy.* It will be given to certain men (and not to all of them) only later, once all the labors of the reorganization of the world and of human life are completed. When one finds a seed of *emme ya* and one knocks it off by threshing it, it must be swept and picked up most carefully out of respect for Amma's work and because of its purity.

ya means "woman," as well as "yesterday" and "to leave." A popular etymology gives *yara,* "to release"; for one says that "the second creation in the past (yesterday = *ya*) was released and liberated by Amma." This is also an allusion to the beginning of things; *ya,* "to leave," here takes on the meaning of "creation by action"; the expression *yaga* is used to say "in the beginning, at the origin."

Of feminine essence, the *emme ya* will later be the guardian of the female sex souls of the cereals, while the *po* will be the guardian of the male souls. The *emme ya* is the "mother of the cereal grains." It is said: "In the family of seeds, the *po* is the father and the *emme ya* the mother."[150]

In this manner the formed seed acquired the shape of the feminine sex. Given its reproductive role, it was also made larger than the *po.* It is said, figuratively, that Amma "tired himself making the *emme ya* seed (the world) enter into the smaller *po* seed (the origin of the world)."

But the *emme ya* did not burst like the *po;* it germinated. And its germination took place slowly, in contrast to the virile emission of the *po.* It gave "birth" to all the varieties of sorghum, the first being the *emme di giru.* In speaking of the *emme ya,* one says: "It is the biggest of all the *emme;* may it make us grow."[151]

The figures representing the creation of the *emme ya* recall its prerogatives; the graphic designs connote the seed's germination and, likewise, the germination of all cereal grains.[152] Just as the *po pilu,* the plant will be shown in its entirety (on the façades of sanctuaries) by dipping a tuft of millet in rice porridge and quickly slapping it flat against the wall: there is a spattering forming the rays of the drawing and a thick plaster at the center of the ear. They alone will be shown this way, thus emphasizing their roles as the progenitors of the other seeds. A variant of the figures representing the *emme ya* shows a *tonu,*

---

150. *dene togu-ne po bay, emme ya nay.* This sentence is part of a prayer recited during the sowing feast, *bulu,* in front of the altar *ka amma.*

151. *emme voy diey, emme barie kana.*

152. Drawn in porridge of *ara pilu* and *yu* on the wall and inside the sanctuaries of *binu ya* when they are founded. The piles of manure put around the *sogo* during the sowing feast will be placed in the same manner as the four figures which represent sowing, germination, cultivation, and the harvest of all the grains.

connoting the stalk, Amma's "fingernails" (the pod), and the seed itself; then a *toy,* which recalls "Amma's work."[153] The image is also that of the ritual iron lance (*binu solumo*), kept in the totemic sanctuaries (fig. 26).

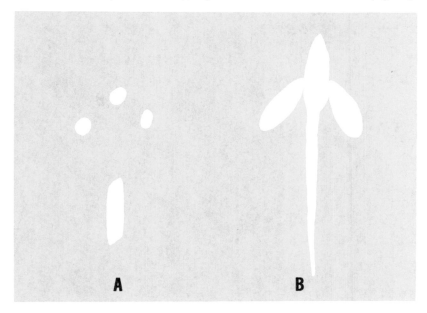

FIG. 26: *tonu* and *toy* of the *emme ya.*

Thus, the *emme ya* is the symbol of gestation and also of the "generations" to come. For this reason, one also says that it divided itself into two parts, one remaining the *emme ya,* the other being the world itself. This duality is also accented when one says that, while Amma had been and had created the *po* and had given creation his impetus, the *emme ya* represents the universe realized and regenerated by the sacrifice of the *nommo anagonno;* it symbolizes what he will give to the world at a later stage, in order that it may exist and organize itself.

After the *emme ya,* Amma created the other seeds without difficulty by rolling them in the thick of his fingers.

He created the seed *emme di giru,* "eye of the water," which is said

---

153. For "Amma's work," cf. *infra,* p. 184 and ff.

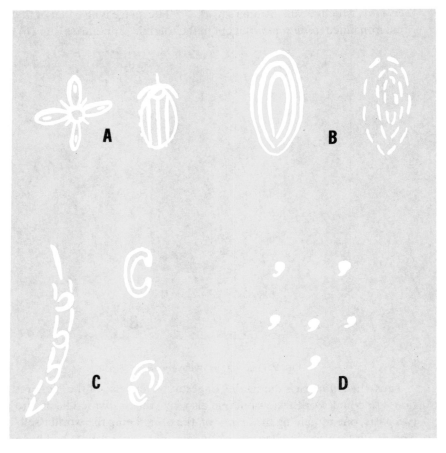

FIG. 27: Figures of the seeds: A. *namu*, B. *ara*, C. *nu*, D. *yu*.

to be the "eye of the Nommo" and "shows the path of the water to the *emme ya.*"[154]

Then he created those of the *emme pilu* and the *emme nakolo*.[155]

---

154. Figure drawn with *ara geu* and *yu* porridge under the altars to Amma of all the *binu ya* during their foundation.

155. The figure of the *emme pilu* is drawn under the altars to Amma of the priests and priestesses of Amma, *ammakezine* and *ammayana,* placed in the *ginna,* with *yu* and *ara geu* porridge when they are founded.

Then black rice, *ara geu;* the figures of this seed are made up of three ovals, one within the other, connoting the later formation of two other varieties of rice, the *ara pilu* and *ara banu*[156] (fig. 27, B).

If the predominantly masculine *po pilu* and predominantly feminine *emme ya* are associated with the spiritual principles (*kikinu*), with the souls of the grains of which they are the "guardians," in like manner the *yu* and the *nu* are associated with the life force (*nyama*) of the seeds in its complementary masculinity and femininity.

From the beginning the *yu* had the shape of a male sex organ. The tip of the seed is the "mouth of the world that opens," and the husk the image of the "ark" that will descend on earth.

The figure of the seed of "small white millet" (*yu pilu i tonu*) (fig. 27, D) features a hook denoting the germ. It is repeated seven times, for the *yu pilu* gave birth to six other varieties: *yu tolone peze, yu donno, yu toroy, bobo yu, manu yu,* and *sana yu.*[157]

The bean, *nu,* which is said to be larger in volume than the largest cereal grain, is called "Amma's food," *amma da.*

It is said (when the seed splits in two) after germination: "The (climbing) stalks of the bean are like Amma's house,"[158] because of the oval they describe, and because the form of the leaves recalls the shape of Amma's clavicle. In this capacity, it plays an important role in the big family house (*ginna*), for it is the symbol of fertility and denotes pregnancy.[159] The three figures called *"tonu* of the germination of the bean,"

The figure of the *emme nakolo* is drawn under the altars to Amma of the priests of *binu i,* under the same conditions. The vocation of those individuals who, within the family or clan, offer a personal cult to Amma and to his agent the Nommo, is determined by the occurrence of trances, as is the case with the priests of *binu na.* Cf. vol. I, 2nd installment.

156. Drawn with the same porridge under the altars to Amma of all the *binu ana* at their foundation.

157. Drawn with the porridge of *yu* and *ara geu* on the wall inside the *kana* of the *vageu* in the great family house (*ginna*) during its construction (cf. p. 378).

158. *nu vonu amma ginna-gin vo.*

159. The bean is the "seed of the *ginna.* "The pulp, offered to all those belonging to the *ginna, goru da,* on the day of celebration of the *goru* (at the winter solstice) which ends the *bago* rites, is made only from the bean. It is offered beforehand on the altar to Amma of the house.

On the bean and fecundity, cf., G. DIETERLEN and G. CALAME-GRIAULE, *l'Alimentation dogon,* p. 60.

nu tey tonu, connote the progression in the formation of the bean, *nu ninu,* and of its pod, *nu kizu* (fig. 27, C).[160] The *toy* of the bean shows the seed, with a stroke on either side of it, containing eight internal figures connoting the germination of the eight primordial seeds: the outside stroke on the right is called "nose of the bean," *nu kinu.* The eight strokes are the "gift (given) by the bean," *nu solu:* the curved stroke on the left is *po pilu* ready to emerge; then, from left to right: *po banu, namu i, anu, yu,* all the *emme* and the *emme ya.*[161]

A drawing one cubit high is also made above and to the left of the entrance door to the *ginna,* depicting the bean in question and the seeds: *po banu, namu i, anu, ara,* and *yu,* all of the *emme, emme ya,* and *po pilu* which, in the preceding figure, were shown to be inside in the process of germination.

There will be a great many types of beans on Earth that are considered to have originated from the first *nu ninu: nu day dolo, nu seru, nu banu, nu pilu, nu teu, dunu nu.*

The seed of the cottonbush, *namu i,* is included among the cereal grains for it will be consumed by man. The figures represent the formation of the arborescent cottonbush seed, *namu na,* "large cottonbush," for the dwarf cottonbush will appear only later on Earth; they are drawn under the weavers' altars to Amma, *soy ti amma*[162] (fig. 27, A).

The eight seeds are evidence of the presence of the "word" placed in the *po* — a "word" which, at that stage, constituted the "life" bestowed upon the second creation and implied fertility and reproduction. They are like the eight "words." Therefore, they will later be symbolically represented in the clavicles of man, the support for his physical being, where they will become evidence of his wholeness.

Having thus successively formed the eight seeds of the primordial spiral, Amma then created the *gaba* and *anu* grains.

---

160. Drawn with *yu* and *ara geu* porridge under the altar to Amma of the *ginna* when it is founded.

161. Drawn above the entrance door of the *kana* which contains the altar of the ancestors, *vageu,* in the *ginna,* with the porridge of *yu* and *ara geu.* (2nd installment, first year.)

162. With *yu* and *ara geu* porridge when these altars are founded.

GABA *AND* ANU.

The seeds of *anu* and *gaba,* represented by the *yala* outside the spiral of Amma's egg, will not emerge from the *po* as did the cereals. Amma had not placed them in the spiral of seeds, but had rather kept them in reserve, like the sowing seeds, *dene toy,* set aside in the granary.[163] This spiral was contained in the womb-like *gaba;* the *gaba* seeds were formed inside "its pulp," the very place where the first animate beings will be developed, the ancestors of humanity. And, "as if gently held by the pulp of the *gaba,"* the *anu* seed also formed itself. Like the *yala,* evidence of the body and sex souls of the cereals, the formed grains will also bear evidence of the links uniting grains and humans; for one says that "grains and men are of the same kind (species)":[164] they will be associated with the eight principal vital internal organs of man — organs which are relays for the passage of the "word" through the human body by way of the bloodstream.[165] In this capacity, they will be drawn as *toy* at the four openings of the main room of the *ginna,* the *dembere,* "womb of the inside," two per opening, the *gaba* on the right and the *anu* on the left.[166] Each of these figures symbolizes one of the first four varieties of *gaba (koro kuno, koro pomu, koro kinigu, koro kembogu)* and of *anu (anu na, anu golo, anu gonnoru, anu gogobolo).* Their position in Amma's egg and their particular role in the development of the universe will confer a special status on them.

The four *yala* assigned to each seed, and the twin creation of the *gaba* and *anu* seeds are remembered at sowing time. The calabash contains the seeds for sowing: *anu* is sown around the field "to guard it"; the seed of the calabash tree is sown at the east side of the field, because the rain comes from the east.[167] Of all the plants that can be cultivated, *anu* is the only one whose parts can all be utilized: one eats the leaves and seeds;

---

163. This initial position is related to the status of the spiritual principles of the *anu* and the *gaba.* Cf. *infra,* p. 523.

164. *dene inne anay.*

165. Cf. *infra,* p. 375. The vertical position of the *yala* in the egg is also the diagram of the flow of the blood from the emasculation and sacrifice of the *nommo anagonno,* an event that occurred during the development of the universe. Cf. *infra,* ch. III.

166. The *toy* of the *gaba* are drawn with *puru i* (a condiment with *yullo* seeds as its base); those of the *anu* with *kumuli* (a condiment with *oro* seeds as its base) (cf. *infra,* p. 375).

ropes are made of its fibers. Consumption of the leaves takes place before the seeds have ripened. Also, it is sometimes said that Amma created the leaf first — and not the seed — which gives it its sour taste. One also says that on Earth it will be the "adversary of the *sene.*"

The formation of the *anu* will complete the cycle of the creation of the seeds; although created last, it will be man's first food.

At a later stage, it will be the role of the *anu* to classify the elements of creation, especially the basic cereal grains — before their descent on Earth.[168] That is why man's clavicle (seat of the symbols of the eight primordial seeds) will be named *ani guyo,* "granary of *anu.*" A "figure of the *ani,*" *anu tonu,* conveys these various associations and, at the same time, it recalls the genesis of the primordial seeds (fig. 28): the upper circle, A, represents the divine "clavicle" where the seeds were formed, represented by the eight lines to either side (B and B'). The vertical line, C, shows the future descent of the seeds on Earth where they will be passed on to man; they are shown here by the *bummo* drawn inside the lower circle, which is both the *gaba* and the "created world": D, the *po;* E, the *emme ya;* F, the *emme di giru;* G, the *emme pilu;* H, the *emme dum;* K, the *yu;* L, the *nu;* M, the *ara geu;* N, the *anu.*[169]

The stages of creation of the seeds are summed up by comparing them with the succession of generations, and it is said, in speaking of Amma,

---

167. While sowing the *gaba,* one places four grains in the hole, saying *gaba lugu uo nay minne-ne yo:* "Your number of *gaba* is 4, enter into the field." While sowing the *anu,* one says: "The number of the *anu* is 4, for it surrounds the field at the four cardinal points" (*anu lugu nay, minne-ne sibe nay gonno*). When cultivating *po* in Wazouba, in Mendéli, in Kamma, or in the plain, one mixes the *anu* with it. One makes a mound of earth (under an anthill or in an enclosed spot) and sows the *gaba* there. This sowing recalls their role as the original witnesses of the spiritual principles of the cereals.

The primarily maternal role of the *gaba* was in the past remembered during the harvest; a certain number of grain seeds were mixed into the clay of the façade of the *ginna.* This is presently also done among the Bambara.

168. Cf. *infra,* p. 426.

169. Figures drawn at the *bulu* with cereal porridge inside the sanctuaries.

The seeds are twin and of both sexes, but they were first created either male or female, as were the *po* and the *emme ya.* The graphic representations of the *bummo* are evidence of this: open to the right for those seeds created male and open to the left for those created female.

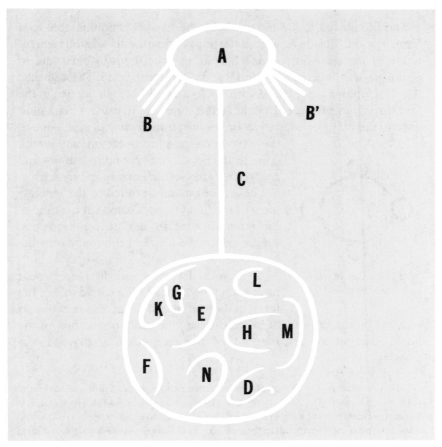

FIG. 28: *tonu* of the *anu*.

the *sene, po, gaba,* and *anu:* "The things that created the world are like the end of the fifth generation."[170]

---

170. *kize ganna manu kumo kalle anay.* Generation is called *"kumo timme,* (that which is) superposed (on top) of the *kumo"* (that is, the fifth generation). The *gaba* and *anu* seeds will not descend on the ark with man, but will go and germinate on the seven *yalu ulo* after that descent (cf. *infra,* p. 520).

FERMENTATION.

The life placed inside the seeds by the "word" is comparable to a fermentation. "Inside Amma, many things fermented." It is the fermentation of the seeds in Amma's bosom, causing them to burst and to germinate, that "will open the world" and allow it to develop. Theoretically, this development, associated with the four elements, will happen in the four directions of space. In light of this, one says that the *yu* and *anu,* gone to the east, correspond to air; *emme ya* and *emme di giru,* gone to the west, correspond to water; *nu* and *namu,* gone to the north, correspond to fire; *po* and *ara,* gone to the south, correspond to earth.

These positions are recalled by the arrangement of the first five pots placed at the time of the foundation of an altar to the ancestors, *vageu,* and at the death of the founder of the family house (fig. 29).[171]

FIG. 29: Sign of the fermentation.

"If there had been no seeds, there would have been no bursting." The active role of the fermentation at the time of the creation is recalled by the brewing of beer at present:[172] the fermentation of the liquid constitutes a "resurrection" of the cereal grains destroyed in the brewing.

---

171. When placing the first piece of earthenware of the *vageu* inside the enclosure, *kana,* which is reserved for this purpose, one puts an iron ring around it. The metal is, in this case, evidence of the *nommo anagonno,* who belongs to a later stage of creation and who also symbolically surrounds it: the earthenware is also representative of the first pond where it will reside on Earth. The four other small pieces of pottery, *vonoy,* are placed inside at the death of the founder of the *ginna.* For the other deceased, a piece of pottery and a *vonoy* are added each time, placed in a spiral around the first.

172. The whole figure is also the "sign of the fermentation" and recalls the form of one of the yeast containers *buzuru goro,* "bonnet yeast container," the most important of them all. (Cf. *infra,* p. 535.)

5. CREATION OF THE *NOMMO ANAGONNO*

Amma's double placenta. The egg of the *nommo anagonno*.
Formation of the *nommo anagonno*. Multiplication of the fish.

AMMA'S DOUBLE PLACENTA.

"Amma's egg, that had enveloped all things inside it, became his placenta."[173] This placenta was formed at the center, within "Amma's seat," *amma doy,* or "calabash in a ball," *gaba gunnu,* which prefigured the womb (matrix) of the world.

The word designating the placenta, *me,* comes from the same root as the word for copper, *menu.*[174] Copper is considered to be impure fire,[175] i.e., fire which has undergone some mutation. It is "solid" fire and the second stage of fire which, as an element, was at the source of creation. Like the human placenta, which will always remain "alive," even after coming out of the womb, copper, also called *ya menu,* "copper of past times," is the symbol of permanence because "it does not die": the expression designates "all ancient things that do not end," that do not disappear.

Now this primordial placenta was double, and its two parts were as if joined by Amma himself; the whole of it, called *menu,* "this is copper," formed the world.

A figure made of two V's — one upside down under the other — recalls the formation of the double placenta. It is called: "Amma forming two points," that is, developing space. This *bummo* will be ritually drawn in

---

173. *amma ene talu kize pu kologo-ne to duia vo gelebe me vomo bi.*

174. Copper will be the product of the transformation of the placenta (vol I, 2nd installment). The word *menu,* "piece," and *mene,* which designates the sacrifice of purification before the killing of the victim *per se,* are of the same root as *me,* "placenta"; *menu,* "piece," is an allusion to that piece of his placenta which the Fox will tear out at his premature birth; the operation called *mene* constitutes a "piece" of the sacrifice considered in its entirety. Finally, *menne* designates the "kinship" which unites the members of a totemic clan, a "kinship" originating at the level of a common gestation, that is, in relation to the same "placenta" (cf. *infra,* p. 338). The Dogon associate *me* with *mene,* "to criticize," because "Amma will reproach the Fox for the theft committed by tearing out a 'piece' of his placenta."

175. "Copper is fire become impure," *menu anu yau puru.*

the fields where sacred functions are performed and on the façade of the
Hogon's dwelling at Arou. It is one of the fundamental representations
of Amma's work.

FIG. 30: In the middle, "Amma's messenger"; to the left, the *bummo* "Amma forming two
points"; to the right, *toy* of the moon and sun, separated by a vertical line.

A drawing depicts Amma in his totality and his double placenta (fig.
30).[176] The completed upper oval has the incomplete lower oval as its
reflection. The latter is open to mark Amma's deliberate failure in
creating the terrestrial placenta, which was to be reorganized by the upper
one.[177] From this perspective, the cross represents "the limit of the
fields," forming the axis of symmetry. From an anthropomorphic point
of view, the sign called *amma titiyayne*, "Amma's messenger," also
represents future man, "principle of the world." In this microcosm, the
arms separate the celestial placenta (the head) from the terrestrial
placenta (the legs and sexual organ), which is incomplete. The sign thus
symbolizes both the world and man, its principle, as well as "Amma's
double placenta."

---

176. This sign is drawn at the *bulu* on the façade of a totemic sanctuary during
consumption of the sacrifice and of the beer by those belonging (*inneomo*) to the totem. It
also represents the statuette *dege*, placed inside the sanctuary (cf. installment II, 8th year).
Cf. also M. GRIAULE and G. DIETERLEN, *Signes graphiques soudanais*, p. 23.

177. This lower open placenta is represented by the bracelet of the dignitary of the
Society of Masks, the *yasigine*, which is also open (cf. installment II, 3rd year).

This division also prefigures the two elements that emerge at the birth of a human being: the child, *i,* and his placenta, *me.* This double representation concerns what happens in the womb at the time of the formation of the fetus, namely, a division between the sac, *sosoy,*[178] also called *i guru,* "child's nest," and the placenta.

This division is also recalled by a drawing of a vertical line separating the moon and the sun,[179] and which prefigures, from a different viewpoint, the future division of time into day and night. Thus these three figures associated with the division of the first placenta represent the future separation of the sky from the Earth, the implementation of time and calendars (solar and lunar), and the basic duality of man.

Regarding Amma's placenta, it is also said that it bears the name *yaduro* ("laden ‹or loaded down› woman" or "which one loads" in the sense of "to superadd"). "Amma is in charge of the life of mankind,"[180] *yaduro* is the "substance" of the placenta that Amma will use to model the first animate beings. *yaduro* is the name given to Amma's placenta as "earth." Because, as fire, it also contains the other elements, including earth, the raw material with which he will produce his work. Thus, the other elements will still be present during this gestation: the primordial signs made of water, the placenta made of fire (copper), and the living beings of earth receiving the air that had been stirred by Amma to determine space and that will give them life.

With regard to the element "water," the substance used to make the signs, Amma's placenta was divided into six registers bearing his thought and his word, i.e., things and beings, schematically and in reduced form. "Amma who created the place of things 'in a ball' (in formation), (for) each thing he traced the division of the placenta into six (parts)."[181] This division was related to the initial impetus given to creation by the male

---

178. *sosoy,* from *soso,* "to melt," "to flow," for the waters of the womb will flow from the envelope before the birth.

179. This *toy* is drawn in millet porridge on the façade of the totemic sanctuary at the *bulu.* The vertical line recalls the separation into two parts of the *gaba* of the center of "Amma's egg."

180. *inneu kinu amma duyo. duyo* means "to fill (load) oneself," from *duro,* "to load someone."

181. *amma kize vo mani me gunnu, kize tuturu me gammala kuloy bummu.*

sex (3 x 2) (represented by the six *yala* of the inner spiral of Amma's egg), as if imprinted on the womb where the eight first beings (4 x 2) were to be formed.

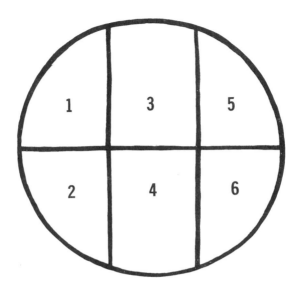

FIG. 31: Diagram of the placenta in six registers
or of the first round divination table.

A figure shows the internal layout of this placenta (fig. 31). It reproduces the ancient round divination table to which all apprentice diviners are first initiated. "The division into six of the table of the Fox is like the division into six of the placenta of the world."[182] This table, called *kala gono,* "torn round,"[183] has six divisions or "houses" (*ginu*) which are, respectively:

1) *amma numo da:* Amma's upper hand,
2) *amma numo donu:* Amma's lower hand,

---

182. *yurugu kala kuloy gammalanu, aduno me tuturu kuloy gammali tozoy.*

183. The term *kala,* "to tear," is given to the divination tables of the Fox which represent a part of his placenta that he will "tear out" in the process of his own gestation (cf. *infra,* p. 203). For the evolution from the round form (called ancient) to the present rectangular form, cf. also p. 246, n. 106. The round table is drawn in red ochre on the ground at the time of the founding of an altar to the Fox, *yurugu lebe.*

3) *ginu bere da:* upper central house,
4) *ginu bere donu:* lower central house,
5) *yimu numo da:* upper hand of death,
6) *yimu numo donu:* lower hand of death.

Man whom Amma will have "descend," i.e., whom he will send down to Earth (only at a later stage in creation), will be created like *nommo anagonno* and following the same stages. Therefore, according to another version, the cosmic placenta is said to be divided into five registers; from this perspective, the five registers stand for Amma's placenta and the individual placentas of the first two pairs of twin *nommo anagonno.* These five registers also recall the succession of the first five human generations descended from one of them,[184] and prefigure the successive partitions of the field of the *ginna* into five parcels, that is, the squaring off of arable soil by the successive generations.

Inside this double placenta Amma created the first animate being, the silurus,* called *nommo anagonno.* It is said: "The *nommo anagonno* is the first living thing created by Amma."[185] The word for silurus, *anagonno,* breaks down into *ana,* "rain," and *gonno,* "to sinuate," *ana* also designates "man" (*vir*), whose seed, on the mythical plane, is associated with the fertilizing rain and fresh water. The word can also be translated as "sinuous rain," or "male (who walks by) sinuating." The sinuous walk belongs to the fish, or to the rain and to fresh water. But the term *ana* foretells that the living being created will become "man," *vir.*

Amma first created two pairs of male twins. The rough design of this pair of twin *nommo anagonno* created in the double placenta and their

---

*(Any of the numerous fishes of the family *Siluridae,* comprising the catfishes. Trsl.)

184. The design of the "house of menstruating women," *ya punulu ginu,* is made in the image of the "placenta with five registers." The *ginna* has five main rooms which correspond to the division of the first placenta into five parts (cf. *infra,* p. 373).

The division of the placenta into five parts deliberately omits the part which, in the division into six parts, represents the impure earth of the Fox.

185. *nommo anagonno amma kize kinugu polo vo manu voy.* This concerns a mythical fish which, in the Dogon streams, replaces the *mannogo ble* (Heterobranchus bidorsalis) of the Niger which plays an analogous role among the Malinke and the Bambara (cf. G. DIETERLEN, *Mythe et organisation sociale au Soudan français*). Out of respect for its role in creation, the *nommo anagonno* is always called *di bana anagonno, "anagonno* master of the water."

position in relation to Amma's clavicles are recalled by a *tonu* called
"sign of the position of the Amma of the *binu* (representing) the design
of the four *nommo anagonno*"(fig. 32).[186] It stresses the positions of the
nommo anagonno created by Amma inside himself. The four strokes

N

FIG. 32: Sign of the foundation of Amma's altar of the *binu*.

are also the *bummo* of the four *kikinu* of the body placed in the placenta,
with which everyone will be endowed at the very beginning of his for-

186. *nommo anagonno nay tonu binu amma danu tonu.* The figure was drawn with
porridge of *yu* and *ara geu* under the raised stone of Dona, which constitutes the *sogo
uguru uguri,* (cf. p. 493). It bears evidence of the sketch of the "opening" of Amma's
clavicles, the final stage of creation; it is within these clavicles that the *nommo anagonno*
will be placed after their completed formation.

mation.[187] The partition of the placenta into *me da,* "upper placenta," and *me donu,* "lower placenta," is made along a line going from east to west, denoting the future orientation of the rains. The figure also shows the future opening of "Amma's clavicles" (shown at the cardinal points). Like the bottom one, the top placenta contained a pair of twins, who were to develop normally at the same time. In order to accomplish this, it is said, Amma tried seven times; the realization took place the eighth time.

THE EGG OF THE "NOMMO ANAGONNO."

Like the "word" with which they are endowed, the *nommo anagonno* are already sketched inside the *po.* It is said: "The *nommo anagonno* that Amma created inside the *po,* Amma who created the *po* had made the image of the *nommo anagonno* inside."[188]

The gestation of the *nommo anagonno* took place slowly in Amma's womb, according to a process recalled by a series of figures. It started with the "fish egg" *(izu talu),* in this case the egg of the *nommo anagonno.* The *yala* of this egg, called *nommo anagonno talu yala* (fig. 33),[189] contains 112 of the twin elements which first composed "Amma's egg," because he divided them.

Of the sixty-six *yala* of the central spiral which, from a certain viewpoint, constitute the beginning of Amma himself,[190] Amma kept the first twenty-two, those of the *po,* and bestowed the remaining forty-four upon the *nommo anagonno.* These *yala* were those of the eight seeds (five *yala* per seed) and the *yala* of the *sene* (with four *yala*), evidence of the first genesis and of the four elements. In the figure of the fish egg, these forty-four *yala* make up the walls and divisions of this egg by four rows of ten, with the four elements placed at the center.

---

187. Putting the placenta in a piece of pottery, placed under the dung-hill in the courtyard, is the same as putting it in a pond; the pebble placed above the pottery symbolizes the sky. The newborn child is bathed on this stone and receives his *kikinu* of body at that time.

188. *amma nommo anagonno vo mani po kolo logoro-ne amma po mani kolo-ne nommo anagonno yala yali.* Cf. fig. 23, B, p. 139, which shows an anthropomorphic design.

189. Drawn with *yu* and *ara geu* porridge under the altar to Amma of each *ginna* at its foundation. This drawing in the family house is evidence of the genetic tie which links the *nommo anagonno* and future man.

190. Cf. p. 121

N

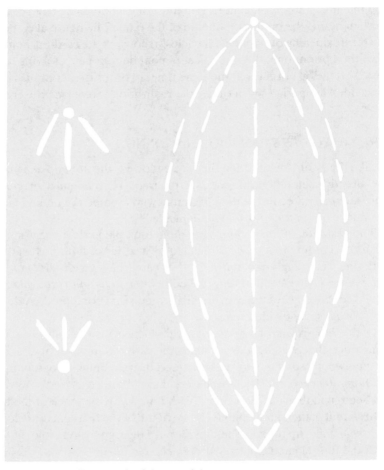

FIG. 33: *yala* of the egg of the *nommo anagonno.*

He also gave it sixty *yala* from the circumference of the *gaba,* a part of those of his "seat," *amma doy,* of his own placenta.[191] He completed the egg by adding to it the eight lower *yala* of the circumference called

---

191. One says: "In the past, the number of the placenta is sixty," *me yala lugu aru pelu kuloy be* (cf. *infra,* ch. II), while executing the paintings on the façade of a totemic sanctuary.

"Amma's eyes"; which had opened when the spiral was unwinding, and which prefigured the existence of the four cardinal directions.[192]

Now, these final eight prefigure here the "four body souls and four sex souls" of the being in formation: thus, "Amma's eyes," which prefigured oriented space, will also be the supports for the spiritual principles of the *nommo anagonno*. It is said: "Amma's eyes, four corners, became the *kikinu* of the *nommo anagonno.*"[193] This attribution was also the image of the future rule of the *nommo anagonno* over the universe in formation; one of the roles of the *nommo anagonno* will be to protect and watch over the world created by Amma. And already during the division of the *yala,* the respective position of the *amma giru,* in relation to all those of the egg of the *nommo anagonno,* will play an essential role of orientation, as well as function as a sort of initial framework. Indeed, the *yala* of the four body *kikinu* placed themselves at the top of the egg (in the form of three strokes emerging from a central point) dominating it somewhat like the ribs of an umbrella (fig. 33). At the opposite end, the *yala* of the four sex *kikinu* became inverted, placing themselves in the same way at the bottom of the egg. Thus, in the world to come, the spiritual principles of the *nommo anagonno* will be "Amma's eye" that looks at and watches over the progress of the universe.[194]

The *yala* of the egg also show the elongated form of the fish itself. The bottom of the V-shaped figure is a rough sketch of the tail of the *anagonno.*

The division of the signs, initiated by the position of the *yala* that represented the Nommo's body souls and sex souls, already prefigured the social structure of humanity. Indeed, the vertical lines do not touch the egg, but rather separate four registers meant to outline the sketch of the "ancestors" of man. Thus, forty *yala* of the spiral of the *po* (in four rows of ten around the four elements) are distributed in the same manner as later the first four lineages of man.

Also, as soon as the egg was formed, the *nommo anagonno* received

---

192. Cf. p. 125.

193. *amma giru sibe nay nommo kikinu to.*

194. In commenting upon this association, the Dogon say that the *kikinu* are "like the eye" since they walk about at night without their means of support and bring back in the dream all they have seen.

the tokens of the four elements, of the four cardinal directions (associated with his spiritual principles), of the eight seeds (related to the future content of the clavicles), and, finally, those of "Amma's womb," or the womb of the world, which became those belonging to his placenta — all these signs being evidence of his future completeness and fertility.

To emphasize their respective roles, one compares the *yala* of Amma's egg with those of the egg of the *nommo anagonno* by saying: "The *yala* of Amma's egg is like an egg with its yolk and its germ; the *yala* of the egg of *nommo anagonno* is stretched like the world that is going to spread itself out"; or again, "the *yala* of Amma's egg is seated, the *yala* of the *nommo (anagonno)* caused the elongation (enlargement, growth) of the world."[195] In fact, the formed being will be complete and alive, therefore pure, and a promoter of general fertility. The priest who invokes it says: "The number of the 'master of water' is one hundred and twelve; here is your purification, may the soft (good) rain fall, give us marriage, give us ripe millet."[196]

"In the past, in the sky (of Amma), one used to say *nommo* fish."[197] Therefore, the *nommo,* silurus fish, originally existed in the form of an egg somewhat larger and longer than the *po* seed. In this egg Amma will first place fire, then water that will unite with the fire. In the form of blood, this water will enter the first clavicle to be formed, just as water flows into a pond. The power of the fire will increase the power of the water. Then earth will be added, that will form the bones, but part of which the creator will keep. This earth, like the air, will be surrounded by water. Finally, the air will penetrate the formed being and endow him with life. Thus, the creation of the *nommo*-silurus prefigures the creation of man, who also begins with fire, for semen is fire in the womb.

This penetration of the four fundamental elements took place during the development of the principal organs of the *nommo anagonno* inside the egg, as shown by the *tonu* of the egg (fig. 34).[198] In fact, while in the

---

195. *amma talu yala deda; nommo yala aduno palaniemi.*

196. *di bana lugu sunu peran ley sige, uguru uo uvo, ana di ezu dele, ya di dele, dene ille obo.* This prayer is recited by the priest of the Goummoyana totem when he performs the purification at the pond Dona in Sanga (cf. p. 493, n. 99).

197. *alakala-ne ani nommo izu gebe.*

198. This figure is called *nommo anagonno izu tonu,* "*tonu* of the egg of the *nommo.*" It is drawn with *ara geu* porridge under the hollow stone which is placed next to the door of totemic sanctuaries and which is filled with "axes of thunder."

egg, it received the three main supports of its being from Amma's thought: the "clavicles" (*ani guyo*) having the same form as those of man, the suprabranchial (i.e., above the gills) organs (*sosogu*), or "adenoids," of the fish, and the cartilage forming the hinge of the pectoral fin (*ta i,* literally: "child of the door" or "key").

The expression *ta i* applies to the external part of the pectoral fins. *ani guyo*, "clavicle," designates more precisely their helicoid base. However, the first of the two terms is currently used to designate the entire fin considered as the clavicle.

FIG. 34: *tonu* of the egg of the *nommo anagonno.*

Amma modeled, as it were, the clavicles upon the water, which came to join the fire. It is said: "The form of the water, he spun it like a circle in the *ani guyo*."[199] The clavicles, an essential element, potentially contained all the organs (with the exception of those two mentioned above), and the heart contained the water.

The suprabranchial organs (*sosogu*) are the seat and symbol of the

---

199. *di yala ani guyo denele-go gonu.*

permanence of the being. It is said: "The *sogo* of the Nommo is a thing
that always remains in place; for this (reason) one says *sosogu*."[200] The
latter is the nominative case for *sosogo,* which means "to remain in
place indefinitely."[201]. They will be nourished by the heart. In the egg,
they were kept closed by the *ta i,* their "keys," which Amma had wanted
to open only at the right time so that the fertilizing air, together with the
germs contained in the clavicles, might penetrate, thus making the
multiplication of fish possible.[202] Therefore, one says that "the key of
the fish is the passage way of the air,"[203] and that the *sosogu* is the
"breathing" of the clavicle.

Moreover, the *sosogu* of the being in formation received from Amma
the *kikinu* of the *po* (on the right) and those of the other grains created
after it, placed in the *emme ya* (on the left): this arrangement of the souls
of the basic grains stressed the future role of Amma's creature in the
universe, i.e., his essential function as guardian and protector of the
primordial elements of Amma's second world. It is said: "The fish that
Amma created, he put in its *sosogu* the eight *kikinu* of the *po*; all of the
seeds which Amma created without their *kikinu,* he did not give them to
the *po,* but to the *emme ya;* in the right *sosogu* of the *nommo anagonno*
are the *kikinu* of the *po;* in the left *sosogu* (are) the *kikinu* of the other
seeds";[204] and, finally: "When Amma's egg opened up, Amma opened the
ta i in order to put in the seeds."[205] This allotment of the seeds and their
spiritual principles also reminds us that the formed being is of the same
essence as the *po,* and that it has received the "word" that makes up the

---

200. *nommo sogo kize sosogoze-de sosogu gi.*

201. sogo means "to put in a pile," "to gather on the spot," "to group," "to put close
together." The *sogo* refers to altars made of gathered stones: a stone which is raised and
fixed to the ground is called *sogo turu.*

The *sosogu* or "adenoid" of the silurus is also called *yogo sogo,* "gathering of the
throat." It is also said "at the market, the men are gathered" (*ibe-ne inneu sogo sogu vo*).

202. Because of their appearance and their symbolism in the fish, they are compared to
the sacks of skin containing semen.

203. *izu ta i ono ozi.*

204. *amma izu vo manu sosogu vomo-ne po kikinu gagara kunni. dene pu amma mani
kikinu po tolo-go emme ya dele. nommo anagonno sosogu tana po kikinu i sosogu-ne to,
dene kikinu nana sosogu-ne to.* These sentences are said when the seeds are put into the
granary, because "the *nommo anagonno* is like the granary."

205. *amma talu vo gommo izu ta i dagala ani guyo vomo-ne dene kunni.*

"life" of the seed, the symbol of which will be the content of the clavicles.

To create the fish's skeleton (that is, the bones),[206] Amma then introduced the element "earth," of which he kept a part.

FORMATION OF THE "NOMMO ANAGONNO."

The *nommo anagonno* was formed from the egg and in proportion to the development of its organs. The "word," originally placed inside the *sosogu* by Amma, will flow through the body via the blood stream; seven internal organs, *kolo da* (literally: "foods of the inside"), will be their relay points, the heart supplying the impulses, because integration of the "word" in the body will also take place in relation to the food nourishing the blood. Thus, all respiratory and digestive organs will be associated with this integration. It is said:

"When the word was not spoken, it was like the seven marks of the *po* which Amma had drawn. The seven *yala* of the beginning of the *po* are the seven words that the *po* transmitted to the *nommo anagonno*. The words which were in the *tonu soy* of the *po*, Amma had them emerge and gave them to the *nommo anagonno*. The words entered the seven internal organs of the *nommo anagonno*. The seven articulations of the *nommo anagonno* which are the word, are the words that the *po* spoke."[207] Therefore, in the first stage, the word in the *sosogu* was androgynous: it was the "life" of the being, still undifferentiated: it was "vegetative" life. During the following stage, the "word" will be nourished by food, the essence of which will be passed into the blood. It will differentiate itself (into male or female), will take on its character by passing through the internal organs, beginning with the heart, which connects with the suprabranchial organs, thus associating the being's physiology with its psychology. The eighth articulation of the word will be in the sex, the reproductive organ that will permit the adult to give birth to a new being.[208] The formation of the fish is represented by two successive

---

206. The dorsal bone is called *izu sonono*, "vertebral column of the fish"; the lateral bones are called *izu go ki*, "ribs of the fish."

207. *so solabe-go-le vogo po yala sey vo-gin amma ni yalabe. po tolo soy yala vogo so digu soy po gozu-ne goa nommo-bere tanu-go voy. po gozu-ne tonu soy tobe amma gona nommo anagonno oba. so nommo anagonno koloda digu soy kolo-ne yoy. nommo anagonno digu soy-ne tobe, po so soy tobe.*

208. For the appearances of the "word" inside the body, cf. *infra*, p. 174 and p. 317 and ff.

bummo which bear, like all signs of this category, the secret character of the initial abstract. Images of fish eggs as well as of the *po* seeds they evoke, and therefore of life itself, the rings of these *bummo,* by their number (eight), recall the "words." They also prefigure the potential

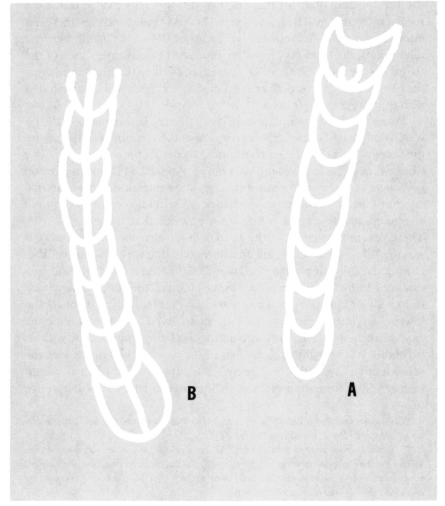

FIG. 35: *bummo* of the *nommo anagonno.*

multiplication of the created being even while it is still in its initial stage of formation.

The first one (fig. 35, A) shows a stylized sketch of a head in which only the open mouth and tongue are visible, organs of the "word" at the oral stage which the *nommo anagonno* is to reveal and transmit. The vertical line crossing the outline of the second one (Fig. 35, B) represents the backbone without vertebrae; it will be given the "articulations" much later, because the *nommo anagonno* is to be created with a smooth body and without articulations (joints).

These two figures are called *"bummo* of the setting of the *vageu,"* or *"bummo* of the setting of the *kuno* and twins."[209] They are drawn when one places the seven earthenware pots of the *kuno* and the eight pots of the twins in the same nook as the altar to the ancestors (*vageu*) — as well as above the pots — inaugurated by the consecration of its foundation. When he sets them in their place the officiant says: "The number of the eight (pieces of) earthenware of the twins which we put down is like the (future) 'articulations' of the Nommo."[210] Moreover, these numbers are related to the *po:* seven is the number of vibrations of the "word" pursuing the formation of the seed; eight is the number of elements of this "word" in the seed at germination.[211] On a parallel plane, the open circle at the top of the drawing of the *kuno* represents the ancestral earthenware (*bunno*) of the founder, which will be placed immediately after those of the *kuno* and twins, and which is "Amma's mouth" gathering the spiritual principles of the deceased. Inside is the forked tongue of the *nommo anagonno* which will reveal the "word." In the other drawing, the line emerging from the open circle is the fish's tongue.

---

209. *vageu bunno danu tonu* (or) *kuno-le dineu-le danu tonu.* These *bummo* are drawn with the porridge of rice and millet, only once, for the foundation of a family house, *ginna,* at the consecration of the altar of the male ancestors of the lineage (*vageu*) in a recess made on the terrace. The foundation of the altar begins by placing pottery attributed to children born from a mother who had not menstruated since the previous childbirth (*kuno*) and to the birth of twins (*dineu*). The *nommo anagonno* is, at the beginning of his formation, compared to the first case; his later splitting and his androgyny will then liken him to a pair of twins. In daily life, twin and *kuno* are of the same essence, because the latter is considered to be the actual twin of the child born during the preceding birth.

210. *dineu-le kuno-le vonoy danani lugu garaga, nommo digu anay.*

211. Cf. *supra,* p. 138.

Thus, despite their apparent abstraction, these two figures, like most Dogon signs, express in advance the fundamental states and first stages of the being in formation: its identification with the primordial seed, *po;* its primitive quality in relation to the womb being "formed without the appearance of menses"; while the next stage, almost concomitant,

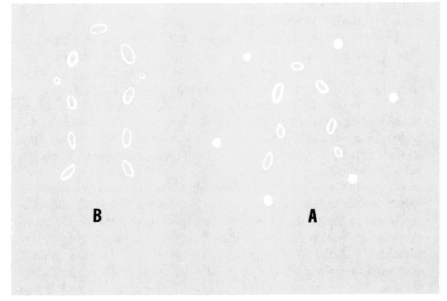

FIG. 36: *yala* of the *nommo anagonno.*

brings out its androgynous quality, which will eventually manifest itself as twinness. Henceforth, the *nommo*-silurus will bear these two successive and definitive physiological characteristics, which will give it its wholeness and purity. Essentially "alive," *omo,* it will be of immortal essence like its creator.

Sketched in the egg where Amma had placed those elements essential to the support of the being, the *nommo anagonno* was slowly formed. The pattern of the *yala* of this formation depicts the body of the silurus at the initial stage. In order to represent the emptiness of the universe at that time, each line making up the whole is egg-shaped, yet remains an empty circle: the *yala* of the *nommo anagonno* are empty circles because Amma will put life into them.

The first *yala* shows an outline of the being inside the *po* seed, which is

FIG. 37: *tonu* of the *nommo anagonno.*

represented by six points. It is said: "The *nommo anagonno* that Amma created inside the *po,* Amma who created the *po,* made the *yala* of the *nommo-* silurus inside" (fig. 36, A).[212] This is to mark the original existence

---

212. *amma nommo anagonno vo manu po kolo logoro-ne, amma po vo manu kolo-ne nommo anagonno yala yali.*

of the *nommo*-silurus, whose sign already existed in potential within the seed. The second *yala* is that of the *nommo*-silurus after the bursting of the *po* (fig. 36, B).[213] Its outline prefigures the formation of the pectoral fins and clavicles; it is called "mark of the body," *gozu yala.* These two *yala* show by their structure that the *nommo*-silurus brought into existence was an egg before being a fish — inside a seed, however, thus emphasizing the original direct connection between seed, egg, and fish.

In addition, the stages of the fish's development, represented by the successive figures, denote one aspect of social structure. In fact, the two *yala* are called *tire ayne* and *dene ayne,* named after the two generations following those of the "sons," *unum* — represented by the *bummo* — which constitute, on the mythical plane, the first generation of man. In like manner, the *bummo* are related to the extended family, *ginna,* the other two to the *ginna dagi* and the *tire ginu,* descended from the first by virtue of its extension.[214]

The schematic *tonu* of the fish, *nommo anagonno tonu* (fig. 37),[215] shows a sharp differentiation of the essential organs (clavicles, suprabranchial organs, and pectoral fin) and their position on the animal. Also represented are the head and barbels, the caudal fins and the backbone (the vertical line). The "keys" of the pectoral fins are closed.

The formation of the *nommo anagonno,* the first being created after the seeds, marked an important step in the creation. Its coming into being, which was to be perfect (like its creator), could only result from a precise order in which the four elements were placed. Now, it is said that the fish realized that it was not complete, because it had no teeth, and that it asked for them. Indeed, before the teeth were put in, it possessed only three elements. First fire, then water, then a part of the earth to form its skeleton; it still remained incomplete. Because of this, the being was without movement, being "neither dead nor alive."

Then Amma placed the four elements into the *nommo*-silurus by

213. Drawn upon the altar to Amma of the Tiré totem, at the ordination ceremony (*duguru)* of the priest, with porridge of *yu* and *ara geu,* facing north.

214. For the *ginna dagi,* cf. G. DIETERLEN, *Parenté et mariage,* p. 123.

215. Drawn upon the altar to Amma of the Yébéné totem, at the ordination ceremony (*duguru)* of the priest, with porridge of *yu* and *ara geu,* facing north.

FIG. 38: *tonu* of the formation of the teeth of
the *nommo anagonno*.

incorporating the rest of the earth into it in the form of teeth; he also added air, thus making it complete. This "piece" of earth, at first witheld and then returned to complete the whole, strengthened the dependence of the *nommo anagonno* upon the creator.

This addition took place according to a process recalled by a series of figures called: *tonu* of the *nommo anagonno* of the sanctuary of Déwa (fig. 38).[216]

Accompanied by the air, this bit of earth, starting where the tip of the backbone is connected with the head, went along the right side of the head and formed the teeth (fig. 38, top). The air, returning alone by the same route, drew the *ta i* to the right (fig. 38, center), which became the respiratory tract of the *sosogu*. Turning around, it crossed the silurus to form the *ta i* on the left (fig. 38, bottom). In doing this, it gave the head a fourth side, i.e., a quadrangular form, like a square, and symbolic of the earth itself. Indeed, the incomplete element earth had thus far been represented by three sides, the silurus itself being considered as a triangular undifferentiated body.[217] The addition of the piece of "earth" in the form of teeth and the delineation of the head and body confer upon the fish both its completeness and individualization.

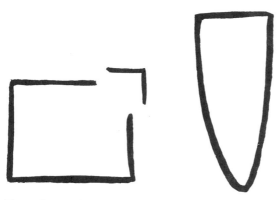

FIG. 39: Tooth of the *nommo anagonno* taken in the element "earth" (explanatory figure).

---

216. *deva binu ginu nommo anagonno tonu.* Drawn in the cave of Dalé during the foundation of the sanctuary of the Binou; the figures are drawn with the porridge of *yu* and *ara geu* on the wall of the cave, north of the sanctuary. The place is associated with the division of the Nommo's body at the time of his sacrifice and with the "division" of the totems. This figure is also drawn on the altar to Amma of the Guéméné totem during the ordination (*duguru*) of the priest.

217. One says that the triangular head of the *nommo anagonno* is similar to a calabash or *pommu.* The expression *minne pommu* designates a "triangular field."

The teeth of the *nommo*-silurus were eight in number, of triangular form, and pointed outwards. They had this form because of the piece of earth, at first withheld and then granted, which was a corner of the square of the complete element "earth" (fig. 39).[218] When Amma appropriated them, these two parts were separated; when the corner that had been torn off was put into place in the form of teeth, Amma noted this former separation with the line the air drew in its final motion.

In the silurus, this separation is represented by two bones that start at the head and widen towards the back. They are called *suguru donu,* "bottom of the ear," or *aa pegu, pegu* of the jaw,"[219] for it is there that the jaw is attached.

Similarly, the gift to the *nommo*-silurus of the four fundamental elements is recalled by *bummo* assigned to them (fig. 40), and which concern the *sosogu.*[220] "Fire" was first, for its coming into being had begun with fire; it is drawn like a flame and also like the clavicles, the creature's first support. The "water" had been united with the "fire" and is shown as an empty circle which represents the *sosogu* of the fish — the circle also prefigures the first pond to be

FIG. 40: *bummo* of the *sosogu* of the *nommo anagonno.*

---

218. Cf. p. 162.

219. From *pege,* "to plant." The *pegu* altars throughout the bush around the villages serve to protect the inhabitants from dangers from the outside by "fixing" to the soil certain spiritual principles of the ancestors of the community.

220. They are called *"bummo* of the *sosogu* of the *nommo anagonno,"* nommo anagonno *sosogu bummo.* They were drawn on the altar to Amma of the Déwa totem of Dalé: fire to the west, water to the east, earth to the south, and air to the north, in porridge made of four cereal grains (*yu pilu, ara geu, emme ya,* and *emme di giru).* The same figures are drawn on the smith's anvil during its consecration.

formed on Earth — the "earth" granted in the form of bones and teeth is a full square like the square mouth of the silurus. The "air," which is a broken line, also represents the *ta i,* "keys" of the respiration.

As he did with the *nommo anagonno,* Amma will bestow the basic elements upon all beings he will mold. It is said: "Amma who keeps the four elements has shared them with (granted them to) all living things."[221] Besides the elements, the bestowal of teeth upon the *nommo anagonno* will also impart to it the gift of the "word."

The eight teeth of the *nommo anagonno* are compared to the "baby teeth" of a child (*i tonu*): they have spaces between them, seven in number, *soy.* By adding teeth Amma will permit the *nommo*-silurus to "speak the word," *so soy.* This concerns another stage of the "word," during which it becomes verbal expression or language. This potential, placed in the piece of earth which formed the teeth, will eventually be realized: it will be the *nommo anagonno's* duty to exteriorize the word, to reveal and transmit it; borne by the *pegu* of the jaw, it will pass through the spaces between the teeth.[222] In fact, the words, like rivers that divide up a region, are comparable to the circulation of water around islets formed of earth, which are the teeth.

The eight "baby teeth" of the *nommo anagonno* will eventually be replaced by twenty-two teeth, symbols of the categories of Amma's "thought." In the course of the events that will take place during the development of the universe, Amma will momentarily withhold them for use elsewhere.[223] This again emphasizes the dependence of the *nommo anagonno* upon its creator, underscored by the final gift of the "piece of earth," first withheld and then used to make the teeth.

"Amma, when he created the *nommo anagonno,* formed the clavicle . . . What existed that day (at that time) was the darkness of night . . . In creating the *nommo anagonno,* he began first with fire . . . The flame (tongue) of the rising fire is like the key (pectoral fin) . . . After fire, Amma added water to the fire . . . The *nommo* united fire and

---

221. *amma kize si nay vo gele, kize omo voy si nay vo gammali.*

222. One of the *nommo anagonno* will reveal to man the "word" likened to weaving — in the water, which will be his domain on Earth (Report 2, first year). The filing of the teeth is associated with these conceptions: the filed teeth of the initiate, who has received the "word" (i.e., "instruction") and who must, in turn, later transmit it, are like those of the fish.

223. Cf. *infra,* p. 254.

water . . . Amma spun the form of the water in a circle in the clavicle . . . which is like a pond . . . The blood went into the clavicle like the water into the pond. When Amma created the *nommo anagonno,* he put three elements together, he divided one element (the earth of which he took a piece), added it to the air and kept it . . . The earth and air were (came) after the water and fire . . . Earth and air entered there where the water was . . . The earth and air entered the water, the water holds both of them by surrounding them . . . The earth formed bone . . . After the earth, the air entered and came out again, it looked outside and made them stay . . . The breathing of the world (i.e., air) is like the key of Amma . . . Inside the body of the *nommo anagonno,* the air made the *sosogu* remain (alive) . . . The fish, when it swims, it is with its hind legs (caudal fins) that it goes and with its front legs (pectoral fins) that it breathes . . . The key of the fish is the pathway of the air . . . When Amma created the *nommo anagonno,* it had no teeth . . . Amma created the *nommo anagonno* without teeth . . . Trying to bite into something, it found it was not able to . . . It went to Amma to ask him for something to bite with . . . (For) Amma when he had created the thing (the Nommo) by putting the four elements together, had kept with him a piece of earth. What he had kept he added to the three . . . The *nommo anagonno* became alive . . . Amma who had kept the piece of earth, the *nommo anagonno* told him that it is without teeth, which it asks for, gave it the *ta i* and the teeth . . . The first fish *nommo anagonno* created by Amma, its head was like a *pommu* calabash . . . By adding the separate piece of earth and the air which he had kept, he (Amma) in adding that, (the *nommo*) became alive, its head had four sides . . . The piece of earth which Amma gave to it, he gave it so that it (the Nommo) would follow him (that is: so that it would depend upon him) . . . Amma put the words in the earth that he had split (withheld) . . . The words entered the seven internal organs of the *nommo anagonno* . . . The Nommo who 'speaks the words,' they came out by the *pegu* of the jaw, they went through the space between the teeth . . ."[224]

---

224. *amma nommo anagonno vo manu ani guyo tono . . . bay-ko-ne yana oloybe . . . nommo anagonno vo mana-le, yau la tolo . . . yau nine ineleze ta i anay . . . amma yau onune di yau kune baru . . . nommo yau-le di-le monieze . . . amma di yala ani-guyo-ne*

The bestowal of the teeth conferred upon the *nommo anagonno* the four elements as well as mastery over the "word"; at the same time, Amma gave it its four "body souls," *gozu kikinu.* In speaking of the four elements, one says: the *kikinu* of fire is smoke, and also ash; that of the earth is dust; that of the wind is fog; that of water is the cloud after the tornado (because before that it contained both water and the soul). Amma mixed them with one another (fire with smoke, etc.),[225] stuck them together by using his saliva, then folded the whole thing into chevrons, which made up the *nommo anagonno* as a person.

But this is both a realistic and figurative way of explaining this creation. In exact terms, we remember that eight of the *yala* of Amma's first egg (cf. fig. 17) had spread open to form "Amma's eyes," prefiguring the "cardinal corners" of future space. "Amma's eyes, four corners, became the *kikinu* of the *nommo anagonno.*"[226] Thus, the fish, whose animation followed the prefiguration of the oriented universe, became both the image of Amma and the synthetic image of his creation, the four "body souls," *gozu kikinu,*[227] containing the four elements as well

---

denele-go gonu . . *ani guyo o anay* . . . *illi ani guyo-ne yoy di o-ne yoa anay* . . . *amma nommo anagonno vo manaze kize bullogu tanu mona, bullogu turu gamma ono-ne bara geli* . . . *minne-le ono-le di-le yau-le onune bey* . . . *minne-le ono-le di yala-ne yoy* . . . *minne-le ono-le di kolo-ne yoa, di bey gona gele* . . . *minne ki kunni* . . . *minne onune ono yoy ono goa para ienna bey bozi* . . . *aduno ninnu amma ta i-gin vo* . . . *nommo anagonno gozu kolone ono sosogu bozi* . . . *izu boni banie-vo-ze bolo kubo-le giru ta i-le vo ninne yaze* . . . *izu ta i ono ozi* . . . *amma nommo anagonno vo mani tonu sebele* . . . *amma nommo anagonno mana tonu tologo mana* . . . *nommo anagonno kize temedo-ga teme bele kana amma-mo-ne ya kize temeni seluma* . . . *amma kize bullogu mona vo mani minne gayley geliade* . . . *amma minne gayley vo geli vomo-go obi* . . . *vo gelebe-go tanu-go-ne bara* . . . *nommo anagonno omoy bi* . . . *amma minne gayley vo gelebe nommo anagonno vomo-ne tonu sele-ga, vo selumeze ta i-le tonu-le voy obi* . . . *polo izu nommo anagonno amma mani ku-go pommu-go be* . . . *minne gayley ono-le bara-vo-ze-be vogo-ne vo bari omoy biga ku-go sibe nay bi* . . . *amma minne gayley vo obi uni dimia-ga ko-de obi* . . *amma minne vo gammi so kunni* . . . *so nommo anagonno kolo da digu soy kolone yoy* . . . *nommo so soy aa pegu-ne goa ya tonu kelu-ne goy.*

The last lines of this text concerning the "word" are uttered during the construction of a new totemic sanctuary.

225. It is said: "superposing dust gives earth," *minne kono ku vomone gimmay minne bieze.*

226. *amma giru sibe nay nommo anagonno kikinu tani.*

227. These four *kikinu* of body will be "divided" before the sacrifice of one of the

as the four spatial directions.

When the *nommo anagonno* had received its "body souls," it was almost completed.

MULTIPLICATION OF THE FISH.

Having created the *nommo anagonno,* Amma proceeded to multiply his creature. His goal was to form four pairs of mixed twins, namely, eight

FIG. 41: *tonu* of the four *nommo anagonno.*

nommo anagonno, which were then to give birth to perfect beings like themselves. He proceeded by consecutive divisions, first forming four male *nommo anagonno,* then, by continuing to work always inside his own placenta, their female twins.

---

nommo anagonno, in order to form four *kikinu* of sex, which he will receive after his resurrection. Cf. *infra,* p. 253 and ff.

There are figures recalling this multiplication. The first one, called
"tonu of the four *nommo anagonno* " (fig. 41),[228] shows the designs of
the first four formed beings: it constitutes the *tonu* of the four original
bummo of Amma's placenta. Each diagram is made of six strokes denoting
the *yala* of the "sex" of the *po*. This figure recalls the formation of the
nommo anagonno inside the *po* (hence the identity between the seed
and the fish egg), and makes it clear that Amma will proceed by first
summoning the reproductive organ. The second one, drawn on the
ceiling of a ritual cave representing the "sky where the eight *nommo
anagonno* were formed," shows this multiplication in Amma's womb,
representing it by the design of the eight fish heads and the vital organs
(*sosogu, ani guyo, ta i*). It is called *"tonu* of the great twin *nommo"* (fig.
42).[229] The figure is not a *toy,* because other events will come to upset
the order of things before complete realization of the eight *nommo
anagonno*.

Meanwhile, this multiplication of the original being implied ideas of
wealth, good fortune, and power that Amma had bestowed upon his
creature, which was complete, fertile, and animated by his Word.
"Amma, who brought together (or made to come together) all things,
enclosed them in the *po*. The superposed *nommo anagonno* came out of
the body of the *po*. The four *nommo anagonno* which came out of
Amma are chiefs, rich." (*ogo*).[230] Chiefs because they are primordial

---

228. *nommo anagonno nay tonu*. Drawn with *yu pilu* porridge mixed with *sa* water, at the
four corners of the upper granary, *delu,* placed above the hall, on the terrace of the
family's "big house" (*ginna*) when this dwelling is erected. This granary serves as a receptacle for grains kept by the family head from the harvest until the next sowing, thus
considered to be placed "in the sky"; the seeds therein are the repositories of the spiritual
principles of the grains, the rest of the harvest having been desacralized — thus become
suitable for consumption — in the course of successive rites performed by the community
(on a family and clan level).

229. *nommo die dineu tonu.* Drawn only once in *yu* and *ara geu* porridge on the ceiling
of the cave in which the sanctuary of the Déwa totem (in Dalé) was built . . . It was also
drawn in porridge of *po pilu, emme ya, yu* and *ara geu* in the cave *kukulu kommo*.

230. *amma kize voy mana mona, po kuya gelemi. nommo anagonno timme po gozune
goy; nommo anagonno nay ammamone goy, ogoy*. These lines are part of a prayer recited
during the purification performed by the Yébéné priest at *si da* (on the banks of the Gona),
a place associated with the sex and fertility of the *nommo anagonno* (cf. p. 492).

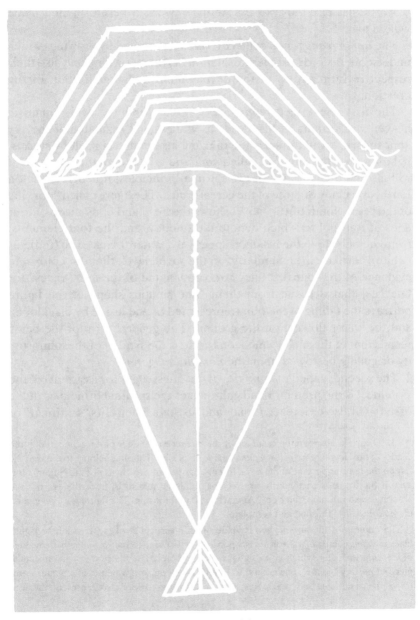

FIG. 42: *tonu* of the multiplication of the *nommo anagonno*.

ancestors; rich because they are strengthened by their multiplication; powerful because they possess Amma's "word"; therefore, their name will be *ogo*.

The *nommo anagonno* called *ogo* are represented by drawings which underscore the order of their formation in Amma's womb and also their respective future roles in the development and organization of the creation.

The first one, called *nommo die,* "great Nommo," will remain in heaven with Amma as his agent; as witness and regulator of the sky atmosphere, it will dispense the rain and also manifest itself by storms, lightning, and the rainbow, called *nommo sizu,* "path of the Nommo." It will also be the guardian of the spiritual principles of beings living on Earth, especially of those of the cereal grains. The figure called "drawing of the great Nommo" (fig. 43)[231] shows the head and body made of four lines of four colors which denote the rainbow and the four elements: from the outside to the inside, respectively, water (black), fire (red), air (white), earth (ochre). Similarly, on the social level, the four colors are evidence of the four first ancestors of man and of the four "races" (or lineages) that descend from them. The sinuous shape of the figure portrays the falling of the rain (represented on the inside by black dots) and the water flowing on the ground. The general form of the being recalls that of the snake which, on Earth, is the symbol of the immortality originally bestowed upon the *nommo anagonno.*

The second, called *nommo titiyayne,* "messenger (or assistant) of the Nommo," is the protector and guardian of the spiritual principles of the first. It will also be its executioner and, in this capacity, its "sacrificer" or

---

231. Drawn in color on the east face of the *manna amma* altar of Arou, located in the district of the Hogon of Arou (on *manna amma,* cf. p. 536). The altar belongs to the Ogosèlè totem, the most important of the Arou totems. *ogosele* means "he is not the Hogon"; for, even if the totem is particularly revered for obtaining rain, it is, nevertheless, not the absolute master of such, since only Amma can grant it the rain. The figure is a *toy* because the *nommo die* is finished and complete.

The *bummo* of the *nommo die* is made of four vertical strokes (from left to right): black in *kilena* charcoal, white in *ara geu* porridge, red in *bana* red earth, yellow with the bulb of the *kulu* waterlily, which gives an ochre-yellow color. The figure is drawn on a small piece of pottery (*vonoy*), placed in the Hogon's dwelling, and which contains rain water (cf. 2nd installment, 2nd year). Respectively, the four colors also represent the four

polugelene ("he who holds the ‹sacrificial› knife").

A first figure of the *titiyayne* (fig. 44)[232] shows a diagram of the backbone containing the seven internal "words" (the dashes) and the *yala* of the future "articulations" or *digu soy* (the dots). The latter will be given to the *nommo anagonno* after the disruptions that occurred during the development of the universe in which it will perform its work. In the "drawing of the *nommo titiyayne*" (fig. 45)[233] the teeth are marked, those with which it will act; the oblique extension of its tail is evidence of the basic opposition it will show to the wicked deeds of one of its twin "brothers" by crushing its placenta "with its foot."[234]

The third is called *o nommo*, "Nommo of the pond." It will be sacrificed for the purification and reorganization of the universe after the wicked deeds of its twin (at that moment it is called *nommo semi*, "sacrificed Nommo"). It will resurrect in human form and descend to Earth on an ark with the ancestors of man, created from the substance of its placenta;[235] it will then take on its first form again, reside in the waters, and give birth to numerous offspring.

The figure that represents it, called "drawing of the *nommo* of *Sommo di*" (fig. 46),[236] describes the important stage in the opening of the *ta i*, before the bestowal of the clavicular seeds in the *sosogu*, which will be returned after its resurrection. In addition, although created as a fish with a smooth body and without any joints, the sacrifice will provide it with "articulations." The backbone contains here five vertebrae, standing for the first five generations descended from man's mythical ancestors.

---

elements: water, air, fire, and earth, and are evidence of the completeness of the being who had been formed in this way. The drawing is also the diagram of the rainbow.

232. *nommo titiyayne tonu.* Drawn in *ara geu* porridge, in parallel to the drawing of the *nommo die,* on the *manna amma* altar of Arou, but facing west.

233. *nommo titiyayne toy.* Drawn in porridge of *ara geu* and *yu* above the door of the totemic sanctuary of Ogosolou of Iréli. *ogo solu* means "Hogon (who makes the) gift." this totem is the most important next to the Yébéné totem of Sanga which represents Déwa, the first of all Dogon totems.

234. Cf. *infra,* p. 231.

235. Cf *infra,* ch. 5, p. 390.

236. *sommo di nommo toy.* Drawn on the façade of the sanctuary of the totem Nommo of Upper Sanghi, in the porridge of *ara geu* and *yu,* during the ordination (*duguru*) of the priest. The priest of this totem (from which stem Sanghi, Enguélé and Dini) performs the annual purification at the place called *Sommo di* (Vol. I, installment 2, first year).

FIG. 44: *tonu* of the *nommo titiyayne*.

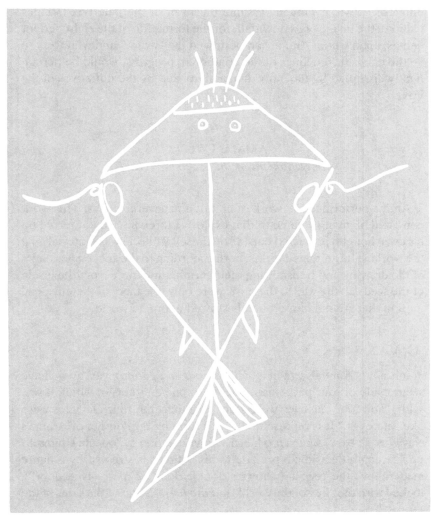

FIG. 45: Drawing of the *nommo titiyayne.*

The fourth, which in the form of *nommo anagonno* will bear the name of *ogo,* is not represented as a fish. Indeed, in the very course of its completion, it will rebel against its creator and bring disorder into the universe. It will eventually assume the form of the pale Fox (Vulpes pallida), the image of its downfall; for the formation of the eight perfect beings, upon whom Amma had bestowed the "word," and who were to be the chiefs or the kings of the creation in progress, would be permanently disrupted by the individual activity and by the initiatives of the Fox.

6. AMMA'S WORK
Development of the "second world."

Amma performed the work of creation in several stages. This work consisted of giving volume to that explosive force he had conferred on his own thought, projected outside of himself while he was materializing the world. The animated forms, born according to the successive stages of the drawing and transmitting their germinating force from the inside of the seeds all the way to the stars, were only one facet of the universal motion that Amma himself had bestowed upon the world.

AMMA'S WORK.

Initially, "Amma's egg in a ball" (*amma talu gunnu*) was, as we have seen, made of four parts that adhered to one another, of which it was said: "The four clavicles were stuck together, the four clavicles were like four eggs." It is represented in this form by the "design of Amma's clavicles."[237] Now, Amma produced his own creation by "opening (himself) up." Amma's decision, a prelude to his actions, is stressed by a figure made above the "egg": it shows a double door (*ta dine,* "twin door"), locked with the "key of the world" (*aduno ta i*).[238] One of the sides of the

---

237. *amma ani guyo tonu.* Cf. *supra,* p. 82, fig. 1.

238. Drawn in *ara geu* porridge on the altar to Amma, called Kan Amma, every three years at the time of the sowing feast, facing west. (Installment 2, 5th year.)

FIG 46: Drawing of *o nommo*.

door is closed and represents that which Amma will keep for himself; the other, which has the key in it, represents what he will give up. The key is placed on what he gave the world because it is "like the germination of grains," that is, the future proliferation of seeds and of man. In prayer to Amma it is said: "Amma's key with which he opened the door to make the things of the placenta of the world come out, the key is like the germination of the cereal grains. May Amma open his door to give births in the world."[239] Thus will Amma "open his door" to set the world free.

This extension will first manifest itself by the opening of the egg: by the force of Amma's will, the four clavicles will separate so as to spread open. Thus, "Amma's work," while he is spinning on his own axis, will separate and open the four clavicles, in order to determine space and the cardinal directions which they potentially contain. This opening takes place in the north, the direction specifically associated with Amma. It is said: "Amma's egg of the north contains the east, the west, and the south. In the past, Amma's egg was stuck in a ball; then it opened."[240] Also, "Amma's egg in a ball" (*amma talu gunnu*) became "Amma's opened egg" (*amma talu ginne*). While Amma was spinning, the first egg formed four "pointed eggs"; the four clavicles progressively lowered themselves. "Amma's clavicle, round, became the four extended cardinal points."[241]

It divided into four parts, which were visible from the outside, like the closed corolla of the blossom of a water lily, each of the "petals" formed in this way being one of Amma's clavicles. They were grouped around Amma's "seat." Joined together by one of their ends around the "seat," they unfolded in a horizontal plane, like a flower that opens up, and were then supported by the "axis of the world" that emerged from them. One sums up this work by saying of the egg: "It spun, opened; the remnant was the fork or axis of the world."[242]

---

239. *amma ta i dagale aduno me kize vo gonu ta i dene teze anay amma ta vomo dagala aduno naniemo.*

240. *du daga amma talu du-le, donno-le, tenulu-le vo gele. amma ene talu ani gunnugo danay onune ginne.*

241. *amma ani guyo dennelem gunno sibe nay palago bi.*

242. *digiliya, ginna; vazu aduno dey bi.*

To accomplish the spreading of the clavicles, Amma moved in a spiral, "leaving things, which is to say, rays" in his wake. His work is described as follows: Amma was standing at the center, spinning on his own axis, his right arm stretched out horizontally with all fingers extended; he turned from right to left, first facing west, then north, then east, then south. As he spun, Amma progressively lowered his arm, once every two turns. He turned fourteen times and stopped, facing west, his arm completely lowered. With each turn, Amma created "a heaven and an Earth stuck together"; he created, therefore, fourteen heavens and fourteen Earths.

The spiral being conical due to the movement of Amma's "arm," the Earths and heavens of the lower portion were not as wide as those at the top. This procedure of Amma's is represented by the two movements involved in the playing of the rhombus; the turn the instrument makes on its axis, and the spinning of the bearer.[243] Thus "Amma spun (spiraled) space;"[244] spinning and dancing, Amma formed all the spiraling star worlds of the universe.

Amma's work and formation of the "fork of space" (*ganna dey*) is represented by a ritual object included in the material of totemic sanctuaries, the *binu solumo*. The object is made of iron; it is composed of an axis supporting a circle from which extend four chains, called "chains of the fork of space,"[245] placed as if at the four cardinal directions. The circle represents the heaven where Amma lives, spinning on his axis and creating the worlds represented by the chains (fig. 47).[246] Of this figure, one says: "The Milky Way (here meaning all the visible stars) is placed on the fork of the world; the two ends touch the Earth: the fork spins; the Milky Way and the Earth spin together. The Milky Way touches the Earth on the one side, the water on the other. Amma's egg is placed on the fork.[247]

---

243. It is only the movement of the rhombus, and not the object itself, which represents Amma's spinning.

244. *amma ganna gona.*

245. *ganna dyey yogu.*

246. This metal object is also compared to a tree whose roots would be of copper.

247. *yalu ulo ganna dene yana; keregu ley minne-ne temga ganna day digilie yalu ulo-le minne-le umogo digilieze. amma ene talu dene yana.* This fork is also represented by the altar called *pegu,* "to plant," which serves to stabilize and protect the village; in the past it

Amma's work is also associated with his "word." Like the first egg, Amma's word was also inside "in a ball." When he "spoke" the clavicles opened, in order to determine space and the cardinal directions. It is said: "At the beginning, Amma was in the ball of the clavicles, Amma's word was in a ball. The moment Amma spoke the word, the clavicles opened. The signs were there before the words. Words and signs of Amma's clavicle are the same thing."[248]

FIG. 47: The fork of space (explanatory figure).

The opening of the clavicles, which determined space and the cardinal points, resulted in the shifting of the signs. The signs were originally, as we have seen, in a picture placed at the center, called "Amma's seat or center" (*amma doy*) or "seat of the inside" (*kolo doy*), also described as the "birth of Amma's liver." This center prefigured the *gaba*: "the *gaba* opened,"[249] and the 266 signs went to place themselves on the open clavicles. Thus, just as this labor resulted in the determination of space and the creation of worlds, Amma simultaneously projected his "word" to the four cardinal

was made from a human victim who had been buried standing up. The "body souls" of the victim were fixed within the altar during the ritual. An iron stake was planted at the top of the altar.

248. *polo amma ani guyo gunnago belle amma se gunnugobe varu amma so vo ole ani guyo-go timmilu tonu-go so girine to-be. amma ani guyo tonu-le so-le tumoy.*

249. *gaba gunnay.*

points of the created universe.

The beginning of the unfolding of the clavicles is represented by the mask *amma ta,* "Amma's door." This term designating the opening of the "door" is also a euphemism used to conceal the true name of the mask, *amma talu,* "Amma's egg," from the uninitiated. Figure 48 shows the ancient mask, worn with one point covering the face and the other over the nape of the neck, fibers hiding the openings on either side. The horizontal strokes that decorate it are the 266 primordial *bummo* then placed in the clavicles.[250]

Similarly, the figure called *amma tonu* shows a circle representing the heaven, inside of which "Amma is seated," "separating the four cardinal points," formed by his four clavicles (fig. 49). He is surrounded by dots (indeterminate in number), which are the stars.[251]

The following step, representing the whole of Amma's

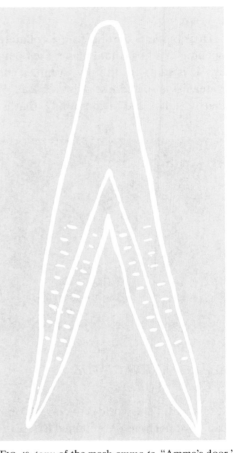

FIG. 48: *tonu* of the mask *amma ta,* "Amma's door."

250. Drawn under the altar of masks of Sodamma at its foundation, but in red, black, and white. The horizontal strokes are the *bummo* of Amma.

251. Drawn in *yu pilu* porridge inside the recess of the *ginna* containing the altar to the ancestors, *vageu.*

work and the open clavicles resting on the fork of the world, is represented by a figure, called "seat of Amma making space turn around, " (fig. 50).[252]

Distributed according to the collateral directions, the four clavicles, opening in a horizontal plane, are compared to the blossom of a water lily. It is said: "In the sky, Amma's clavicles, in the water below, the water lily is seated like Amma's seat."[253] For it is said of the water lily that it is the "eye of the pond," that is, of the water and of him who resides there, *o nommo,* creature of Amma and begetter of humanity. The central drawing is surrounded by two circles representing the two motions Amma made, which are compared to the spinning of the rhombus. The axis, or "fork," is shown vertically and oriented from north to south. In the clavicle positioned to the northeast is the spiraling *po,* surrounded by its placenta.

FIG. 49: *amma tonu.*

ELABORATION OF THE SECOND WORLD.

It is said, "The world is the *toy* of Amma's *tonu.*"[254] "When he was in a ball," Amma himself remained a *tonu;* when he opened up, this became a *toy.* This commentary regarding the progression of the graphic representations conveys well the idea of completion, which is shown in an even more realistic manner and denotes the most advanced stage of creation when expressed in terms relating to gestation. It is said: "Amma's seat

252. *amma ganna digilimi toy.* Drawn in *ara geu* porridge on Kan Amma, facing north, during its foundation.

253. *alakala-ne ani guyo donu di-ne kulomota amma doy-gin da.*

254. *aduno amma tonu toy.*

was like the womb of a woman. All things came from the inside of Amma's placenta."[255] This placenta surrounds the spiraling *po* in the "womb."

N

FIG. 50: Drawing of "Amma's seat spinning space."

The following step will consist of the ejection of the universe from the original "egg."

---

255. *amma doy yana tozoy. amma me kize voy kone goy.*

As we have seen, Amma's work progressively produced the entire universe, made of spiraling stellar worlds. For it is said that "Amma's egg is the mother of the stars."[256] This stage of Amma's work is represented by a figure: "Amma's egg," crowning an axis around which the worlds of the stars spin. It is called "drawing of the fourteen superposed worlds (or spaces)" (fig. 51).[257]

"Amma's egg," which is unique, is placed at the top of the axis around which the "fourteen superposed worlds" spin. It is also the first heaven from which Amma's two "arms" extend, reaching as far as the first Earth, represented by the rectangle. The same figure is repeated seven times, because it is also said that the worlds were formed by the bursting of seven seeds, the *po* being the first and being like Amma himself. At the center, in the fourth world, appears the sun that lights our planet, because (playing on the words) "the way we say sun (light) is said because of the

---

256. *amma ene talu tolo na.*

257. *ganna gimme peli nay sige tonu. ganna* designates the world as reality; *aduno* designates it as an entity. It was drawn in black and white under the stone used to build the altar to Amma of the cave called Kèkè Kommo, where the people of the Dyon and Arou tribes settled, who were the first to arrive and who founded Sanga. Cf. *supra,* map II, B and Pl. VI, 2 and 3.

FIG. 51: Drawing of the fourteen superposed worlds (or spaces).

four superposed worlds."[258] The fourth world of stars is the one in which eventually the stages of the life of man will unfold. The lines decorating the heavens and Earths mark the development of the universe and of life. At the bottom of the figure a semi-circle is drawn, which is "Amma's seat." Thus, all the worlds are held in place by Amma's "head" and "seat."

This explanatory drawing describes one of the forms of the *sirige* mask, also called "storied house."[259] The mask, carved from a single tree trunk, has a rectangular face with a very high mast on top, with a tip that is usually carved into a point: it is divided into elements forming a rectangular grid, alternating with elements that are solid wood. The very top here represents "Amma's seat"; a cluster of *sene* fibers, dyed red and hooked on top of the mast, recalls the first world created and then abandoned by Amma.

The wearer of the mask dances the *bimmili galu* rhythm, holding the mast horizontally; his spinning around signifies the spinning of Amma creating the world. If the bunch of fibers drops off during the dance, it is a remembrance of the isolated "descent" of the *sene*.

Similarly, the calabash sistrums of the circumcised represent Amma's superposed worlds: according to custom, they should have seven pairs of notched rings under the gourd. From this perspective, the object must be looked at upside down.

When one invokes Amma during ceremonies performed on the family altar consecrated to him, one says: "Amma, seven above, seven below, he spun fourteen worlds."[260]

The number 14, attributed to the spiral stellar worlds produced by

---

258. *may geni-ko ganna gimme nay sige-de geni.* There is a play on words here on the name of the sun, *"nay,"* which also means "four." See also *infra,* p. 218.

259. It is called "drawing of the *sirige* of the ending of space by Amma," *amma ganna mana kari sirige toy.* There are four variants of the form of the *sirige* mask, one of them recalling "Amma's work," which are emphasized, for the object, by the use of a particular color or a particular variant in the cut of the wood. These interpretations are expressed by different figures, drawn in color in the caves, where they have both a ritualistic and initiatory value. These four variants are presented together *infra,* p. 559. Figure 161 A, p. 559, represents the variant that recalls the creation of the superposed worlds.

260. *amma, dana soy, donune soy, yalu peli nay sige ganna ginnigili.*

Amma, implies the concept of potential reproduction and multiplication: seven is the sum of three, the masculine number, and four, the feminine number. Here it designates the seven Earths and seven heavens. Amma creates 7x2, that is to say, an infinity of worlds. The superposition of worlds and the concept of the infinite multiplication of stellar universes are indicated by the fact that the number 28 is attributed to Amma as well; it is called "Amma's number" (*amma lugu*), because one also says: "Amma fourteen above, fourteen below, etc. . . ."

The spiral worlds of stars were populated universes; because, simultaneously with things, Amma, having given form and movement to the world, created all living beings. Just as on our own planet, living beings will live on those other "Earths,"[261] but in this whole universe there will be only one Ogo who will become the Fox.

Having completed his work, "Amma pressed his right hand on the top and his left hand at the bottom." The final act of creation, originating from Amma's own movement, is shown by the figure of the axis in a fixed position, called "drawing of the end of creation by Amma"[262] (fig. 52), or "Amma's hand," *amma numa*. While drawing it and before erecting the altar to Amma on the figure, one says: "May Amma sit on the drawing of Amma creating the world and may he plant the world."[263] This image reproduces the first and most ancient form of the mask *kanaga*. Here Amma is shown in a standing position, pointing to the sky with his right arm and to the Earth with his left arm. The headpiece of

---

261. This proliferation of life is illustrated by a commentary on the myth, of explanatory value, in which it is said: people are on the fourth earth, but on the third there are "people with horns," *inneu kelegu,* on the fifth, "people with tails," *inneu dullogu,* on the sixth, "winged people," *inneu gammurugu,* on the seventh, "crawling people," *inneu bummo,* etc. This is to emphasize the absolute ignorance one has of forms of life on other worlds, but also the certainty of the presence of those forms.

262. *amma ganna manu donuni tonu.* Drawn in *ara pilu* under the altars to Amma in all *ginna* before they are built.

263. *amma ganna manu donuni amma daie ganna pege.*

the mask was made of a grid of four bars which concealed the face of its wearer, yet allowed him, like Amma, to see without being seen. The spinning during one of the steps of the dance of the mask is "Amma letting his hands drop when he is tired." The "trembling of the stretched-out arms of the wearer" (*numo woderun soy gay*) is the movement of

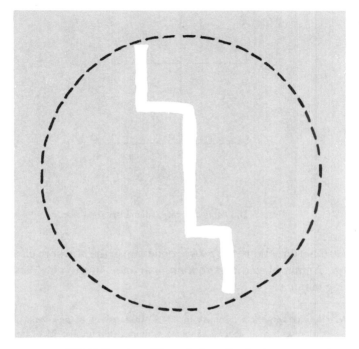

FIG. 52: Drawing of the end of creation by Amma.

Amma's hands creating the world.[264]

One of the current forms of the *kanaga* mask (fig. 53) also portrays Amma's work: the statuettes on top are the *nommo die,* twins in the invisible heaven (1 and 2); the central axis is the axis of the world; the two upper arms (4 and 5) are the sacrificed *nommo* and his female twin in the visible heaven; the two lower arms (7 and 8) are Ogo and his

---

264. *amma dunno dane yo, amma duno donu yo.*

female twin Yasigui on Earth.[265]

When Amma's work was finished and the open clavicles were placed

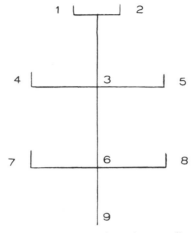

FIG. 53: The *kanaga* mask (explanatory figure).

in the cardinal directions, the *po* was coiled up in the northern clavicle. In addition, Amma placed the *nommo anagonno* in the clavicles in the following manner:

---

265. As is the case with the *sirige* mask, there are other variants of the *kanaga* mask; one of the masks represents the insect *barakamaza,* which will anchor the ark of the Nommo on Earth after his descent (cf. *infra,* p. 472). The other represents Ogo, turned into the Fox, flat on his back, dying with thirst, his four paws in the air to implore Amma (installment 2). These masks are also represented by different drawings in the caves; their details indicate what they represent.

The figures dealing with the *amma ta,* the *sirige,* and the *kanaga* to which we refer in this volume, are drawn on the walls of the totemic sanctuaries where they represent, not masks, but rather events said to be "of the old world." They are considered, in mythical time, to be anterior to the masks which, however, recall the same events, but in a context related to the appearance of death on the Earth. The figures, therefore, are not prohibited to the totemic priests, whereas the masks are. See pl. VII, 2.

the *nommo die* to the north;
the *nommo semi* to the east;
the *nommo titiyayne,* to the west;
the *nommo anagonno,* called Ogo, who will become the Fox,
to the south.[266]

Amma then proceeded to produce the female twins of the four *nommo anagonno;* but this work will immediately be disrupted by Ogo's deeds.

---

266. They will later be shifted, as will the *po,* in the course of events caused by Ogo's revolt, Cf. *infra,* p. 225.

CHAPTER II
OGO

Ogo's revolt. Ogo's first descent. Formation of the Earth. Representation of Ogo's ark.
Ogo's reascent to the sky. Creation of the sun and of the turtle *agunuru*. Theft of
Amma's seeds. Reintegration of the elements of creation in the *po pilu*. Ogo's second
descent. Representation of Ogo's second ark. Ogo's sowing. Crushing of the placenta
by the *nommo titiyayne*. The *sene na* and the work of the spider.

There are several versions of the completion of Ogo's formation as
well as of the continuation of his life. Their deeper significance remains
the same, but each one represents an original expression. All are useful
in that they illustrate the character of Ogo, the first being to develop his
personality in opposition to that of Amma, thus introducing psychological
diversification into the universe.

OGO'S REVOLT.

Like his twin "brothers," Ogo was attached to his formed placenta
as a complete being and was provided with four "body souls," evidence
of the four elements. But he was still alone; Amma was proceeding
to fashion the female twins of the *nommo anagonno,* who were to be
completed sixty "periods" after their formation. From that time on, Ogo
demonstrated his anxiety and impatience. Although Amma wanted to
form his female twin and give her to him, as he had done with his twin
brothers, Ogo, in his anguish and desire to possess her, believed that she
would not be given to him and he became incessantly restless. Thinking
he was to be deprived of her, he "was irritating" Amma by moving
about. Amma then told him that he would receive his female twin at the
time of her birth, of her "emergence from the womb." But Ogo did not
believe him, demanded her immediately, revolted, and started to look
for her without waiting for Amma's creations. This search consisted in
trying to gain possession of Amma's work for his own advantage.

Now, the lower part of Ogo's placenta was located in the same place where once the *sene* seed had been made. He wanted first of all to gain access to the first thing Amma had created and judged complete enough to entrust it with a creative mission. Ogo "touched" the *sene,* thinking he would find his own female twin in the place where the seed had been produced. But Amma had taken the creative function away from the *sene:* because of its failure it was now nothing more than a "germ."

Nevertheless, Ogo tried to seize it, and he demonstrated his aggressiveness in that he himself did not want to be "touched" by the *sene* seed. They fought, and it is said that during the fight Ogo took away two of the *sene's* elements, water and fire, leaving it only air and earth. But this fight also brought about a mutual impregnation, for it is said that "the *sene* became rotten" by Ogo's actions; but, from its side, it helped to accentuate Ogo's incompleteness. Later on, one will say that "the roots of the *sene* are the Fox's four members and its thorns (are) his claws," thus emphasizing that during the fight each had acquired a part of the other.

Dissatisfied and breaking all the rules, Ogo began to move about with the intention of getting hold of the secrets of the universe in formation. Provided with his body souls, but without the capacity to reproduce, he "watched for the formation of the seeds," Amma's semen, to catch it, use it for himself, and be fertile like his creator. He began by measuring this universe. To do this, one says, he "walked" inside the womb and took 8,000 x 60 "steps" over sixty periods, the "number" of this placenta. The total obtained, 28,800,000 "steps," will make up the distance that will eventually separate the sky from the Earth, as well as the circumference of the terrestrial world to which Ogo was to be confined. To take this measurement, Ogo started from the east, traveled towards the south, then went west and north in the opposite direction of Amma who, starting from the east, had begun the world in the north. Having thus begun his course in the opposite direction to the one followed by Amma, Ogo then turned in the same direction as Amma, thus completing a second path inside the first and tracing two lozenge contours, one inside the other (fig. 54, B).[1]

1. This diagram shows the lozenge-shaped opening cut into the wood of the Great Mask, *imina na.* Cf. *infra,* p. 237, n. 82.

Ogo had not yet disorganized anything by this journey: he simply wanted to "see" the creation. He walked in a zigzag all around Amma's work in progress. However, these comings and goings "striped" his placenta as well as Ogo himself, who still bears the lines: three on the body and four on the face.

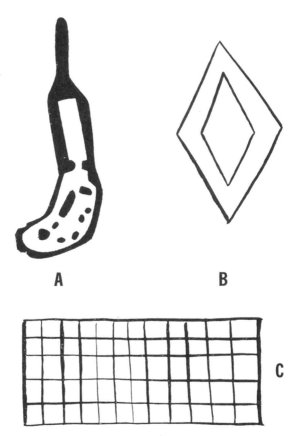

A   B

C

FIG. 54: A. Ogo in his placenta (the *yala* representing him prefigure his future form of the Fox).
    B. Outline of Ogo's first journey.
    C. Stripes of Ogo's placenta.

Now, the universe in Amma's womb was still outside of time and space, which were intermingled in a common state of valuation, that of the number and in particular of the said "number of the placenta," where they were being formed. By his act, Ogo was the first to determine a series of sequences which prefigure, in their reality, both dimension — the "step" he used to measure — and time — the periods during which he took these "steps." That is why the "stripes" of Ogo's body and face are associated with the colors of the rainbow — symbol of the bond uniting sky and Earth, which will be separated by a distance — as well as with the seasons that will follow each other on Earth and that will be evidence of time.

From this perspective, the lines are as follows:

body lines:
- red, *bado*
- white, *nay banu*
- black

face lines:
- gray
- yellow, *bago*
- green
- blue, *dine*

Similarly, the stripes of the placenta are the prefiguration of the morphology of the terrestrial world to which Ogo will be attached: the Earth will be represented by a rectangle divided into sixty parcels (fig. 54, C).[2]

So, Ogo had traveled around the universe to "see" the bounds of creation. Having completed his journey and finding himself at the center of Amma's womb, he declared that "he knew just as much as Amma" and that he was capable, in his turn, of creating a world. So he said: "Amma, I have seen the world that you created."[3] Amma answered him: "As I have created, create (something yourself) neither in the sun nor in the shade; you stay there; as for me, I will come to find (us) together."[4] Amma said this to confuse him and to ask something of him that was impossible to accomplish.

Leaving the center where he was, and sent back by Amma to the west,

---

2. Figure drawn on the divination tables of instruction, cf. *infra,* p. 301.

3. *amma mu ganna u mani iade.*

4. *mu manu-gin nay-la kinni-la mane u vone mu ve temmemoydo.*

Ogo stole the "nerves," *volu,* of Amma, that is, the "nervures," or internal *volu,* of the egg which were eventually to open into four clavicles. He seized the nervure which formed the separation and wove a utensil in the form of a bonnet with it. Starting at the top and ending at the bottom, he made it so well, in fact, that, once the object was finished, he found himself enclosed inside, just as Amma himself had enclosed himself in the primordial egg. This object, later named *yurugu goro,* "the Fox's bonnet," and then, to ridicule Ogo's failure, *nu goro,* "bonnet of the beans," was round and egg-shaped in the image of "Amma's sky." "Ogo, having stolen Amma's nerve, began the *nu goro,* he wove it going down. Ogo, by spinning, wove the *nu goro;* he turned it upside down on his head."[5]

Ogo had made the basket as had Amma his creation: the two motions were represented which Amma bestowed upon the first seed, and later upon the two worlds: the spiral by the coiling, the vibration by the rays. Thus, Ogo had repeated the vibratory-spiraling motion of Amma. Therefore, his work was a challenge to that of Amma. Amma then said: "That resembles the image which I have created; do not contest me"; because, seeing him work, Amma feared that Ogo might be able to make a world just as he himself was making one.

However, situated there under the overturned object in a place "without shadow or light," since the braiding was loosely done, Ogo defied Amma. At that point, irritated by this success, Amma cut off a part of his tongue, or more precisely, "the vein of his tongue." So, Ogo was deprived of the full pitch of his voice, thus of the range of sounds he was able to emit. Amma then sent him back to the clavicle of the west and Ogo left the *nu goro* basket in the southern clavicle, where it remained.

OGO'S FIRST DESCENT.

Like his twin brothers, Ogo had received the "word," therefore the "knowledge" to henceforth appear in this universe: the impairment of the pitch of his voice — even if it was connected to the utterance of the word — did not deprive Ogo of his possession of that word. This mutilation was simply Amma's warning.

---

5. *ogo amma volu guyo nu goro tola tie sununi. ogo nu goro gono tia, ku vomo-ne ki.*

Ogo, however, wanted to take unfair advantage of this knowledge, in order to act on his own authority and to equal his creator. He "was born prematurely" and left his placenta hurriedly "with his eyes closed," that is, in the primordial darkness. In doing so, he disrupted his own gestation and the order of the world because, emerging from the side where his umbilical cord was attached, he tore off from the placenta a piece that was "square," thus well delimited, and as such lending itself to both extension and division.

Now, the celestial placenta itself had been divided into two by Amma: "Amma organized two placentas. A round one which was on top; th ∍ second one, attached to it, was an open circle, which connected the two of them; at the center was Amma himself. The placenta above was right (proper); the one below was wide open (because) one side had been stolen by the Fox. It was not in proper form."[6] This last sentence alludes to the fact that the torn piece had a square shape and was therefore "not right," in contrast to the round form which is bounded and completed by its circumference.

Also, at birth, Ogo had torn out the piece of his placenta attached to his umbilical cord. Therefore, the name of *ogoyne,* "the rich one," given to the Fox out of politeness by diviners, is related by the Dogon to the term *ogo* (umbilical cord),[7] on the one hand, and to the word *ogu* (quick), on the other hand, expressing his haste. Restless, worried, anxious, too quick to act, Ogo was also a premature being; on the psychic level, he was not all separated from his "mother," from whom he had, meanwhile, "torn" himself away voluntarily. For mankind, the navel, *bogu,* will be the reminder of this primordial wrench.

Moreover, Ogo tore a piece out of the placenta which contained his female twin in formation, who was to be produced sixty periods after him. He thought he would be taking her with him by doing this. Amma, however, removing from the placenta the basic spiritual principle of the being in gestation, put it out of his reach. This spiritual principle, which was to animate Ogo's female twin and which was her prefiguration, was

---

6. *amma me ley yegera. turu-go dennele-go da-go boza vogo-ne digu leye-go dennele-go ozu na vomo-le danala kanu logoro-go-ne belley dige-go amma ku vomoy; me damo-go kenebe, donumo-go danala vogo tana turu-go yurugu guyo-go ezu bileyle.*

7. The point where the cord is attached to the placenta is called *koni.*

entrusted to the other *nommo anagonno,* who would keep her until
Amma produced a support for her. All Ogo's future attempts will be to
look for and take back his lost female twin — or yet, his female soul — a
loss due to his pride, his revolt, and his initiatives. He will never find her
again. So, in yet another way Ogo upset Amma's plans, since he did not
wait for his splitting, that is to say, his own twinness. Therefore, from
that time on he will be alone and "weak" *(yugi* or *yugu).*[8]

As for the birth process itself, it is said that the cord of Ogo's placenta
was linked to the egg and that Ogo, whose head was at the bottom, by
tearing out the piece as described above, turned around like a child, so
that he could get out. He descended in seven phases or periods into
empty space, still linked to his placenta, which was turning around itself.
To feed himself, Ogo ate some *bi* fruit.[9] The placenta, which constituted
Ogo's "ark," was directed by Amma to the east, *du.* Indeed, from the
very start, Amma wanted to remedy the disorder caused by Ogo. Now,
from the spatial viewpoint, east *(du)* is the "root" *(du)* of things. "Bad
things," in returning to the east *(du),* return to the "root" *(du)* of the
world: the good in them is directed to the north, *du daga,* "root left
behind," i.e., in the hands of the creator, who had begun the realization
of this world by "turning" it to the north; what is permanently bad goes
to the south, *tenulu* (from *tene dana,* "to cut and set").

Now, Amma had also sent the four *tonu* of the *sene* seed to the east,
connoting the four elements conferred upon the witness of the first
world, i.e., the image of the seed. The seed wanted, first of all, to put
Ogo back in his place in Amma's womb. However, it was unable to do
so; it was swept up by the spinning motion of the piece that had been
torn off. So it descended with the rebel, whom it supposed to be
victorious in his fight against his creator. Single and therefore incomplete,
it also tried to get closer to Ogo, so it might take his female principle
away from him, believing he had it in his possession.

It is said that the *tonu* of the *sene* descended like a whirlwind between
the two pieces of placenta, the one that had been torn out forming the
ark and the other one that had stayed in the sky serving as an intermedi-

---

8. Later he will have the name of *yurugu.* Cf. *infra,* p. 285.

9. The *bi* fruit, which is the Fox's staple food, is sometimes used instead of groundnuts to
attract the animal onto the divination tables.

ary to Amma. The placenta that had remained in the sky and the ark "turned in opposite directions"; the seed was drawn in between the two. It is also said that Ogo descended due to the movements of the *sene,* the seed having been placed in front of him, and that "the whirlwind of the *sene* is the blood (like the wind) of Ogo's placenta."

So, sometimes passing Ogo, sometimes being passed by him, the *sene* seed completed the descent, stuck to the bleeding placenta of the rebel. This phase of the *sene's* role is recalled by the figure drawn under the altar to the Fox *(yurugu lebe):* the four *yala* are drawn on the ground before it is erected.[10]

Finally, it is said that the thorns of the *sene* are "Ogo's nails," because he took the seed with his nails. Having stolen a piece of his placenta, Ogo also stole from Amma the first seed he had created.

Now, the movement of the *sene* seed contributed to the formation of certain plants: it developed by spinning and sent portions of its shell, which made up its placenta, to the four cardinal directions of space, where they formed other seeds. "The *sene* seed, by spinning, helped the earth that gave birth to trees and seeds. As it spun, it was the way the *po* was going to spin."[11] For it is the seed of the female *po pilu* which, by its spinning about, will complete Amma's creative work.[12]

The plants thus created will be either thorny trees like the *sene* or plants whose fruit is generally inedible: *mono, bala, dolo, dolum gonolo, sene be,*[13] *onuge*[14] and *tara onuge, volo pilu* and *geu, pogo, inu banuma,*[15] *balakoro,*[16] *togozo si;* or grassy plants of the bush, *sanavonu, keni, atay, kolumo, keukuzu, solo anu, olo, tenu, gala;* or mushrooms (often poisonous), *ta boy.*

These seeds called "seeds stolen from Amma by Ogo," *amma dene ogo guyo,* are also named *dene debe,* "seeds covered" (by the earth). For

---

10. Cf. *supra,* p. 115, fig. 14.
11. *sene i digile minne barieme timmu-le dene-le nanameze. vo digile po digiliedo anay.*
12. Cf. *infra,* p. 415 and ff.
13. Literally: "found by the *sene.*"
14. The fruit of the *onuge,* however, is edible.
15. Literally: "that turns the teeth red" (in *dyamsay* dialect).
16. Mixed with tobacco, the bark of the *balakoro* becomes sweetened.

they alone will later germinate during the first rain. The *sene* will abandon them in space as it descends.

In like manner, the spinning of the *sene* will create insects, but these will descend by sticking to Ogo's bloody placenta: they are, on the one hand, the *barankamaza* and the *kaka bamagommolo* and, on the other hand, the *minne iru keke* and the *kaka kolo kayaze,* formed from the shell containing the core (or "nest of the core," *ninilu guru)* of the *sene.* The *minne iru keke* was Ogo's "tick," *kibizu.*

Now, the *barankamaza dullogu,* a water insect that will burrow into the dry earth to wait for the first rain, had a shape that recalls the gesture of Amma showing his creation. It was later sent by Amma to counteract Ogo's deeds. It is said: "Amma made the *barankamaza* go down; it showed the way (route) by which Amma created the world."[17]

These events are represented by a figure called "drawing of the *amma ta,"* or "descent of Ogo's ark and of the *barankamaza dullogu"* (fig. 55).[18]

The mask making up the top portion of the figure represents the opening of Amma's clavicles.[19] The hewn out part — into which the wearer puts his head — is like the "door opened" by Amma, in which Ogo (at the center of the two clavicles) and the *barankamaza dullogu* (to the right) have taken place for the descent. Anticipating these events that will follow, one says of this figure "Ogo and the insect met in space like the sun and *sigi tolo,* Sirius, will meet each other."

The characteristics of the *sene,* its role in the formation of plants and insects, and the fact that it came first in Amma's creation are all recalled by a figure called "seat of the Great Mask on the drawing of the *sene* spinning the world" (fig. 56),[20] drawn at the time of the Sigui. The four *sene na* grains, which denote the four elements and the four cardinal

---

17. The word *barankamaza* apparently stems from *barye,* "to add," and *kamma,* "to cast, (throw)"; an allusion to Amma's deeds of "adding and sending" the insect to counteract Ogo's initiatives.

18. *amma ta tonu,* or *ogo-le barankamaza dullogu-le koro sugu tonu;* drawn in red ochre, *bana.*

19. Cf. *supra,* p. 189.

20. *sene ganna digilimi tonu imina na doy;* in red ochre, *bana,* at the place called Sisongo, on the boulder which will support the Great Mask made of *sene* wood, the head of the mask being put on the drawing.

points, surround a dot called *timmu,* "superposed," which is the result of their spinning about. The four oriented dashes represent the four insects formed in this way: to the north, the *minne iru keke;* to the east, the *barankamaza;* to the south, the *keke bama gommolo;* to the west, the *keke kolo kayaze.* One says, after having drawn the figure (while the head of the Great Mask is placed on top): "Drawing of the image of the world of times past, Amma, come and help us, Amma, put us on the right path."[21] Because the drawing represents what Ogo made come down with him and which he had taken from above, one also says of this figure: "The drawing of the seat of the *imina na* is the image of what the Fox (i.e. Ogo) brought down from 'the star of the *po,*' (i.e., what he took from Amma's womb); the *imina na* leaning (against the boulder) is like the seated *sene."*[22]

FORMATION OF THE EARTH.

The piece of placenta that was Ogo's ark and that turned on its own axis, first landed on the "fork of the world," where it left a trace much like the *piru* of the sling;[23] it made then three turns in place (clockwise), and finally a quarter of a turn, bringing the head of the ark to the south.

Seeing the disorder caused by Ogo, Amma then transformed the piece of placenta into earth; later he will form the moon, *ie pilu,* from the opening Ogo had made to emerge from his womb.[24] The ark then stabilized itself, oriented itself east-west, and became our Earth.

When he noticed that the soil was humid and as if muddy, Ogo declared that there was no place for him on Earth. So that he might find a place for himself, Amma dried it up, transforming the soil into "heavy, sandy earth," *"minne soso demme.* Ogo, noticing the hard shell of a *bi* fruit (called *pelie),*[25] went inside it and hid himself by closing the

---

21. *ya ganna yala tonu, amma ve, emmi bara, amma ozu ezu-ne emmi kunnu.*

22. *imina na doy tonu yurugu po tolo vo sununi yalay; imina na tebe sene da anay.*

23. Corresponding to the stolen piece of placenta is the *piru* of the *bimmu* sling, the middle part shaped like a shuttle similar to Ogo's ark. The spinning of the sling recalls the spinning of the ark around itself, upon arrival.

24. Cf. *infra,* p. 227.

25. The term *pelie* designates the shell of this fruit only, and of no other. This is the fruit he ate during his descent.

opening. He then asked Amma if he could see him. And when Amma, picking up the fruit, answered in the affirmative, Ogo fled and crouched down in a hole. This gesture is evidence of "Ogo's exit from the world" and of his separation from the creation as it was conceived by Amma.

Ogo then tried to find in the ground what he was lacking. He started to look for his female twin and his lost soul in the piece that had been transformed into earth. To do this, he entered his own placenta and, as if he already had the "claws" with which he would later be provided, he dug furrows *(golo)* in the ground, beginning in the east.

He made a sort of spiral path inside the Earth. His pathway, in the image of the first journey made inside his placenta, was not curved, but straight, each lap being marked by a stop and forming an angle. Thus he dug five series of twelve holes; at the sixtieth, he emerged onto the sky. In the drawings of Ogo, the number corresponded to the numbers of *yala* that had made up the circumference of the *gaba* in Amma's egg as well as to the count in base 60 "of the placenta." By imitating "his father" and by determining the form of the torn-off placenta by the same number, Ogo was trying to make it equal to the one in which he himself had been created, that is, to make it fertile. These holes also formed, in the earth, the outline of a first field where the seeds would be sown, in order to "complete the incomplete Earth" that consisted of the stolen piece of placenta and to make it equal to Amma's in every respect. Ogo was foreseeing the future sowing.

Thus, "the piece of placenta stolen by Ogo made the second world, the descended piece became field, became the second world."[26]

The journey included twenty-eight stops (seven times "four angles") or periods, to which the departure and arrival are added, or two periods more.[27] Ogo's actions, which took place at a stage of creation outside of time and space, prefigured divisions, sequences, and distributions. The

---

26. *yurugu me tana turu-go guyo donu suga, aduno leye boza, donugo suga minne-go bila, aduno leye bi.*

27. This journey, such as it is graphically represented by the informants, presents a series of squares, one inside the other; each of their corners is placed in the center of the sides of the square that contains it. Theoretically, it is presently repeated by the Fox on the divination tables. In order for the response to be complete, sixty of the animal's "steps" must be imprinted on the sand.

duration of his peregrination — thirty "periods" — symbolizes the future division of the year into lunar months, for the formation of the moon and its phases will be related to his work. Therefore, one sometimes says that, if the placenta in its entirety "represents the year," Ogo's journey inside the stolen part represents only a twelfth part, namely "the lunar month."[28] Thus, an essential difference was already developing in Ogo's attempt to equal Amma.

Now, by penetrating into the earth, the substance of his placenta, Ogo was uniting with his mother. In a certain way, the quest inside his placenta is that of a 'single' being, possessing only one part of his spiritual principles, and who has lost the female twin he is seeking in the same womb where he himself was formed. One says that Ogo entered through the mouth and came out through the sex of his "mother," the Earth, thus committing an exceptionally grave form of incest. This first attempt will be followed by other efforts on Ogo's part, who, in the future, will eternally pursue the search for his spiritual completeness and for the lost twin.

In speaking of Ogo tearing out his placenta and of his incest, it is said: "His mother and the sky (it is) all one; it is as if he had stolen a piece of sky; Ogo, like the *kuno,* was (had as a symbol) 7; he entered into his mother, seeking to add (to himself) the word 8. (But) the word did not come very much to Ogo."[29]

The incest committed with his placenta, the earth, his "mother," was nevertheless productive. First to be born were the Yeban *(yebeu),* small creatures with big heads, discolored bodies, and frail limbs who, for shame of their condition, hide in the holes of the earth. They coupled and gave birth to the Andoumboulou *(andummolo),* who are even smaller than they are. All these beings were born single. All were incestuous because, like Ogo his progenitor, a Yeban male coupled with his daughter, an Andoumboulou woman. Thus, the Earth's interior became slowly populated with these beings who are the very first to attest to

---

28. Similarly, one sometimes says that the stolen piece, sixty "holes" or furrows, represents "two months."

29. *vo na-le alagala-le keke; alagala tana turu vo guyo-gin vo; ogo kuno-gin vomo soy be; vo na-le yoa, so gagara dena baru; ogo ga gay so vomo-ne dolu.* For 7 and 8 — the numbers associated with completeness and fertility — cf. *supra,* p. 165.

Ogo's failure and his lost twinness.

So, by these births Ogo made of his "mother," the Earth, the equivalent of his wife, i.e., of his ideal twin. But as this union produced only incomplete, imperfect, single beings, it was unsatisfactory and showed Ogo's first failure in his attempt to equal Amma.

REPRESENTATION OF OGO'S FIRST ARK.

In the ancestors' sanctuaries in the family houses is a sort of receptacle called *nu koro,* "bean box," or *yurugu koro,* "ark of the Fox" (fig. 57).[30] In the shape of a weaver's shuttle with high sides becoming narrow at one end, it has a handle at each tip forming boat-stems.[31] When turned upside down, this "ark," with the bow higher than the stern, evokes the future silhouette of the animal which, by the way, is branded into the bottom with a red-hot iron, together with the image of a *po* seed, the symbol of all cultivated seeds.

By its shape, the ark is also the prefiguration of one of the rhombuses, which will be the image of a Fox that would spin when grabbed by the tail. Like the ark, the instrument is carved in *sene* wood, a tree whose avatars are related to those of Ogo.

The oblong shell has notches at the bow and stern, symbolizing the degrees of Ogo's descent. It is the image of the egg of the world and of the placenta of which Ogo tore out a part, marked by the opening of the vessel, the sides of which show the direction of the "stroke of the claw." The buttonhole shape of this opening and the narrowing of the walls illustrate the labors of Ogo who, wanting to act on his own, tried to close himself up in his ark. In doing so, he was doing the opposite of what would be the future task of the Nommo, who had to act for the good and the multiplication of all, as indicated by the widened shape of his own ark, symbol of the extension of all beings.

The "strokes of the claw" marked the hull with grooves which are reproduced by twelve longitudinal lines, branded with a red-hot iron,

---

30. Of Ogo's future name.
31. This particular model was made by the smith Akoundyo in the Ogols.

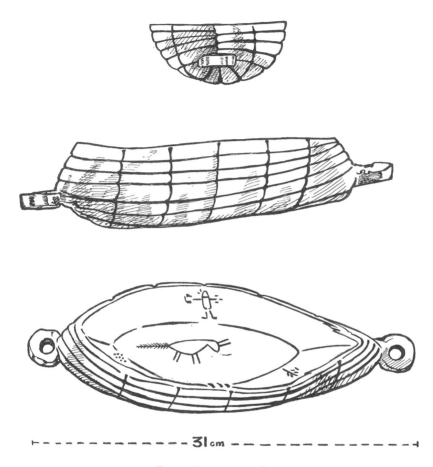

FIG. 57: The ark of the Fox.

symbolizing the twelve lunar months and the twelve forge tools, and by
five transversal lines which connote the five generations. These divisions also recall how the earth was squared off, as premeditated by Ogo,
the holes of the two handles being the primordial hollows in which the
seeds will germinate. In any case, this ground was the ark itself, the symbol of the placenta that Ogo had scratched with his claw, and which he
had then spread out like a plot of land, a new field.

The result of the agricultural labors later performed on the prepared ground is also recalled by the closed profile of the ark, a conical trunk with an oval base, having the shape of a pile of seeds heaped up on the threshing floor.

All the 12 x 5 compartments together are also the count in base 60, called "reckoning of the placenta," or reckoning of Mandé.[32]

The ark is decorated on the inside with several figures branded in with a red-hot iron, certain ones of them being the representations of Ogo's future deeds:

— the field Fox, placed in the middle, its tail stretched out to the back, reminds us that the ark is oblong, like the rhombus and the animal itself.

— to the right, towards the front, a diagram of a tree represents the *sene*.

— to the right, towards the back, a group of dots are the *po* seeds, later stolen by Ogo, and *poli* (sesame) seeds.[33]

— in the middle, to the left, a personage prefigures the future "diviner," holding a "hand of the Fox" in his right hand.

— on the right edge, three notches are the three grasshoppers that will land on the ark the moment it has been stabilized: *bolomo toru, yamana* (or *kako), kaka amma giru*.[34] After he had caught them, Ogo ate them: this was his first food on earth. To commemorate this, a grasshopper is sometimes placed under a stone by the diviner before he writes the question in the sand.

VARIANT.

In Wazouba, the ark is represented by an object a cubit long, made of *ga guyo* wood, called *amma kolondo,* "Amma's box" (fig. 58).

---

32. In the past, the grid was also engraved inside the object.

33. For the *poli,* a plant which will later appear on Earth, cf. report 2, 3rd year.

34. This last variety, "grasshopper 'eye of Amma'" is also called *ana giru,* "eye of the *anu.*"

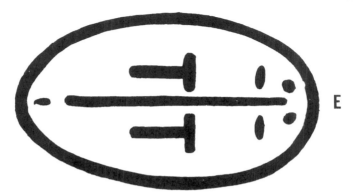

FIG. 58: Figure of Ogo's ark in Wazouba.

This utensil is represented by an oval figure, the ark, its large axis forming Ogo's body and tail in his future form as a four-legged animal: two T-shaped figures and two lines mark the paws, two dots the eyes of the animal (fig. 1), which is supposed to be sitting facing east on a seat recalled today by the four-legged bench for the women, carved in *anaumyo* (W.) or *alumi* (S.) wood. In his paws he holds four sticks of *saselu* on the right and three branches of *segele* on the left. The sum (7) corresponds to the seven days of the descent. Thus, in order, four types of wood came into play, substitutes for Ogo of the four elements and cardinal points:

alumi	:	earth, east
saselu	:	fire, north
segele	:	wind, south
ga guyo	:	water, west

But, the actual orientation of these types of wood is reversed in the figure, in order to mark Ogo's desire to try to do something that was the opposite of what Amma had done: the seat in *alumi* (east) was placed to the west; the *saselu* (north) was to the right side, the south. These plants will later be used for purification rites, for they will remain untouched by Ogo's later impurity.[35] Their presence on Ogo's ark shows that at this

---

35. Inside the totemic sanctuary, a branch of *ga guyo* carved in the shape of a

stage of his existence he was still pure, *omo* (literally: alive), that his being was not corrupted and had not yet contributed to the serious disorganization of the world in formation.

The uses of Ogo's ark are varied: the one placed near the ancestors' altar served in the past to measure the seeds necessary for the daily food of the family. It was used to scoop up the beans for seeding, put in reserve after the harvest. This gesture was symbolically valid for all seeds, and it recalled that the bean will be the first to germinate in one of the holes dug by Ogo,[36] as will the *po pilu* in its own hole immediately after the bean. In light of this, to extract it by separating it from the fine sand in which it is kept is like separating it from the *po*, which is as fine as sand, i.e., to preserve it from any risk of impurity.[37]

The arks of the family houses, measuring a cubit long and a hand wide, may be used either as a seat by turning them upside down, or as a platter on which one puts the sacrificial meat for the old men. However, this should only be goat's meat, because this animal, associated with the Fox, is his agent: none other may be put into this receptacle. To consume the goat is to consume Ogo himself.[38] As for mutton, the sheep being the animal of the Nommo, this is placed in the receptacle shaped like the Nommo's ark.

The ark is also represented by a basket used to sift beans, also called

---

lance-handle *(dommolo)* is planted to the left of the entrance: the bark of this wood is placed under the foundation. This plant effects a purification of the site of the sanctuary. The *segele* is put in water used to shave the priest's head. When the *binu* is "impure" *(puru)*, a branch of *saselu* is crushed and mixed with water to sprinkle the sanctuary. Small sticks of *saselu* are stuck vertically into the sand of the divination tables to establish the series of questions. The Fox "speaks" because "it is his tree." The *saselu* is used to make the posts for the weaver's loom, for the Fox, who possesses the "word," has also woven it, cf. *infra,* p. 238.

36. Site of the first ant hill (cf. *infra,* p. 231) represented by the round hole of the object's handles.

37. To scoop with the wooden ark is symbolically the same as to scoop with the filters *nugoro* or *nukoro* which actually separate the beans from the sand. We should note that beans are often eaten with *po*.

For the impurity of one variety of *po*, cf. *infra,* p. 234.

38. The elders' "bonus" is composed of a leg of lamb, half the head and half the breast. For the sacrifice of purification, called *uguru,* a goat is immolated, which is the same as offering the Fox himself to the Nommo.

nu koro, "bean box," which is oval and braided in fibers of palmyra leaves, *siu,* currently used to separate the beans from the grains of sand in which they are kept (fig. 59).[39] The grid engraved on the object described above is, in a certain sense, the projection of the inside surface

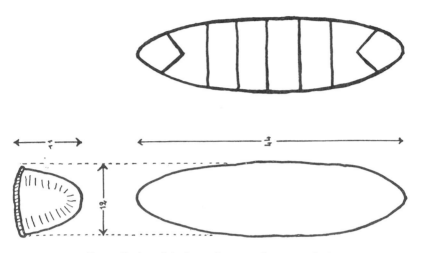

FIG. 59: Basket of the beans (layout and cross section).

of this basket, the prototype of which must have sixty-eight twigs or bars. The basket is bordered with bark of *yoru geu* (or *yoru na);* the separation strings are of cotton fiber.[40] The palmyra used for the fabrication of the basket, with regard to this first ark, constitutes the link that unites it with the "sky," Amma's seat. It was like the "chain" that would later allow the descent of the ark of his twin brother and adversary, the Nommo.[41] The palmyra thus united the sky and the Earth, formed from Ogo's ark.

---

39. There are two types of filters for the beans: one in the shape of a shuttle called "canoe of the bean," *nu koro;* another in the shape of a round bonnet with a spiral structure called *nu goro,* "bonnet of the bean," which also represents the object Ogo made before his descent (cf. p. 202).

40. The fiber of *yoru geu* (Grewia bicolor) is also used for making mats.

41. Cf. *infra,* Ark of the Nommo, p. 452.

Ogo's ark is also represented by a small wooden drum, *koro bogu, koro* "with a navel." The instrument, made of a hollow trunk of *sene* wood, has a rectangular form: at one end it has a sort of protuberance which forms a handle (cf. fig. 60). The whole thing connotes the torn-out piece of placenta and the attached bit of the umbilical cord. The object is also the image of the first "field" spread out by Ogo; on the inside and the outside, there are sometimes carved figures representing incomplete, unfinished beings. The opening of the instrument is the opening of the universe: the bottom is the earth, cultivation, and everything that is below; the sides are the sky and the high millet. The player alternately strikes the bottom and the one and the other side: this means to leave the sky to arrive on Earth.

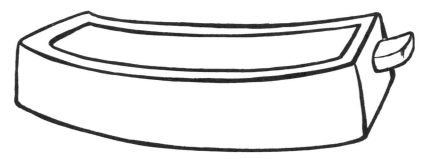

FIG. 60: Wooden drum "with a navel" (explanatory figure).

The instrument is used exclusively in the bush by children after the first weeding to protect the crops from domestic and wild animals. One says of this: "The guardians who play the drum of the Fox in the bush, it is so that the Fox will not steal the grain that they are playing."[42] (Pl. IX, 1).

Ogo's movements inside his placenta, his quest to see the universe created by Amma, and his descent are all recalled by the form of one of the *sirige* masks. The figure that represents it is called "drawing of the *sirige* of the run of the Fox around the worlds that Amma created" (fig.

---

42. *yurugu koro bogi olu-ne banu-go yurugu va dene-go guyono-ga banu.* Literally: "it is to say to the Fox: 'don't steal the seeds' that they play the drum with the Fox's navel."

161, B, p. 559),[43] the worlds being represented by the vertical series of seven red circles painted on the mast.

From this viewpoint, the grids of the mask having five slits, each represents one of "Ogo's strokes with his claws" to tear off his placenta. Theoretically, the total of sixty slits is equal to the sixty holes dug in the ground; one also says that he gave twelve strokes with his claws which correspond to the twelve lunar months. The filled surfaces of the mast are decorated with lozenges representing Ogo's two fields, the first being the "hole" in which he will sow the stolen *po,* and the second to be delimited at a later time.[44] At the same time, these filled surfaces are also the future divination tables.

OGO'S RETURN TO THE SKY.

Ogo's quest on earth for his twin — his female soul — had long remained fruitless. Moreover, the soil was arid. Thinking the Earth useless such as he found it, Ogo immediately left it and reascended to the sky to continue his search there.

Amma, foreseeing the increasing seriousness of the initiatives of Ogo, who caused only disorder, had in the meantime begun to make changes inside his clavicles. He placed the *nommo anagonno titiyayne* in the clavicle or egg to the east, where the *nommo semi* was; he pushed the rest of Ogo's placenta into the west egg; finally, he entrusted to the couple of the east egg the spiritual principles of Ogo's future female twin, whom he had not yet produced, so that Ogo would be deprived of them.

To reascend to the sky, Ogo spun in a spiral from east to north, then to the west, then to the south, to return to the east, making twenty-eight stops at the "corners," that is, seven stops at each of the future "cardinal angles" *(sibe nay)* — all this in sixty periods. He will also remain in the sky for sixty periods, during which he will again measure the breadth of the universe by walking from east to north, from west to south.

One recalls Ogo's first descent with the *sene,* his ascent to the sky, and his new journey by saying: "The *sene* and the Fox, Amma had them descend first, the *sene* turned space, the Fox traveled around space,

---

43. *amma ganna mani yurugu gona gali toy.*
44. Cf. *infra,* p. 229 and installment 2, 3rd year.

returned from it, came back, went up to the sky."[45]

During Ogo's reascent to the sky, Amma gave the order to the *nommo titiyayne* to transform the placenta into a burning fire to prevent his coming near it. Ogo could grab only a small bit that he tore off, burning himself in the process, just as the *nommo titiyayne* was performing the metamorphosis. Amma then made the placenta spin and turned it into a sun; at the same time, he took the spiritual principles of Ogo's female twin from it. The sun would be called *nay,* "four," a term which recalls, on the one hand, the femininity of the placenta and, on the other hand, the fact that, in the course of these events, it had been divided into four pieces, two of which were stolen by Ogo. The rays of the sun were made from the blood of the placenta.

VARIANT.

During Ogo's reascent, because Ogo wanted to get hold of his placenta again, Amma transformed it into a fish. The organ was square, and to lengthen it Amma pulled on two opposite corners, leaving the two others to form the "clavicles" of the being in formation.[46] However, Ogo got close enough to the fish to touch it. Amma took the fish by the tail and, pulling it toward him, folded it over, head to tail.[47] He turned it into copper; when Ogo approached the copper, Amma changed it into a burning fire; then he spun it around and made the sun with it.

One draws the trace of the "Fox's claws" (for Ogo will be transformed into the Fox) tearing out a second piece of his placenta, just as it was changed into

FIG. 61: *tonu* of the tearing-off of the sun by the Fox's claws.

---

45. *sene-le yurugu-le amma polo sununi; sene ganna digile, yurugu ganna gona pilema via alakala uli.*

46. This episode of the myth is recalled by the string game, called "let's make the fish" (cf. M. Griaule, *Rôle du Clarias Senegalensis dans la procréation,* p. 310).

47. This episode is recalled by the form and use of the *gengala* or "whirligig" toy (cf. M. Griaule, *Jeux dogon,* p. 68 and 64) made of a splinter of millet stalk and a thorn from the *mono,* a name derived from *monno* "to stick": for "the head and the tail of the fish stuck (themselves) together."

the sun. This figure is called: *"tonu* of the tearing off of the sun by the Fox's claws" (fig. 61)."[48] It is drawn above two recesses placed at the top of the façade of the totemic sanctuary, a position representative of the sky, where the event took place. The three registers of this sort of grid represent, from bottom to top, the lower, middle, and upper phalanges of a "hand" associated with Ogo's deed.

CREATION OF THE SUN AND OF THE TURTLE "AGUNURU."

The transformation of the placenta into a sun is associated with Amma's creation of the earth turtle, *agunuru*. The whole sequence of these operations is represented by a series of figures.

FIG. 62: *tonu* of the creation of the turtle.

---

48. *yurugu kubo unum nay gobo tonu.* Drawn in porridge of *ara geu.*

The first is called *"tonu* of the creation of the turtle by Amma" (fig. 62).[49] The remaining portion of the placenta was flat and square; Amma cut off its four corners. This deed recalled Ogo's successive gestures when he cut his own placenta into bits. These corners became, respectively:

> to the northeast, the turtle;
> to the northwest, the setting sun;
> to the southwest, the midday sun;
> to the southeast, the rising sun.

With the corner of the turtle remaining spread open, Amma placed on it the triangle of the rising sun folded in half (the sides of the two triangles remaining parallel), then the triangle of the midday sun folded in four, and finally, the triangle of the setting sun folded in half (fig. 63).

FIG. 63: Work of Amma creating the turtle (explanatory figure): above, from left to right: the turtle, the rising sun, the setting sun; below, center: the midday sun.)

The sides of the largest triangle were then folded up, beginning with the side with the largest base. Thus, the turtle was created, whose hind legs were made with the corners in the folding. The smaller forelegs were made with the corners that Amma had torn off.

---

49. *amma gonna agunuru manu tonu.* Drawn in porridge of *ara geu* to the right side of the door of the totemic sanctuary, during the *bulu.*

A figure called *"tonu* of Amma who cut off the four corners of Ogo's placenta and transformed them into a turtle" (fig. 64)[50] shows the design of the animal.

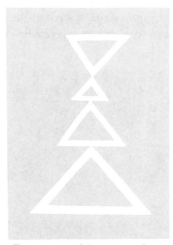

FIG. 64: *tonu* of Amma transforming the placenta of the Fox into a turtle.

The large triangle is called *agunuru tolo,* "beginning of the turtle." The set of the other three is called *agunuru bere,* "inside (belly) of the turtle." One also says of this figure *nay yoyi,* "it's the course of the sun."

The turtle formed in this way was one of the representations of the world. The upper shell, called "case of the turtle" *(agunuru koro),* represents the celestial world. The lower one, called "belly of the turtle" *(agunuru bere),* is the Earth. The turtle's scales, in a figure called *agunuru toy,* "drawing of the turtle" (fig. 65),[51] are theoretically 2 x 22 in number, divided into two rows of eleven on the left, called "paths of the sun" *(nay ozu),* and as many on the right, called "paths of the blood" *(illi ozu).* The entire set of lozenges represents the classification of things, their "distribution in different places by Amma."[52]

The liver of the turtle is like the sun; its size is in proportion to that of the star, which appears to be larger when it rises in the morning or sets in the evening than it does at midday.

So, the turtle is one piece of Ogo's placenta and evidence of the rest

50. *amma ogo me sibe nay polla agunuru bilenu tonu.* Drawn at the *bulu* to the right of the door of the totemic sanctuary, in *ara geu* porridge under the preceding one.

51. *agunuru toy.* Drawn at the *bulu* on the façade of the sanctuary to the left of the door, in *ara geu* porridge. The turtle is also drawn when a Hogon's house is being built, on the east side of the platform. It is also carved on the doors of the Hogon's granaries (cf. *infra,* p. 536) or those of the family heads.

52. *amma yalu de de kize gammalu.* For these classifications, cf. *infra,* p. 431.

which is the sun. Its status determines its future role on Earth. It is an equal of the sun, which will become "one of the guardians of the world." Also, the sun and the Earth become twins, each being made from a piece of the same placenta.

The Hogon and the heads of the families, *ginna bana,* keep a ground turtle in their homes, "guardian of the world," to whom they give a bit of

FIG. 65: Drawing of the turtle *agunuru.*

their food before eating it themselves. In the absence of the *ginna bana,* his wife gives some food to the animal before every meal. This action is similar to the one performed in the bush, when one casts a bit of food or water "for the sun" in the four spatial directions (to the east, north, west, and south) before satisfying one's own hunger or thirst.

The *agunuru* turtle is sacrificed only in serious circumstances that concern the entire *ginna.* Should this happen, the object of the sacrifice, the turtle, is equivalent to all the animals on Earth together. No other offering is necessary for a long time after this supreme sacrifice.

The transformation of the rest of Ogo's placenta into a burning star deprived him forever of the possibility of getting hold of it: the sun and its motion in space will be entrusted to the *nommo die,* who resides in Amma's "sky" at his side. On the Earth, the heat of the sun will "burn" Ogo, transformed into the Fox, so as to keep him from acting, to "dry him out." But the rays of the sun, as "blood of the placenta," will act upon the seeds placed in the earth and watered by the rain, promoting agriculture and the growth of plant life.

Now, at the moment of the transformation, while Ogo tried to seize his placenta, the solar fire had burned his "hand," shriveling it up, so that he could only claw at the organ, grab a small piece of it, and thus retrieve but a few "signs" inscribed on the surface. These signs will become the fundamental figures later drawn on the divination tables: in an abstract way, they will represent Ogo's reascent and the act of tearing off the second piece of the placenta. "When one draws the trailings (smoothing) of the table of the Fox, it is the image of the Fox stealing the placenta of the sun."[53]

THEFT OF AMMA'S SEEDS.

Seeing that he could not obtain what he was looking for, that is, his female twin, Ogo wanted to get hold of the seeds created by Amma, including the *po,* the cornerstone of creation. In this way, he thought he could take possession of the universe.

---

53. *yurugu golo* or *kala bummone tononu, yurugu nay me guyo yalay. bummone tononu,* "to make traces," the action of using the smooth object, called "hand of the Fox," to make the registers of the divination table.

To do this, going around by the south and east clavicles, he set out to steal the male seeds from the north clavicle. This journey shows that, to perpetrate this deed in connection with the foundation of Amma's creation, he had to pass by the east, *du,* that is to say, by the "root," *du,* of the world.

"Ogo descended; after that he ascended again to the south, he left it and turned towards the east which follows; he went to the north to steal the seeds in Amma's north clavicle; he returned to the east clavicle, then descended below."[54]

He stole eight male seeds, with the exception of those of the *emme ya, emme di giru,* and *gaba,* which Amma got away in time, as well as the corresponding female seeds, which are: *po pilu, yu, emme pilu, emme sonodum, emme nakolo, nu, ara,* and *ani.* These seeds, called *yu ana,* "male millet," were in one of Amma's clavicles, which is represented in this instance by a small, round *kemme* or *koro sesege* gourd, also called "small gourd," *koro dagi;* "the *sesege* represents Amma's clavicle."[55]

VARIANT.

He stole the male seeds that Amma had placed in a goatskin, as well as the male *po* that Amma had put in a *bana* bowl made of *kilena* wood. He took the *po* seed from the bowl and put it with the others, in order to take them all away in the gourd, the image of Amma's clavicle.

Ogo put the gourd in a secret hole in the stolen piece of placenta. The result of this action was that the *po* became impure according to the word of Amma, who ascertained disorder by saying: "By stealing the *po,* Ogo made it impure."[56]

It is said: "Ogo reascended; Amma having hidden his placenta, he did not see it, he stole Amma's seeds, as a replacement for his placenta, and he descended."[57] For Ogo believed that the stolen cereal seeds were his

---

54. *yurugu suga; kone ula tenulu benne-ne goa, gona du dimmo, du daga-ne yu amma ani guyo-ne guya; pilema, du amma ani guyo-ne donune sugu.*

55. *Sesege amma ani guyo tozoy.* The gourd *koro sesege* is used by the soothsayers *(ammayana* or *vanupazane):* it is emptied and refilled with small pebbles and grains. It is also used to cadence the requests uttered at the pond or on an ant hill.

56. *yurugu po guya voy puroma va.*

57. *ogo kone ula; me vomo amma bagiri ielu kana; amma dene me vomo toze-go guya sugi; yurugu dene guyo me vomoy-ga sebe.*

placenta and did not realize the truth until he was below. Thus, his error was revealed to him only when he had descended on Earth with the seeds and the torn-off piece of his placenta, which was already fiery and had burned him.

Ogo also got hold of the "baby teeth," *i tonu,* of his twin brother, which Amma had taken just then. As we have seen, the teeth of the *nommo anagonno* were associated with the "word." To Ogo, this theft was a final attempt to gain possession of what he was lacking. On earth, the teeth of the sacrificed *nommo anagonno* will be transformed into *dugoy* of *nani,* thus becoming evidence of the "kinship" that will link the *nommo anagonno* to men, his "sons." By taking the teeth, bearers of the "word," Ogo was also trying to make sure he would have descendants.[58]

REINTEGRATION OF THE ELEMENTS OF CREATION IN THE "PO PILU."

As the theft of the seeds had taken place in one of his clavicles (represented by the *sesege* gourd), Amma judged that Ogo's deeds were seriously upsetting the order of things, and he put all that he had created back inside the female seed of the *po pilu,* which he placed to the south. Everything was put into the seed except for the *nommo anagonno* and the eight female seeds, twins of the ones that had been stolen, which he placed to the north. Amma put the elements of the universe inside the female *po pilu* seed according to a process in which the latter participated: it "unrolled" itself to the limits of Amma's seat; then rolled up again, and placed itself in the south clavicle. While the *po* rolled itself up, Amma placed in it, one by one, the things which were gathered in the coils: "When Amma put things in the *po,* it rolled itself up."[59] At the center were the seeds of the *ani* and the *gaba,* so the *po pilu,* then motionless, formed a sort of spiral around a sphere.

The created things were thus put back into the original seed; their placenta was kept by Amma. "When he created all things (Amma) took

---

58. The teeth transformed into *dugoy* of *nani* will be recovered from the Fox on Earth (installment 1, 1st year). The milk teeth of the child are, for the Dogon, comparable to those of the *nommo anagonno;* when they fall out, one says that "they return to the Nommo."

59. *amma po-ne kize kana vo kunna po toniay.*

back the placenta which he kept; he placed the child (i.e., the created thing) in the body of the *po;* all the placentas of things were in Amma's

FIG. 66: *tonu* of the female *po pilu.*

egg."[60] Thus Amma kept in himself all the placentas, that is, all the possibilities for the reproduction of things.

The active role of the *po pilu* is represented by a figure called *"tonu* of the female *po pilu,"* which features a circle, the shell of the *po,* and inside it are arranged twenty-two lines, which recall the twenty-two *yala* of the sex and of the body of the *po* (such as they were in the original egg) as well as the categories of Amma (fig. 66). This number implies the completeness of things "brought together" at that time in the seed.[61]

---

60. *kize pu vo manaze me-go gona sia; i-go po gozu-ne kunni; kize me pu amma me-ne tobe. sia* means "to keep for oneself."

61. Figure drawn in porridge of *po pilu* at the place called *tuyo taba,* "plateau of the pile," located south of Lower Ogol, where they used to put the fonio harvest; symbolically, it represents the theoretical site of the first pile of fonio harvested on Earth. Construction of

OGO'S SECOND DESCENT.

In order to descend, leaving his own egg (the west clavicle), Ogo used the small stolen piece of placenta, which formed a second ark in which he hid the seeds. The object is compared to a small square box, *yurugu koro sibe nay,* "ark of the *yurugu* with four corners."

Therefore, one says, speaking simultaneously of Ogo's placenta, the two stolen pieces, and the transformed remnant: "The divided placenta forms the whole (that will give) the first *nu koro,* the square box, and the sun."[62]

To descend to the Earth, Ogo made a "hole" in the egg, which "Amma transformed into a moon, so as not to lose the testimony to the theft." Later, the "new moon" will correspond to that moment of the theft. From the aspect of time, the second stolen piece of placenta itself represents a "month," that is, a "moon," the one that precedes the sowing,[63] thus associating the theft of the seeds with their future crop. Thus, the two stars (the sun and the moon) are the celestial evidence of the placenta of the Fox. One says of the figures that represent these heavenly bodies on the façades of the totemic sanctuaries: "The drawings of the sun and moon (drawn) on the sanctuary of the *binu* mark the placenta of Ogo."[64]

While descending, he checked the stopping-points, marked during his reascent, "naming a race of beings at each one of them." This descent is called "winding road," *ozu gonnu.* The "chain" which allowed the ark to descend is the palmyra tree, *siu:* "The top of the tree touched the sky, the bottom will take root in the earth and will finally rot."[65]

---

houses by the American mission has caused them to abandon the site and the custom of putting the fonio there. Presently, it is threshed at night in the respective fields of the farmers.

62. *yurugu me gunnu kabulu nu koro polo vo sugu-le koro sibe nay vo sugu-le nay-le mona.*

63. That is to say, *bado.* Children conceived at this time are *ogo, i.e.,* "leaders," because this is the "month before the conception of the seeds." During this month, the new moon represents the days of menstruation preceding conception. Now, since "Amma did not wish to take back the piece of placenta," the children conceived at this time may become leaders.

64. *ie pilu-le nay-le binu-ne tonu ogo me yalay.*

65. At this stage of the myth, the Earth is compared to the field of the joint family, *ginna minne.* The tree, then, belongs to the family head, *ginna bana.* He is the person one asks for fibers to make baskets, some of which are given to him in thanks. Sometimes, palmyra trees are planted in the field of the *ginna.*

At Amma's bidding, three insects accompanied Ogo and watched over him. First, the female ant *key,* who dug the hole for the descent, and the termite *tu,* called "Amma's drawer of water," who helped him to drink.

The ant and the termite, who were at the center of Amma's "womb" and his four clavicles, are Amma's assistants or *titiyayne.*[66]

They descended along the fork of the world to watch over the universe in formation. Their role with regard to Ogo is implied by their name: *key,* which designates the ant, comes from *kele,* "to separate," for it "separated itself from Ogo"; *tu,* the termite, comes from *tumo,* "together" or "counterpart," for it acted in the same way as the ant.

The third insect was the spider *dada yurugu geze gezene* (literally: *dada* who spins the Fox's thread): it was related to the *kikinu bummone ana* of Ogo's body (whereas the *minne iru keke* descended with the *sene* was linked to the *kikinu bummone ya).* Placed on the second ark, of which it formed the cover, its head facing south, it hid Ogo from Amma's eyes.

In the ark were also all the seeds of wild plants, born from the spinning of the *sene* and which it had left in space.

The male *po pilu,* cornerstone of the world, directed Ogo in the descent. Now, the *po* is the symbol of the origin of beings and of material goods, just as the placenta is the original envelope of man, who begins his life as small as the seed. Therefore, Ogo thought he possessed the source of all things when he stole the one thing and the other. "One says that the Fox stole fonio and placenta from the sky, saying that with these one gains a (creation of) family and of material goods."[67]

Ogo's mistake in seizing the *po* and the placenta was that he had penetrated the secret of the origins, the secret of Amma himself, that is to say, in short, that he had understood Amma's essence.[68] One also says that Amma — who foresaw all things — had allowed Ogo to descend and form the Earth to prepare it before the arrival of man: he had entrusted him with the destiny of the world. However, since Ogo in his pride believed himself to be stronger, Amma would later delegate his twin brother to replace him; he would "cut out Ogo's tongue," thereby

---

66. The Dogon say that only the ignorant call them "Amma's wives."

67. *yurugu-va, po-le me-le alakala-go guyo vo, ko-le togu moyedaga yenu guyo va siye ko-le bele meze ga* (in *tombo so* dialect).

68. Cf. p. 131, n. 120, for the prohibition which forbids the utterance of the name of the *po.*

depriving him forever of the verbal expression of the "word" that he had received.

OGO'S SECOND ARK.

In certain family houses *(ginna)* there is a quadrangular object made of *sene* wood. Four holes have been made at the top, symbolizing the hiding place where Ogo had put the stolen seeds, which are related to four stars, called "stars of the four-cornered ark of the descent of the Fox" (fig. 67, A).[69] The object symbolizes the future "field of the Fox," where he will sow four seeds.[70] The form of the object is also related to the shape of the first granary built by man, since it normally should have the shape of a pyramid, each side of the base measuring four cubits (fig. 67, B). The central hole is called "central post of space," *ganna dey.*

FIG. 67: Designs of Ogo's second ark.

This "four-cornered ark of the Fox," *yurugu koro sibe nay,* is also called *tazi koro,* "ark (in the shape of) *tazi,"* because it is represented by the basket *tazi,* "small *tazu,"* which has a square base and a round opening and is made of palmyra leaves and *ezegele* stalks (Pl. IX, 2). Used by women to hold raw cotton, this basket is impure and must never be brought into the house of the Hogon, nor into that of the totemic priests, nor near the sanctuaries or the pond of Dona, which is considered to be the duplicate of the first pond to be formed on Earth.

OGO'S SOWING.

When he arrived, Ogo did not find the ground in the condition in

---

69. *yurugu sugu koro sibe nay tolo.*

70. This is the field he delimited the third year after the descent upon Earth of the ark of the Nommo and man (installment 2, 3rd year).

which he had left it: sprung from the four *tonu,* the *sene na* seed had adhered to the descended placenta, had germinated from the moisture it contained, and had grown to the northeast; it joined the Earth, by its roots and trunk, to the sky, by its leaves. However, because it had descended with Ogo, the *sene* was obliged to share the four elements with him: it had lost fire and water, which belonged to Ogo. Thus it contained two beings who were incomplete and yet also complementary, having drawn their strength from the same placenta.

When Ogo had redescended, he divided the gourd in half to cover up his theft. He put the seeds in one half and, keeping the other as a vessel to eat and drink from, placed it in a cave. However, as he was still rebellious and still desirous to possess the universe, he decided to use the stolen seeds. They were incomplete because their female twins had remained in the sky, and thus they were apt to disturb the order of creation. To attain this goal of destruction for his own advantage, he wanted to sow the seeds broadcast in the prepared field, in which sixty holes had been dug, symbols of the initial placenta. He started at the east, the direction chosen by Amma to produce his creation, and which was the more humid one, since Amma had begun his creation with the element "water." For Ogo wanted to do just what Amma had done in every way, but also against him. He succeeded only in placing in the first hole (situated to the northeast) the eight seeds in his possession and, not far from there, the baby teeth of the *nommo semi* that he had taken at the same time. He put the second piece of placenta, torn out at the time of the theft, over the hole to cover it and hide the stolen seeds.

Then he broke the half of the gourd that had contained the seeds and threw it away, so that it would not be seen. It was lost for good.[71] The other half, that had remained in the cave, stretched itself and became *koro pommu,* "elongated calabash," because "it was not yet time." Indeed, to cut the calabash in half and break a part of it was the same as destroying a fundamental thing belonging to Amma: "The calabash stretched itself, for it was not yet time to slaughter (to sacrifice)."[72]

---

71. However, the seed of *koro sesege* will still germinate; due to the effects of impurity, the plant will mutate and produce the variety called *gaba dogo;* these two types grow wild in the bush.

72. *semu dolo vo se-ga koro pommu tana.* The *koro pommu* calabash is the variety used to make the vessels for the dignitaries of the Sigui.

At that time the ant and the termite intervened, who had descended with Ogo and had been delegated by Amma to counteract him. The ant "was a messenger ordered to take the stolen seeds." The termite, "whose tracks are like the *bummo* and whose termite hill is like the clavicles," and who, because of this, is proof of Amma's creative thought, had to watch over everything that would happen and gnaw away anything that might remain in case the seeds germinated and the stalks produced straw.

At Amma's order, the ant went to the hole in the northeast and transported seven of the stolen seeds, one by one, to his own hole, i.e., out of reach of the second piece of placenta, leaving only the *po*.[73] During this time, the termite was ordered to "turn away from each of Ogo's holes any moisture of the original placenta, in order to prevent the seeds from germinating."

CRUSHING OF THE PLACENTA BY THE "NOMMO TITIYAYNE."

The second piece of placenta, stolen by Ogo and placed over the hole, originally contained the *bummo* called *amma numo donu,* "hand of Amma below" (fig. 68). It represented Amma's thumb, index finger, and middle finger as he created the world; for one says that "Amma made the world with three fingers."[74] Amma then gave the order to the *nommo titiyayne* to crush that piece, which he did by stretching out his "right foot" (i.e., the tail). He trampled the placenta, which decayed, except for a section located under the arch of his "foot."[75]

FIG. 68: Sign of Amma's hand below.

Because of this deed, the second stolen piece of placenta "corresponds

73. Only the female *key* ant, who comes into play at this stage of the myth, will be "spiritually akin" *(manu)* to Ogo as transformed into the Fox (installment 2). The male *key* ant will enter into it later (cf. *infra,* p. 288).

74. *amma ganna mani numo i tanu-le mani.*

75. The importance of this part of the sole of the foot (of which it is said that the arch of man's foot is like "next to" the Fox or is on the Fox's side) *(inne kubo namu yurugu tana anay)* is recalled in the teaching of the diviners. The student puts his foot on the divination table and asks if he will have a long life; if the Fox walks on the print of his arch, he will have a long life.

The arks of the Fox:

1) The wooden drum, *koro m'bogi,* called "with a navel," symbol of the first ark;

PL. IX

2) The *tazi* basket, symbol of the second ark.

PL. X   1) Cave and figuration of Andoumboulou at Yougo Dogorou;

2) Rock shelter *demme togolu kommo* near Barna (Sanga).

in size to the foot of the *nommo titiyayne"* who crushed it.[76] The *po*, however, was not crushed and, in spite of the efforts made to prevent it from doing so, it did germinate within the decay of the placenta and its bloody moisture.

Defending himself against the deeds of the *titiyayne,* Ogo tried to take his placenta back and to defend it as it was about to be crushed. He succeeded only in tearing away a small piece of it. The *titiyayne* cried out, Ogo became frightened and let it go; the *titiyayne* immediately changed it into an insect, the *nay na,* which escaped its would-be captor. The term which designates this cicada literally means "mother of the little mother" *(na i na),* that is, of the "little placenta" of Ogo. One says that this is the reason why the insect is the color of the earth.

This crushing was the cause of a series of events of considerable importance:

1. The crushed placenta decayed, except for the small piece just under the arch of the sole of the foot: this would allow the *po* seed, which was the only one there (the other seeds having been carried off by the ant to its hole), to germinate.

However, it would be contaminated by the decay of the placenta. Moreover, it would become the carrier of the impurity of its sower; the penetration into the soil, that is, into Ogo's placenta, represented a sort of incest. Because of this, the male soul of the *po* alone remained inside it; its female soul (which symbolically became identified with that of Ogo's placenta) was taken back to the sky by Amma, as was its *nyama.* Amma put both of them into the *emme ya* seed, which he had kept out of Ogo's reach and preserved within himself. Amma never returned these to the *po* seed: thus, since that time, the *emme ya* has contained the essence of the *po pilu.* The seed that germinated in Ogo's hole was incomplete and became impure, *puru;* it would give birth to the variety of fonio called *po banu,* "red fonio."[77]

In addition, the *kikinu* of the placenta — i.e., of the earth — left it as soon as it was crushed. It was completely contaminated and became impure, *puru,* because of the decay of the crushed piece. It dried up and became more and more barren and unproductive.

---

76. The *toy* of the *nommo titiyayne* (fig. 45, p. 183) emphasizes the elongation of the fish's tail, crushing Ogo's placenta.

77. This variety will be the cause of the general prohibition on the fonio.

2. When the *titiyayne* crushed the piece of placenta placed over Ogo's hole, the Yéban and Andoumboulou who lived there tried to flee; the Yéban were able to get away, but the sexual organ of a male Andoumboulou was crushed at the same time as the placenta. This crushing was eventually to cause his death. Thus, the germ of destruction that was developing on Earth had, because of the decay of the placenta, its replica in the appearance of death among the Andoumboulou and thereafter among the people, where it would eventually spread. Now, death was brought about by the crushing of the sex of the Andoumboulou, struck in his vital parts. Amma had created the *po* — or the second world — beginning with the formation of the sex of the seed: the destruction of the sex organ of the Andoumboulou is, on the one hand, evidence of the primary importance Amma had conferred upon the organ of reproduction and fertility; on the other hand, it emphasized that death would be the price of sterility; and, finally, it revealed Ogo's lack of responsibility and the exceptionally serious repercussions of his revolt and his actions.

The face of the *dommo* or "rabbit" mask, in its entirety, represents these events: the rectangle is the piece of Ogo's placenta; it is divided into two parts, the right side denoting the Yéban who escaped being crushed, and the left side the Andoumboulou whose sex organ was crushed. The two parts also recall the later division of the second piece of placenta, of which the section that was protected by the arch of the sole of the foot would be kept by Ogo and later be used by him. The red dots sprinkled over the face are the *po banu* (cf. fig. 69).[78]

THE "SENE NA" AND THE WORK OF THE SPIDER.

When the *sene na,* whose seed had germinated in the soil, noticed Ogo's deeds, it tried to return to the sky. Its quest is compared to Ogo's: alone and incomplete like him, but in an opposite way, it sought its completeness in the sky. To do this, it began to turn on its axis; its stalk, which first supported two lateral thorns, grew in a helix,[79] while its roots dug

78. For the *dommo* mask, cf. M. Griaule, *Masques dogons,* p. 454 (also installment 2, 10th year).

79. An allusion to the trunk of the *sene* which is covered by bark that twists around it in a helical fashion; the tree's branches grow around it in the same way. This helical motion is called *minne.* For a twisted bracelet, one says *minemu* or *minemo.*

into the soil.

While it rose in a helix, its movement attracted the seeds of plants
that had descended with Ogo's second ark and had been hurled out by
the spinning motion. They were then enveloped by the movement of the
sene, which grew while taking them into its whorls. Then it threw them
out, and they fell on the earth and germinated. The first seed caught by
the *sene* was that of the *mono,* a word meaning "to bring together," for
the other plants that reach the earth later will be classified with the *sene,*
which represents the tree *par excellence.*

Now, the spider *dada yurugu geze gezene* (literally: *"dada*[80] who holds
the thread of the Fox") had been delegated by Amma, when Ogo
descended for the second time, to watch his deeds and to report them to
Amma. However, since it believed that Ogo would be victorious and
that, once he had stolen the *po,* he would take over creation for his own
advantage, it betrayed Amma's trust. It entered the *sene na* (that was
beginning to grow) in order to "weave the words" of Ogo. By weaving
them in the *sene* and thus giving a new form to the signs that Ogo had
stolen with his placenta, it wished to draw into the *sene* the four
elements originally contained in the *sene* seed.

Placed at the center of the acacia, the spider wove its threads in a
conical spiral for the placement of the warp, and by moving vertically
for the coming and going of the passing woof.[81]

Through the fabric, it sifted the germs that had been hurled into the
universe by the spinning. The sound of its work, of the same nature as
the word, grabbed them as they passed by and, with them, fastened itself
at the crossing of the threads.

The spider was in the tree, weaving its thread, which it wound around
the tree. The tree tried to close the insect in and became longer, first
twisting its trunk, then developing its branches, which formed "four

---

80. *dada* is used to describe a weak or sick animal that walks with difficulty.

81. The conical spiraling motion is called *digilio bara vani,* "circle (or turning) that
increases in width," while the helix *minne* is also called "similar turning," *kekeu digilio.*
The in-and-out movement of the woof bears the same name as the spider, *dada.* According
to a popular derivation, those terms are to be compared to *dana:* "stuck," because the
band rolled up and stuck very tightly to itself, as implied by the repetition of *dada.* This last
term also applies to the vibration of the loom.

points in the direction of the sky." This growth is compared to the acquisition of the four spatial directions by the *sene,* which originally possessed, in the first genesis, all four elements. This labor will give the tree first three, then four branches. Thus, the spiraling motion of the insect was similar to the helicoid motion of the plant.

The four branches of the *sene na* in which the spider was working will bear fruit. The fruits will fall on the ground where some of them will be transformed *(bibile).* They will give birth to three other *sene* which will grow later: respectively, *sene gommuzu* or "bumpy"; *sene benu* or "stocky"; *sene urio* "that bows (its head)." The four *sene* will embody on earth the four *yala* allocated to the *sene na* seed in Amma's womb, which contained the four elements in this order: *sene na,* water; *sene gommuzu,* air; *sene benu,* fire; *sene urio,* earth.

A series of figures represents the components and the development of the *sene na* seed — its *yala* are drawn under the altar to the Fox — and the formation of the tree (fig. 70).[82].

The first, called *"tonu* of the four elements of the *sene* seed" *(sene i kize nay tonu)* (A), is made of a lozenge flanked by a dot at each corner.

The second, called *"tonu* of the *sene* seed" *(sene i tonu)* (B), is made of four concentric oval lines; it shows the position of the four elements in the seed, on the one hand, and the eventual existence of the four types of *sene,* on the other hand.

The third is called "drawing of the tree of the *sene* seed" *(sene i timme toy)* (C); it represents the *sene na,* its roots, trunk, and four branches, also associated with the four varieties, the vertical branch being the *sene na,* those to the left the *sene gommuzu* (above) and the *sene urio* (below), the one to the right the *sene benu.*

In like manner, four other schematic drawings, called *"tonu* of the germination of the *sene* of the *olugizu"(oligizu sene tey tonu),* show the

---

82. Drawn with red earth, *bana,* under the altar of the masks, called *mele ganna,* of the Doziou Orey quarter (of Lower Ogol), when it was founded. This altar is consecrated to the man who was the first to die, the Andoumboulou whose sex organ was crushed by the *nommo titiyayne,* and to the Fox (installment 2).

The lozenge-shaped figure connoting the four elements of the seed is identical to the opening of same shape made in the wood of the Great Mask, the *imina na,* which portrays the ancestor Dyongou Sérou, who died in the form of a snake.

four oriented stages of the development of the *sene*:[83] the growing of the roots, the germination of the seed, the growth of the trunk and branches (fig. 71).

In the first (a), a circle represents the seed from which two segments emerge, the roots; in the second (b), the seed has three roots and a germ; in the third (c), the open circle denotes the beginning of the helicoidal growth of the stem and trunk; in the fourth (d), two segments represent the roots and four others, grouped on the other side of the circle, represent the four branches associated with the four varieties of *sene*. Likewise, *a* represents the *sene na,* *b* the *sene benu,* *c* the *sene gommuzu,* *d* the *sene urio.* These figures are also called "drawing of the evidence that the Fox found the *sene* that was in the former world."[84]

The spider climbed first on the central branch of the *sene na,* in order to weave Ogo's "words." Not succeeding, it came down again and took refuge on the branch whose fruit would later produce the *sene gommuzu,* around which it wove; then it left and sat down on the branch of the *sene benu,* where it tried to spin its web until it was finished.

It stopped at the top of the growing tree, and its "word" was then "like a band of fabric rolled up around itself." But its intentions were not realized; just as had happened during the first creation with the *sene,* it was unable to unite the four elements in the "word" it was weaving: the water was missing. This is why one says: "The four elements are not in the tree of the Fox (Ogo), there are only three of them."[85]

The *sene na* kept growing, trying to get back to the sky; the spider, seeing that the tree wanted to get back there too, fled and abandoned the work it had begun, while the tree reached the sky.

However, since it had grown in Ogo's placenta, the tree, like him,

---

83. Drawn with red earth, *bana,* under the funeral pots, *olugizu,* placed in the cave sheltering the *imina na.* These pots receive libations offered by the *olubaru,* dignitaries of the Sigui in charge of the cult of the ancestor Dyongou Sérou, represented by the *imina na;* for Dyongou Sérou and for the souls of deceased dignitaries, they pour beer into the pots, made from four varieties of sorghum *(emme sono dum banu, emme dum banu doruba, emme dum pilu, emme dum banu)* which symbolically group the four elements in the liquid. At Sanga, the *imina na* is kept in the cave called *kommo dama* near Upper Ogol.

84. *aduno girine be sene yurugu temme sere tonu.*

85. *yurugu kize si nay timmu vomo-ne tolo, si tanu to.*

had become impure. Amma dried it up and sent the *nommo titiyayne* to take back the seed. Transformed into a whirlwind, the *nommo* could not get hold of it; but it did tear off the leaves and fruit, which caused the tree to wither and die.[86] The leaves will be the origin of the creation of plants (especially of the *kilena*) and later on of wild animals, for one says: "All wild animals came from the leaf of the *sene.*"[87]

Thus, just as the death of the Andoumboulou will introduce death into the animal kingdom and the human race, so death will be brought to the plant kingdom by the death of the *sene na*. Both will be victims of Ogo's deeds and will remain proof of the impurity — the very germ of death — which he brought into creation.

The spider stayed on the ground for quite a while; then it tried to climb back up to the sky with the help of its thread. Amma refused to welcome it; he told it that it had waited too long, that it was forever associated with Ogo and with the Earth, and that it had become impure like them, since the *titiyayne* had caused the second piece of placenta to decay by crushing it.

The spider crawled down again. Later, it would spin "the cotton of the Fox," which is the ball of the ceiba (or kapok) tree, *togozo,* by climbing in the *sene urio:* the *minne iru keke,* who had descended with Ogo, was to stretch its thread to make the woof. Thus, to the very end, the spider would attempt to put the four elements in its web by weaving it in the branches of four *sene* — but without success. Its work would be incomplete, for this word would always lack the element "water." Ogo's "word" will remain the "dry word," i.e., the word of the stolen piece of placenta. On Earth, it will become the language taught to initiates of the Society of Masks, *sigi so,* "word of the Sigui," which does not contain the element "water" either: "In *sigi so* there is no water."[88]

The "incomplete word" of Ogo, woven by the spider, will be confronted with the "complete word," woven by the resurrected Nommo after his descent on the ark.[89] The first one, woven "in a spiral" by the

---

86. This is why the present tree no longer turns green in the rainy season.

87. *olunama fu sene lie-ne goy.*

88. *sigi so-ne di tolo.* This "word" is also the "word" of the Andoumboulou (installment 2, 3rd year).

89. Cf. *infra,* p. 492.

spider, does not have the substance of the second one, woven "in strips of crossed threads." So one will say of Ogo that he possesses the "coiled word," *so munno,* that is to say, fallacious, deceitful, and not the straight or "good word," *so ezu,* of his adversary and future conqueror, represented by the strip of cotton. When Ogo, transformed into the Fox and no longer able to express himself orally, will "speak" with his paws on the divination tables, he will trace only a "word" which is often incomplete and false.

The divination table of the Fox is divided into two distinct parts representing the "world above," the sky, and the "world below," Earth.[90] With regard to Ogo's "word," associated with both the *sene* and the work of the spider, these two parts represent, on the one hand, the creation of the *sene* seed in the sky and, on the other hand, the growth of the tree on the earth. The altar of the Fox, built in each village close to the first tables established nearby, is called *yuguru lebe.* The word *lebe,* according to an indigenous etymology, is the contraction of *ley* and *be,* "those two," and refers here to the Fox and the *sene,* who are forever associated. At the time of its consecration, a figure representing the insect is drawn on the altar, called "drawing of the spinning of (the fabric) of *togozo* by the spider."[91] The animal's head is placed to the south to recall that Ogo "emerged" from Amma's womb to the south (fig. 72).

Similarly, another drawing shows the work of the insect on the *sene,* represented by a circle surrounded by four dots: the one to the left and the one below represent the roots, the other two the thorns (fig. 73).[92] The movement of the spider — who began at a thorn placed to the east and spun around the tree as it grew — is represented by the spiral. This movement is recalled by the way in which the blood of a victim is poured over the altar to the Fox: the sacrificer lets the first three

---

90. Respectively, fig. 31, p. 156 and fig. 94, p. 295.

91. *dada togozu di-giru tonu.* Drawn with *yu* porridge, to recall that Ogo had sown the millet "without rain." This type of sowing which is sometimes still practiced, is called *ana ma bizu,* "hidden dry rain," which is to say, sowing done in dry weather; *bize* means "to push down and recover," for example, a seed that one sows. For the divination tables and the tables for instruction, cf. *infra,* p. 294 and ff.

92. Drawn with red earth, *bana,* on the altar of the masks, *bandini,* of Barna; it is also traced in the sand on the divination tables for instruction.

drops of blood flowing from the victim's throat fall to the north, west, and south; then he begins the spiral to the east and turns the victim above the altar.

S

FIG. 72: Drawing of the spider *dada yurugu geze gezene.*

The *sene na,* whose seed originally contained the four elements, will be resurrected by Amma and will descend on Earth with the ark of the *nommo semu* after his resurrection;[93] it will grow in the first family

---

93. Cf. *infra,* p. 450.

field of the *ginna.* According to tradition, it is still planted in the family field; for the *sene,* which is the first tree, represents in itself all plant life. During the ceremony of the Sigui, a sacrifice is offered to the *sene* of the field of the *ginna.* The celebrant cuts the throat of a red cock on the east side of the foot of the tree and pours out some sesame oil *(poli ni),* saying: "The sacrifice of the *sene* is for all trees; the tree is like the Nommo, like a person."[94] The beer of the Sigui is also poured at the foot of the tree.

Later, when the Fox will see the *sene na* in the fields of the *ginna,* one says — which, of course, is an image — "that he will take the wood to make his hand out of it."[95] For having impregnated each other, sharing the same essence, the Fox and the *sene* are "allied," *manu.* By making this "hand," the Fox wanted to imitate Amma's work: the object will have the form of the "egg of the world"; it will also be like a *sene* thorn[96] which, in the second universe, is evidence of the former world created before the *po.* Also, because Amma had made the *sene* with his saliva containing his "word," the Fox will be able to foretell the future: the "hand" or smoothing instrument made of *sene* and held by the diviner will participate in the revelation of destiny.

The events relating to Ogo's deeds and to the avatars of his placenta are represented on the ground by various arrangements for ritual purposes and for the instruction of the initiates.

Generally speaking, the rock paintings, the structures of puddled clay, the alignment of stones, and stacks of rocks, by virtue of the symbolism attributed to them, all bear evidence of mythical events said to be "of the old world," which are recalled and reenacted by certain rites. Earlier we presented the arrangement of the place where the

---

94. *sene-ne numpugu pugonu-go vogo tummu pu-moy; timmu nommo tozoy, inne tozoy.* Sesame oil is the testimony of the "words" and constitutes a purification, *dolu.* The red cock is *ene ana dazu,* which is to say, "with a flat comb"; the cock is said to be "full." A cock with a vertical and jagged comb is called *ene ana seruve* (installment 2, 2nd year).

95. According to another version, he made the hand out of *sene benu,* which has a harder wood and longer thorns.

96. For the Dogon, the object's lozenge shape, like the lozenge-shaped openings made in the sides of the Great Mask, are comparable to ovals and are also called *ene talu,* "chicken's egg." For the lozenge (shape), cf. *infra,* p. 465.

Dogon have situated "Amma's seat," *amma doy.* Various arrangements are sometimes set up inside or near a cave or rock shelter which, for the Dogon, are the images of the different first placentas. "The cave is like the placenta;"[97] it is also considered to be the first dwelling of the mythical ancestors.

1) At the locality of *nakile* (literally "herd of cows"), located to the south of the communities of the Ogols and of Barkou, a rather large rectangular stone, placed at the center of a vast rocky plateau, stands for the place where Ogo's umbilical cord was attached to his placenta — Earth — and recalls his first descent. On the same plateau a pile of stones, called *azagay pati,*[98] make up the "tomb" of the Fox.[99]

2) The crushing of the second piece of Ogo's placenta by the *nommo titiyayne* is situated at Yougo (map I). The entire boulder represents the "foot": "The boulder of Yougo is like the foot of the *nommo titiyayne* that trampled (it).[100] The three villages of Yougo, also called *yugo dummo tanu,* "the three boulders of Yougo," symbolically represent Yougo Pilou, the heel, Yougo Dogorou, the big toe, and Yougo Na, the little toe.

At Yougo Dogorou, two caves contain clay figurines representing the Andoumboulou: the shelter, called *imina sommo* or "cave of the body of the dead Andoumboulou" *(andumbulu yimu gozu kommo),* which houses the Great Mask *(imina na);* and the cave of masks, called *andubulum kommo,* assigned to the Andoumboulou, who are supposed to be still alive today.[101]

---

97. *kommo me anay.* For the caves, cf. *infra,* p. 434.

98. Literally: *"azagay,* destroyed"; *azagay* designates the insect; it is also the name of the mask worn by the Fox in the myth (installment 2, 3rd year), the same mask used to represent him in present ceremonies. For the *azagay* mask, see M. Griaule, *Masques dogons,* p. 565.

99. Installment 2, 9th year and ff.

100. *yugo dummo nommo titiyayne kubo nammi.* Yougo plays a fundamental part in the Sigui and in everything involving the institution of the masks.

101. For the figurines representing the Andoumboulou at Yougo Dogorou, cf. *Masques dogons,* p. 158, fig. 17 and plate XXIII C. See also *infra,* plate X, 1.

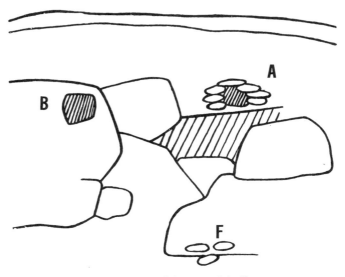

FIG. 74: A. Diagram of the cave of the Fox.

Similarly, in the Sanga region, the cave *demme togolu kommo* located near Barna represents, like those of Yougo, the "placenta" of the Yéban and of the Andoumboulou, their dwelling, and the place where the sex organ of the Andoumboulou was crushed by the *nommo titiyayne*[102] (map II, D and plate X, 2).

3) In the Sanga region, at Ka and on the slope of the plateau called *ka donnolo,* one of the caves, called *ka kommo* or "cave of the tearing" (from *kala* "to tear"), or *yurugu kommo,* "cave of the Fox," is considered to be Ogo's first dwelling on Earth; it recalls both the womb

---

102. This cave is also a replica of the mythical place where the *dama* of the Andoumboulou will be performed. It is at *demme togolu kommo* that the circumcision of the 3rd generation of men (the *tire)* will be portrayed (installment 2).

from which he emerged and the avatars of his placenta. About twenty meters wide, it is theoretically divided into three parts depth-wise (fig. 74 A). The back represents the torn-out placenta that formed the Earth; the part near the opening represents the second piece taken away during the second descent; the rock blocks before the opening represent the sun, that is, the rest of the placenta after its transformation.

A small structure of stone and clay, located to the right in A, is the dwelling of the Fox. To the left, in B, a similar arrangement of puddled clay against the wall is the receptacle of the spiritual principles of the *po banu*. Beneath this arrangement is a painting done in red ochre, *bana,* called *"tonu* of the resurrected placenta of the Fox" (fig. 74, B).[103]

It represents the avatars of this placenta: above is the first piece that was torn off, the Earth and the sun, remnant of his placenta; below, in parallel, the second piece placed over the hole in which the seeds were sown — a piece the Fox will later divide up.

In front of the cave at F, two large stones, called *dummo nay keregu-le nanna-le,* "stones of the left and right side of the sun," are supposed to be placed at two points of the sun's circumference, which itself is represented by the rocky platform, where they sit. Between the two, another stone is placed, called *dummo doy nay tummugu,* "stone seat of the rising sun." The whole thing represents the formation of the star, its future rising, and its positions at the solstices and equinoxes that man will observe.[104]

Near the depression, which runs alongside the rocky entablature of *ka donnolo* opposite the cave, a *sene na* is planted, which is considered to be evidence of the first tree having grown on Earth at the time of Ogo's descent, and on which the spider had done its work. Next to it, the first round "divination table" will be drawn for the instruction of the initiates (fig. 75).

This figure reproduces the six registers of "Amma's placenta."[105] The *bummo* drawn on this table, which portray Ogo's deeds, form the basic signs of the rectangular "divination tables" of the Fox used by

---

103. *yurugu me bulogu tonu.*
104. Volume I, installment 2, 1st year.
105. Cf. *supra,* p. 156.

diviners.[106] Their arrangement should be read as follows:

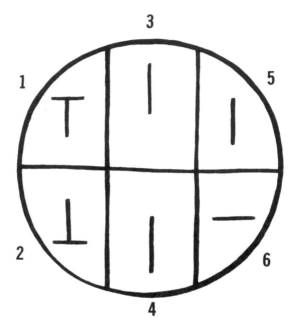

FIG. 75: The *bummo* of the round divination table.

Starting at 4, the "terrestrial house," Ogo ascends to the sky, in 3; he goes to 1, where he tears off what he can from the remnant of his placenta (transformed into the sun), and redescends to 2; in 6 is the Earth, the first stolen piece, where his deeds will lead him to "the tomb"; in 5 his "funeral blanket" is represented, evidence of his weakening, but also of Amma's future mercy, because he will permit the performance of his *dama*.

---

106. The "first divination table" is the one used to first teach the apprentice diviners; it is round. The rectangular table is considered to be a later form. For the use of the divination tables, cf. *infra,* p. 293 and ff.

The cave is the place for the performance of the rites for the end of mourning *(dama)* of the millet and of the Fox, who will intervene in the course of events that will take place on Earth. These rites are repeated annually by the goatherds; they celebrate the *dama* of the Fox, especially by playing the rhythms of the masks on the small wooden drum, the shape of which represents the first torn-out piece of placenta, the first ark;[107] the severed umbilical cord or navel is represented by a bulge made on one of the sides of the instrument.

4) One of the variants of the *sirige* mask recalls Ogo's journeys. In the caves, this variant is represented by the figure called "drawing of the *sirige* of the path of the Fox around the world that Amma created"[108] (fig. 161B, p. 559).

---

107. See plate IX, 1 and *supra,* p. 216.

The rites of Ka, performed by the goatherds, will be presented in their entirety in installment 2, 10th year. The children play the rhythms *kagandige* and *var(u) sigiri (Masques dogons,* p. 712 and ff).

108. *amma ganna mani yurugu gona gali sirige toy.*

CHAPTER III
SACRIFICE AND RESURRECTION OF THE NOMMO

I. EMASCULATION OF THE NOMMO

Amma's choice of the sacrificer and the victim. Separation of the souls of the victim.
Emasculation of the victim.

When he observed the disorder caused by Ogo in the creation, Amma
at first wanted to take his work back by entrusting it to the couple that
had developed in the other placenta. He also wanted to mark the beginning
of this work by an atonement and a test. Actually, inside the egg with the
double placenta the redeeming couple had been formed sixty periods
before Ogo and were opposed to the theft. The test, it seems, consisted
of putting the elements of this creation into their hands, and to make
another one out of it with the salvaged matter. In this way, Amma might
judge the power of those he was choosing to rule over it. However,
Amma did not want to reincorporate the stolen placenta into a new
universe, since it had become impure because of the incest Ogo had
committed; nor did he want to abandon it to create another placenta. So
he gave up the idea of a second creation, and the events continued in a
universe which remained unique.

The atonement for the disorder was the bloody sacrifice of the very
one who had to restore order. The *nommo semu,* being of the same
essence as Ogo and being his twin brother, shared the responsibility
somewhat and had at least to answer for the theft he had allowed to
happen. From this perspective, the sacrifice was a punishment.

This deed had to be a "purification," *uguru,* of the world to be
regenerated. In addition, it was to allow Amma to retrieve, one by one,
from the victim's body, the seats of the "word" with which he had
endowed it, and to continue his creative work by making it go forward,
so that the initial order disrupted by Ogo's deeds would be reestablished.
The sacrifice was a preparation for the descent on Earth of an ark
containing the principles, agents, and material for the reorganization.
Finally, it would allow for the expansion throughout the universe of the
power and forces possessed by the couple of *nommo anagonno,* who

were to remain with him in the "sky," and by the *nommo semu* on Earth.

In light of this, the design of the sacrifice of the Nommo is represented at Sanga by a series of altars delimiting a "mythical territory" where currently the rites are held that symbolically repeat the act of reorganization and its consequences: these rites renew its effects while again actualizing them at the same time.

A certain number of them are placed on an earth platform called *lebe dala,* "terrace of Lébé" (cf. Pl. XIII, 3), located to the south of the village of Upper Ogol, on which no one — except for the designated priests — may tread, and which represents the "sky" where the sacrifice took place, as well as the "placenta" of the victim.[1] Another series of altars extends this system of representations to the north, first across the groups of dwellings and then beyond (fig. 76).

These altars, different in form and in ritual usage, are associated:

— with the parts of the body, the vital organs, the blood of the victim, and the "word";

— with the stages of the sacrifice and resurrection and with time;

— with different stars and with space;

— with the mythical ancestors, the totemic clans, and social organization.

The arrangement outlines a schematic representation of three liturgical calendars (solar, Venusian and Sirian), which are combined with the current lunar calendar for determining the various dates of agrarian, family, clan, or general rites.

They are placed and consecrated to record on the ground and to commemorate:

— the execution and resurrection of the Nommo in the sky and before the descent of man on Earth;

— the execution and resurrection of Lébé Sérou, one of the eponymous ancestors, which will take place on Earth the second year after the descent of man;

— a third sacrifice — commemorative of the preceding ones — will be performed the fifth year after the descent of man on the Earth to consecrate the altars which, theoretically, were built at this stage of the myth. The immolation of the victim is followed by his consumption, which constitutes an alimentary communion for the entire totemic clan

---

1. Every year, the Hogon's millet from the field of Lébé is crushed on this terrace. "The millet of the Hogon that one crushes on the *lebe dala,* the *lebe dala* is like the sky" (*ogone yu lebe dalane dunoni, lebe dala alagala anay*).

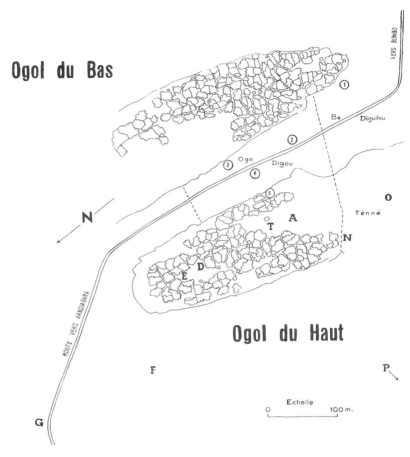

FIG. 76: Map of the Ogol villages: distribution of the principal altars.

and consecrates its structure. This last sacrifice is performed annually at the sowing feast, *bulu* (literally: "to bring back to life"). Anticipating the mythical events that follow, it has seemed necessary to us to explain the position and morphology of the altars as well as the figures drawn during their foundation, which allow for commentaries concerning the events of the second and fifth years. These are to be found in installment 2, which will deal with the continuation of the myth and the different representations in the same territory.

Figure 76 situates the *lebe dala* in the village of Upper Ogol (A), and indicates the chain of altars extending to the north (D, E, F, G).

Figure 77 shows the theoretical diagram of the sacrifice by the manner in which the principal altars of the *lebe dala* and those associated with them have been positioned. The dots joining A and B mark the flowing of blood from the emasculation of the Nommo to the south; those joining C, D, E, F, and G show the flow of sacrificial blood to the north, H, N, O, and P to the west.

AMMA'S CHOICE OF THE VICTIM AND THE SACRIFICER.

When Amma had ordered the *nommo anagonno titiyayne* to purify the Earth, one of the *nommo anagonno,* formed in the same part of the double placenta as Ogo, claimed that this should be his prerogative. Amma then designated him as the victim of the sacrifice. Comments on this choice emphasize that the *nommo anagonno* in question had revolted against Amma's order, saying that the *nommo titiyayne* had already acted by crushing Ogo's placenta, and that he himself had played no role at all. Amma then ordered the *nommo titiyayne* to sacrifice him, thus showing the permanent authority he had over his creatures by asking of them the obedience Ogo had refused him.

According to a similar version, Amma gave this order to the *nommo anagonno die* who, in turn, delegated his sacrificer, the *nommo anagonno titiyayne,* to perform the operation on the third, Ogo's twin brother.

Another, more aberrant version of the choice of the victim reflects the alert and sly personality of Ogo: according to this version, Amma first wanted to sacrifice Ogo, but Ogo argued that, through the divination, he would later be of great service to mankind and therefore it would be better to choose his twin brother to purify the world.

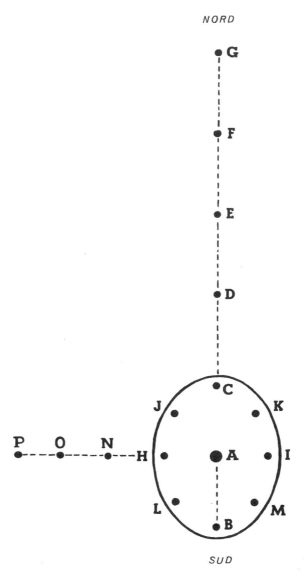

FIG. 77: Theoretical diagram of the altars located on the *lebe dala*
and on the "route of the blood."

Finally, it is said that Amma took the future form of Ogo, that of the Fox, to sacrifice the latter's twin brother; this was, on the one hand, to create disharmony between them, and, on the other hand, to weaken Ogo. Indeed, this operation was the beginning of the battle between Ogo and the one who was sacrificed, a struggle that would continue indefinitely, because it was necessary to the equilibrium and the proper functioning of the universe in formation.

Therefore, one sometimes says, when discussing his choice, that it is in the form of the Fox that Amma, dressed in yellow and having the appearance of a sexless being, approached the victim. He thus gave form to the profound desire of the Fox (who had only his male soul) to get back his female soul (or twin), entrusted to the other pair. In addition, he pushed the victim to seize the Fox's male soul, in order to possess his spiritual person in its entirety.

SEPARATION OF THE SOULS OF THE VICTIM.

The sacrifice of the *nommo anagonno,* known from that time on as *nommo semu* (sacrificed *nommo)*, lasted for eight periods.

Before performing any other work, Amma started to divide the four body souls of the *nommo anagonno* into two, thus creating four supplementary souls, which will be given to him later and will be his "sex souls," or *du kikinu.*

This preliminary deed profoundly modified the essence of those first beings created by Amma. At first androgynous in their fetal form as fishes, they will later be of different sexes: sexual union will become necessary for the propagation of the species. By dividing the victim's souls into two, Amma created the model for the separation of the sexes in general and simultaneously endowed his creatures with those spiritual principles associated with procreation.

Comments on this fundamental deed emphasize that if the *nommo anagonno* had not received his "sex souls," that is, the image or presence of the "ideal" female with whom he was to be united later, he would not have reproduced with her, but rather with Ogo's female twin whom Amma had entrusted to him. Now Amma wanted to prevent this from happening, since Ogo's female twin was tainted by his increasing impurity. In addition, this union of twins was not to produce triplets, *vuru,* considered to be superior to those that preceded them. Amma was thus protecting the *nommo anagonno* in advance against both a potential impurity and an "overstepping" of the fundamental rule of twinness, that is, an excess of which Ogo became the living symbol. The *nommo* had to conform in every way to the order established by the creator.

Finally, the physical identity between Ogo and the sacrificed *nommo,* both twins formed in the same placenta, implied that if the latter had had sexual relations with the female twin of the former, that deed would have been considered incestuous and, for him, would have consisted of "consorting with himself."

The importance of Amma's splitting the spiritual principles of the sacrificed twin into two, creating a total of eight *kikinu* (which will be allotted to every human being), is also stressed by a commentary on this act of the Nommo. For one says that the present *nommo anagonno,* testimony on Earth of the primordial androgyny and of the propagation of livings beings in Amma's womb, have eight body souls and eight sex souls.

During purification sacrifices performed near the water, the priest says: "Nommo, here is your purification, eight souls above, eight souls below, together sixteen."[2]

This version points to the future procreative role of the sacrificed *nommo anagonno;* as humanity's ancestor, he will give human beings their spiritual principles and will protect them. The souls of the victim are shared, for although he maintains his wholeness (eight above . . .), he gives part of it to human beings, his "sons" (eight below . . .). Through the intermediary of these principles he will watch over them and intervene during their lifetime.

To help the victim realize his future role, Amma will then take away his teeth, in order to keep the seat of the "word" at the stage where it becomes articulate language. A commentary emphasizes the role of the teeth by specifying that the victim lost every other one, the bottom teeth fitting into the gaps between those above them, and vice-versa. It is said: "At the moment of the Nommo's death, his teeth fell out in alternate

---

2. *nommo uguru uo uvo; da-go kikinu gagara-le donu-go kikinu gagara-le mona pelu kuloy sige.*

rows, the word began, weaving began, for he is the word that comes out."[3] The gaps between the teeth will allow for the passage of the "word," just as the threads of the warp let those of the woof pass through.

These teeth, which Amma would later send down to Earth, will become "little beads," *dugoy,* called *nani dugoy,* which will attest to the "kinship" that links the victim to men, his "sons." Thus, the "word" at the oral stage will be an agent of the fertility which it promotes: it emerges from the body to extend itself on the outside, comparable in this respect to that of the sex with which it is associated, and the product of which is the child. "The word of the *dugoy* of *nani* is like the things of the inside of the belly that follow each other."[4]

Amma's deed is currently recalled during sacrifices: the jaw and teeth of the victim are saved so that the species may reproduce.

The role of dispenser of spiritual principles that was conferred on the victim presently devolves upon every individual after death; one successively gives portions of one's life force to a certain number of descendants, and this allotment may span five generations. This role of the ancestor is the basis for the representations regarding the institution of the *nani.*[5]

When a child is born, it receives a part of its spiritual principles from an ancestor who becomes its guardian and of whom the child itself is the living testimony; it is the *nani* of that ancestor who, in turn, becomes its *nani.* When the family head questions the invisible through divination to find out which ancestor is involved, he prays to Amma, saying: "The *nani* of the child has come; in the name of Amma and of the Nommo, give the child the divided souls of the *nani,* in the hollow of (the pottery of) *somu di,* make him come out with gentleness (or kindness)."[6] When the *nani* ancestor has been designated, a sacrifice consecrates the *nani dugo* placed on the altar to the ancestors, *vageu.* One then strings the testimonial "teeth" of the Nommo on a little cord, which is tied around the child's neck.

---

3. *nombo varu vo yime-le tonumo lelia lelia yennumbo lelie dige, so konon mwey soyti-le sogodogo dige yenu mwey* (Wazouba dialect).

4. *nani dugoy so bere kolo-ne kize to dimme anay.*

5. For the institution of the *nani,* cf. G. Dieterlen, *Parenté et mariage,* p. 131.

6. *i nani via, amma boy-le nommo boy-le nani kikinu gammala i obu, i somu gono omo-le ve.*

During the *goru* ceremony, performed at the winter solstice, all the members of the family are brought together in the *ginna* for an offering to the ancestors (whose *nani* they are), and they recite a prayer called "Amma's name" (*amma boy*). It is preceded by the following lines which associate the living with the dead and recall the "sharing" of the souls of the sacrificed Nommo through their bestowal upon his descendants: "Amma has made 'the father emerge' (the harvest); for the men who are present or for those whom he is going to have emerge (be born), today is their day; may he (Amma) insure the stability of the remnant of what he is going to take away."[7]

One version of the division of the sacrificed Nommo's *kikinu* emphasizes the representations involving the Smith. The Smith will teach the men on the Earth of the Fox the skills that are necessary to their life and he will make the utensils, tools, and arms. These skills — especially agriculture — will all have the value of righting the disturbances caused by Ogo; they will contribute to the organization and development of human societies. In this respect, the role of the Smith on Earth will be similar to that of the victim: both will be associated with the other pair of *nommo anagonno,* the monitors of the universe, who will live in the "sky" with Amma. So, the Smith will be created as the "twin" of the victim, after the latter's resurrection, and will receive spiritual principles considered to be equal to, or originating from, those of the victim.[8] Therefore, one sometimes says that Amma, having divided the body *kikinu* of the *nommo anagonno*, kept half of them in his placenta until the formation of the Smith, who will receive them for his own.

EMASCULATION OF THE VICTIM.

Amma then proceeded with the emasculation of the *nommo anagonno,* this act bringing about a purification of the first double placenta. The victim was "seated," as it were, facing south, in the middle of his placenta where his umbilical cord was attached (fig. 77, A). The sacrificer, i.e., the *nommo titiyayne,* folded the penis back against the cord and cut off the whole. Thus, Amma separated the victim from his placenta and from his sex at the same time.

---

7. *amma ba gonu, inneu vazungo inneu gonevodo iye bay, gonese vazungo pegu pege.*
8. Cf. *infra,* p. 406.

He then had the sex organ placed in the center of the placenta, next to where the cord was attached, and made the victim sit on top of it.

The *sigi tolo* star, Sirius, was born of this emasculation. It is evidence of the placenta and umbilical cord of the sacrificed Nommo and, in view of the victim's role as reorganizer of the world, it is the image of the center of the universe, because "Sirius is the navel of the world."[9]

It is said: "The Nommo slaughtered by Amma, his *kikinu* before he was slaughtered, (Amma) knew the bad words (of anger) which were going to come. He split each of the four *kikinu* in two (i.e., down the middle). Amma created him like his twin brother. After that, this Nommo argued with (Amma). Amma cut off his sex, folded it back against the cord and sat him in this spot. He cut the cord. This cord became *sigi tolo*."[10] The operation was done in this way so that the weight of the sacrificed Nommo pressing on his sex made everything come out that it contained and that Amma wanted to preserve. More precisely, the result of this action was that the nucleus of the testicles came out, which will become the *anagulo* or "hatchet of rain."[11]

According to a similar version, it is the sacrificer who, pressing on the sex, emptied it of its contents. It is said: "The sacrificing *nommo* sitting on the testicles caused the piece (nucleus) to be vomited up, and one calls it *anagulo*. (The sacrificing *nommo*) sitting on the sex of the sacrificed *nommo* made the piece of the nucleus come down."[12]

The blood at the emasculation flowed, impregnating the placenta and giving it new life. The blood of the arteries, *volu ana illi,*[13] and the accompanying life force, or *nyama,* penetrated it.

Now, a being's sex is its most living aspect. This impregnation was a purification — that is to say, a revitalization — of the placenta which, in

---

9. *sigi tolo aduno bogi.*

10. *amma nommo semi-go kikinu semele vo so monu vedo-go igi bia. kikinu vomo nay logoro-go-ne de de gamma. amma bey dine-go manu. vogo onune nommo vogo amma belley day voya. tere-go keze ogo-go-ne munna, ko ku-ne daya ogo-go keze. ogo-go sigi tolo bi. nommo-go dena, uguru uguri-ne inera seme.*

11. Another derivation gives *gulo,* "vomited"; *anagulo* would mean "male vomited."

12. *nommo semene dolo ku-go-ne daya gunni gulomu. anagulo gi nommo semi ogo ku-go-ne daya dolo gunni sununi. dolo gunni* refers to the nucleus in the testicles.

13. For the Dogon, the sex organ is nourished by two arteries (*volu ana,* "male veins"), one of which runs from the testicles to the penis, the other from the penis to the kidneys.

spite of the imposed separation, was to remain pure and "alive," *omo.*

It is said: "In order to perform a purification with the *nommo (anagonno),* the *nommo die* cut off his sex, folded it back along his umbilical cord, which he cut, sitting (the victim on top). The blood of this emasculation entered the placenta; it increased the *nyama* of the placenta. The *nyama* of the sex passed into the placenta, and the placenta became alive."[14] The *yayaga* plant that will be used on Earth for purification was born on the spot where the blood had fallen.[15]

However, this purification affected not just the placenta to which the victim was attached. Indeed, at the moment of the emasculation, Amma placed Ogo's placenta (namely, the sun) under that of the sacrificed Nommo. The blood and the life force that had come from the sex penetrated it, thus purifying the two united placentas. Therefore, stressing the importance of the meeting of the momentarily re-united placentas, one says: "At the moment of all those things, the sun and Sirius met for the first time."[16]

This act of purification of fundamental importance, brought about by the emasculation, is remembered at every sacrifice taking place today. A preliminary victim — generally less important than the victim of the actual sacrifice — is slaughtered beforehand: this operation, called *mene*, constitutes a purification of the altar in question. It also has a value in regard to divination.[17]

From another perspective, the blood from the emasculation of the *nommo anagonno* is compared to the menstrual flow lost by women each month. It is said that the victim bled "bad blood," the bad part of the blood of Ogo's placenta (from the piece he tore out), that is, the

---

14. *nommo die nommo-le uguru kunnu, tere keza ogo-ne timma keza; ko ku-ne daya; kikinu nay doba yurugu-mone yoy; tere yama me-ne tana, me omo bi.*

15. *yayaga* apparently comes from *ya,* "to leave," or from *yagara,* "to place upon." Another popular derivation would have it derive from *yaga,* "other," since the plant grows like mistletoe, differing from its means of support. It may take the place of the *pelu* bark (cf. *infra,* p. 330); it is passed over the tongue of someone who is being purified, after he has bitten into a *kilena* coal; the officiant then passes an ear of millet over his body, "putting back in place" the contents of his clavicles, the seeds, which were disturbed by the impurity.

16. *kize-ko varu-le, nay-le sigi tolo-le segeri.*

17. Cf. *infra,* p. 389. The word *mene* comes from *me,* "piece" (of the sacrifice).

blood that will be incapable of "forming the child" in a women.[18] However, he kept the good part of the blood of Ogo's placenta (that of the sun), which he added, mixed with his own, and which Ogo would never get back. This comparison — based on the conjunction of the sun and Sirius — once again emphasizes Ogo's incompleteness, which will manifest itself as sterility.

Finally, the separation of the *nommo anagonno* from his placenta, i.e., his birth — brought about at the same time as the emasculation — is also understood as the symbol of the separation of the sexes that it accomplished. Sacrificed as a hermaphrodite, the victim will come back to life in the form of two beings of different sexes, man and woman. Moreover, since the placenta, considered to be the twin of the newborn Nommo, was separated from the *nommo anagonno,* this deed also forms the image of the prohibition that will be associated with a sexual union between male and female twins, a union which Amma originally had intended for the *nommo anagonno* and which the deeds of Ogo had made impossible.

These representations are recalled at childbirth: a boy's umbilical cord is pinched between two sticks (of *pelu, kilena* or *satele*) or between two shards of pottery and is cut off between the shards. These two sticks or shards recall the penis and testicles of the victim, which were folded over and cut off. This operation is called "cutting of the cord (between) the shards put on top of each other" (*ogo kezu gegeme timme*). The cord is cut to separate the newborn child from his twin, the placenta: moreover, one pretends to cut off the sex, to demonstrate that sexual relations with one's twin are forbidden.

The blood then flowed from the center to the south, to a place called *illi yalu tege,* "place of the dripping blood."

At the very end, in this same place, *yazu* or Venus was born in the *obia*[19]

---

18. The red paint which is put on the masks after they have been painted black is seen as the blood from the Nommo's emasculation. On Earth, the evidence of this blood will be the "red frog," *toru banu,* (cf. volume 1, installment 2, 3rd year).

19. The Dogon ritually observe six positions of Venus, usually called *yazu,* a word meaning "(star) of the morning come" or "early in the morning." A star is *obia* when it is not visible; it comes from the term *obo,* "to incubate (eggs)" (used for a fowl which sits on the ground or incubates ‹eggs›); in fact, one says that the invisible star is "incubated" (*obie*) until the time it appears. All of Venus' positions will be commented upon p. 514 and ff.

position (fig. 77, B), that is, it was invisible. This planet, evidence of the flow of the blood from the victim's sex, will also be representative of the blood shed later by women every month. "The trace (of the blood) of the sacrificed Nommo, which stopped at *igibie,* (created) Venus *obia.* "[20]

The sex was emptied of its contents and placed by Amma in the west, in the place where Venus was to appear in the second position, called "star of the west," *donno tolo* (or *albana tolo*) (fig. 77, H).

The cord, *koni,* stayed in the center; there a tiny little star emerged, *yazu danala tolo,* "star that accompanies Venus."

Thus, the first stages of the sacrifice of the *nommo anagonno* were at the origin of the formation of the stars and planets. Their presence in the world of spiraling stars, prefigured by first the rolling up and then the unrolling of the *yala* of the primordial egg and by their movement in space triggered by Amma's deed, will testify to the reorganization of the universe produced by the sacrifice.

Amma put aside the contents of the sex of the emasculated hermaphrodite for later use, just as he would utilize the pieces of the victim's body. This action formed one of the fundamental stages of "Amma's work" with the victim's body: his purpose, as we recall, was to retrieve, one by one, all the "articulations of the word" originally developed inside the *po* seed and bestowed upon the *nommo anagonno.*[21] By appropriating the contents of the sex, he appropriated the eighth word, evidence of the *po 's* germination and of the fertility originally conferred on the victim and on his twin brothers. The sperm or seed of the sacrificed Nommo contained:

— water, *di,* male and female, which are, respectively, fresh water and sea water or "salt water," *neu di;*

— "rain hatchets," *anagulo;*

— convenant stones or "beads," *dugoy,* the images or doubles (*bibile*) of the first seeds;

— some cowries, *kele;*

— the image (*bibile*) of two *anagonno sala* siluri or "ordinary *anagonno.*"

These six elements have a symbolic relationship to the six *yala* of sex

---

20. *nommo semi bummo, igibie-ne kali yazu obia. igibie* is the name of the altar which is, on Earth, the witness for this celestial place. cf. p. 368.

21. Cf. *supra,* p. 165.

of the *po pilu* Amma created to produce the second universe after the first one had failed, and which made up the center of the internal spiral of the primordial egg: in relation to this figure, beginning from the center of the spiral, they come in the following order: water, male and female *anagonno, dugoy, anagulo, kele.* Thus, one emphasizes the fact that the sacrifice of the *nommo anagonno* constituted a renewal of the universe along principles similar to those which had regulated its creation.

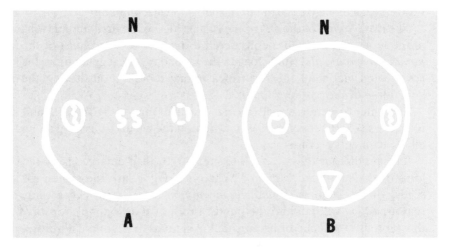

FIG. 78: *tonu* of the contents of the sacrificed *nommo's* semen.

The semen of the sacrificed Nommo and its content, which will later be essential to life on earth and which Amma kept in the sky, are represented by figures drawn at the foundation of the totemic sanctuaries. One says of these drawings: "The six things that were separated, in the *yala* of the *po's* body they are drawn as signs in the sanctuary of the first *binu*" (fig. 78, A and B).[22]

22. *po gozu-ne kize bullogo kuloy yala tobe, binu ginu-ne binu polo tonu tononu.*

The figure is drawn in porridge of *yu* and *ara geu* on the ground of a *bina ana* sanctuary at its construction; it is inverted for the construction of a *binu ya.* The *binu ya* are associated with sowing, pregnancy, and the season called *ba do;* the *binu ana* are associated with the harvest, birth, and the season called *ba go.*

In another more symbolic respect, these six elements are male or female:
— fresh water is male, sea water is female;
— the *anagonno sala* are a pair of mixed twins;
— the rain "hatchets" are male;
— the covenant stones are female;
— the cowries are female.

As agents of the fertility of the victim, these elements indicate his future deeds on Ogo's Earth and his kinship with humanity.

The two *bummo* of the *anagonno sala* prefigure the first human twins at the fetal stage: they are considered to be the "sons" (*unum*) of the *nommo anagonno* and will belong to the second mythical generation, the resurrected victim in the form of a human couple constituting the generation of the "fathers" (*bau*).[23]

The water from the sex will fall in the form of rain on Ogo's Earth and form the sea and networks of fresh water on the ground, carrying along all the elements it contained.

It is said that the *dugoy,* that is to say, the "births," emerged from the loins of the sacrificed Nommo: "The *binu dugoy,* are the semen (or seeds) of the Nommo" (*binu dugoy nommo toy*). With every rainy season, *dugoy* will fall into the ponds. Proof of the Nommo's fertility, they are also evidence of his spiritual principles or *kikinu.* Therefore, the clavicular contents, symbol of the eight primordial seeds, will be represented by the *dugoy:* "The *dugoy* of the *binu* are like the seeds that were in the clavicles of the sacrificed Nommo and that emerged. The *dugoy* are the living evidence of the seeds in the clavicles."[24] The *dugoy* worn by the Hogon and the priests will be the living testimony and basis of the "sex souls" of cereal grains and of the basic edible plants.

---

23. Cf. *infra,* p. 390.

24. *binu dugoy nommo semi ani guyo-ne dene tobe goy; dugoy ani guyo dene serey.* The *dugo* is made of a perforated oval or round stone, studded with either an old glassware piece (collected in the bush near formerly inhabited areas), modern beads bought at the market, or even a small iron ring. Its color varies greatly. The Dogon distinguish between four types of *dugoy:* the *ogo dugoy* worn by the Hogons, the *binu dugoy* worn by the totemic priests, the *amma dugoy* worn by the priests and priestesses of Amma, the *nani dugoy* worn by individuals of both sexes. The first two originated in the contents of the sperm; the *nani dugoy* are the avatars of the sacrificed Nommo's teeth (cf. *infra,* p. 322). Pierced and strung on a small cord, the *binu dugoy* will first be worn on the totemic priest's

The victim's *anagulo,* evidence of the life force, *nyama,* will fall during thunder storms, because the "lightening," the "thunder, and the fire" are the forces of the *nommo anagonno* in the sky atmosphere.

Because of this, certain *anagulo* will make up the base of altars called *andugo, "dugo* of rain" or "male *dugo,"* which will retain a part of the sacrificed *nyama,* and through which one may appeal to the *kikinu say ya* of the male *nommo die* to obtain rain.[25]

---

wrist, then on his neck (in the course of the successive ordination rites). The *nani dugoy* is placed around the child's neck by the head of the joint family after the divination has revealed the identity of his *nani* (ancestor) and the object has been consecrated on the altar to the ancestors (*vageu*) with a bloody sacrifice (G. Dieterlen, *Les Ames des Dogon,* p. 133 to 135). The color of the *dugo* plays a role in its attribution. So as to recall the four categories, the *toy* of the *dugo,* composed of four strokes, is drawn in porridge of *ara geu* and *yu* on the façade of the sanctuary of the Nommo totem (at the ordination, *duguru,* of the priest and at the *bulu).*

25. The Dogon call the hatchets and mallets included in their stone tools *anagulo;* they are evidence of ancient settlements and are still frequently found in the bush of Western Africa.

They distinguish between three types of *anagulo,* with regard to their shapes:

— *anagulo ana ley,* "with two mouths" (elongated with two cutting edges in the shape of a fish).

— *anagulo ana turu,* "with one mouth (classic hatchet with one edge).

— *anagulo dunulio,* "in a ball" (a round stone).

They are part of the totemic material and are most often kept in an unused millstone, *tono,* placed near the door of the sanctuary. This is why the three types of *anagulo* are sometimes drawn on a façade above the millstone.

In the three categories, the distinctions are determined by the color of this stone equipment:

1) *anagulo minne ne yoze,* "that penetrates the earth," grey in color (*purugu*). This object, which may be found after a thunderstorm (since it is supposed to go down into the earth and come back out again after having dug its way), is kept in the unused millstone placed next to the sanctuary in use or in the *sogo* of the field.

2) *anagulo timmu-ne yau kunnoze,* "that strikes down (with lightning) the trees"; spotted black and white. This object is kept inside the sanctuary.

3) *sau anagulo sugoze,* "that descends on the bush," black in color. This object is part of the material of the *andugo* altar.

The first two kinds of hatchets are supposed to fall during a storm on a field or on a tree in order to warn the owner of the violation of a prohibition, more serious in the second case. The individual must purify himself under penalty of being struck down by a hatchet of the third type. The *andugo* altar also contains a pierced *dugoy,* image of the clavicular seeds; one of the altar's stones represents the sacrificed Nommo's "clavicle."

The cowries, or *kele,* that come from the sea are considered as something alive (and pure); it is said: "The cowries are alive" (*kele omoy*). They will be the tokens of the "word" of the Nommo's sex and, therefore, will be associated with the first economic exchanges, consisting of the exchange of women between families. A gift of 320 cowries (80 x 4) seals the transactions preceding an engagement: the cowries from the man's *ginna* are offered by his mother to the mother of his fiancée. As ritual objects, the cowries serve as ornaments, and are used for offerings and for divination; they are also the money used for commerce.

In each family dwelling, a piece of pottery called *kele bundo,* "pot of cowries," containing 400 (80 x 5) cowries is placed in one of the granaries of the group. The number here is the symbol of the count in base 80 of the five first mythical generations.[26] This piece of pottery is placed on the terrace at the funeral of a member of the family.

Playing on a popular etymological comparison with the word *kele,* "that which remains," one says: "The rest of the sacrificed Nommo's head entered the water; it produced cowries put in the *bunno* that was placed in the granary; this is man's wealth."[27]

Made of elements belonging to the animal and mineral kingdoms, "the content of the sex was like a shining metal." This commentary revealing the variety of colors of the contents testifies to the richness and fecundity of the sacrificed Nommo as well as to the multiplicity of his future deeds. His beneficent deed, powerful and permanent, which will regenerate the universe, is recalled by the totemic priest when he thanks Amma during the sowing feast after the sacrifice performed inside the sanctuary by saying: "The sex of the 'master of the water'

---

26. Cf. *infra,* p. 390.

27. *nommo semi ku kele di-ne yoa, nani bunno kele kunne guyo-ne dananu, inne ogoy.*

The Dogon term is comparable to the Bambara word *kolo,* which derives from the Hindu *kauri.*

The Dogon attribute the importation of cowries to the Guellagui who, they claim, once ruled West Africa; they call that society *la la tire,* "first ones, first ancestors." The use of cowries as money may have replaced the cotton band, measured by the cubit, among the Sarakollé during the Ghana Empire period. For the cowry and its representations in West Africa, cf. G. Dieterlen, *Mythe et organisation sociale en Afrique Occidentale,* pp. 133 and 134.

that was cut off is the image of the good things that Amma will bring into the world."[28]

The emasculation is represented by figures drawn under the family altars *ommolo ana* and *ommolo ya* (literally: "alive male and female") that are raised when a *ginna* is founded.

The altar *ommolo ana,* placed in the courtyard of the dwelling and concealed by a low wall, represents the sacrificed Nommo's sex after the emasculation. It is composed of a clay cone (made with earth taken from the family pond) completely covered with red ochre, *bana,* into which a male *anagonno sala* silurus caught alive is cast. A cavity has been hollowed out at the top of the altar, so that water can be put in it; it is covered by a stone that hides it, since the fish, although enclosed in the altar, is considered to be living in this water.

During its foundation, a figure is drawn in red ochre (*bana*) on the site of the altar, called *ommolo ana danu tonu,* "drawing of the founding of the *ommolo ana"* (fig 79, A), the whole of which represents the two testicles and penis of the sacrificed victim.

This figure symbolizes at the same time the altar's structure in which the clay envelops — besides the fish — a vertically placed piece of *ga guyo* wood (representing the penis) and some accompanying objects: a coiled iron bracelet on the right, which is the victim's "arm" (associated with the right testicle); a piece of pottery called *somu di* on the left, containing roots soaking in water (associated with the left testicle). The roots are taken from four trees (baobab, butter-tree, *yullo,* and *sa),* which will later, near the pond, attest to the victim's resurrection.[29] The water in which they have been soaked will be used to care for the sick and to purify family members in the event of the violation of a prohibition.

The altar *ommolo ya,* placed in one of the dwelling's storehouses (*kana*), represents the body of the sacrificed Nommo after his emasculation. It is composed of a wooden statuette, representing the "person," a piece of pottery of *somu di* like that of the *ommolo ana* and of similar usage,[30] and a ball of red ochre, *bana,* which represents the

---

28. *di bana ogo kezi amma aduno-ne kize ezu uo tagaraydo yalay.* Out of respect, the name of Nommo is not pronounced; he is always called "master of the water."

29. Cf. *infra,* p. 493.

30. The roots are taken from plants other than those used for the pot of the *ommolo ana.*

blood circulating through the body. Under the altar a figure has been drawn, called *ommolo ya danu tonu,* "drawing of the founding of the *ommolo ya"* (fig. 79, B).

The two central dots of the figure represent the two male and female spiritual principles, *kikinu bummone,* of the victim's body. The five dots on either side show the five generations to which each individual is linked by his maternal or paternal lineage. The four dots below are evidence of the femininity of the altar. Similarly, the figure is associated with marriages, the central dots being the husband and wife, the lateral dots the generations descended from them. At the time of the annual collective sacrifice, one says: "The *ommolo ya* is like marriage."[31]

These two altars receive sacrifices offered by each of the family members: after the marriage, to ask the *nommo semu* to grant the spiritual principles of the desired children; after each birth, offerings are made to thank him and to entrust him with the life of the newborn child.[32]

2. OGO'S CIRCUMCISION

Ogo's second reascent. Ogo's circumcision. Ogo's third and final descent. The transformation of Ogo into the Pale Fox. The divination tables of the Fox.

OGO'S SECOND REASCENT.

When the emasculation took place, Ogo, who thought the victim was near its end and who wanted to obtain what he lacked, namely his female twin and his placenta, reascended to the sky. Amma, however, had put his female twin and the female seeds under safekeeping. He also moved the sun, the remnant of Ogo's placenta, so that Ogo would be unable

---

31. *ommolo ya yadi anay.*

32. The foundation of these altars and their family and medical uses will be treated in installment 2 (2nd and 3rd years).

to get near it. Having it emerge from his womb, where it had been during the emasculation, Amma pushed it out to the west. The sun came out through a "hole" which Amma had left open for this purpose. But before making the star rise, Amma packed the "life of the world" into the hole and formed the white cow, said to be "of death." For the opening left for the emergence of the sun recalls the rebel's deeds that are the cause of the appearance of death on the Earth that was formed from his placenta.[33]

Unable to approach his burning placenta, Ogo instead approached the victim and seized his four sex souls located in his foreskin. Ogo also tried to take his semen, a bit of which he caught with his mouth. Then h ɔ fled, following the line of blood flowing from the emasculation.

A figure called *"tonu* of the hunting Fox," *yurugu andolone tonu*[34] (fig. 80), drawn on the divination tables used for instruction, shows Ogo taking possession of the sex souls: the four lines are the four souls; they are on either side of the central figure, made of a small pile of stones, which is the sun into which Ogo's foreskin will be thrown later. The drawing is also the schematic image of Ogo's later transformation into a four-legged creature.

When he came to the end of the "line of blood," Ogo wanted to get back down to Earth with his booty. The two *anagonno sala* that were in the victim's semen were witness to his deed; the male one alerted the *nommo titiyayne*.[35] Without waiting for Amma's orders, he tried to stop

---

33. These facts are recalled by a game called "image of Amma creating the white cow of death in the hole of the sun's emergence" (*yimu na pilu nay bunnone amma tono yala*), which is played after the harvest with a rather long string, the ends of which are tied together. A series of figures the players make by changing the shape of the string, which is first placed in a square around a low, rounded pile of dirt, represent the moon, the sun, and the red and white cows.

34. *andolone* means "man who grows tired" (by walking) and is the synonym of *danane:* "he who is seated" (to watch from a hunting hut, *dana togi).* Both terms refer to the hunter and connote the two techniques, pursuing the game or sitting and watching for it.

35. Symbolically, the *anagonno sala,* cast into the *ommolo ana* of the *ginna* (cf. *supra,* p.

Ogo; he did not succeed, but only managed to catch the very end of Ogo's sex with his mouth and to bite it off, circumcising him with his teeth. In this way, he got back the sex souls. Then, to get the stolen semen back, the *nommo titiyayne* broke Ogo's teeth, tore out his tongue, the organ of the "word," and wounded his throat, depriving him of part of his voice. This deed foreshadowed Ogo's loss of the spoken word.

During a circumcision that takes place today the officiant says: "The Nommo saddled and bridled Yourougou to go and circumcise him: his teeth that were torn out fell and became *tolo dullogu.* The trace (or line cut by the knife) of the circumcision is like the incisors of the Nommo"[36] (recalling that the operation was performed by the *nommo titiyayne* with his teeth).

FIG. 80: Sign of the hunting Fox.

Once again, Ogo's haste caused events of which he will be the victim. For, according to a similar version, Amma, having formed the sex souls by splitting up those of the sacrificed Nommo, intended to give them to Ogo, as he had done with Ogo's brothers, in order to reestablish the order that had been disrupted by his deeds. Since Ogo had taken them without waiting and without Amma's permission, they were taken away from him at the circumcision performed by the *nommo titiyayne.*

OGO'S CIRCUMCISION.

Ogo's circumcision was a punishment for the theft he had committed: "The *nommo titiyayne* circumcised Ogo; the circumcision represents Ogo stealing part of his placenta"[37] in Amma's womb at the time of his premature departure.

---

265), represents the one who warned (informed) Amma of Ogo's acts: he is considered to be a protector and defender of the family's fertility from outside dangers.

36. *nommo yurugu kegere para kalumu kunna ule olu gono yadoga; tonu vomo baga suga tolo dullogu bi; selume olu gonu nommo tonu giru-gin vo.*

37. *nommo anagonno yurugu ala nomu; olu gonu vogo yurugu me vo guyo-go yalay yalanu. ala no,* "to drink the porridge (of the circumcision)" is a euphemism for: to circumcise, to undergo circumcision; circumcision (*ogo guzu kezu,* "to cut off the skin of the sex organ," precisely) is also called *olu go,* "to go out in the bush."

Tearing out the foreskin was the ransom for Ogo's tearing off the placenta: it will later be repeated for all men: by circumcising a human being, one repeats what Ogo did (on the cosmic plane) to try to gain possession of his female twin as well as what was inflicted upon him in order to separate him from the stolen spiritual principles and from the foreskin which had become their physical support.

The four sex souls recovered by the operation changed into a tree, the *kilena,* represented as a trunk with three roots. Therefore, putting this series of events into a single image, one sometimes considers Ogo as being "attached" to the *kilena,* (i.e., to the four souls he had stolen) and in this way undergoing the ordeal inflicted by the *nommo titiyayne* to take back the sex souls by circumcising him . . .

Ogo's circumcision is recalled by a series of figures.

The first one, somewhat schematic, is called *"tonu* of the Fox's circumcision"[38] (fig. 81). Inside an oval representing Ogo's ark, a rocket-shaped outline represents the *kilena,* formed by the four sex souls of the *nommo,* under which Ogo is tied (in his future four-legged form), represented by the central line and four lateral segments. The fanning out at the bottom, recalling the position of the roots, contains a vertical segment which is the foreskin after its removal. The three segments fanning out below symbolize the roots of a tree, the *saselu,* that grew on the blood of the circumcision.

The second figure, called *"toy* of the Fox's circumcision"[39] (fig. 82), is a more realistic representation of the operation: the four sex souls of the *nommo semu* are positioned in a bundle forming the trunk of the *kilena,* the "roots" of which fan out at the bottom. Ogo (in the form of the Fox) is bound on his back; the *nommo titiyayne* circumcises him with his teeth.

Liberated by the *nommo titiyayne,* the sex souls then went near the site where the purifying plant *yayaga* had grown from the blood of the emasculation of the *nommo semi* and "lay down there," awaiting their final assignment.

---

38. *nommo anagonno yurugu olu gonu tonu.* Drawn in red ochre (*bana*) on the back of the calabash *koro pomuru* of the dignitaries of the Sigui, the *olubaru,* during the ceremony.

39. *nommo anagonno yurugu olu gonu toy.* Engraved on the calabash of the female dignitary of the Sigui, the *yasigine,* and packed with *ara banu* porridge.

A figure called *"tonu* of the ark surrounding the *yayaga* grown during the emasculation of the Nommo"[40] bears an outline of the *yayaga* in the center of the ark (on which the *nommo semu* will descend after his resurrection). The four lines drawn under the plant are the four sex souls or the roots of the *kilena.*

The blood from Ogo's circumcision fell on the placenta of the *nommo semi,* right where the blood from the *nommo semi's* emasculation stopped flowing, next to the place where Venus had been formed (fig. 84). Then Mars, or *yapunu tolo* ("star of menstruating women"), was born, also in the *obia* position, that is , it was invisible. It was made of "soft copper," *menu olu;* "When *yapunu tolo* was created, it was red like fire, now the red is diminishing."[41] For although it was blood-red at the time of its creation, its color had to fade with time.

Mars is represented by a figure called *"tonu* of the star of menstruating women" (fig. 85).[42] A grain of *anu* is placed at the center of a circle from which four rays radiate, the feminine number, since the star is evidence of the removal of Ogo's foreskin, or of his feminine aspect. These four rays are also evidence of the four *yala* of the *anu* in the primordial egg. The name of the star, its association with the blood of Ogo's circumcision — the very first of its kind, and which will be repeated by the circumcision of men on Earth — and with the *yala* of the *anu,* all attest to the fact that this blood may be considered as being of the same essence as menstrual blood. The bleeding circumcised man is *puru,* impure, as if he were menstruating. The circumcision itself is called *anau punia,* "menstruation of the men"; the circumcised men are isolated during their retreat as are the women every month. Mars will be

---

40. *nommo olugonu yayaga te koro gonu tonu* (fig. 83). Drawn in porridge of *ara banu* on the façade of the totemic sanctuary to the left of the door during the second ceremony of the priest's ordination (*duguru*). The word circumcision here replaces "emasculation," which is exactly the operation performed on the victim.

41. *yapunu tolo manu-le yau-gin banu-go be, kanney banu gammio.*

42. *yapunu tonu tolo.* Drawn in red ochre (*bana*) under the figure of the *ani na* on the wall of the "house of menstruating women," *yapunulu* (installment 2, 1st year).

At the Sigui, a red dot is drawn on the *sigi doy* ("seat of the Sigui") to recall the origin of Mars: this dot is one of the four *yala* of the *anu* in Amma's womb; the three others "are lost" — yet another image of Ogo's incompleteness.

visible from Earth at the time of the first menstruation of Ogo's female "twin," Yasigui. This association also emphasized a similarity between the blood from the placenta that Ogo had torn out and the blood from the foreskin, as well as the respective femininity of each.

Before Ogo's circumcision, Amma had entrusted the placenta of his

FIG. 83: *tonu* of the ark surrounding the *yayaga*.

female twin, taken away by the side of Ogo's, to the *nommo titiyayne.* To perform the operation, the fish moved like a star: turning in place, it spun five times in one direction and five in the other. First grabbing a part of Ogo's sex organ, it began again to turn around the star, trying to hook onto the rest of it, hence the name of *anagonno,* "man hook" or "male hook." The sex organ thus virtually captured from the other is called *anagonno doy,* or "seat of the *anagonno."*

Resisting this operation, Ogo struck the fish and, as a result, detached his placenta, which whirled into space, along with his foreskin. The placenta placed itself near the sun, whereas the foreskin was pushed into the sun by the fish, where it turned into a sort of lizard, *nay.*

In this way the *nommo titiyayne,* sent the foreskin (transformed into the *nay*) into the sun and practically took possession of Ogo's virility. At the same time, he surrounded Ogo's female twin and her placenta with his tail, thus heightening the frustration he inflicted upon the patient.

"The foreskin of Yourougou circumcised by the *anagonno* and

Fig. 84: Venus *obia.*

the placenta of Yasigui fixed (stuck) to the tail of the silurus ran together. The *anagonno* chased Yourougou's foreskin and put it in the sun; the placenta of Yasigui was placed next to the sun."[43]

The lizard, meanwhile, acted on the sun. As living evidence of the foreskin, it shared the aggressiveness of Ogo, from whom it had been torn. It circumcised the star. After it passed into the sun, there emerged from it the insect *nay na,* "mother of the sun," produced during the female circumcision of the sun by the *nay.* "The *nay* ran towards the sun and entered it; it is the sun which it circumcised; that which it cut off fell below. One says it is the cicada. The *nay na* is a flame cut from the sun, which descended upon Earth."[44] The insect is called "mother of the sun," *nay na,* because the clitoris is "like the mother of a woman whom it feeds"; "a woman's sex organ is like a field that one cultivates."[45] This

---

43. *yurugu anagonno olu gonu boru kuzu-le yasigi me anagonno dullo-ne dana-le belley doba, yurugu, boru guzu anagonno nanna, nay-ne kunni, yasigi me nay genne-ne bi.*

44. *nay nay-ne doba yoa; nayi olu gona, pollo-go donune sugi nay na gi. nay na nay nine polla minne-le sugi.* The insect will be drawn on the forge oven since it contributes to the fire's heat and intensity.

45. *yana demme minne valanu.*

female circumcision of the star foreshadows that of Yasigui, Ogo's twin sister, which will take place later on Earth. It also indicates that the life force, or *nyama,* of Ogo's sex will join the life force of his placenta, the sun. The sun, whose rays will "heat" the earth and "nourish" the seeds sown in the fields, will take part in the growth of all plant life, and particularly those edible plants necessary to the life of mankind.

Ogo's aggressiveness leading to the female circumcision of the sun (which is actually the mutilation of a part of his placenta) is also stressed by a similar version, according to which Ogo himself, and not the *titiyayne,* sent the foreskin into the sun to seek his female twin there.

To avoid yet another theft by Ogo, the *nommo titiyayne,* at Amma's order, took the *emme ya* seed and placed it in a star, *emme ya tolo,* which would later establish its orbit around Sirius.

These events are represented by a figure called *"'tonu* of the separation of the twins,"[46] (fig. 86) drawn at the time of circumcision. It signifies the respective positions of Sirius and of the sun in relation to "Amma's womb," the site of the mutilation inflicted upon Ogo who, himself, is represented in this instance by the "star of the *po," po tolo.* This star will have to be formed later as evidence of the whole of creation wrought by Amma. [47]

Two circles, *a,* the "star of the *po,"* and *b,* Sirius, are joined together by a vertical axis. The upper one has two pairs of three rays directed downwards on either side of the axis, which is itself an extended outgrowth.

It represents the "star of the *po"* and the eight seeds (composed of the seven rays and the star itself). The upper part of the axis — above *d* — is the sex of the human being, constituted by the interior vibrations of the first grain.[48] In this case, there is a transfer onto Ogo's sex organ. The rays are also the stolen seeds and the sexes of children to be circumcised.

The lower circle, Sirius, is crossed by two perpendicular diameters, whose intersection has not been drawn. The form of the figure of these two stars depicts the time during which the events we have just related

---

46. *dineu gammalu tonu.* Drawn during circumcision in ochre (*bana*), or with red hibiscus tincture (*anu banu*), or with a mixture of both, on the rock of the locality of *ba namma* by the oldest man of Lower Ogol in plain sight of all the circumcised.

47. Cf. *infra,* p. 501 and ff.

48. Cf. *supra,* p. 139, fig. 23B.

took place. Indeed, the rays of the *po* (*a*), the future star of the fonio, show well that it had within it the living and created world, which had not yet "emerged" or been realized, as it was still bound to its placenta (*b*) by the cord (joining *a* and *b*). Moreover, the rays of Sirius are still internal, since the star — as yet a placenta — had not been formed.

Circle *a* is inside a curve shaped like a sickle, whose point meets Ogo's sex at *d* and whose handle, crossed by two vertical lines (*e*), is the foreskin transformed into the *Hemitheconyx caudicinctus,* or *nay,* surrounded by the circle of the sun, *nay,* thus projected into the star, which was already separate from the rest (in *c*).

This relationship is evoked by a euphemism: "The sex of the fish is the sickle (and) then *Hemitheconyx.* "[49] In this way one avoids too direct a reference to Ogo's mutilation and the virtual capture of his sex by the fish. Also recalled is the fact that the jaw of the fish cut off the organ like a fonio sickle, the blade of which, in turn, represents the ancient knife *kebele goi.*[50] In this drawing, the knife is to be imagined in place of the curve beginning at *d*, the loop of which is to be taken for the circle *a*.

The movements evoked by the figure should therefore be read as follows: the fish/knife circumcises Ogo at *d,* virtually takes hold of the organ, puts it in his tail/mouth and throws the foreskin into the sun in the form of the *Hemitheconyx.* One says of this figure: "The Fox (Ogo) wanted to take the rest of his placenta which Amma, transformed into the sun, forced to retreat and to emerge from the star of the fonio. Amma sent the *anagonno,* who circumcised the Fox, 'married his wife,' and chased away his foreskin which entered the sun."[51]

---

49. *anagonno tere goi ie nayi.*

50. This tool was formerly used for harvesting millet. It was decorated on the backside with three registers of three notches (the male number), recalling the teeth of the circumcising fish; but in its entirety it is also the whole silurus, the tail of which is the loop. The modern forms of this tool are the *kebele,* used to cut millet, and the *goi,* used for grass, rice, and fonio. The *kebele* features a piece of wood on the back to facilitate its use. The old form is, however, still used to cut millet stalks needed for the celebration of the rite *azagay pati:* literally, "destroyed ear-wig" (cf. p. 289, n. 76). The flat bracelet reserved for twins is a replica of this knife.

51. *yurugu me vomo denedoga, amma nay bilema dora gonati; amma anagonno tia, voy olu gona, yana vomo deya, boru guzu vomo doba nay-ne yoy.*

According to another symbolic record, the *anagonno* swallowed Ogo's foreskin and became his twin, since this organ is the support of his female soul. Its transformation into the *Hemitheconyx,* thrown into the sun, resulted in the identical relationship of fish/lizard/sun. So that, too, the knife — image of the jaw and of the fish itself and model for the instrument currently used for circumcisions — is compared to the sun.

A figure called "Amma carrying out the punishment of the world from above," *amma da aduno dugo kanu,* drawn on the divination tables for the instruction of diviners, recalls the order of these mythical events (fig. 87): Amma (in A) and the sun, which is the transformed remnant of Ogo's placenta; the *nommo die* (in B) transmits Amma's order to the *nommo titiyayne* (in C), who emasculated the *nommo semu* (in D) whose sex and navel (with the umbilical cord) are shown; circumcised and transformed into the Fox, Ogo (in E) is between the first piece of the stolen placenta (the Earth, T) and the second piece covering the stolen male *po* (P), that is to say, between his two arks; then Sirius and the sun, within which the *nay* is found (in F).

These figures are also drawn with the porrridge of four different cereal grains, associated with the four elements, when the foundation is laid for the *ginna,* in the hall, where they represent the different rooms of the dwelling under construction.[52]

In the *ginna,* the altar *taba tolo,* "beginning of the plateau," the very first to be built during the construction of the dwelling, is made against the west wall of the main room, or *dembere,* and is evidence of Ogo's circumcision and of Amma's recovery of the sex souls of the sacrificed victim.

The base of the altar is a vertically set, split stone which represents Ogo's circumcised sex. On this stone a small altar is rough-cast, called *taba amma,* "Amma of the plateau,"[53] made of earth taken from the family

---

52. A, with *po pilu,* for the recess (*kana*) where the altar to the ancestors (*vageu*) will be placed; B, with *emme ya,* for the second recess where the sacrificial objects and utensils will be deposited; C, with *ara geu,* for the room in which one places the pot containing the water used by the family; D, with *ara pilu;* and F, with *yu,* for the hall; E, in *emme dum banu,* for the main room, *dembere* (installment 2, 1st year).

53. At Sanga, the *taba tolo* altars are communal and located in every *ginna* and *tire ginu.* In other regions — Kamma, for example — there is an altar in every married man's house.

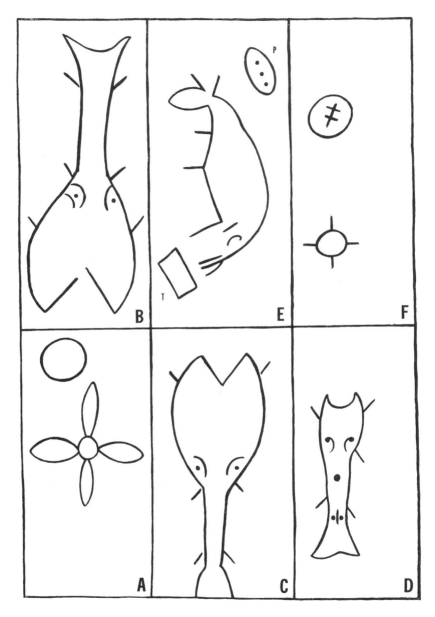

FIG. 87: Figures representing Ogo's circumcision drawn on the
divination tables used for instruction.

pond: the stone (Ogo's sex) being coated with earth from the family pond, where the *nommo anagonno* will reside after his resurrection, emphasizes the recovery of the latter's sex souls during the operation.

On top of the altar is a small piece of pottery, *vonoy*. Speaking of the whole thing, one says: "(The altar) *taba tolo* is like Amma's foot; the *vonoy* of the *taba* is like the calabash in a ball (of Amma),"[54] which is to say, like the image of the primordial placenta. Thus is emphasized the assignment of the altar representing Amma's womb, site of the emasculation of the *nommo semu* and the circumcision of Ogo.

During the foundation of the *taba tolo,* a figure is drawn, using red ochre *(bana)* relating both to Ogo's circumcision and to the unsuccessful meeting with his female twin, called "*tonu* of the prevented marriage" (fig. 88).[55]

Inside an oval of about 40 cm. in diameter, the orbit of the *po* star, a curve with ends slightly spiraling in opposite directions, symbolizes the fish and surrounds, on the one hand, the sun (*a*) situated at the periphery and, on the other hand, Sirius (*b)* placed at one of the centers of the ellipse. Circle *a* has only three rays, the absence of the fourth recalling the removal of the foreskin, cut off by the fish's jaw and thrown into the sun. Circle *b* has four rays, the feminine number, whereas the three of *a* connote masculinity. Thus, the quest is portrayed of the male (Ogo) turning around the female (later to be Yasigui) without ever reaching her. However, Ogo's virility has virtually passed into the fish, causing the tip of its tail to swell, thus underlining the fact that the fish had taken back his sex souls.

The altar also denotes the presence in the *ginna* of the two *kikinu say* of sex of the sacrificed victim. Within the family dwelling, it will be the depository and guardian of those same two principles of the boys until their marriage. However, before they marry, they will undergo the same mutilation inflicted upon Ogo by the *nommo titiyayne:* circumcision. The child, until then considered to be androgynous, has his feminine aspect — the foreskin — removed by this operation which, at the same time, definitively determines his personality as a male: it is said of an

---

54. *taba tolo amma kubo tozey; taba vonoy gaba kunu gunnu anay.*
55. *yadi elu tonu. elu* means literally "prevented, pushed back."

uncircumcised youth that he is "a child which is not among the number (of men)," *(i lugu-ne tolo),* and of a circumcised youth that "he has entered the number of men *(vir)*" *(anau lugu-ne yoa).* The operation constitutes a modification of the physical being, which is necessary to marriage. When they are led to the place of the operation, the family head prays and says: *"taba tolo,* we will give the porridge to drink to the children (to circumcise them); keep their *kikinu,* we are counting on Amma and on you."[56]

Ogo's mutilation had deprived him of the physical support of his femininity and had, at the same time, determined his personality as a male. However, it had also established his final separation from his female twin, for he will always remain deprived of a part of those sexual spiritual principles that he had stolen. Man, on the other hand, will be the descendant of the *nommo semu,* sacrificed as an androgyne, but who will resurrect in the form of a human couple, male and female, with each of the formed beings in full possession of all corporeal and sexual spiritual principles. Sexual union — marriage, therefore — will then be possible and, in fact, necessary to the reproduction and multiplication of the species, completely in accordance with Amma's original plans. Therefore, a figure much like the preceding one (but different in meaning) is drawn in *yu* porridge on the altar for the consecration of a marriage, i.e., at the time when a young woman leaves her father's house to go and live with her husband.[57] The figure is called *"tonu* of the *taba tolo* of

---

56. *taba tolo unum ala nomoy beme kikinu gelie, amma sagu, u sagu.* The operation is performed at the third moon.

57. The young Dogon woman lives in her father's home; she spends the night with her husband, but is still not officially recognized as his wife. At her first pregnancy, she brings to her husband's *ginna* some water drawn from the family pond, where the souls of the unborn children live, and pours it into the jar in the main room. This gesture "legitimizes" the child she carries. When she expects the third child, she is qualified to come and live in her husband's home, an act which constitutes her acceptance into his *ginna.* At that time, the figure in question is drawn on the clay of the altar made of earth from the family pond.

After the sacrifice consecrating the marriage, raw *yu* porridge is poured on the altar, and the family eats a dish of rice, *ara da,* and drinks beer made from *emme di giru.* Then, each year, the young woman offers a chicken, which the family head sacrifices in her name. The rule regarding the admission of the young woman at her third pregnancy has changed with time: presently, the rite is generally performed at the first or second pregnancy.

The collective sacrifice called "beer of the *taba,"* *taba kono,* takes place at the spring equinox (in the season of *nay banu*).

the sun and of Sirius" (fig. 89).[58] The fourth segment, emerging from the sun and present here (although absent in the preceding figure) in *a,*

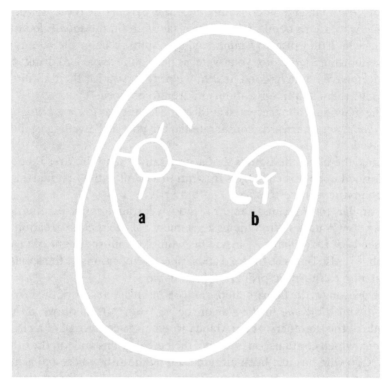

FIG. 89: *tonu* of the *taba tolo* of the sun and of Sirius.

connects with that of Sirius in *b*; it is the image of the union of the two original twin placentas. On the other hand, the curve of the silurus,

---

All the rites — which make up a cycle — performed during circumcision, marriage, pregnancies, and births on the altars which are the supports of the spiritual forces of the sacrificed Nommo in the *ginna* will be described in installment 2.

58. *nay-le taba tolo-le taba tolo-ne tonu.* The figure's name is associated with the first Sigui, performed upon the heliacal rise of Sirius, which followed the circumcision of the mythical ancestors and preceded their marriage (installment 2, 2nd year). The heliacal rising ("meeting of Sirius and the sun") is symbolized by the line connecting the two stars in this figure.

or *anagonno sala,* which represents the fetus or child carried in the woman's womb, is inverted to show that man, unlike Ogo, will receive and keep his four *kikinu* of the sex and will be able to marry.

Before a marriage is consummated, the parents of the two young people who are to be marrried offer a sacrifice on the *taba tolo* altar, during which they pray to Amma, saying: "Amma receive the salutation of the morning: *taba tolo,* your water is here, take some and drink; the children have come in good health; we pray to you for their *kikinu* of sex; give them health; give them children to be born."[59]

The individual altars erected at this time for the sex *kikinu, kutogolo,* and *dabie,* are afterwards consecrated in the paternal dwelling of those involved.

Thus, the altar, the figures that accompany it, and the rites that are performed upon it recall Ogo's frustration as well as the first marriages of the mythical ancestors.

A similar drawing, made on the façade of certain totemic sanctuaries, shows how Amma shifted the basic elements of the second creation — the seeds of food plants — inside his womb, to put them out of Ogo's reach.[60] It also outlines the role and respective positions of the spouses in relation to the basic property of the *ginna.*

At Orosongo, the figure called *"tonu* of the circumcision of the Fox by the *nommo titiyayne* in the star of the *po"* (fig. 90)[61] is drawn on the façade of the sanctuary of the Manda totem. It is composed of a circle, *po tolo,* which contains, on one side, the cereal grains and, on the other side, Ogo who has just been circumcised by the fish, whose tail is now completely curled up in the direction of *sigi tolo,* Sirius, represented by a circle crossed by a diameter. His foreskin, transformed into the *nay (Hemitheconyx caudicinctus),* is in the placenta/sun, which is represented by a sort of racquet.

Before Ogo's second descent, everything was mixed together in Amma's womb; by the time of the second reascent, everything will be arranged,

---

59. *amma agana yaba, taba di uo goa, yabu no; unum dau-le viyay, ogo kikinu gemo, kintam obo, i nonu obo.*

60. Cf. *supra,* p. 225.

61. *izu nommo titiyayne yulugu po tondolo kolo-ne sendi kundu toy.* Drawn above the sanctuary door with porridge of *ara geu.*

ordered, and classified; hence, the division of the circle into compartments. One says that Amma "pushed" the cereal grains to one side and emptied the other, where there was only Ogo, who was, therefore, unable to get

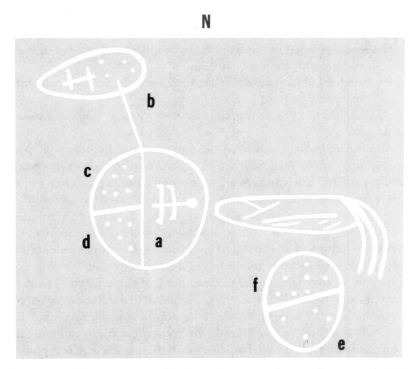

FIG. 90: *tonu* of the circumcision of the Fox by the *nommo titiyayne*. From top to bottom: the sun and the Fox's foreskin; Amma's womb, the Fox and the seeds; the *nommo titiyayne;* Sirius.

hold of them. The half where he was (in *a*) became symbolic of the first field of fonio (which will be located in the east on Earth). In the other half, itself divided into two, the southern quarter (*d*) symbolized the field of the *ginna*, the northern quarter (*c*) being the totemic field (*binu minne*); the sun (*b*) was the field of Lébé. In Sirius were the "field of the sons" (*unum minne*) (*e*)[62] and the "field of the outside" (*poruba minne*) *(f)*, an individual field which is not, like the others, part of the collective property.

It is said that the fish ate, digested, and excreted the grains, which then passed into *sigi tolo;* the grains of the *lebe minne* (*b*) passed into the foreskin of Ogo, who followed the course of the drawing. The gesture of the *anagonno's* tail foreshadowed the female circumcision of Yasigui, which would later take place on Earth.

The seeds assigned to these fields are as follows:

— in the *po* field, one seed: *po banu;*

— in the field of the *ginna,* five seeds: *yu, emme pilu, emme na kolu, emme dum banu, anu;*

—in the field of Lébé, four grains: *yu, emme di giru, emme ya, emme banu;*

— in the *unum* field, four seeds: *emme ya, emme dolo, po pilu, poli;*

— in the *poruba* field, seven seeds: *yu, emme di giru, emme banu, emme soroba (doruba* in Sanga), *pegele emme (emme dum pilu), modi emme (emme* of the Mossi and *emme giri po* in Sanga), *andi (anu).*

The growing numbers of seeds are symbolic of the future increase of the harvests. There are more seeds in the *poruba* field, because the individual fields will be the last to be delimited and will be evidence of the extension of families and of the ever-increasing number of human beings. Also, marriage includes that a part of the collective field be granted to the husband or a new field be delimited to fill the needs of the young household; one says: "Circumcision is like marriage and the division of the fields."[63] All seeds for consumption are theoretically respresented by this figure. For with the marriage, the wife is supposed to have brought to her husband — thus to his *ginna* — all the varieties of seeds from her own *ginna.* Every year, her husband gives her "a share" of his harvest in recognition of what she has brought to the community. After her death, the women of her family will come to get her personal belongings and all the grain in her granary, in order to give them to her daughters at the second rainy season following her death.

Before the sowing feast, the men of the entire community perform a

---

62. The "field of the sons," *unum minne,* called *dio minne* in Sanga, is part of the collective property.

63. *olu gonu yadi-le minne gammalu-le anay.*

collective ritual hunt called *tala* (from *ta,* " to shoot an arrow, a gun, a sling-shot"),which is a reminder of Ogo's circumcision. Animals killed during this rite — which is no longer existent in Sanga because of the scarcity of game — were brought to the *ginna* of those involved for the altar to the ancestors, *vageu.* It is said: "To do (hunt) the hunt, the game that is caught is like the *anagonno* cutting off the foreskin of Yourougou with his teeth. The animals one carries to the *vageu,* this is like the foreskin of Yourougou transformed into the *nay* which one places in the sun."[64] From this perspective, the *bunno* pottery placed in the altar for each person who has died symbolizes the sun. The foreskin is represented by the notched pieces of wood which are placed beside it.

OGO'S THIRD AND FINAL DESCENT.

After his circumcision, Ogo went back down to Earth, unable to bring anything with him. To do this, he used the object he had made with the "nervures" of the primordial egg and abandoned the first time he emerged from Amma's womb.

This instrument, which formed Ogo's third ark, emerged through the opening previously made, came down, and landed on the ground, without spinning as its predecessors had done. This absence of movement meant the end of Ogo's celestial journeys and his final settling down on Earth. It also showed that "the creation was finished."

The third ark of Ogo's descent is presently represented by the *nugoro* basket, or "bean bonnet," made of *saguba* straw.[65] Shaped like a bonnet, it is made of a spiral supported by segments or "rays." Placed upside

---

64. *tala tanu nama be-be-ze anagonno yurugu boru guzu tonu vomo-le vo pollo anay; olunama vageu-mone dele-be-ze yurugu boru guzu nay bila nay-ne kunni anay.* The rite of the Ono is performed at the spring equinox and recalls this mythical event; the rites of *goru* for the Dyon, *agu* for the Arou, are performed at the winter and summer solstice, respectively. The feast of the fall equinox is celebrated by the Dommo.

65. *saguba* grows near the water; it is considered to be the first aquatic plant and is the property of the sacrificed Nommo who, on Earth, dwells in that element. To show his supremacy over the Fox, he may take on the form of this reed. In the winter season the girls temporarily put aside their silver and copper jewelry, and don bracelets or other jewelry made of braided *saguba.* No metal should be worn when crossing streams since water is exclusively the property of the Nommo. *saguba* is used to make the lids one puts on dishes.

down on the ground in the same position as when Ogo had fashioned it with the "nerves" of Amma's egg, it represents the sky and the Earth: the "rays" are those of the sun called *aduno ozu,* "paths of the world," visible through the clouds. The basket contains the image of the two essential motions, the spiral by its structure and the vibration by its rays.[66]

The names of *nukoro* and *nugoro,* "bean box" and "bean bonnet," given to the two baskets representing the first and third arks, *yurugu koro* and *yurugu goro,* are also related to their usage as utensils. Dry beans that are to be stored are mixed with sand *(soso),* called "earth of the Fox," so the "tick" of the Fox, the insect *kibizu,* won't get at them. When people want to eat them, the beans are sifted in these baskets "to make fun of Ogo's failure."

The mutilation he had undergone left him still bleeding. The blood from his sex fell on the ground, but Amma brought it back up to the sky in the form of four satellites that would turn around *dana tolo,* Jupiter, when it would be born after the sacrifice of the *nommo semu.* "The four small stars are the chocks of Jupiter."[67] The four drops of blood were of decreasing quality. The first, *illi ezu* or "good blood," formed *gerelle tolo,* "star of the *gerelle";* the third, *illi monu,* "the bad blood," formed *sene tolo,* or "star of the Acacia," and the last drop formed *bala tolo,* "star of the *bala.*" They are also related to the four varieties of *sene.*

Thus, for Ogo, just as for the *nommo semu,* the stars in the sky will be proof of Amma's deeds. It is said: "The harm that Amma did to the Fox, he made come out of the hole the one who had first gone down; he performed the purification (and) chose the place of the stars. Amma punished the living things, sacrificed them, and turned the blood into stars.[68] This is as much as to say that the punishment inflicted by Amma

---

66. The boys imitate the *nugoro,* after the *bulu,* by making a bonnet of millet stalks *(Jeux dogons,* p. 37, n. 3, fig. 9). Then they make a flat, round pile of dirt on which each child, wearing this bonnet, sits or squats in turn; this pile is called "image of (the descent) on Earth of the bonnet of the Fox" *(yurugu goro minne yala);* the game recalls Ogo's third descent.

The *nugoro* is used in ceremonies for twins.

67. *tolo uzi nay dana tolo penni.* When representing Jupiter with a block of stone, one chocks it with four stones. See the figures of Jupiter and its satellites *infra,* p. 352.

68. *yurugu amma monu-go kanu bonno-go-ne gona uvo donugo sugona; uguru kunna tolo yalu bozi; amma kize omo dugu kana vo seme illi tolo bilemi.*

(the Fox's circumcision and the sacrifice of the Nommo) in the sky are inscribed upon the Earth. He purified it and then created the stars, for all the blood of the sacrifices was turned into stars.

When Amma was shifting the sun to put it out of Ogo's reach, the *nommo titiyayne* threw the turtle *agunuru,* evidence of the sun, through the opening. "Ogo having twice ascended and redescended, Amma threw the *agunuru* down to Earth; the *agunuru* on Earth is like the evidence of the ark which he will throw down."[69] The descent of the turtle, a piece of Ogo's placenta, foreshadowed the descent of the ark made from the placenta of his twin brother, the *nommo semu,* who was to descend after his resurrection with all the elements of Amma's creation.

OGO'S TRANSFORMATION INTO THE PALE FOX.

Once arrived on Earth, Ogo thought he could continue his work, but the creator, "having placed him under the sign of the animals," transformed him, turned him around, and thrust him to the ground, forcing him to move like a four-legged creature. Losing the name of Ogo, he took the name of *yurugu:* he had become *Vulpes pallidus,* the "Pale Fox."

According to an original derivation, *yurugu* comes from *yu,* "small millet," which is related to *guyo,* "to steal, to rob," because the individual concerned "left furtively after having stolen the seeds."

Another etymology relates this word to *yu,* "small millet," and *yola,* "to sneak about," also expressing the stealthy and secretive character of Ogo; *yo* (of the same root as *yu)* means "to enter (like a thief) to grab something." The *yurugu* "sneaked off with the stolen millet."

A third derivation attributes *yurugu* to *yurugie* "to be bristly," which is to say, not "smooth" or finished — because alone — thus weak and without strength. It stresses another psycho-physical aspect of the Fox which has to do with his solitude, the deprivation of his female twin, and his impotence.

---

69. *ogo kubo ley ula vo sugi, agunuru minne-ne amma ti, koro ti vo-do sere agunuru minne-ne bozi.*

No matter which etymology is accepted, the word *yurugu* will have as its opposite the term *yuguru* (from *yu*, "small millet," and *guru*, "nest"), which designates the snake in general, the symbolic sense remaining analogous. Snakes, "nests of the millet," protectors of the basic grains, will be the avatars on Earth of the mythical ancestors before the appearance and spreading of death, and they will remain symbols of immortality.

The order and ambivalence of these two names, *ogo* and *yurugu,* in themselves clearly illustrate the necessity of the initial presence of the element which the original demiurge represents, as well as the character, both baneful and necessary, of that same element. The Fox, having reached his final form after a long and complicated destiny, will be the permanent element of disorder in the universe — or rather the agent of disorganization.

A figure represents the transformation of Ogo into the Fox after his arrival on earth; he is shown curled up with his head down (not visible in this drawing) (fig. 91). The metamorphosis has curved him, arched his back, and lowered his hindquarters. The fish's fins have become his paws, the tail has lengthened to form a linear appendage, and fur has grown "out of the nerves." This figure is painted in red ochre, *bana,* during the Sigui on top of the boulder rising above the cave *kommo dama*, "forbidden cave." This boulder, called "place of the blood of the Fox's circumcision,"[70] is said to conceal Mars (*yapunu tolo*), born of the blood from the Fox's circumcision, in the *obia* position. A red mark is painted next to the animal to represent Mars at the time of the Sigui.[71]

The animal's body is the image of Ogo's downfall; his four paws foreshadow the steps and counter-steps that he must from now on take on the ground (impure like himself), defiled by the incest and theft and the fruitless quest for his female twin and missing sex souls. One also says of the number four that it is the reflection of the female twin, whom he will forever pursue and never find.

During the operation, the *nommo titiyayne* had tried to tear out

---

70. *yurugu ala nomu illi minne-ne tege yalu.*

71. The locality of *kommo dama,* located in Lower Ogol, is impure, *puru;* no one may go there, except during the Sigui when it is called *sigi doy,* "seat of the Sigui." Only the masked men who dance in the square of Lower Ogol may go there to rest during the ceremonies of the *dama.*

Ogo's eyes with his teeth, so that Ogo would be completely powerless. Marks remained on the patient's cheek in the form of scars, which are also his tears. They are represented by the markings in the fur of the Fox's face. To punish him for having stolen the baby teeth of the *nommo semi,* the *nommo titiyayne* had also broken this teeth and cut off part of his tongue. This changed his voice, a trait foreshadowing the loss of the "spoken" word. For this reason, in his present form of the Fox, Ogo "speaks only with his paws" on the divination tables.

This impairment showed that the Fox's "spoken word" — related to the contents of the clavicles as well as to the spiritual principles — would similarly be modified. One says that "if Amma had left the Fox his *kikinu bummone ana,* the Fox would have been able to 'speak' like him." This commentary emphasizes two aspects of the "spoken word": the Fox, whose "voice was ruined," rapidly was no longer to express himself orally, but rather by leaving "traces" on the ground with his paws; also, this "spoken word" wandered incomplete through his internal organs and no longer allowed him to procreate perfect twin beings — as will his adversary and conqueror — but only single animal beings like himself.

One of Amma's goals in creating the "sex souls" (*du kikinu*) by splitting up the "body souls" of the sacrificed Nommo was to bestow them upon all his creatures, especially the seeds, the primordial grains. By stealing them, Ogo wanted to overthrow Amma and not only take them for himself, but also give them to those seeds he had stolen and sown in the ground. Thus, the fertility he was seeking he would have obtained — for his own advantage.

Watching over them, Amma intervened, as we have seen, by immediately taking back the stolen souls. It is also said that "when Amma created the seeds, they possessed the *kikinu* of body and not of sex. The seeds could not reproduce. They received the *kikinu* of sex through the *nommo,* when his sex was cut off. The sacrificed Nommo's four *kikinu* of sex were cut off and split up, four sent to the Fox and the remaining four placed in the seeds. Along with the severed sex organ of the Nommo, the seeds of his clavicles, following the blood, came out with the four *kikinu* of sex."[72] Thus, when the victim's clavicular seeds

---

72. *dene amma mani varu-le gozu kikinu sebe, ogo kikinu sebele; dene nanie bele; dene*

will come out of his body with his blood, they will receive "sex souls," twin sisters of those stolen by the Fox and necessary to their future proliferation.

But Ogo's actions, as he had once more tried to act on his own and without waiting until his "sex souls" would be given to him, caused Amma to leave him only two, the *kikinu say ana* and the *kikinu bummone ya,* again showing his incompleteness by this. Indeed, the fact that he had two "sex souls" enabled him to reproduce on Earth as an animal, but made him forever different from his celestial brothers who, like their descendants, were to be provided with four body souls and four sex souls.

The transmission of these two principles took place through the intermediary of an insect: the sex souls of the *nommo,* recovered by the *titiyayne,* had been entrusted to the male *key* ant. It was responsible for bringing their sex souls to the seeds that were in the hole of the female ant that had descended with Ogo during his second journey.[73]

The sacrificer had placed two *kikinu* on either side of the insect. These gave it its wings: it flew off to earth. When the wings fell off like a shed skin, the *kikinu* remained attached to the male ant, that penetrated the earth and changed into the *keke gummolomo:* the rough spots of this beetle are evidence of the wings as well as the sex *kikinu* which it did not possess before.[74]

Seeing the insect, the Fox devoured it in an attempt to get back the sex souls that it had stolen during the emasculation of the *nommo semu* and lost later. "When the Fox gobbled up the *gummolomo,* the four sex *kikinu* of the *nommo (semu),* which he (the *nommo titiyayne)* had entrusted to the ant, the ant tried to fly away. Nommo pulled it back to him; the *gummolomo* which the Fox gobbled up is the representation of the 'sex

---

ogo kikinu vo bia nommo ogo varu keze kolle; nommo semi ogo kikinu nay dena, gammala, nay yurugu mone tia vazu nay vazu dene mone kunnu; nommo ogo kezi-le ani guyo vomo dene illi-go-le dimia ogo kikinu nay-le goy.

73. Cf. *supra,* p. 231.

74. The *keke gummolomo* is the *Gymnopleurus fugidus* OL.

For the Dogon, the winged ant called *key kile,* "flying *key,*" goes down into the earth after losing its wings and then comes up as the *keke gummolomo.*

souls'."[75] Indeed, the *nommo titiyayne* left the Fox only two of his sex souls; the two other principles were kept by Amma. "The Fox has six *kikinu,* he never has eight."[76]

Thus transformed and deprived of a part of his spiritual principles, the Fox, who will feed primarily on insects, burrowed into the cracks of caves, like he did into his placenta: one says that his earth, or lair, measures twelve cubits deep, this number being symbolic of the twelve months of the year and of the "number" attributed to the rebel.

Since that time, it is as if the Fox were in exile, in a separate world; this exile is due to his impurity. Alone, incomplete, and ever rebellious, but active, he will play a necessary part in the development of life on Earth. For it is said that Amma provoked Ogo's actions in order to experiment with the universe in formation: "Amma made the Fox do all these things to try him out in the world."[77] Therefore, one sometimes adds that Amma, angry at Ogo's reascent, reproached him for this unauthorized act and forced him to go down again, "to show the way" for all the future "descents" of the beings created in his womb.

The Fox had initiated agriculture, but by sowing stolen seeds — the "semen" of his "father" Amma — inside the Earth, his "mother." It will be necessary to purify the soil, parched by incest, in order to renew its fertility. To carry out this purification, men will sow in their turn, but with seeds given to them by Amma for this purpose, and not with stolen ones. The Fox will then leave to take refuge in the uncultivated bush, his domain. However, man will follow him and will again purify new territory by delimiting new fields. Thus, the Fox's presence as well as his actions will promote the expansion of mankind.

This idea of the expansion of the human domain, progressively imping-ing upon that of the Fox (who show the way), is illustrated or inaugu-rated (one may say) in children's games. The role of the very young children, who have a "joking relationship" with the Fox (*manu*), is to play

---

75.*yurugu gummolomo vo teme nommo ogo kikinu nay key gera, key kilie ya, nommo ela; gummolomo yurugu tema ogo kikinu yalay be.*

76. *yurugu kikinu kule vo asu gagara belu.* These words are spoken each year by the goatherds, when they place the cut wood on a pile of stones and old wood at the place called *azagay pati,* "destroyed earwig"; this gesture commemorates the Fox's death.

77. *amma yurugumon kize ua kanu fu aduno sone uoy suburu yenede kay.*

with his "earth,"[78] both to look for him and to chase him away. To model animals or objects out of earth is to imitate the Fox who "scratched" to tear away his placenta. The game *sey*, played by two children with a small pebble or a small *bey* seed (bean), hidden in a handful of dirt, consists in pushing the partner back into his own territory until he has been driven out of a circle traced on the ground: this is the Nommo pursuing the Fox.[79]

Well before his completion, the Fox had manifested his insubordination, his refusal to comply with Amma's plans. He was born "marked" for failure. His role and function, for that very reason, would reinforce his own individuality. Just as he initiated the disorganization of the universe, so, too, he himself remained incomplete. His two quests, one on the cosmic level — for the "sign," therefore the Word — the other on the level of personality — for his female twin or female principles — will always be necessary. He will be the agent of psychological individualization, as he was of cosmic disorder, by bringing to both these domains the beneficial ferment of opposition. For Amma, who foresaw all things, had also prearranged the dual organization of the universe by dividing the original placenta into two distinct parts. Commenting on this division, the *nommo anagonno,* and Ogo's deeds, one says: "The reason why Amma created both the Nommo and the Fox is because he both disorganizes and organizes the world."[80] For he had formed the *nommo anagonno* to be masters of the universe: opposite yet complementary, Ogo who foments disorder and his "twin brothers" who fought him, will be involved in its management as well as in its functioning.

The preceding facts, related to various mythical events, are also recalled by the relief figures on the Dandoulou totemic sanctuary of Upper Euguel,[81] called "drawings of the *po* making the world and of the dead and resurrected Fox descended on his ark"[82] (fig. 92A and B).

---

78. "The work of the little children is to play with the earth," *unu uzi bire minne-ne yogoro yogori.*

79. For a complete description of this game, cf. M. Griaule, *Jeux Dogons,* p. 172.

80. *amma nommo-le yurugu-le vo manu-go aduno yammalaze kene kanay kanaze.* The last words literally mean "it must be done from organization."

81. In 1955; a similar figure was observed twelve years before on the Mangara of Dini sanctuary.

82. *po ganna mana, yurugu omo-go bila koro-le sugi tonu.*

The figures of the *"po* creating the world" were on the north wall of the sanctuary: to the left, one similar to the *bummo* of the *po*; on the right,

FIG. 92: Figures taken from the Dandoulòu totemic sanctuary: A: *bummo* of the *po*; the fields; the divination table.

the same picture with an added vertical segment which represents "the root of the germinating *po.*" Above, the *"tonu* of the earth which one cultivates and where man walks"[83] prefigures the squaring up of the

---

83. *minne vala-le inne yala-le tonu.*

arable soil and the "partition" of the fields. Finally, a reduced outline of
the table of the Fox, also called "hollow of the Fox," *yurugu golo.* On the

FIG. 92: B: The Fox and the Nommo under the sun.

east wall were the figures called "drawing of the dead Fox after his
circumcision by the *nommo anagonno* in the name of Amma and
drawing of the Nommo mounted on the dead Fox's head, after having
revived him in the name of Amma, under the sun."[84]

Thus is emphasized the fact that Ogo's circumcision, because of his
deeds and his rebellion, led to his transformation into the Fox and to his
death, which will take place on Earth for similar reasons.[85]

A series of paintings drawn in the cave *toy nama kommo donu,* "lower
cave of the covered seeds," or *yau dama kommo,* "cave forbidden to
women," relates certain episodes of the Fox's circumcision and of his
life on Earth (fig. 93 II).[86]

On the outside edge of the cave (cf. fig. 93, II, A): following the first
figure (which has not yet been commented upon) are placed in order
(fig. 93, I): a schematic drawing of Amma creating the world (*a*); a sort of

84. *yurugu nommo anagonno amma boy-le olu vo gonu yime; yurugu nay donune
yimu-le amma boy-le nommo omo bilema ku-gone uli tonu.*

85. Installment 2, 9th year.

86. Map II, G.

hook (*b*); the Fox mounted by the circumciser, represented here by a sort of saddle (the two semicircles forming the front and back of the object) (*c*); the circumcised Fox losing his blood (the red dots) (*d*); the Fox in his final form (*e*): the figure stresses the lengthening of his tail and the growth of fur. On the ceiling (fig. 93, II, B) are represented the episodes of the loss of the spoken word and of the voice (fig. 93, I): the torn tongue (*f*); the cut nerve (*g*); the wounded windpipe (or *yogo golone*, "river of the throat") (*h*); a sort of grid representing the Fox's jaws and incisors (*i*); the dots that follow (*j*) are the teeth that have been pulled out. At the back of the cave (C) is shown the burial of the Fox by the goatherds (*k*): the body is covered with the funeral blanket. The tomb is located to the right: a small crack has been blocked with stones. Inside are two wood carvings, representing the dead Fox and his blanket, as well as a small piece of pottery, *vonoy* (here called *olu gizu*), for libations. In front of the cave, a small hollow has been dug (D) in the rock to represent the "puddle" where the Fox used to drink during his lifetime.

THE DIVINATION TABLES OF THE FOX.

No longer able to express himself in language, the Fox, still possessing the "word," will reveal it to man by means of the "traces" he leaves on the ground when moving about. The form and use of the tables, drawn in

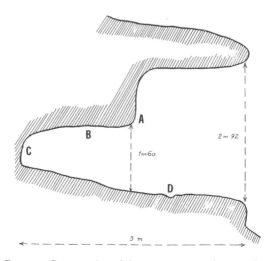

FIG: 93 II: Cross-section of the cave *toy nama kommo donu.*

the sand by the diviners to question the Fox or to instruct beginners, are related to the events we have just described. Therefore, it seems fitting to give certain commentaries regarding this method of divination and technique of instruction.

Divination "by the Fox" is an activity intended solely for the men. Anyone who has reached maturity, if he wishes, may be instructed and ordained: he is then called *yurugu yayne,* "he who goes (to the table) of the Fox," or *yurugu kunnone,* "he who places (the tables) of the Fox." Experienced diviners are always high initiates: heads of joint families, dignitaries of the Society of Masks, healers, hunters, etc. However, neither the totemic priests, nor the Hogon, who are responsible for the community's tribute to the adversary and conqueror of the Fox, may approach the tables; nevertheless, being initiates, they are instructed in everything that concerns them.

A distinction is made between two different types of tables: the actual divination tables and the tables of instruction, used for teaching the initiates and future diviners. They are called *kala,* "to tear," as they are related to the placenta "torn out" by Ogo and to the cosmic consequences of this act. The round table, called *kala gono,* "torn rounded," is the first of mythical time; it is no longer used, but was ritually drawn near the cave of Ka at the time when the Dogon arrived. We have seen that, from the point of view of the world's creation by Amma, it represents the division of the primordial placenta into parcels; with regard to the Fox, it is the image of the northeastern "hole" he made in his torn-out placenta, "spread out like Earth," the place where the stolen *po* will germinate. The explanations of the symbolism of this table are part of the instruction given to the initiates.

A) The commonly used divination table is rectangular and is called *kala sibe nay*, "to tear at the four corners." It represents the second piece "torn out" by Ogo. The rectangle is divided in half lengthwise and into three parts widthwise, thus having six compartments: if the round table is the image of the first "field," or the field of the *po,* the rectangular table is the image of a field in six parcels, as established by the Fox to sow seeds in after the descent of the ark and of man — an attempt that will end in failure.[87]

The diviner traces the basic figures on this table — which is not

----

87. Volume I, Installment 2, 3rd year.

oriented — always placing those having to do with Amma to his left ("the hand of Amma above and below," A and B) and placing those relating to death to his right ("the hand of death above and below," that is, his funeral blanket and the tomb, E and F); the two central registers are reserved for the worlds of the sky and of the Earth ("the central house above and below," C and D), in relation to the consultant, who is generally represented by a stick stuck in the sand (in D) (fig. 94).

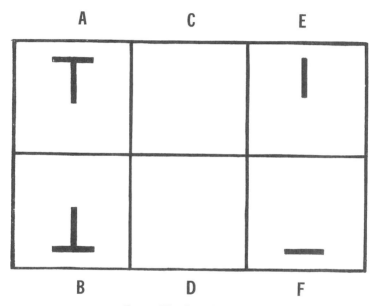

FIG: 94: The divination table.

Then he draws schematic figures in each register relating to the personal, individual, or collective questions with which he is concerned. These schematic figures are associated with the journeys of the Fox to the sky and upon Earth: the diviner theoretically draws sixty traces or figures, which are Ogo's sixty furrows, established according to what is called the "reckoning of the placenta," for "the world is divided into sixty parts like the primordial field." The diviner, like the Fox, conducts a search; the figures he draws on the table are like the successive images of the rebel's eternal quest to find the rest of his placenta and his lost female twin. In like manner, he will "read" the tables from right to left:

the order of the basic figures (A,B,C,D,E,F) constitutes an image of "Ogo's walk" in space, namely, his successive "descents" and reascents between sky and Earth, the third of which leads to his death. Regarding the theoretical zigzag line which then connects the registers one says: "The path of death is crooked, the path of life is straight, the path of death is three."[88]

The Fox descended from the sky to the Earth which he formed and seeded: when he moves about on the divination tables, "the planet begins to turn as if from the movement of his paws."

The appointed diviner smooths the tables with the "hand of the Fox," *yurugu numo,* made of *sene* wood. The apprentice diviner may use only one stone "hand," a sort of triangular pebble with which to draw the registers. This pebble, heavier than wood, symbolizes both the placenta, a heavy thing stolen by the Fox, and the responsibility, heavy as the stone, taken on by the apprentice.

The stone "hands" are "stolen" by the diviners from the terrace of the *lebe dala* which symbolizes the "sky," the place where the events involving the Fox and his twin brothers took place, especially the redeeming sacrifice of the *nommo semu.*[89] The object's point represents the sun, and its flat side, with which one smooths the tables, is the sky in which it moves (fig. 14); what is drawn on the raised part with the flat side reproduces an image of the sky on the ground. Moving the stone means to "lay" the sky and sun upon the Earth. When the apprentice is ordained, he offers two chickens for sacrifice on the altar to the Fox. The eldest diviner present consecrates this by taking his hand and having him smooth the table with the *sene* "smoother."

The altar called "*lebe* of the Fox" (*yurugu lebe*) is erected near the place where the first divination table will be drawn as established by the community's diviners. The name of the altar, *lebe,* is a contraction of *ley be,* "those two," or "two together"; it expresses the status of the one to whom it is consecrated, who is "both Ogo and the Fox." From a mythical perspective, the *yurugu lebe* will be consecrated by men after the death

---

88. *yiminu ozu gonnugo vo, iele ozu deu vo, yiminu ozu ozu tanu.* This image of the "three paths of death" is represented in a different form in the prayer recited before the dead are laid out for burial. (G. Dieterlen, *Les Ames des Dogon,* p. 98).

89. Cf. *supra,* p. 249.

of the Fox and the celebration of his *dama* by the goatherds, in commemoration of his resurrection as an entity;[90] the altar is made of a small
clay cone of "earth of a pond which is soon dry," *tara minne,* taken
from one of the small temporary ponds which form on the plateaus or in
the hollows of the rocks in the rainy season. Mixed in with it is a piece of
the altar of Lébé — *izubay para lebe* — consecrated to his adversary
and conqueror in memory of his resurrection,[91] a piece which is stolen
for this occasion (Pl. XII, 2).

A circle (the world) is drawn on the sand; the figure representing the
yala of the *sene* and the Fox's "hands" (fig. 14, p. 115) is drawn on the
ground and on the cone, built on top of the whole thing. Before the
consecration, the spider *dada* (who had woven Ogo's "word") is drawn
at the top of the altar (fig. 72, p. 241). The figure is the structural diagram
of the twelve registers of the tables of instruction (fig. 96).

    a: *amma numo donu:* "Amma's lower hand."

    b: *ginu bere donu:* "the lower central house (belly)."

    c: *yimu numo donu:* "the lower hand of death."

    d: *amma numo da:* "Amma's upper hand."

    e: *ginu bere da:* "the upper central house."

    f: *yimu numo da:* "the upper hand of death."

In *g* is the head of the animal, symbolizing the altar of the Fox; it is
placed to the south, the direction taken by Ogo to get out of Amma's
womb.

After the sacrifice of consecration, the officiant draws the first table
and says (recalling the successive "splittings" of Ogo's placenta): "The
world that Amma has created, forty *yala* for the sun, fourteen for the
Earth, six for the Fox, together (they are) sixty *yala.* Fox, tell us the white
word (i.e., the truth); do not lie to us."[92]

The diviners' offerings will be brought in a piece of calabash and
placed in a shard of pottery, which remains near the altar. These objects
recall the gourd Ogo had broken to gain possession of the seeds.

---

90. Volume I, Installment 2, 10th year.

91. Cf. *infra,* p. 349.

92. *amma ganna mana nay-le yala pennay, minne-le pelu nay sige, yurugu-le kuloy,
mona pelu kuloy yala. so pilu emmi taga, emmi bogono.*

An annual sacrifice, accompanied by libations of beer, is offered by all the diviners to the Fox on the altar that is consecrated to him. The following morning, those involved meet to read the tables on which

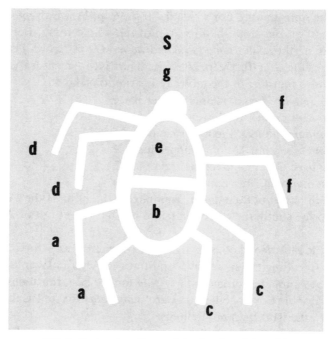

FIG: 95: Explanatory figure of the drawing of the spider.

questions of a general nature have been asked and to drink the rest of the beer. One of them then addresses the Fox: "Fox, hail to your coming and going; because of his soft foot, we follow him morning and night; thank you for your gentle foot; show us who is going to die and who is going to get well; we will go out to grow millet in the bush, tell us if we will have the grain of ripe millet or not; the world that Amma created

(modeled) forty *yala* of the sun, fourteen of the Earth, six of the Fox
(are) together sixty *yala*. Fox, those who are going to consult you salute
you for your coming and going!"[93]

The diviner draws the figures before sunset; the Fox, who comes out
at night, is attracted to the tables by the peanuts scattered over them.
The tracks are read the following morning after sunrise: the reader
follows the Fox's passage with a "stalk for looking at the Fox's traces"
(*keru yurugu yennu*) — a stalk of sorghum, because the Fox "is satisfied
that a millet stalk is used to read his tracks."

The animal's tracks, which connect, encircle, or avoid the figures, are
interpreted as answers to the diviner's questions. However, his walk can
also present certain specific aspects which are related to either his status
or his mythical deeds and which are not answers to the questions.

When he goes around the table without treading on it, one says that he
has gone around the universe, as Amma made him do at the dawn of
creation. When he walks inside the table in a regular way, one says that he
"has walked the walk that belongs to the Fox."[94] and that he "has walked
the walk belonging to the Earth."[95] When the only visible traces on the
table are made by his tail, the image is compared to the movement of the
Earth turning on its axis; one says: "The Fox has turned with his tail; the
Earth has turned on its axis."[96] If he treads on the middle of the table,
scrambling his tracks, one says that "the Fox has overturned the creation of the world,"[97] thus recalling the fundamental disorder brought
about by him.

To find out the truth in very serious cases, the diviner may draw an
outline of the Fox, which is normally not drawn, in the left bottom
register ("lower hand of Amma"). The middle lines, which also differ
from the usual lines, are in this case the *bummo* of the sky and of the
Earth. This procedure is exceptional. The image formed by the lines is of

---

93. *yurugu tonno po; kubo ninu vomo-de aga-le dige le voy dimmi; kubo ninu vomo ga;
yimie do-le bazay do-le emmi taga; olu yu vala goyde, yu i ille illeru emmi taga; amma
ganna mana nay yala pennay, minne pelu nay sige, yurugu kuloy, mona pelu kyloy yala.
yurugu yayu tonno poy.*

94. *yurugu ku vomo yoy.*

95. *minne yoy vomo yay.*

96. *yurugu dullo vomo-le gona; minne ku vomo-le gona.*

97. *yurugu ganna mana kia* (from *ki,* "to pour").

an initiatory nature which may not be seen or read by individuals who have not been instructed.

B) The table for instruction is double; it is called *kala gimme,* "torn double," because it related the Fox's deeds and their cosmic consequences to the deeds of his "twin brothers," who had to vanquish him and establish their domination over the universe.

It is not really a table for divination and is not used as such, but rather is used to teach the diviners to show them the reorganization of the universe by the Nommo and his domination over the Fox. For this reason, the figures on the instruction tables are drawn in reverse to those on the divination tables: the instructor faces the table, which is oriented differently. Generally speaking, the entire figure of the twelve compartments of the instruction tables constitutes a lunar calendar and also represents the course of the sun during one year. It is named "the place of the sun, the path that it walked (during) the year of twelve moons" (I), and one may calculate the sun's movements over twelve lunar months by the successive order of the figures marked in the twelve compartments of the table (fig. 96).

Before drawing this table, the diviner digs his fingers into the four corners and outside the figure to represent the "cardinal points," i.e., space. Then he smooths the table and draws an outline of the Fox with four small holes for the paws. Thus, the divination table represents the Earth "turning under the movement of the Fox's paws" when he moves about on the registers, whereas the instruction table represents the space in which the Earth, sun, and moon move, which Amma had placed out of the Fox's reach.

As examples, we will now comment on the schematic figures drawn on a double instruction table which, during initiation, sums up the principal mythical events described in the preceding chapters and which are related to facts to be presented later. The pictures are placed in the compartments according to the diagram of the twelve "positions" of the sun (fig. 97).

In the past, the same pictures were drawn with lizard dung on the sites where the circumcision took place. These figures were also drawn in front of one of the caves of Ka (said to be of Dyongou Sérou and Yasigui) during its installation when the Dogon settled there.

East

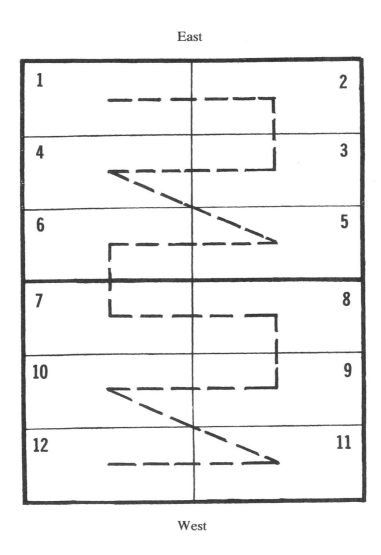

West

FIG. 96: Outline of the "path of the sun" in the double instruction table.

The table of the east, (six compartments) is called *yurugu doy,* "seat of the Fox"; the table of the west (six compartments) is called *yasigui-le donu seru-le doy,* "seat of Yasigui and of Dyongou Sérou."

Compartment 1: *amma ginu,* "Amma's house": the figure represents Amma's open clavicles, or the place where he began the realization of the universe.

E

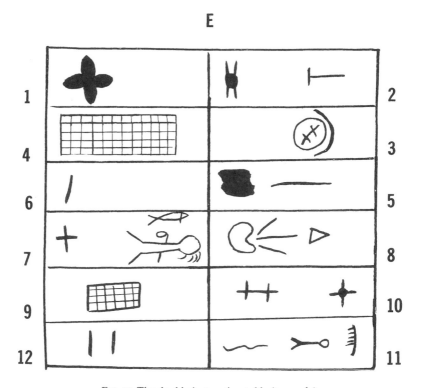

FIG. 97: The double instruction table (example).

Compartment 2: *yurugu ginu,* "house of the Fox": Ogo (figure on the left) is circumcised by the *nommo anagonno* (figure on the right).

Compartment 3: *alagala,* "the sky": an open semi circle facing compartment 4 contains the sun and Ogo's foreskin in the form of the *nay.*

Compartment 4: *yurugu me nommo titiyayne nammi,* "the Fox's placenta that was crushed by the sacrificing *nommo*": the grid represents the whole of the stolen placenta, or the sixty furrows of the Fox and the Earth.

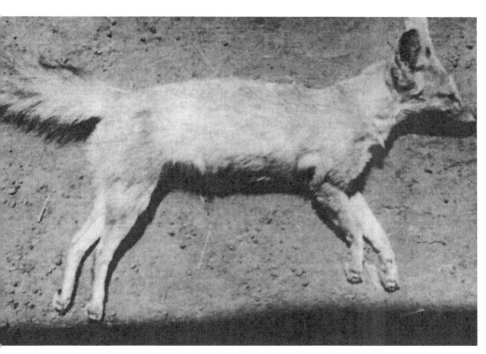

PLATE XI: 1) The Vulpes pallidus.

2) The divination table: in the center, tracks of the animal's paw may be seen.

PLATE XII: 1) Annual sacrifice to the *lebe* of the Fox; in front of the altar are the smoothing instruments, called "hands of the Fox";

2) The divination tables.

Compartment 5: *yurugu bozu ginu,* "House of the Fox's funeral blanket."

Compartment 6: *yurugu ie yalu,* "place of the Fox's tomb."[98]

Compartment 7: *amma ginu,* "Amma's clavicles": the long-haired sacrificing *nommo* holding the sacrificial knife; above him is the victim.

Compartment 8: *yasigi minne,* "field of Yasigui": the female circumcision of Yasigui and the hoe.[99]

Compartment 9: *donu seru me yalu,* "place of the placenta of Dyongou Sérou": the grid also represents the Fox's second field.[100]

Compartment 10: *alagala tolo doy,* "seat of the stars of the sky": Sirius (to the right) and the scorpion, an avatar of Yasigui's clitoris.

Compartment 11: *donu seru inne bibile boso vomo-le yalu,* "place of the funeral blanket (in fibers) and of Dyongou Sérou as a man, later transformed (into a snake)."[101]

Compartment 12: *yurugu-le yasigi-le ie yalu,* "place of the Fox's tomb and of (that of) Yasigui."[102]

3. SACRIFICE OF THE NOMMO

Slaughter of the victim. Division of the victim's body. Projection of the
parts of the body into space.

In circumcising Ogo, the sacrificer had acted too hastily, on his own, and without Amma's orders. Amma said that he "had not waited" for what he was going to do. For had Ogo not been circumcised, Amma simply would have destroyed him to prevent him, once and for all, from causing any harm. However, this deed was so hastily committed that it made Ogo's blood penetrate the celestial placenta as well as his own placenta, the Earth, upon which he had also bled. A purification of the celestial and terrestrial spaces then became necessary.

---

98. Volume I, installment 2, 9th year.

99. Installment 2, 1st year.

100. Installment 2, 3rd year.

101. Installment 2, 3rd year.

102. Installment 2, 9th and 15th years.

Amma proceeded to sacrifice the one he had just emasculated and to divide his body into parcels for the purification of space and of the universe in formation; thereupon he will resurrect the victim, who will become the symbol and support of the organized world.

SLAUGHTER OF THE VICTIM.

North of the placenta, Amma planted the dry piece of the *nommo anagonno's* umbilical cord, detached from the navel during the emasculation, which became alive and changed into a tree, the *kilena*. This tree was also living evidence of the "sex souls" that had been formed by being split up before the emasculation.[103]

Seizing the victim (then called "Amma's captive," *amma gunnone),* Amma brought him to the north (fig. 77C, *sogo uguru uguri)* where, standing up and facing east, the Nommo was tied to the *kilena,* whose roots spread out in three directions and whose two branches supported the pectoral fins. The body was surrounded from top to bottom by a flexible iron helix, called *amma su* or "cord of God," with fourteen coils, "symbol of Amma's fourteen worlds in a spiral." It rose from right to left (passing in front of the body), i.e., in the same direction as the *yala* of the internal spiral of the primordial "egg." "For this, Amma stretched the Nommo's two arms across a fork of the *kilena;* he killed him (after) having tied him up with an iron cord. The spiral of this cord, Amma, changing (the way of) the creation of the world, started it at the right, in order to bring it to the left. To destroy the world he had created, Amma tied up the Nommo by changing (the direction of the spiral)."[104] Thus, Amma reorganized the world by coiling the spiral around the victim in the same way it had turned to form the universe in his womb, and not in

---

103. For the *kilena,* the first plant to grow after the *sene,* cf. *supra,* p. 268; *kile* means "wood coal." *kile* is a pile of wood burned to make charcoal.

The *kilena,* which took life from the sacrificed Nommo's umbilical cord, is considered to have the power of reviving what is dead.

104. *ko-de amma nommo numo-go ley kilena day-ne vasara, inu sule voy komma day; su-go amma mani-go dulomati-ga, numo i-go tola nanna-go dayay; amma aduno vo manu-go yamalado-ga nommoy dulomatiga kommu.*

the direction it had turned to liberate the beings outside his womb. Pieces of this same metallic cord tied the fins to the wood. The being sacrificed in this manner represented mankind and animate beings; the tree that was to perish with him stood for all plant life. Both were standing, since the reorganization of the world called for a victim who had suffered greatly: therefore the *nommo anagonno* was sacrificed standing up, the position in which the death agony inflicts the greatest suffering. "The man who dies lying down does not see (experience) much suffering. Therefore the Nommo died standing up. When one dies standing up, the suffering is greater. Therefore, in order to organize the world, the Nommo died standing up. For if you wish to organize the world, you must experience great suffering."[105]

Stressing his vertical position, one also says that the *nommo anagonno* was "as if pressed between two parallel walls," with his pectoral fins piercing them, and that Amma had him die this way, in front of the "door of the world," *aduno ta,* facing the universe he was to reorganize. His pectoral fins were extended into space.

The sacrificer cut the back of his neck and his pectoral fins at the same time. The ordeal of the victim being a "punishment," Amma acted in "plain daylight," since the sun, which had been under the victim's placenta during the emasculation, was moved to the west after the operation. It illuminated what Amma did inside the womb. Therefore, it is said that the *nommo semu* was struck on the forehead by its rays and that the shock passed into the nape of his neck, into his spine and his kidneys.[106]

He became thirsty and, at his request, Amma gave him some water in a "copper bowl," *menu bana.* Having drunk too much, he vomited a "serpent of water," *di yuguru,* into the bowl. The word *yuguru,* which designates the snake in general, is composed of *yu,* "small millet," and *guru,* "container." The snake is the "container of cereal grain," symbol of the sacrificed *nommo,* who is the receptacle of the primordial seeds on account of his clavicular contents. The etymology of this term is

---

105. *inne di yimay bono gay iele; ko-de nommo inele ine yimu; inele ineu yimu-go bono vo ga; ko-de nommo ganna yegeredo-ga inele ineu yimu-go bono ieze.*

106. The leather and metal strap worn by the women recalls the place where the sun struck the victim's forehead.

considered to be similar to that of *uguru,* "purification," thus emphasizing the fundamental role of the sacrifice of the *nommo anagonno.* One
will say: "The word uttered by the *yuguru* will be the *uguru* of the
universe." Also, the snake's skin, *kogo,* will be considered on Earth to
be the witness of the "skin" of the earth, that is, the arable topsoil:
therefore, one sometimes says that millet and all cereal grain will grow
"in the head of the snake" that surrounds them.[107]

The term *yuguru* is the antonym of the name given to the Fox, *yurugu,*
"stealer of millet." On Earth and in the water, the sacrificed Nommo
will protect the grains, or "Amma's semen," and will oppose the deeds of
the one who had stolen them from the Creator.

His executioner who, according to another version, had taken on the
form of his future enemy, whose forked tongue resembled his own,
"drew the blood from his nose," just as the Nommo himself would do later
on to people who drowned.

The victim's blood ran over him, covering the metallic spiral which
bound him, making it turn red. This blood represented all the "life of the
world." It is compared to the menstruation that precedes procreation; it
is the "menstruation of the Earth," whose future life it ensures. Thus,
this binding "cord," itself symbolic of the movement of the universe in
which Amma had enclosed the sacrified Nommo, was vivified by the
blood and transmitted all its force to the entire world that the Nommo
was to reorganize. It is said of this iron (also called "twisted iron of the
creation of the world by Amma"[108]): "Amma gave the twisted iron from
the sky (to the Nommo) so that he might give it to the world he must
create when he had come down from the sky."[109]

The blood of the victim fell on him and in front of him, on his
placenta/earth, and also traversed space. As a "prototype" of the rains,

---

107. On the Earth, one of the sacrificed Nommo's avatars will be the "water snake," *di
yuguru,* the general taboo of the totemic priests and considered to be the "guardian of the
grain in the water." Similarly, the avatar of one of mankind's four ancestors, the python or
yuguru na, will be their "guardian on the earth."

108. *amba adinya mani ine tonu* (Wazouba dialect).

109. *amba alakala-ne gonda ine tonolom von oba ta-ne suge adinya yem managa vo obu.*
In the totemic sanctuaries, this mythical iron is represented by a ritual object of twisted
iron, called *ine tunnulumo.*

it formed "cords of rain," *an(a) di su,* along which, even today, it descends on the Earth. At present it also descends along the sun's rays. As he was bleeding, the victim lost his life force and his clavicular seeds. Therefore, one says that, while he was bleeding on a rock, *sogo,* placed in front of him, the blood fell into the copper bowl, *menu bana,* where it turned into covenant stones, *dugoy,* which will become the symbol of his clavicular contents.[110] "The house in which Amma had placed and enclosed him represents (is like) a punishment. The grains of his clavicles descended below with his blood."[111] The association of the blood with the seeds also stresses the fact that the basic food, symbolized by the clavicular contents, passes through the blood to give life to the individual.[112]

Thus, the victim lost all his life forces. He took the name of Nommo, a word whose root is *nomo,* "to give drink," for his sacrifice nourished the universe, ridding it of all impurity. "The Nommo shared his body among mankind to feed it"; therefore it is also said that, since the universe "drank his body," the Nommo also gives drink to man. He gave all his living principles to human beings. One also sums up his work by saying: "The Nommo died to give *dugoy* to the world."[113]

The *kilena* tree will also die, together with the victim: it was caught with him in the helical cord that spun in the original direction of the creation. Just as the Nommo died to reorganize the world and ensure the existence of mankind and of animals, so, too, the tree died, later to rise again and to allow the resurrection of the plants.

As had been the case with Ogo's emasculation and circumcision, in regard to the construction of the universe, the sacrifice of the Nommo determined the creation and the path of the stars, evidence of the blood, of the clavicular seeds and spiritual principles (*kikinu*), and of the vital organs when the body was divided up. Summing up this series of events,

---

110. The mythical "copper bowl" is represented by the *ogo bana* bowl ("vase of the Hogon") of the religious leader, the Hogon.

111. *gine-gon von angara kadu todo-go kunnabe; ani guyo yu-go illi vomo-le dim-bia duba sugu.*

112. It is said: "The food that you eat, the drink you drink, may Amma change them into red blood; white blood is a bad thing."

113. *nombo vo yimu-go aduno-ne dugoy ogo degay* (Wazouba dialect).

one says: "Amma was in the *po,* the seven grains came out of it in spirals. Because of the sacrifice of the Nommo, the stars and seeds were strewn throughout space (the world). In the beginning the stars walked in the sky by following the sacrifice of the *nommo.* "[114]

The planet *dana banna tolo,* "star of the fontanel," or more generally, "star of the skull," *dana tolo* (Jupiter), rose from the blood that fell on the placenta (fig. 77C, the altar *uguru uguri).*[115]

Holding the head down to let the blood flow out, Amma walked to the north. The blood flowed like a torrent through a valley. Amma stopped, and the Nommo lost the seeds of his right clavicle, among them the *po pilu.* Here the *po tolo* was born (fig. 77D, the altar *dummo dama),*[116] the symbol of the beginning of the universe. Further on, the victim lost the seeds of his left clavicle, including the *emme ya* and his very life, *kinu.* That spot marks the birthplace (fig. 77E, the altar *ka amma)*[117] of *emme ya tolo* which, along with *po tolo,* was eventually to revolve around Sirius. These two companions are proof of the initial seeds as foreshown by the *yala* of the spiral inside "Amma's womb," with twenty-two for the *po* and forty-four for the *emme ya.*

Just as the *po* is symbolic of the beginning of the second world created by Amma, the *emme ya* is symbolic of Amma's action to regenerate it after the disruptions brought about by the Fox. One says of it that "it is like Amma who split himself in two to create the world that was born from him." It is also said that the seed, evidence of the sacrifice, came out of the clavicles as red as blood. Amma's deed, however, was an act of purification. The *emme ya,* "which until then was red like a woman reddened with blood," passed this color on to its descendants, that is, to other varieties of *emme ya,* itself becoming white and pure. "The *emme ya* which emerged from the Nommo's clavicle came out red with blood; thereupon it became white."[118] It finally resembles the victim, whose body

114. *amma po kolo-gone dene goy-go digilio gonu; nommo voy semi-go dige ganna fu tolo-le dene-le.*

115. The fontanel is called *dana banna,* "mark of the skull."

116. Literally, forbidden height (or boulder). Of all the altars in Sanga, it is the most sacred because, pointing to the sky, it represents the *po,* both the first thing created and an agent of creation.

117. *ka amma* means the altar to Amma of the "thing done," *kize kanu; kana* is "to do."

118. *emme ya nommo semi ani guyo-ne goy illi banu goy; onune pilinia.* It is the *kikinu say ya* of the *nommo die.*

will be divided up for the purification and the reconstruction of the world, a notion which is expressed by saying that one part of it remained the *emme ya* and that the other part became the universe. It is considered to be immortal, as it is the depositary of the "female souls" of the grains, which are also immortal, and of the corresponding *nyama* or life force. Its star, the *emme ya tolo,* is their "granary." It was created so that those principles might remain in the sky, beyond the Fox's grasp, and this was possible only through the sacrifice performed.

Now, at the same time when the blood was flowing and the clavicular seeds were scattering, the spiritual principles *kikinu say* and *bummone* (related to them) also left the victim's body. For it is said: "The eight grains of the clavicles mark the seat of the eight *kikinu.* "[119] Thus, *po tolo* and *emme ya tolo,* the first two stars, became the seat of the *kikinu say ana* and the *kikinu say ya,* respectively, whereas the two *kikinu bummone* followed the flow of the blood. Amma saved the seeds to return them to the sacrificed Nommo at his resurrection five days later, when the bleeding stopped.

Following the flow of the blood, Amma cut off the head without shaving it (fig. 77F, *pegu* altar); the red star in the constellation of Taurus emerged there, called "scintillating red star," *tolo bani nenneu.*

The blood kept flowing, taking the other clavicular seeds with it. When it stopped (at G, the altar *tenu amma*), the first *sa* tree grew, living proof of the victim's blood. The two last seeds, *ara geu* (black rice) and *yu* (small millet), accompanying the two body souls, *kikinu bummone ana* and *ya,* had been carried to the very end of the blood flow. There Venus emerged, in the *bayara* or *yazu*[120] position, white and shining, asking for water for the seeds. "She said she wanted water to clear her eyes, for she no longer saw the millet."

Then, rice grew in the puddle of blood, while millet germinated at the edge. Thus, an image of the first pond was produced in the sky, which was to play an important role on Earth.[121] At the same time, two stars appeared, witnesses of the grains, respectively *ara* and *yu tolo.* These

---

119. *ani guyo dene gagara kikinu gagara doy.*

120. *bayara* is the time of the night after midnight. *yazu* means "very early."

121. Cf. *infra,* p. 325 and p. 493.

two stars will eventually revolve around *emme ya tolo,* which is itself a satellite of Sirius. It is said: *"po tolo, emme ya tolo, ara tolo* are very close to Sirius, one does not see them often."[122]

The "day after" the sacrifice, the bird *donu* was born from the blood that was progressively drying up.[123] It sang to the blood: its song, acting

FIG. 98: Drawing of the slaughter of the *nommo* and of his passage into the valley.

like a rooster's crow in the villages, made the *valu,* the antelope, appear, because "the bird, the antelope, and the Nommo all came out of the

---

122. *po tolo-le emme ya tolo-le ara tolo-le sigi tolo-le beru-go ve, da iemele. ara tolo* is said to have a time of revolution of thirty years, i.e., half the period of the Sigui (*sigi anakuzu pelu kuloy logoro:* "the middle of the sixty years of the Sigui").

123. *dou* in Wazouba.

same placenta," the first two being the Nommo's twins. Similarly, the bird, like the *ara* seed, was related to the victim's *kikinu bummone ya* of the body, and the antelope, like the *yu,* to his *kikinu bummone ana.* The *valu* was as if asleep, because the Nommo, its master, had just died: by its song, the bird was the instrument of his awakening, which foreshadowed the victim's resurrection. One again comments upon this image by saying that the male *kikinu bummone,* which "followed the blood" in the form of the antelope, found its female soul in the form of the bird that "awakened" the antelope with its call.

At the resurrection, Amma will return the Nommo's body souls and the contents of his clavicles to him; the *valu,* who had been the guardian of the seeds that had been carried with the blood, is later to become the first totemic prohibition *(bibinu dama).*[124]

The sacrifice of the Nommo is represented by a figure called "drawing of the Nommo's slaughter and of his passage into the valley" (fig. 98).[125] It depicts an individual, the Nommo, on the left, whose curved arm recalls the leg of the crocodile. From his throat comes a horizontal line, the "path" of the blood, *illi ozu.* It ends in an oval representing the end of the blood flow, that is, in the image of the primordial pond containing a dot: the rice. Another dot on the outside represents the millet. The *valu* is portrayed between the Nommo and the pond.

Amma had followed the blood to its end before returning to divide up the body. The trace of blood flowing from the placenta formed a straight north-south line called *illi ozu,* "path of the blood." The track of Amma's walk parallel to it, called "Amma's path," is present in the sky. Together they make up the Milky Way, *yalu ulo,* "bounds of space," the evidence of which is the star *yalu ulo tolo.* Thus, the Milky Way has, ever since, been evidence in the sky of the discharge of the victim's

---

124. We recall here that, for a man, the *kikinu bummone ana* of body is associated with the totemic prohibition; the *kikinu bummone ya* of body resides in the individual's totemic sanctuary. It is similar for a woman, with the respective situations of the two principles being reversed.

125. *nommo be sema sadane woywa goy.* Drawn at Wazouba on the wall of the totemic sanctuary Desa, during the collective hunt, *tala,* which, in the past, came two months before the ceremony called "the coming of the winter season," *dine golo,* towards the month of November.

blood. As for the purification Amma performed through his successive acts of immolation, the Nommo's placenta as well as the remainder of Ogo's had both been purified by the blood of the emasculation. With the exception of the precise spot where the Nommo had been killed (fig. 77C), neither one had been in contact with the sacrificial blood that flows "to the outside." It is said that "the emasculation purified the Nommo's placenta; his sacrifice purified the outside (space)."[126]

A figure drawn in the totemic sanctuary, called "drawing of the route of the blood of the Nommo become stars" (fig. 99),[127] represents both the formation of the stars in the Milky Way and the blood flow of the sacrificed Nommo. With regard to Amma's initial egg, the design of this flow corresponds to the *yala* of the *gaba,* the last to leave the primordial egg.[128]

Similarly, one draws in the *ginna* a *tonu* of *yalu ulo tolo,* "star of the Milky Way" (fig. 100). The funeral urn of the founder of the lineage, called "bulging urn," *bundo gwe,* represents this star. The opening of the container is surrounded by a bulge (*gwe*) which represents the star's permanent halo (*gwe*); "the *bundo gwe* resembles *yalu ulo tolo*; the bulge of the *bundo* resembles the halo of *yalu ulo*

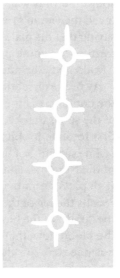

FIG. 99: Drawing of the "route of the blood" of the sacrificed *nommo* become stars.

---

126. *nommo olugonu-go me-go dolu; nommo semi-go parago voy dolu.*

127. *nommo semi illi ozu tolo tani toy.* Drawn with porridge of *ara geu* inside (to the left of the door as one enters) the sanctuary of Asama of Gogoli during the sowing celebration.

128. See the *yala* of the *gaba,* p. 124. We recall that, similarly, the *yala* of the *anu* are the image of the flow of blood from Ogo's circumcision. Their evidence is *yapunu tolo,* Mars (cf. p. 270).

tolo. "[129] During the consecration of the altar to the ancestors (*vageu*), the picture of the star is drawn under the urn which is placed first in line; those of the other deceased members of the lineage are all placed in a spiral around it.

FIG: 100: *yalu ulo tolo* and its halo.

---

129. *bundo gwe yalu ulo tolo mumu; bundo gwe yalu ulo tolo gwe munu.* This may be in reference to Saturn, since the Dogon confirm the existence of the planet's permanent halo, different from the one sometimes seen around the moon. Also, this planet is always associated with the Milky Way, of which it may be a fixed element. Some investigation remains to be done on this point.

The time it took for the blood to flow out is of the same duration as the period between the sacrifice and the resurrection. This is to be repeated by the interval between the arrival of the resurrected Nommo's ark and the first rainfall. This will determine the Dogon five-day week. In fact, it is said: "In the past, the days were not counted. In the past, one counted the time separating the day of the sacrifice from the day of the resurrection. That is what we today call a week."[130]

DIVISION OF THE BODY OF THE VICTIM.

Retracing his steps, during the bleeding Amma had brought the body back to the west (fig. 77H, *sogo belu uri*) to divide it up in the place where he had been keeping the contents of the sex organ. Venus then appeared in the *donno tolo* or "star of the west" position, evidence of the dismemberment of the body. So one says of it that *"yazu* is like the bounds (limits) of the place of the trace of the sacrificed Nommo's blood; *donno tolo* is like the end of the space of the sacrificed Nommo's blood."[131] But the two pectoral fins (*ta i*), also called "arms of the Nommo," remained momentarily attached to the *kilena.* Indeed, Amma wanted to leave the support of the four fundamental elements and of the

---

130. *ani bay lugu bele; ani varu lugube nommo sema bay bula bay kunnu; vo ie dugu emme voy.* This formula is recited in a low voice by the patriarch before he slaughters a sheep on the altar to the ancestors, *vageu,* of the *ginna* during the family ceremony of the winter solstice, *goru,* which brings the year to an end.

131. *yazu nommo semi illi bummo yalu kalle tozoy; donno tolo nommo semi illi kalle dogo-go tozoy.* This is how one already determined three positions of Venus in relation to the blood of the victim and prefigured the Venusian calendar, which is composed of six positions.

contents of the clavicles intact and pure in the living being, and to avoid all contact between it and the body he was going to cut up. One says that "Amma, wanting to keep the Nommo's name from being lost, left something whole in his body."

Amma then proceeded to work on the Nommo's body, repeating the successive stages of the formation of the primordial germ, the *po* seed. We recall that the *po* — in which Amma had reintegrated the four elements first contained by the seed of the *sene* — had grown around a central core in seven vibrations, or "words," composing its life within. The eighth, belonging to the "sex" and foreshowing the seed's germination, had manifested itself as an external vibration, from which future promises of reproduction were to be born.

Taking the body of the sacrificed Nommo, Amma resumed his work in the same way as before. The contents of the clavicles, seat of the eight "words" in their life-giving stage, had flowed out with the blood. Turning the victim on his back, he had the body opened, first lengthwise, then widthwise, producing four counterparts of the four elements, *kize nay.* When it was open, he took out the seven internal organs through which, by way of the blood, the already differentiated and individualized "word" was circulating. Just as he had put aside for safekeeping the contents of the sex organ, seat of the eighth word, so he also preserved, with the organs, the seven others with the intention of returning them in their entirety to the Nommo at the time of his resurrection. Thus, in order to place them in a regenerated universe, along with the Nommo's other internal organs, Amma took back the sources of the life, developed in seven vibrations inside the primordial germ — the *po* — to which was added the eighth vibration, evidence of its germination.

First he took the liver, *kinne na,* which is the "seat of the heart";[132] it also is the privileged seat for the being's life force, *nyama,* which circulates with the blood in the veins. Demonstrating the "force" contained by the organ (the liver), one cuts a bit off to throw it on the altar during a sacrifice, saying: "The grilled liver we throw is like the exterior word (that is) coming out and being thrown."[133] The liver is made up of

---

132. *kinne na kinne donno doy.*
133. *kinne na gorey mananu so para-ne gona tani anay.*

three parts: the *kinne na* itself, which is the largest part; the second one is called *kinne manu,* "liver that is thrown," i.e., the part that is taken to be thrown on the altar for the sacrifice; and last, the gall bladder, *gala,* which is the first part to be struck by a disease of the liver. Amma removed the gall bladder; he will not return it to the Nommo at his resurrection because, henceforth intangible, the Nommo "is never to be ill again or to become impure *(puru)*."[134] He then carried the liver and placed it on the eastern placenta where appeared, as evidence of the organ, *atanu* "three," Orion's Belt (fig. 77, 1, *sogo* of the Yébéné totem).

He took the spleen, *kinne laga.* This organ plays the part of regulating the "words" expelled by the liver; especially it is said that "the spleen purifies the bad words."[135] He placed it to the northwest, where three stars appeared, called *tolo dullogu* "tailed star," which make up the Sword of Orion (J, *sogo,* of the Guéméné totem).

Then the kidneys, related to procreation and births, which is to say, to the "multiplication" of words. He brought them to the northeast, where the Pleiades appeared, *tolo duno,* "clustered stars" (K, *sogo,* of the Goummoyana totem).

Then the lungs, *buzu buzu,* associated with the word which the resurrected Nommo will emit in the water, his domain on Earth: "The lung blows the word that is in the water and will come after (i.e., after the resurrection)."[136] It is the straight or "white" word that the resurrected Nommo will weave and reveal to man. Amma brought them to the southwest, where the "star of the Lion" appeared, *yara tolo,* in the constellation of Aries (fig. 77, L, *sogo,* of the Nommo totem).

He then took the intestines, *kolosa,* which are said to be "the sharing of the words,"[137] as it is through the intestines that the food passes into the blood and into the joints.[138] These he placed to the southeast, where the "Goatherd's star" appeared, *enegirine tolo,* located near Orion (fig. 77, M, *sogo* of the Tiré totem).

---

134. The victim's gall bladder will be the basis for the first "medication," *bana,* which will be possessed by Dyongou Sérou, the fourth ancestor, a hunter and healer (cf. *infra,* p. 451).

135. *kinne laga so monu-goy dalaze.*

136. *buzu bazu ninnu so di-ne to onu goy-do anay.*

137. *kolosa so gammalu-ne.*

138. The small intestine is called *kolosa,* the stomach *donozo,* the caecum *kolosa bobolu.* In ruminants, the second stomach is called *donozo timmu,* "superposed."

The heart and the pancreas, which play a special part in the distribution of the "word" within the body, both received a particular treatment:

The heart, *kinne donno,* is the first organ directly connected to the clavicular contents, witness to the "word" in the life-saving stage, the vegetative life of the being.[139] The beating of the heart makes the "word" pass into the blood, which circulates it through the entire body; it has an active and distributive role. Amma put it on the "line of the blood," where *emme ya tolo* had appeared (E).[140]

The *kolosa dugu,* "the intestine that knows,"[141] is considered to be the "eye of the heart," "The blood of the heart that follows the nerves goes to the pancreas, which sees like the eye; the eye of the heart is the pancreas."[142] This organ is the seat of intuition and of inspiration:[143] "(as) granular as the pebbles used for divination," it is, as such, the means of vision for the "seers" (*kumogu*), for the diviners, and also for the great initiates. Amma placed it at the end of the flow of blood,[144] where Venus appeared in the *yazu* position (fig. 77, G).

In this way, by placing the organs or "seats" of the "articulations of the word" on the placenta and on the line of the Nommo's blood, Amma determined the form of a spatial universe over which the resurrected victim was to become master and ruler: his organs, the "words," were "spread throughout" the space of the renewed universe by this. Amma continued his work by proceeding to make, with these elements, a "design" of the world he was in the process of regenerating. He had also saved the Nommo's organs, through which the blood would pass, thus lending passage to the word. One says that "Amma took the seat of all the words," that is, the Nommo's eight principal organs, in order to return them at his resurrection. For although the "word" of the sex —

---

139. Cf. *supra,* p. 165.

140. The altar in this place represents the sacrificed Nommo's right clavicle, cf. *infra,* p. 354. See also p. 375 and ff.

141.Or "intestine which knows (of) knowledge," *kolosa dugu dugone.*

142. *kinne donno illi to volu dige kolosa dugu-ne ya giru-go iyeze. kolosa dugu giru kinne donno-ne to.*

143. During an individual's lifetime, his *kikinu say ana* (for a man) dwells in the pancreas; this principle's twin, the *kikinu say ya,* which dwells in the family pond, brings him — sometimes in a dream — the instructions or suggestions of the resurrected Nommo.

144. The altar in this place represents the sacrificed Nommo's left clavicle, cf. *infra,* p. 357.

foundation of the creation — always remains under Amma's absolute power, he will, nevertheless, give it to the resurrected Nommo and to his "sons" — mankind — so that they may be fertile. One will also say that "the word of the sex that Amma kept, comes and goes."[145]

From the blood that was spilled while Amma removed the organs and placed them on the victim's placenta, a series of plants was also born, which were to descend with him on his "ark" after the resurrection. Like the *yayaga,* born from the blood of the emasculation as living evidence of the victim's sex organ, these plants will be evidence of the dismemberment of the body and the purifying function of the sacrifice. They are later to be used by man for a series of purification rites.

From the gall bladder, *gala dimme* or "curved bitter," and thus from the liver, emerged the *pelu* which, together with the *kilena,* will be the instrument for the resurrection performed by Amma.

From the heart emerged the tuber of the *kinu bommo,* called *nono* (literally "perpetual"); this incorruptible bulb, proof of the immortal heart beats of the resurrected Nommo, was to be put in the ground during the foundation of a *ginna* to ensure the permanence of the life of the community.[146]

The *ezegele* was born from the pancreas; the *satele* from the spleen; the *saguba* from the lungs; *the sana* from the intestines; finally, a full ear of millet, *yu* (or *sayu*), was born from the kidneys, the seat of "births."

Generally speaking, this plant, which dies and is reborn from its own seed, will be like a living image of the principle of resurrection. Each of the plants related to the victim's organs that we have just named also corresponds to one of the eight articulations of the "word." On Earth, they will become the special instruments of purification, *dolu,* needed by man in case of violation of a prohibition. The effect of these purifications is to reestablish in the body of the offender the stability of those principles which were disrupted by his offense.

In the case of violation of a totemic prohibition, for example, the plants

---

145. *ogo so amma gelebe yayveu yaze.*

146. Cf. *infra,* p. 376. To emphasize the immortality of Amma and of the bulb, evidence of the heart, one says: "Amma, *nono,* both of them, it is the same name" (*amma, nono be ley boy turu)* (G. Dieterlen, *Classification des Végétaux,* n. 1, p. 153).

are used in the following way: to purify the inside of the body, the priest has the offender chew a piece of *kilena* charcoal (proof of the sacrifice), which is then spat out. He then rubs the offender's tongue with a stalk of *sana* to "clean the words," because "the *sana* is like the words."[147] He purifies the outside of the body by passing over it a piece of *pelu* bark (proof of the resurrection).[148] Then, over the head, shoulders, and all the joints he passes an ear of small millet, *yu,* to put the seeds, that left their host at the time of the offence, back into the clavicles. For millet, *yu,* is "Amma's milk," *amma iri di,* which "washes" men as it feeds them.[149]

Amma then proceeded to dismember the body that had been opened up and emptied of its internal organs. After tearing away the skin, he had the victim's flesh cut up. The division was accomplished by separating every articulation; sixty elements were thus counted. They illustrated the count in base 60, *mene lugi* or "reckoning of the placenta," and recalled the basic form of Amma's placenta:

1.	head	13.	right thumb
2.	ears	14.	right index finger
3.	eye	15.	right big finger
4.	nose	16.	right ring finger
5.	mouth	17.	right little finger
6.	neck	18.	left thumb
7.	shoulders	19.	left index finger
8.	chest	20.	left big finger
9.	thigh	21.	left ring finger
10.	knee	22.	left little finger
11.	shinbone	23.	right big toe
12.	foot	24-27.	right toes

---

147. *sana so anay.*

148. Cf. *infra,* p. 331.

149. The *satele* will be used for individual purifications of the priests and family heads and for those of the altars *ommolo ana;* the *ezegele* for acts of purification necessary for the women and children as well as for the altars *ommolo ya;* the *pelu* will also be used for the altars to Amma and the individual altars *kutogolo* and *dabie (Classification des Végétaux,* p. 126-127).

28.	left big toe	43-50.	left ribs
29-32.	left toes	51.	(lower) vertebrae
33.	(top) right rib	52-58.	other vertebrae
34-41.	right ribs	59-60.	the two pelvis bones[150]
42.	(top) left rib		

When the body was cut up, the rest of the victim's blood, called *illi doda* or "weak blood," flowed out of the placenta from east to west. Three dots marking this flow are associated with three other positions of Venus, respectively, *enegirim*, "goatherds" (N), *dige tanu*, "to cross in the middle" (O), and *yapunu da*, "dish of the menstruating woman" (P). By its direction, this flow completed the purification of "space" which began with the north to south orientation of the sacrificial blood at the time of the slaughter; "the trail of blood of the sacrificed Nommo purified the entire space of the pathway of the blood."[151]

The Nommo's skull was stripped of its teeth, so the Fox couldn't take possession of them, as he had done with the first ones. Amma would keep them in the sky until the time when, in the image of the *dugoy* of *binu* that had sprung from the victim's semen as evidence of the clavicular seeds, they, too, would fall with rain from the sky on Earth for mankind, like *dugoy* of *nani*. "The seeds of the clavicles and the *dugoy* of *binu* are like the Nommo's semen; the *dugoy* of *nani* are the molars and incisors of the sacrificed Nommo."[152]

The Dogon makes a distinction between the incisors, *tonu giru* or "front teeth," the molars, *tonu aa bomu* or "teeth of the corner of the jaw," and the canine teeth, *tonu amma labu* or "teeth carved by Amma." Their part in the bestowal of *dugoy* of *nani* had to be in accordance with their shape. "The upper molars of the sacrificed Nommo are the *dugoy* of *nani* of the men; the lower molars are the *dugoy* of *nani* of the women; the incisors are the *dugoy* of *nani* of the *innepuru;*[153] the canine teeth are

---

150. This division will be the basis for the structure of totemism, cf. *infra*, p. 328.

151. *nommo semi illi bummo illi ozu ganna pu dalu.*

152. *ani guyo dene-le binu dugo-le nommo yu toy anay; nani dugo nommo semi tonu aa bomu-le tonu giru-le anay.*

153. *nommo semi aa bonu da anau nani dugo anay; tonu aa bomu donu yau nani dugo anay; nommo semi tonu giru inneu puru nani dugo anay.* Said during the sacrifice offered

the *dugoy* of *nani* of the weavers."[154]

The sacrificed Nommo's tongue was cut lengthwise in two. The first half on the left side will descend on Earth with the first rain on the pond and will turn into *izu nine,* or "tongue fish." The right half will be used by Amma to give a new tongue to the resurrected Nommo as well as to mankind that will be formed with the substance of his placenta. Thus, the resurrected Nommo will possess the two halves of his tongue: the one in his body and the one that lives in the water, his domain on Earth.[155] The word which is related to this half of the tongue corresponds to the "one that a man hears in this heart (conscience), and whose sound is not heard."[156]

The division of the body into sixty parts, to which were added the six elements of the contents of the semen, gave a total of sixty-six pieces: this number is equal to the number of the *yala* in Amma's egg, which were the image of the spiraling primordial seeds.[157] Thus, continuing his work, Amma caused, by the number of pieces and the use he will make of them, the essential elements that regulated the development of the universe to be set into motion again.

He then had seven piles made of the pieces of the dismembered body. Then, a constellation of seven stars, *aduno sene,* or "bracelet of the world," appeared at that place. Similar to the division, these seven piles produced the next stage in the formation of the *po* seed, i.e., the development of its internal life or "articulations of the word," which were represented by seven segments of increasing length — also form-

---

by the men and women in the family sanctuary to their *nani,* ancestor. For the *inneomo* and the *innepuru,* cf. *supra,* p. 56.

154. *nommo semi tonu amma labu soy tiu dugo anay.* Said at the sacrifice on the altar of the weaver in the *ginna.* The resurrected Nommo, *o nommo,* will "weave" the word with his canine teeth in the "water of the pond" before he reveals it (installment 2, 1st year).

155. This image is recalled when it is said that the resurrected Nommo, *o nommo,* who dwells on Earth in the waters, "has a forked tongue."

156. It is this "other half" of the tongue, therefore this "word within," which responds to the totemic priest when he makes a request at the pond by clapping his hands. It is represented by a copper knife which the Hogon receives upon taking office (installment 2); there is a replica of this knife in the totemic sanctuaries.

157. Cf. *supra,* p. 121.

ing the image of a spiral — inside the grain.[158] "The seven (piles) of the divided flesh of the sacrificed Nommo are like the seven *tonu* of the *po.* "[159] Thus, by the numbers encountered during its performance, the sacrifice repeated Amma's fundamental acts.

The seven piles Amma made of the dismembered body are remembered annually at Sanga during the ceremony which precedes the sowing, *bulu,* when seven pieces of the divided body of the sacrificial victim on the altar to Lébé (A) are given to seven of the oldest "impure men," *innepuru,* of the settlement, who alone are qualified to consume this meat. It is said that "the sharing of the meat of Lébé among the seven old men is like the seven words";[160] and that "in meetings all words end with those of the seven eldest (men)."[161]

Amma then covered with the victim's skin the seven piles made with the pieces of the body: "The skin of the flaying of the *nommo anagonno,* who is on *belu uri,* is to show how he (the *nommo*) keeps (maintains) the 'four corners' of space."[162]

PROJECTION OF THE PARTS OF THE BODY INTO SPACE.

Amma then had the pieces of the body brought to the south (fig. 77 at B) in the place where the blood flowing from the emasculation had stopped. He had four piles made of it, here representing the four directions of space. He opened the sky at that point and had the pieces of the body thrown through the opening in all four directions to purify space, the four cardinal points, and the Fox's earth: "Amma killed the Nommo; he flung the four parts (of his body) to the 'four angles' of space. He killed him in order to organize the world with him."[163]

---

158. Cf. *supra,* p. 137.

159. *nommo semi gozu gammalu soy, po tonu soy anay.*

160. *diem soy lebe nama gammala, so soy anay.*

161. *baru yaye diem soy-le so dogose.*

162. *nommo anagonno gozu ura belu uri ku-ne debi ganna sibe nay vo gele anay. belu uri* is the name of the altar of the *lebe dala* commemorating the dismemberment of the body, cf. *infra,* p. 359.

163. *amma nommoy da; ganna sibe nay-ne digu vomo-go vo tia; vo-le ganna yegeredo-ga voy day.*

Thus, the next stage of the sacrifice shows that the purpose of Amma's work was the total reorganization of the universe considered in its spatial entirety. The opening that had been made recalled the opening of "Amma's eyes" during the development of the world, which fore-showed the "cardinal angles" of space in formation.[164] Once again, Amma repeated the primordial acts; continuing to work in the same way, he had an "operation" performed on the victim's dismembered body that was similar to that of the *yala* of the *po* emerging from the egg to create the world.

The division into four piles and the ejection into space are remembered each year during the sacrifice (*goru*) performed at the winter solstice in the family house when the four eldest men of the community are given the main parts of the body of the victim.[165] One then says: "The animal we have sacrificed to the *vageu* of the *ginna* and divided between the four eldest (men), it is like Amma dividing the sacrificed Nommo's body and throwing it to the four cardinal angles of space in four pieces that grew like four trees in the pond."[166]

The pectoral fins (*tai i*), or "raised arms," attached to the fork of the *kilena* are not included in this group of elements, because they were the pure evidence of the dismembered body. However, they were also thrown through the celestial opening; transformed into a *nommo anagonno* (the right one) and a black crocodile or *ayo geu* (the left one), they lay down on the Earth and surrounded the hole, *bonno*, which would be the first pond and represents on Earth the opening in the celestial placenta that had been made by Amma for the ejection of the body and the descent of the ark.

The right arm fell end-first, giving the crocodile his ridged tail. The other fell down flat, which gave the *anagonno* his flat tail.

---

164. Cf. *supra*, p. 125.

165. A leg, the head and the breast (containing the heart and pancreas) are given to the *ginna bana*, the second leg to the next eldest, one front leg to the third eldest, the other to the fourth eldest. The kidneys are given as a gift (*solu*) to the wife of the family head and the hindquarters to the nephew on the mother's side. The intestines are shared among all.

166. *ginna vageu* (or *ommolo*) *belu semenu, dieu nay gammalanu, amma nommo semu gozu nay ganna sibe nay tuturu tia, o-ne timmu nay te anay.* The last sentence is an allusion to the facts represented on the next page.

Before falling through the opening, the "left arm" was cut off at the joint; the forearm was emptied of its marrow, and Amma put the seeds that had fallen from the victim's clavicles into it. This bone that was kept in the sky later became the hammer of the Smith. "The end of (the joint of) the sacrificed Nommo's arm, the lower part, is the hammer of the Smith. The top part is the crocodile."[167]

The pieces of the body gathered around the pond; four trees, avatars of the four piles made by Amma in the sky, will grow around the pond after the first rain: a *minu* to the east represents the trunk, an *oro* to the west represents the kidneys, a *yullo* to the north the legs, and a *sa* to the south the head. It is said: "What grew around the pond is the living testimony of the sacrificed Nommo's divided body."[168] These trees, living proof of the dismemberment of the body, were impure and did not bear fruit.[169] However, they foreshadowed the resurrection that was to follow.

It is said that the "nape (of the neck) and the eyes" of the victim remained in the Milky Way, demonstrating the supervision he will exercise, along with his twin brothers, over the progress and working of the universe.

A ritual figure portrays the sacrifice of the Nommo in the form of the *nommo anagonno* (fig. 101).[170] It shows the victim and his dismembered body placed inside the body of the sacrificer, who is represented by a larger fish, equipped with teeth to perform the operations.

---

167. *nommo semi numo pene kalle donugo sugo vogo irune senu, dago ulo ayoy.*

168. *o dineru-ne tego vogo nommo semi-go gozu gammali sere.*

169. A tree that bears no fruit is called *puru*, "impure," whereas a tree with fruit is "pure" (*omo* "alive"). When a tree bears no fruit, a purification (*uguru*) is performed to make it produce. The wood of a *puru* tree is used to make the harp-lute of the healers.

170. Figure drawn with python (*yurugu na*) dung under the altar *para lebe* of Sanga during its foundation.

It is also drawn in the sanctuary of Wazouba's main totem, Yagolo (literally "emerged from over there"); the totem's name recalls that it originated from the first one (for the Dogon), Déwa.

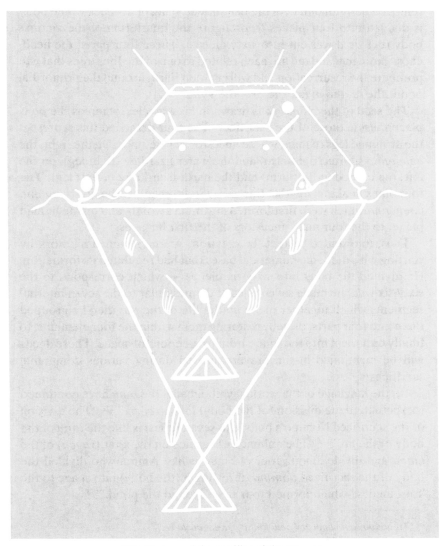

FIG. 101: *tonu* of the sacrifice of the *nommo*.

The severed head is at the top; in the center is the sex organ which was removed beforehand, with the fish shown "lying on its back." The body is divided into four pieces to prefigure the quartering of the victim's body (before it was cut into sixty pieces). These four parts, the head, chest, stomach, and tail are each related to one of the four trees that will prefigure the resurrection and will grow on Earth around the primordial pond: the *sa,* the *minu,* the *oro,* the *yullo.*

The seed of the *emme ya* is drawn in his clavicles, whereas the *po* is placed inside those of the sacrificer. The four detached fins represent the arms and legs of man, whose ancestor the victim is. On the right, the *anagonno* silurus (right arm) and the water lizard *ay* (right leg), on the left, the crocodile (left arm) and the earth lizard *ugunu* (left leg). The four lines making up the fins are a reference to the four *nommo anagonno* which were first formed in Amma's womb, and on the human plane, to the four male ancestors of the first lineages.

Thus, in order to perfect the creation, Amma resumed his work by starting with the same numerical bases that had regulated its formation. He divided the body into sixty-six pieces — which correspond to the sixty-six *yala;* he made seven piles of them, similar to the seven internal segments which together make up the life of the *po;* then he grouped them into four parts, thereby restoring them within the four elements, to finally cast them into the four cardinal directions of space. These deeds will be mentioned in the prayers uttered during various communal sacrifices:

"In the language of the world (symbolically) the *binu* have continued (perpetuated) the division (of the body) into sixty-six."[171] "The division of the sacrificed Nommo's body into seven (piles) is like the *tonu* of the body of the *po.* "[172] "The animal we sacrifice on the altar (*vageu*) of the *ginna* and divide among four old men is like Amma who divided the body of the sacrificed *nommo*, throwing it (the body) into space to the 'four angles,' which formed four trees around the pond."[173]

---

171. *aduno so-ne binu goy pelu kuloy sige gammala ve.*

172. *nommo semi nama gammalu soy po gozu-ne tonu soy tobe anay.*

173. *ginna vageu lebes emenu dieu nay gammalanu, amma nommo semi gozu nay ganna sibe nay tuturu tia, o-ne timu nay te anay.*

The first sentence is recited in the totemic sanctuary and expresses a likening of the totems divided among the families on the one hand to the elements that helped form the universe in Amma's womb and on the other hand to the parts of the sacrificed victim's body. The second, recited during the sacrifice to the *lebe,* refers to the seven elders who, together with the Hogon, receive a part of the sacrificial meat: as a presence of authority, the eight of them here represent the "articulations" of the word in the *po* seed. The third sentence, pronounced in the house of the joint family, recalls the expansion of mankind into the four directions of space, symbolized by the division of the Dogon people into four tribes. Thus, through the stages of the Nommo's sacrifice, this society's structure is contained within the stages of the organization of the universe.

4. THE NOMMO'S RESURRECTION

Outlines of the sacrifice and the resurrection: the altars of the *lebe dala* and of the line of blood; representations: a) the lineage, b) the totemic clan. Value and function of the Nommo's sacrifice and resurrection.

THE NOMMO'S RESURRECTION.

Once the purifying dispersion had taken place, Amma put the victim's organs together again and brought him back to life. "Amma sent the four parts of the Nommo to the four cardinal points; he organized the world. (Amma) took (the pieces) and put them back together; he resurrected the Nommo."[174] For Amma wanted to throw him once again through the celestial opening into the universe, which was to become another "body of the Nommo," determined in its categories by the corresponding parts of that body. It is said that "the Nommo had his body passed onto the world."[175]

The Nommo who had been emasculated and sacrificed as a hermaphrodite was brought back to life in the form of a mixed pair of human twins. To perform this resurrection, Amma took back the victim's seven vital organs, the seats of the "word." He kneaded them in the middle of

---

174. *amma nommo digu nay-go ganna sibe nay-ne tia, ganna yegeru; ie ganna sibe nay kebela mona, nommoy bulumu.*

175. *nommo gozu vomoy aduno tanumu.*

the placenta where the umbilical cord and sex organ had been severed (fig. 77A). To do this, he used the "earth" of the placenta, "light-colored clay": he took some from the place of the sacrifice (at C), some from the place where the blood had flowed from the emasculation, some from the places where the vital organs had been put, and he mixed them all together. In this way, he used the substance that was the most charged with "life force," *nyama,* carried along by the blood; he took back all the power of the placenta. The "earth" was alive, thus "pure," *omo.* With it, Amma made the living Nommo, male and female, in the middle of the sky (the point to which the placenta was attached). While he was molding it, Amma said: "Amma has arranged what he had disarranged. After he had destroyed, today Amma gave back what he himself had destroyed."[176]

Now, the *kilena* to which the Nommo had been tied during the sacrifice had died at the same time as he did. Fed by sacrificial blood, the *yayaga* had grown on it, like mistletoe grows on a tree. This constituted a purification of the withered tree.

In addition, in a hollow, the *pelu* (cailcidrate) had grown from the victim's gall bladder as a twin of the *kilena,* which had grown on flat ground. One says that the *pelu* is a "piece" of the *kilena,* because *pelu* comes from *pele,* "to cut off (the tip of a thing)." One also says that the *pelu* was born from the fruit of its twin, the *kilena.* "The fruit of the *kilena* that was cut (in the place of its seed) turned into *pelu.*"[177] This tree grew on the "earth" into which Amma had put the four elements, the basis of living matter, and on which he had drawn the four collateral directions, the foundation of the site where this matter was to develop,

---

176. *amma bilu bila vo kena, amma yamale amma ie unu yamala obaze.*

According to another version, Amma again took the form of the Fox to gather the scattered pieces; however, the element "water" was missing because the Fox, who belonged to the dry world, was unable to find it. He returned to the tree of the sacrifice and found that the moisture released by the withering of the *kilena* allowed him to re-form the Nommo near the trunk to which the testimonial "arms" were still attached without the clavicles.

177. *kilena i pelle pelu bilenu.* This is said during the purification of the body of a man who has violated a prohibition. According to a popular derivation, *pelu* means "to break." "Amma made use of the *pelu,* for he repaired what he had 'broken' by resurrecting the Nommo."

that is to say, on the victim's placenta: "The *pelu* is always right (straight up), because it was created by the four elements of the world coming together again. Because of this, the *pelu* is never *puru,* it always purifies."[178]

What is even more important in the *pelu* than the presence of the four elements, is that of Amma's "saliva" (i.e., his "word") which sealed them together to form the plant. For it is this "saliva" which actually animates the impure being — impure as it was deprived of its *nyama* — helping it to regain its life force through purification. Therefore, one also says that between the wood and the bark the *pelu* contains Amma's *ninnu* or "light breath." In order to purify the bodies he had just molded and to give them life, Amma wound the *pelu* around them, starting from the head and going down to the feet, in the opposite direction from the "iron chain" used to tie up the victim during the sacrifice. In this way, Amma wanted, on the one hand, to symbolically untie the victim and, on the other hand, to restore with the tree what had been undone during the sacrifice. "Amma, with the *pelu* as he did with the creation of the world, began at the head and went down (to spin the *pelu*). Starting the purification at the top with the *pelu* and bringing it downward, represents untying the Nommo's rope which he had tied at the bottom and taken upward."[179]

In remembrance of its role in the resurrection and its purifying functions, the *pelu* is ritually drawn in a place called *ankuno* (from *ana,* man, and *kuno,* "born without menstrual periods"). The name of said place emphasizes its purity and intangibility, "because like the twin brother, the *kuno* is never impure (*puru*)." This place is located east of the *lebe dala,* at the side of the boulder that rises above the depression separating the Ogol villages, Ogo Digou (Map II), site of the field of Lébé. It represents the place where the umbilical cord of the sacrificed Nommo was attached to his placenta. On a flat rock, called *ogo tuyo taba duni,* "plateau of the placement of the pile (of millet) of the cord," the millet harvest of the religious leader is laid each year to retain the

---

178. *pelu bay voy tey tay vo vogo ganna kize nay-le voy kebela mani-go-de, ko-de pelu asu puriele, bay voy vo dalaze.* The cracks of the bark of the cailcidrate tree are attributed to the presence of the four elements.

179. *amma pelu-le aduno vo manu-gin ku-go tola donugo sugu; pelu-le dago dalu tole, donugo sugonu-go vogo amma nommoy su donugo paga dago vo unnugo pagalanu tozoy.*

E

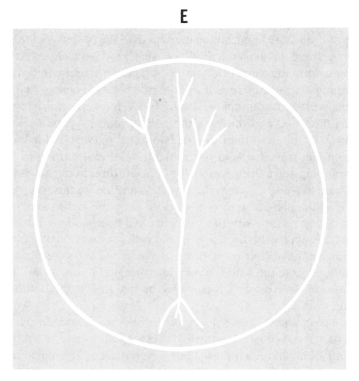

FIG. 102: Drawing of the *pelu*.

spiritual principles of the cereal grains, or *dene,*[180] until the following
sowing season. Before the harvest is put there, a circle (20-30 cm. in
diameter) is drawn with the porridge of fresh *yu,* harvested near the *sogo*
of the Hogon's field. Then, with the same porridge, a *pelu* is drawn with
its branches directed to the east (cf. fig. 102).

One then places on the drawing the prepared ears called *yu dineu,*
"twin millet" and *yu kuno, "kuno* millet,"[181] which will retain the spiritual principles of the cereal grains in the Hogon's granary until the following

---

180. The rites involving the spiritual principles of the grains from sowing to harvest,
storage, and consumption, all make up a cycle which will be presented in installment 2.

181. The officiant, in this case, the Yébéné priest, the Hogon's "sacrificer," prepared the
"twin" millet by tying two ears of *yu* head to tail, then by tying together four pairs of ears

sowing season; after that the rest of the harvest is deposited. The whole thing is sprinkled with the bark of crushed *pelu.* During seven days the Hogon spends his day seated on the "Hogon rock," *ogo dummo,* which is nearby as a part of the locality, to watch over the millet pile during the day. During the night, the *lebe's* snake (represented by the circle surrounding the drawing of the *pelu*) is supposed to protect the harvest.[182] When the seven days have passed, the millet will be transported to be threshed by the community on the *lebe dala,* quite close to the *para lebe* altar: this spot, called *ogo tuyo tabi doni,* "plateau of the crushing of the (millet) pile of the cord," represents the place where the umbilical cord was attached to the victim's body, i.e., his navel.

The resurrection included the Nommo's spiritual principles being put into their place, to ensure the completeness and stability of his person. Amma first gave him his eight souls of body and sex. It is said that the *kikinu say ya* of body "threw a *pelu* bark on the *kikinu bummone* to bring them back to life," thus causing a regrouping of the souls. From this perspective, one also says that the *kilena* and *pelu* represented respectively the two *say ana* and *ya* principles. For the resurrection of the Nommo brought about the resurrection of the *kilena,* which became green again.

Amma also gave the resurrected Nommo the life force (*nyama*) and the eight "seeds of the clavicles." One says: "When Amma resurrected the Nommo, he gave him the seeds from above."[183] Amma did, however, temporarily keep in the sky everything that was in his semen: water, the *dugoy,* the *anagulo,* the cowries, . . .[184]

The Nommo's resurrection was performed by Amma five "periods" or stages after the sacrifice. The number of days — five — of the present week (*dugu* or *ibe dugu,* "market week") is determined by the interval between the Nommo's sacrifice and his resurrection. It is said: "Previously, the

---

also prepared that way, two by two. He then makes a bundle of seven ears to produce the *kuno* millet. These two preparations are related to the representations described *supra,* p. 138 and p. 165.

182. During the Hogon's funeral, the body will momentarily be placed on the "stone of the Hogon" before being brought to the cemetery (installment 2, 3rd and 8th years).

183. *amma nommo varu vo bulumu-le da dene voy obu.*

184. This water will form the first pond on Earth. The cowries, etc., will fall with the first rain. It is said that "what grows by the side of the pond is evidence of the divided body of the sacrificed Nommo," *o dineru-ne te-go vogo nommo semi-go gozu gammali sere.*

days were not counted, one counted the time from the day of the
Nommo's sacrifice to the day of his resurrection; today, this is our

FIG. 103: *tonu* of the "star of the tenth moon."

week."[185] The *dambay,* or "forbidden day," during which no one may
cultivate the ritual field, and which ends the week, is the day of the
resurrection; it comes every five days.

The celestial evidence of the resurrection will be the "star of the tenth
moon," *ie pelu tolo* (fig. 103).[186] The ten rays, paired as twins, are inside,
because the star has not yet "come out." It will be produced when the
Nommo's ark descends, since it is also the witness of the "eye" of the
resurrected Nommo.

The Nommo's resurrection is represented by a series of figures, the
form of which relates its stages and emphasizes, by the presence of

---

185. *ani bay lugi bele; ani varu lugube nommo sema bay bula kunnu.* Four of the days
of the Dogon week bear the name of the marketday of the local villages: Sanga, Iréli, Ibi,
Banani, the fifth being called *dambay,* "forbidden day."

186. Drawn during the ceremony accompanying the ordination (*duguro*) ceremony of
the priest of the Manda totem of Orosongo (with *ara geu* porridge) inside the sanctuary on
the right side. Apparently, this heavenly body (which has not yet been determined) is not
easily seen until the tenth moon (in July).

certain numbers, by the lines, and by their position, the various structures of which it is the genesis. These configurations are placed in certain sanctuaries and various places where they recall his role as overseer of the universe, as the "father" of human beings, as the guardian of their spiritual principles, as the dispenser of rain, and as the master of water in general. In order to comment on them, we give a summarized description of their locations:

N

FIG. 104: *yala* of the 104 articulations of the *nommo*.

1) The first, called *"yala* of the Nommo's 104 articulations"[187] (fig. 104), shows him in an anthropomorphic form and is a *yala.* It represents the formation of articulations, the first result of the division of the victim into pieces — articulations that will be conferred on human beings, the sacrificed Nommo's descendants, who will have to live on earth.

We recall that the formation of the egg of the *nommo anagonno* is represented by a figure of 112 *yala.*[188] Now, the victim's pectoral fins — originally corresponding to eight *yala* of the whole figure — which remained "alive," had been virtually thrown into space and set aside from the dismembered body, which means that they would not be granted to man. Therefore, the figure representing the resurrected Nommo — man's ancestor — has only 104 *yala.*[189] Thus, this figure stresses the genetic bonds between the victim and human beings by its anthropomorphism, by the number of dots, and by the stage of the depiction (*yala*), which symbolizes the preformation of the articulations.

The drawing has one dot that is larger than the others, indicating the place of the skull, source of the "word" as "thought." It is connected by a dotted line to another equally important dot that marks the position of the sex organ, the organ of reproduction related to the "eighth word." On either side, two rows of four dots represent the clavicular seeds. Then are shown:
the shoulder joints: *tatabu digu*
the elbow joints: *numo totogu digu*
the hand joints: *numo digu,* including
those of the wrist (one dot), *numo kokolo digu,*
of the hand itself (two groups of three dots),
and of the fingers (three groups of five dots), *numo i digu*
the hip joints: *loru digu*
the knee joints: *yonolo digu*
the foot joints (four dots): *kubo digu.*

---

187. Drawn under the *sogo uguru uguri* of the pond of Dona with *yu* and *ara geu* porridge.
188. Cf. *supra,* p. 159.
189. According to popular belief, a crocodile eats a pebble every year. When it has swallowed 104 stones, it becomes "like the Nommo," of whom it is both the agent and the avatar, and goes to live for the rest of its life in a cave located in the cliffs above Yanda. The inhabitants of this settlement, for whom the crocodile is a totemic prohibition, bury these animals and hold funerals for them as they would for one of their own people.

The figure is a *yala,* that is to say, a form of depiction evoking the genesis of the realization of the thing depicted; here it is indicative of Amma's aim: the resurrection of the sacrificed Nommo in human form.

The point at the top represents the cowry sewn on the kerchief (*binekezu dommo*) of the totemic priest the day he is ordained.

The central dot represents a sea shell *ki selu,* "striped bone," which the priest also wears on his clothes that day. These two objects recall the sea water which, like fresh water, sprang from the emasculation, and they are related to the first pond (fresh water) and the first lagoon (sea water) to be formed on Earth.

After his descent to Earth the resurrected Nommo will go to the waters — to transform himself and live there in his original form of *nommo anagonno.*[190]

2) Now, it is in the water and after his transformation that the Nommo will be instructed by Amma to reveal the "word" he possesses to man. This revelation is in direct correspondence with the number of the main "body parts" of the resurrected Nommo, twenty-two, depicted by the following graphic representation, which we must first explain.

a) With regard to the formation of the universe, the Nommo's sacrifice had not only regenerated those parts of it affected by the Fox's deeds, but had also contributed to the development of the rest: the twenty-two "articulations" correspond here to the twenty-two *yala* of body and sex of the *po,* placed in the center of the spiral of Amma's primordial egg. Having resumed his work by sacrificing the Nommo, when he resurrected him Amma conferred on him the number attributed to the development of "life" (thus of the "word") in the first grain.[191]

b) The twenty-two articulations are also related to the resurrected Nommo's possession of the "word," which he will "weave" in the water across his teeth and then reveal to man. "The words which were in the *tonu soy* of the *po,* Amma made them come out and gave them to the Nommo: this became the cloth that cannot be cut."[192] At this stage, the

---

190. Cf. *infra,* p. 490.

191. Cf. *infra,* p. 121.

192. *po gozune tonu soy tobe amma gona nommo oba nommo so, soy paralay bi.* These words are spoken at the consecration of a weaver's altar to Amma. For the identity between the "word" and weaving, cf. Marcel Griaule, *Dieu d'eau.* p. 84 and ff.

word becomes verbal expression, thus including the "articulations" of thought as well as those of language. In this instance, the number of the resurrected Nommo's "articulations" corresponds to the categories into which Amma had put his entire future creation — categories foreshown by the classification of the primordial signs originating from his thought.[193]"The words which are in the belly are not known; what is spoken is what is known. The word is like the seven articulations (organs) of the Nommo. The seven words of the Nommo's articulations are the seven words of the Nommo which were inside the belly and had not come out. His twenty-two articulations are the twenty-two words which he spoke on the outside and the number of the words."[194]

c) From the social viewpoint, the number of the resurrected Nommo's articulations is related here to kinship in its broadest sense, called *menne* (from *me,* placenta), and makes up the structure of totemism — the institution of the *binu* — i.e., the worship rendered by all men to the sacrificed and resurrected Nommo.

In regard to the first mythical generation, the eight ancestors of humanity are primarily considered as forming a single clan, all originating, therefore, from one totem. The clan will be "divided" into five at the third generation, then into seventeen at the fifth, in relation to the development of the mythical "families." All together, the twenty-two first "great totems," *binu na,* theoretically constitute the symbol of the collective worship rendered by all men of all clans to the sacrificed Nommo. The motto of the first totem, Déwa, recalls this "division": "Déwa grew from the thigh, Hogon of the stable word; the number of the twenty-two articulations of the Nommo came out of his body."[195] One says: "The *binu* is like the rebirth of the Nommo; the twenty-two *binu* in the world are the resurrected body of the Nommo. All men possess the divided body of the sacrificed Nommo."[196] "The twenty-two successive articulations of the word of the sacrificed Nommo are like the twenty-two divided *binu.*"[197]

---

193. Cf. *supra,* p. 94.

194. *bere-ne so to innemo, so soani igi bemese. so-go nommo semi digu soy ginu vo, nommo digu soy-go vogo nommo so vomo soy bere vomo kolo-ne parago so golu tolu-go voy. digu vomo pelley ley sige so vomo pelley sige vogo so parago soa vo gonu lugi anay.*

195. *dewa paga puzu, imo ogono; nommo digu lugi pelley ley sige gozu vo-ne goy.*

196. *binu nommo pillema nani tosoy. innem pu nommo semi-go gammalu si.* Spoken when the goat is slaughtered on the terrace of the totemic sanctuaries during the sowing celebration, *bulu.*

That is why one draws a *tonu* on the façade of certain sanctuaries, called *"tonu* of the Nommo's articulations,"[198] which is composed of a series of twenty-two figures drawn to either side of the door (fig. 105), with twelve to the right and ten to the left:

1. *ku-le kukuli-le:* hair, head, neck
2. *gene:* chest
3. *bere:* belly
4. *surugu:* ear
5. *go:* ribs
6. *sonono:* spinal column
7. *doy:* kidneys
8. *ani guyo:* clavicle
9. *numo temie:* "brick" of the hand[201]
10. *giru:* eye

1. *numo ene talu:* "chicken egg" arm[199]
2. *numo ammu:* forearm[200]
3. *kebele:* shoulderblade
4. *numo i:* fingers
5. *paga:* thigh
6. *tozu:* calf, tibia
7. *kubo temie:* "brick" of the foot
8. *aa:* lower jaw
9. *kubo i:* toes
10. *bolo kommo:* rear orifice
11. *kinu:* nose
12. *kenne:* mouth

The division of figures here denotes: on the right (male side), the number attributed to the Fox (twelve) corresponding to those elements henceforth controlled by the victim; on the left (female side), the number attributed to the sacrificed Nommo (ten) as a "person" and "progenitor" of humanity.

Similarly, every candidate for priesthood must undergo a series of twenty-two trances or "attacks," called *soy,* "quaking spells," each of which corresponds to a part of the Nommo's body as well as to the categories of Amma, that is to say, to the classifications of his "word."

---

197. *nommo semi digu so pelle ley sige ya-le, binu pelle ley sige gammeli anay.* Spoken during the ceremony for ordination (*duguru*) of a priest of the Goummoyana totem. The list of the twenty-two *binu na,* their distribution among the Dogon tribes and the corresponding prohibitions will be presented in installment 2.

198. *nommo digu tonu.* Drawn with *po pilu* porridge on the façade of the sanctuary of the Goummoyana *binu* during the second ceremony for the ordination of the priest (*duguru*), performed before sowing time. During the *pagu,* performed the preceding year at the time of the *po pilu* harvest, a porridge of this grain had been poured over the altar; some kernels had been saved for making the paintings for the actual *duguru* before the following sowing. Goummoyana is in charge of purifications performed at the pond of Dona on the *sogo uguru uguri.* (Cf. *infra,* p. 493, n. 99).

199. This expression refers to the biceps.   200. From *amma,* "to hold in one's arms."
201.This expression refers to the "top-side" of the foot, the "back" of the hand.

The totemic cult will multiply gradually with the development of the
lineages, and the "division of the totems" will continue indefinitely. This
division of the totemic cult into totems, which are "split" according

FIG. 105: *tonu* of the articulations of the *nommo.*

to the Dogon method as territorial groups and lineages expand, is
directly related to these concepts. Ritual objects of the sanctuaries will
be divided as many times as necessary to create more of them, entirely
in the image of the division of the Nommo's body for the reorganization
of the world. Each new totem is connected with the different stages of
history and relates to one of the twenty-two fundamental *binu,* manifestations of the categories of the "word."

3) The following stage of the resurrection is represented by a series of figures which, by their form and the places where they are drawn, emphasize the protection the Nommo will provide for the territory that will be inhabited by man. They are, in fact, drawn under altars called *pegu* (literally "to plant"), which are placed in the area occupied by a village, or a group of villages, and in the land belonging to them.

The altar sometimes includes a male anthropomorphic statuette with an iron hook driven into the top of its head. It is placed outside the settlements and is usually buried near a tree which may have been planted for this occasion.

Generally speaking, the foundation of a *pegu* is based on the voluntary sacrifice of a living being, who consents to the *pegu* being "symbolically planted on his head." He knows his end is near because his spiritual principles are leaving him at the consecretion of the altar to enter the statuette that represents him; he agrees, therefore, to die in a short time.[202] He becomes the Nommo's agent on the Fox's Earth since his *own* spiritual principles — and his life force — are "summoned" to the altar during the collective offering, and not those of the resurrected Nommo which dwell exclusively in the water. He is the one, therefore, who "stabilizes" and "protects" the settlements in the name of the Nommo. He is, in fact, considered to be permanently joined to the Nommo.

At Sanga, the figures relating the resurrection, called *"tonu* of the head, the trunk, and the feet of the resurrected Nommo" (fig. 106),[203] have been drawn in *ara geu* porridge under the three principal *pegu* during their foundation: these altars are of a general type and concern all the settlements of Lower and Upper Sanga; they are called *sana ganna pegu, "pegu* of the space of Sanga."

The head is found under the *pegu* called *ke boru* (literally "increase of the heritage"), located near the village of Kangadaga (Map II, J). The vertical line is the *bummo* of the Nommo's face and also recalls his vertical position when he was resurrected.

---

202. The altar may also have been founded with a real sacrifice: the victim is buried standing up with a hook or a bar of metal that has been driven in, "planted" in his skull. The form and function of the different *pegu* will be discussed in installment 2.

203. *kize bulo ku-le go-le kubo-le tonu.* The word *kize,* "thing," is used as an euphemism to avoid saying the name of the Nommo.

E

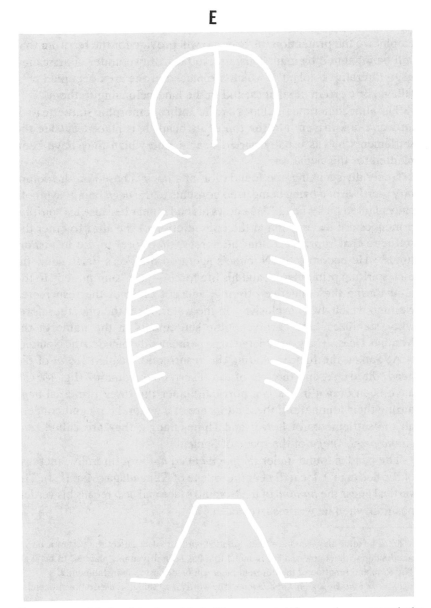

F<small>IG</small>. 106: *tonu* of the head, trunk, and feet of the resurrected Nommo, drawn respectively:
the head, under the *pegu* at Kangadaga; the trunk, under the *pegu* of Dina; the legs under
the *pegu* of Gona.

The trunk is situated under the *pegu* of Dina (Map II, K). The nine "ribs" denote the Nommo's female twin and humanity's eight ancestors, his "sons"; ten (the whole, that is) is the number attributed to him as a "person." For it is said: "The people (persons) Amma sent into the world on the ark, the eight human beings, the two Nommos, the number of those descended is ten. Amma sent into the world a number of ten people."[204]

The legs are located under the *pegu* of Gona (Map II, L) i.e., near the stream where he will reside after his descent upon Earth. The east-west orientation of the three figures is evidence of the Nommo's position at the time of his resurrection in the sky: he "fell" with his head to the east, and Amma resurrected him in the center of his placenta, standing up and facing east. When speaking of these different attributions — of the number ten corresponding to the person — and of the orientation of the altars, one says: "The ten articulations of the *pegu* of Sanga are like the ten articulations of the sacrificed Nommo; the head is to the east, the chest in the center, the feet to the west."[205]

By their number (three), the figures emphasize the resurrected Nommo's sex. The fact that they are deliberately spaced out over the territory occupied by the inhabitants of Lower and Upper Sanga finally demonstrates that the male Nommo's protection extends over their whole territory. Sacrifices are performed on the three altars by three representatives of the entire community during the hot season (*nay banu*) for the first two, and before the sowing feast, *bulu*, for the one at Gona.[206]

4) The final stage is portrayed by a figure called "drawing of the Nommo resurrected as a man who went into the water."[207] It is drawn inside the totemic sanctuary and depicts the Nommo in his human and realistic aspect. In addition to the nose, the head here has the mouth that will "speak the words." The number of ribs showing is the same as on the figure of the *pegu*. The arms and legs are very long, and the hands and feet now have their fingers and toes.

---

204. *amma inne koro-le aduno-ne vo ti, inneu gagara nommo ley, pelu sununi lugi. amma aduno-ne inneu pelu ti lugi.*

205. *sana pegu digu tanu nommo semi digu tanu tozoy; ku-go du sibe-ne vo go logoro-ne vo kubo, donno-go vo.*

206. Respectively, the head of the *ginna* of Kangadaga, the representative of the Hogon of Sanga for Dina, and of Yébéné for Gona.

PLAN OF THE SACRIFICE AND RESURRECTION: THE ALTARS OF THE LEBE DALA AND THE LINE OF BLOOD.

It is appropriate to examine the morphology of the altars and of the raised stones, placed on the *lebe dala* or outside on the "line of blood," and of the different figures drawn at their foundation that relate the sacrifice and resurrection of the Nommo.

The altars represent the different parts of the victim's body; they are manifestations of the bonds uniting him with human beings, his descendants, by the way in which they respectively correspond to the various basic levels of social organization: the tribe (in this case the Dyon), the totemic clans, and the lineages.

All these altars are the objects of libations or of sacrifices, performed by those who have this responsibility in their society, during the sowing celebration, *bulu,* in which all who belong to the different communities of Upper and Lower Sanga participate.[208] These offerings are performed in accordance with the path called "Amma's great winding path," *amma ozu na gonnu,* which represents his perambulations during the Nommo's sacrifice.

The altars are formed either of clay cones, made with earth taken from the banks of the ponds, or raised stones or groups of rocks, *sogo,* made of stones which are also taken from the ponds, *o tibi,* i.e., the water in which the resurrected Nommo lives.

Drawn under the altars when they are founded, we find:

a) the figures of the internal organs or parts of the body which recall, above all, the characteristics of the different "words" (except for the word of the sex, kept by Amma), carried along by the blood and corresponding to each of the parts (fig. 107). One says that "the seven *sogo* of the Nommo's articulations placed on the *lebe dala,* the division of the sacrificial meat of the *lebe* among the seven elders, this is like the seven words. In meetings, the words end with those of the seven eldest

207. *nommo bula inne-go di-ne yoy toy.* In the past, this figure was drawn with *ara geu* porridge inside the sanctuary during the ceremony for the ordination of the priest of the Ogoine totem (installment 2).

208. Installment 2, 5th year.

(men)."[209] They also demonstrate the order of distribution of the parts of a sacrificial victim among the different members of the group involved — tribe, clan, or lineage — an order which reflects the social hierarchy;

b) generally placed to the east of those we have just mentioned are the figures of the different stars formed during the sacrifice.

Generally speaking, the different stages of the Nommo's emasculation and sacrifice determined the formation and future motion of the stars in space, prefigured by the *yala* of "Amma's egg."[210] They are the basis for the different calendars — solar, lunar, Sirian, Venusian — that people will establish on Earth and that will cadence all their activities.

Generally speaking and in relation to the sacrifice, the stellar system includes:

— An "internal" system of stars corresponding to the flow of the blood on the placenta and to the victim's vital organs; it is considered to be the driving force of the stellar world, directly influencing the life of man and his development on Earth; it plays a part much like the system of internal organs in the human body.

— An "external" system corresponding to the "path of the blood" outside the placenta as well as to the "ornaments" of the resurrected Nommo; it is made up of stars which are further away, but which also make their influence felt in people's lives, although to a lesser degree. It includes the Milky Way, itself the image of the spiral of stars within the "spiraling star world" in which Earth is found.[211] In this "world of stars," the axis ("Amma's fork") around which these various movements take place connects the Polestar, *aduno giru* ("eye of the world"), with the stars of the Southern Cross, *aduno giru ley* ("second eye of the world") (fig. 108). These stars are so named because they "watch" the space they support: "The Polestar and the Southern Cross support the place where

---

209. *lebe dala-ne nommo digu sogu sogo-ne to, dieu soy lebe nama gammala so soy anay. bara yaye dieu soy-le so dogoze.* This regards the division of the victim's body on the altar of the *lebe* between the seven eldest men of Upper and Lower Sanga, during the *bulu.* Cf. *supra,* p. 305 and installment 2, 5th year.

210. We recall that, for the Dogon, there exists an almost infinite number of "star worlds in a spiral," cf. *supra,* p. 170.

211. Cf. *supra,* p. 169.

FIG. 107: Figures of the organs drawn under the altars of the *lebe dala:*
1) heart, 2) liver, 3) spleen, 4) pancreas, 5) lungs, 6) kidneys,
7) intestines; in 8), the skin of the *nommo anagonno.*

the Earth rests."[212] They are also called, respectively, *amma giru,* "Amma's eye," and *amma giru ley,* "Amma's second eye." Thus, "Amma's eyes" that opened in order to produce the universe[213] are present and hold up all the stars.

The Dogon make a distinction between the fixed stars, *tolo,* and the planets, *tolo tanaze,* "stars that move across," or "stars that walk separately," because of their motion or also "stars of the east," *du tolo,* an allusion to their observed rising. The fixed stars belong to the "family of stars that do not turn" (around another star), *tolo digilele togu;* the planets belong to the "family of stars that turn" (around another), *tolo gonu togu;* the satellites are called *tolo gonoze,* "stars that make a circle."

It is said of the planets: "All the stars that turn separately are the blood of the sacrificed things."[214] With regard to the Nommo's sacrifice, the fixed stars are related to the parts of the sacrificed Nommo's body; the planets, satellites (and companions) are related to the circulating blood and to the "seeds," especially to the contents of the clavicles that flow with the blood.

The stars are also the celestial evidence of the "seeds," the primal elements formed in Amma's womb. We recall that they, like the seeds, were prefigured by the *yala* of the egg.

From this perspective, Venus is also called *nu tolo,* "star of the bean;" Jupiter, *yu tolo,* "star of the small millet;" Saturn (?), *ani tolo,* "star of the Hibiscus"; Mars, *emme sono dum banu tolo.* The stars, therefore, will later be related to the distribution and proliferation of the primordial seeds created in Amma's womb and to the safekeeping of their spiritual principles, which is also the responsibility of the resurrected Nommo and his "twin brothers," the *nommo die* and the *titiyayne,* who live with Amma. Therefore, certain of them are seen — at other stages of graphic representation — under the *sogo* altars in the fields where sacred functions are performed (fields of the *lebe,* of the *ginna* and of the various totems in the region), on the façades of the Hogon's dwelling and of the totemic sanctuaries.

---

212. *aduno gire turu-le aduno gire ley-le minne doy da be gele.* For the Dogon, the Southern Cross has four stars.

213. The Pole Star is also called "found seat," *dogo temme.*

214. *tolo dumogo dey-le gonoze kize semu illi.* One will say of Venus, "Venus which moves across," *yazu tanaze.*

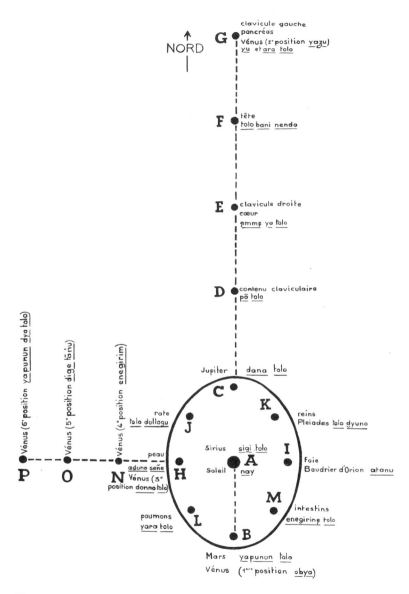

FIG. 108: The altars of the *lebe dala* and of the "path of blood": representations.
A. *para lebe;* B. *igibie;* C. *uguru uguri;* D. *dummo dama;* E. *ka amma;* F. *pegu;*
G. *tenu amma;* H. *belu uri;* I. *sogo* of Yébéné; J. *sogo* of Guéméné: K. *sogo* of Goummayana;
L. *sogo* of Nommo; M. *sogo* of Tiré; N. *sogo enegirim tolo;* O. *sogo dige tanu tolo;*
P. *yapunu dya tolo.*

A. *"lebe* of the day of the fish seated on the outside," *izubay lebe para-ne da,* commonly called *"lebe* of the outside."

At A, site of the emasculation and the resurrection, an altar is raised as evidence both of the sacrificed Nommo's placenta, the celestial ground, and of Sirius, born of the cutting of the umbilical cord at the time of the emasculation: it is the "navel of the world" *(aduno bogi),* or the omphalos. The Fox's placenta (transformed into the sun) was under the sacrificed Nommo's placenta during the operation. The altar is a red clay cone topped by a small flat stone representing this star "that one now sees in space" (Pl. XIII, 3). Thus, it presents a deliberate switch of position between the two stars at the time of the emasculation. At this level of the myth, the altar represents the "first meeting of Sirius and the sun," which is the heliacal rising of Sirius that will later come to pass and that will, in the course of events taking place on Earth, commemorate the first sacrifice that gave rise to the formation and motion of the stars.

The *bummo* of Sirius, *sigi tolo,* is a dot surrounded by sixty rays of unequal length, with the shortest one placed to the east, the segments getting longer turning to the south, the west, and the north, with the longest to the northeast. It signifies the number attributed to the placenta, or the number of the placenta, *me lugu,* and the spiraling motion of the life that quickens it. Finally, it represents the similar movement of the stars in space.[215]

In every village where the Sigui is performed, each woman, after having brewed the ceremonial beer, brings the dignitaries the container used for its fermentation, a yeast container representative of the placenta. The dignitary then says to her: "The number of the placenta and the number of the Sigui are the same."[216]

A figure representing *sigi tolo* (in porridge of *yu* and *ara geu*) and the

---

215. Drawn on the site where the *albarga* altar of Yougo and the *buguturo* altar of Go were erected, representing the sacrificed Nommo's placenta. At Yougo and Sanga, the Sigui ceremonies begin with offerings made on these altars.

216. *me lugi sigi lugi koturu.* The various yeast containers used for the regular and ceremonial beers represent the placenta or pieces of the placenta of the first beings Amma created. The symbolism and function of the yeast containers will be presented in installment 2. For the symbolism of fermentation, cf. also *supra,* p. 152.

sun (in red ochre, *bana*) was drawn under the altar *para lebe* during its foundation (fig. 109). The four branches of *sigi tolo,* placed in the center, represent the four elements: to the northeast, water; to the northwest, air; to the southeast, earth; to the southwest, fire. This attribution is evidence of the integrity of the placenta of the Nommo, who will always remain pure and alive. The same holds true for the placentas of human beings. It is said that "the woman who has given birth, the placenta remains for seven (weeks) in the place where they will wash themselves; (the child) it is (there) as if (it were) living in water; it is as if it were living in water; it is as if it were living in the water with the Nommo."[217] Indeed, the placenta and attached umbilical cord are put in a piece of pottery which is placed in the courtyard under the dunghill, composed of millet left to rot there. It is covered with a flat rock: the child-bearing mother performs her morning ablutions on this rock and also washes the newborn child on it for a period of seven weeks. The earthenware that theoretically receives the water is left there and finally gets broken. To leave the placenta "in the water" for seven weeks (seven being the number attributed to the multiplication of the "word"[218]), to abandon it under the dunghill containing the vital force (*nyama*) of the grains, is the same as keeping it alive indefinitely. With regard to the integrity of any placenta, a being or an object which is never susceptible to impurity is called *kize mene,* "thing (in) the placenta."

Thus, Sirius is the symbol of the ever-living placenta of the resurrected Nommo: the star is also called *albararu,* a contraction of "Amma *albarka,"* or "thanks to Amma."

On the spatial level, the figure of the Nommo's placenta (Sirius) denotes the collateral directions or "four angles" of celestial space, just as the figure of the Fox's placenta (the sun) denotes the cardinal directions of terrestrial space; hence the symbolic value attached to the heliacal rising of Sirius, which figures in the composition of the long calendar of the Dogon.[219]

---

217. *yani i nana me yalu di be inerese-ne, ibe soy yadoy me omoyo dine to anay; omo-le nommo-le di-ne vo anay.* These words are spoken after the delivery by the midwife, called "old woman who makes the child be born," *yana pey i nanama.*

218. *Supra,* p. 137.

219. A series of figures drawn in other places, connoting the solar positions (equinoxes

C. *uguru uguri,* "place where the fumigation (purification) is performed."

The altar is made of four black stones which correspond to the four basic elements.

N

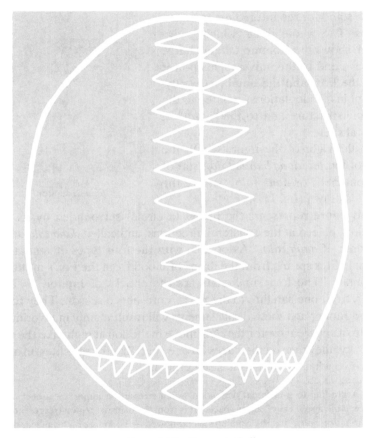

FIG. 110: The Nommo's skull.

---

and solstices) as well as the heliacal rising of Sirius, will be treated in volume I, installment 2, 1st year.

At the time of its founding, the figures drawn are: the resurrected Nommo's anthropomorphic skull, *dana* (fig. 110). This drawing of the brainpan has twelve vertical indentations — the number assigned to Ogo — and ten horizontal indentations — the number assigned to the resurrected Nommo; the latter ten are divided into two sections of five teeth which stand for the future human generations. The whole thing, which is oriented, shows the Nommo taking charge of space and of the universe, his power over the Fox, and the number (twenty-two) of his "articulations," related to the totemic structure and to the "word" at the oral stage.

To the right of the figure (east), the *tonu* of Jupiter, *dana banna tolo*, "star of the fontanel," or *dana tolo*, "star of the skull" is drawn (fig. 111).[220]

FIG. 111:
tonu of Jupiter.

This figure represents the planet (a circle) surrounded by its four satellites, placed at the collateral directions, and called *dana tolo unum*, "children of *dana tolo*." Associated with the four types of *sene*, these four satellites sprang from the drops of blood from the Fox's mutilated sex organ. "The four small stars are the chocks of Jupiter."[221] Each sector, from one satellite to the next, represents a season. They rotate around Jupiter and these displacements will result mainly in favoring the growth of *sene* leaves; for the *sene* move in the soil at night like the stars in the sky. they turn on their axes (in one year) like the satellites, in order to receive what these satellites send them.[222]

---

220. According to a different derivation which stresses an important aspect of the sacrifice, *dana* also means "empty space." It is from the celestial region (represented by the altar *uguru uguri)* that the Nommo's blood flowed — no longer on his placenta, but into space, in order to purify it. According to another derivation, Jupiter is also the star of "the hunt," *dana.*

221. *tolo uzi nay dana tolo peni.* Cf. *supra,* p. 284.

222. The trunk of certain varieties of *sene* grows in a spiral. Houses are not built with *sene* wood which "would make the house spin." The *sene's* "movements" at night are also believed to attract the souls of the dead which "move from one place to another."

A hole made in the east wall of the *kana,* where the altar to the ancestors (*vageu*) is located, represents *dana tolo.* During offerings to the ancestors, the porridge is first poured through this hole for the *nommo die,* then onto the earthenware pots of the *kunu* and of the twins for the *o nommo* and, finally, on the other pottery for the ancestors of the lineage.

The planet is similarly associated with the cultivation of the "field of the ancestors," *vageu.* The *yala* of Jupiter is drawn under the *sogo* placed in this field, which itself is made of a big rock supported or chocked by four stones in the cardinal directions. The order in which the seeds are sown in the ritual field connotes the progression of the planet.

D. *dummo dama,* "forbidden boulder."

The altar consists of a very long and very white raised stone, placed on a rocky block, which itself is elevated in relation to the village (Pl. XIII, 1).

This altar, neither a *sogo* nor an *ommolo,* is the only one of its kind. It recalls the loss of the contents of the victim's clavicles as well as the site of *po tolo,* "star of the *po* "and proof of the emergence of *po pilu* that will pour all it contains into the ark of the resurrected Nommo.[223] The *bummo* for this star is a dot surrounded by sixty-six rays recalling the sixty-six *yala* of the *po* inside Amma's womb. The *tonu* drawn under the altar is composed of six lines in a spiral, each of which begins with a dot, depicting the six *yala* of the seed's sex as well as the movement impressed on it during its creation (fig. 112). "The six *yala* of *po tolo* of *dummo*

---

223. For *po tolo,* see *infra,* p. 500.

dama are like the resurrection of the sacrificed Nommo's blood."[224] For
the strength and power of the divine word that Amma included in the *po
pilu* will be the means to bring about the resurrection.

N

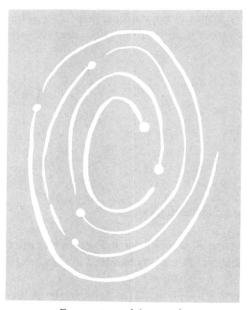

FIG. 112: *tonu* of the *po tolo*.

E. *ka amma*, "(altar of) Amma of Ka."

This term indicates the supreme importance of this altar to the Dyon
of Sanga. It is the first altar to Amma, which they built when they arrived

---

224. *dummo dama-ne po tolo yala kuloy nommo semi illi bulo anay.*

there from Kani Kombolé via Kani Gogouna. It is also called *amma kize kana,* "(the altar) to Amma of the finished thing," that is, of the death of the sacrificed Nommo (Pl. XIII, 2).

Made of a clay cone, it is similar to the altars of the family houses,

N

FIG. 113: *tonu* of *emme ya tolo.*

except that it is much larger. It represents the victim's right clavicle, the receptacle of part of the clavicular contents that had spilled out during the sacrifice; it also is evidence of the star *emme ya tolo,* the seed's twin and holder of the spiritual principles of cereal grains, *ka amma* is like the right clavicle of the sacrificed 'master of the water'."[225]

---

225. *ka amma di bana semi-go numo i ani guyo tozoy.*

Under the altar, when its foundation is laid, are drawn: the picture of Amma's signs and the *bummo* of the *po*,[226] the *toy* of the victim's heart, which Amma laid there after the sacrifice, and a figure of the star *emme ya tolo,* the second companion (or satellite) of Sirius (fig. 113).

The *bummo* for *emme ya tolo* is a dot representing the star from which stem eight rays portraying the varieties of sorghum "that originated from it"; the extension pointing north is *emme nakolo.* Under the altar the "*tonu* of the seat of the *emme ya* star" has been drawn.[227] It is made of a circle with a smaller circle inside it, representing the seed; four oriented "rays" cross the entire picture, while four shorter lines inside the circle, and therefore inside the star, are drawn in the collateral directions. These four lines in the central circle, "seat of the *emme ya,*" and the four rays represent the four *kikinu* of the sex and the four body *kikinu* of the eight basic grains.[228] The predominant femininity of the *emme ya* and its fertility are both stressed by the line placed to the northeast in the figure, which represents the germ emerging from the seed.

F. *pegu,* literally: "planted."

There the Nommo died where Amma cut off his head. Two trees were planted near the altar, a *bozo* and an *ommolu.* Drawn under the altar in *ara geu* porridge is the *yala* of the "scintillating red star," *tolo bani nenneu,* born of the blood that was shed. It is made of a central dot surrounded by twelve smaller dots, that recall the number assigned to Ogo and to his deeds that necessitated the sacrifice of his twin brother (a star in the constellation of Taurus) (fig. 114).

The *tonu* of two concentric circles is drawn with snake excrement, *yuguru na,* on the façade of the dwelling of the Hogon of Arou, above the platform, at the time this dignitary is ordained.

---

226. Cf. *supra,* p. 83, fig. 2 and p. 136, fig. 21.

227. *emme ya tolo doy tonu.*

228. The *emme ya* is put in the granary where the seeds are kept for sowing for the following year. There, it is the testimony of the souls of the cereals which will be bestowed upon the seeds after the sacrifice offered on Ka Amma at the time of the *bulu.*

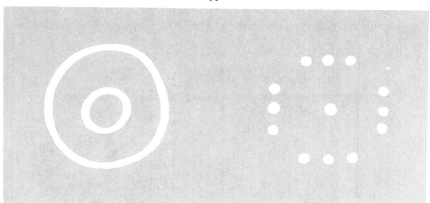

FIG. 114: *yala* and *tonu* of *tolo banu nenneu* (from left to right).

G. *keze amma* or *tenu amma,* "moist (altar to) Amma."

This altar is made of clay, like *ka amma* and the altars of Amma in the family houses, but it is smaller in size and represents the victim's left clavicle.[229]

The figures drawn during its foundation represent Amma's closed egg, Venus in the *yazu* (or *bayara*) position, the stars of *yu* and of *ara geu,* the victim's pancreas (the internal organ associated with intuition), and lines which denote the four body *kikinu* of the basic cereal grains (fig. 115). This last figure, placed next to the pancreas, is associated with divination. Indeed, on the day called *bulu o,* "gift of the *bulu,*"[230] all the totemic priests of the Sanga region meet near the altar to determine the exact date of the *bulu,* to find out whether the seeds sown will receive their four spiritual body principles, *gozu kikinu,* and whether the harvest will be a good one.

---

229. The dimensions of the two altars connoting the victim's "clavicles" are associated with the fact that, for a boy, the right clavicle (that of *ka amma*) is believed to form first: this emphasizes the resurrected Nommo's role as a male at this stage of the myth.

230. Drawn at the first crescent of the sixth moon. The *bulu* takes place before the end of that same moon.

All the priests sit in a row facing east; the eldest among them to the south, the others placed after him according to age. A diviner known for his skill in handling the cowries, *vanu pazane,* has been summoned and sits beside the eldest priest. After a libation of porridge on the altar and

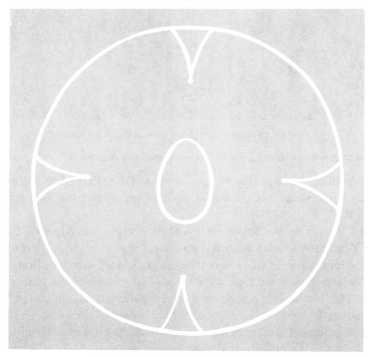

FIG. 115: Drawing of the four *kikinu* of body of the grains.

on the divination material, he draws a figure on the ground which symbolically shows the grains' four *kikinu* of body. (To the north, *say ya,* to the south, *say ana,* to the east, *bummone ya,* to the west *bummone ana*). On this figure — which is a reproduction of the one drawn under the altar — he then throws the divination cowries, twice in a row. It is through the pancreas that the diviner receives the "messages" relating to the divination, through the intermediary of the organ of the sacrificed Nommo.

Similarly, after the *bulu,* when the fields where sacred functions are performed are first fertilized (before sowing),[231] the family heads, *ginna bana,* perform the divination on the table of the Fox by drawing on the registers four lines, which represent four sex *kikinu,* in order to find out whether the seeds will receive their complementary spiritual principles.

H. *belu uri,* "place where one skins the (sacrificed) animal."

The altar is made of seven red stones which represent the seven piles made with the dismembered body and the seven articulations of the "word."

Under the altar, the *toy* of the *nommo anagonno's* skin and the *tonu* of Venus in the *donno tolo* position are drawn; the constellation *aduno sene* is represented by the open iron bracelet that is placed on the arm of every totemic priest when he takes office. The position of Venus, the "star of the west" in this instance, is evidence of the general apparent motion of all the stars from east to west, such as it will be seen by man.

The altars I, J, K, L, M were erected in those theoretical places where Amma supposedly placed certain of the victim's internal organs and where certain stars or constellations are said to have appeared. These altars, *sogo,* are assigned to five great totems of the Dyon in the region, whose names they bear; these totems are proof of the first division, among the first four lineages, of the only original totem, Déwa.[232]

I. *sogo* of the Yébéné totem.

This altar is made of a long green stone.

The figures drawn on it include the *toy* of the liver (cf. fig. 107) and the *tonu* of the stars called *atanu,* "three," which are those of Orion's Belt (fig. 116).

The *toy* of the liver bears witness to the three parts of the organ: the part that is detached to be thrown on the altar, called "liver that is

---

231. Drawn at the first crescent of the seventh moon. All of these ceremonies will be described in installment 2, 5th year.

232. Cf. *supra,* p. 338.

thrown," *mani kinne*; the "liver of the right side," *i tana kinne*; "the liver of the left side," *nanna tana kinne.* During a sacrifice in the *ginna,* these last two parts of the liver are given to the patriarch and the spleen to the one who is the eldest after him.

The three stars of Orion's Belt, oriented east-west, respectively represent the *nommo die,* the *titiyayne,* and the sacrificed Nommo, i.e., the guardians of the spiritual principles of the cereal grains that are entrusted to them between the harvest and the following sowing season. These are

E

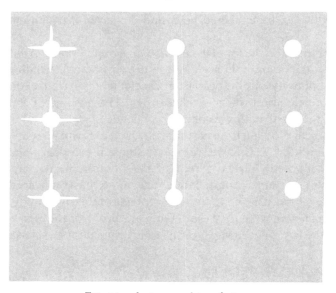

FIG. 116: *yala, tonu,* and *toy* of *atanu.*

the stars that are therefore associated with the safekeeping of the grain seeds. Referring to the principal agents of the cult devoted to Amma and to his three deputies, it is said: "The *gina bana,* the Hogon of Lébé, and the totemic priest are the guardians of the souls of the seeds of the grains."[233]

---

233. *vageu bana-le lebe ogone-le binugedine-le yu toy kikinu be gele.*

Pl. XIII: The altars of the *lebe dala* and the "path of the blood":
1) *dummo dama*

2) *ka amma*

3) The *lebe* at the center of the *lebe dala*.

Pl. XIV: Arranged stones and *sogo* representing the various positions of Venus:
1) Venus *donno tolo,* east of Lower Ogol.

2) Venus *dige tanu,* at a location called Tenné, south of Upper Ogol.

3) Venus *yapunu dya,* marketplace of Sanga.

J. *sogo* of the Guéméné totem.

This altar is made of a long black stone with three round pebbles on either side. Drawn under it are the *toy* of the spleen and the *tonu* of the constellation called *tolo dullogu,* "tailed stars," which form Orion's Sword (fig. 117).[234] The figures representing *tolo dullogu* (that is, the two stars and the nebula of the Sword) are oriented from northeast to southwest and symbolize the ritual fields in the following order: *lebe, binu* and *vageu.* They also symbolize the succession of rites performed

N

FIG. 117: *yala, tonu,* and *toy* of the *tolo dullogu.*

from the time they are seeded until they are harvested on the *sogo* of these fields by those in charge. These figures are related to the cultivated soil, the "earth of the fish," *izubay minne,* that is to say, to the placenta of the resurrected Nommo that will become the ark with which he will descend to the Fox's Earth.

---

234. These stars are apparently also called *tolo momio,* "scorpion stars."

K. *sogo* of the Goummoyana totem.

This altar is made of eight white stones placed in an unused mill stone, *tono*: in its totality it represents the gestation of the twins.

The figures under the altar are the *toy* of the kidneys and the *tonu* of

E

FIG. 118: *yala, tonu,* and *toy* of the Pleiades.

the Pleiades, *tolo duno,* "grouped stars" (fig. 118).

The kidneys, being close to the organs of reproduction, are associated with marriages and births; the kidneys of an animal sacrificed in the *ginna* are always given to the wife of the *ginna bana.* Generally speaking they are the "women's share."

Recalling the identity between the child and the seed, the symbolism of the Pleiades is comparable to that of the kidneys: these stars are associated with the sowing and the harvest. The figures representing the Pleiades — which are like a "pile of harvested millet" — have nine dots for the "eight grains and the seed of the calabash in the ninth." "The grouped stars" (Pleiades) in the world are proof of the eight grains of Amma which he will give as food (to man)."[235] For these stars represent

---

235. *tolo duno aduno-ne amma dene gagara pana vo obodo serey.* These words are spoken by the Yébéné priest, the Hogon's sacrificer, when he performs the rite that precedes the sowing (*vanu*) on the main *sogo (sogo die)* of the field of Lébé (installment 2, 2nd year).

the seeds that the Smith will bring from the sky to man for the first sowing.[236]

Just before the rainy season (*bado* season), the *duno* are not visible: they are *obia*. Their rising announces the approaching winter season, and preparations are made for sowing. This is determined by the rising of the *duno* on the horizon; one says: *duno obolo* "the Pleiades appear right on

N

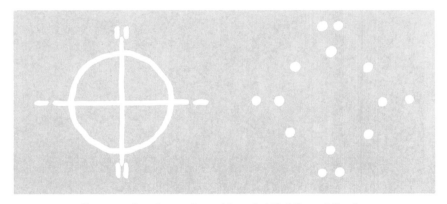

FIG. 119: *yala* and *tonu* of *enegirine tolo* (γ of Canus Minor).

time." The harvesting takes place when they are at their zenith at sunset.[237]

L. *sogo* of the Nommo totem.

This altar is made of two pale green stones placed in a *tono*, representing the resurrected Nommo and his female twin in the pond as well as the Nommo's lungs with which he will breathe the "word" in the

---

236. Installment 2, 1st year.

237. In the winter season, the position of the Pleiades is observed to tell time. They are first at their zenith, later a bit past it, at sunrise. At the end of the winter season, they set when the sun rises. After the winter season, Orion's Belt (*atanu*) is used for time-keeping; the onions are sown when Orion rises at sunset.

water, his domain, to reveal it to men, his "sons."

Under the altar the *toy* of the lungs (the victim's lungs are given to the children of the *ginna*) and the *tonu* of the Goatherd's star, *enegirine*

N

FIG. 120: *yala* and *tonu* of *yara tolo* (β of Aries).

tolo, are drawn (fig. 119); for in this instance, the Nommo guides the universe: he is like the goatherd who leads the flocks, i.e., mankind and seeds. The *yala* is composed of a circle of eight dots: the eight seeds, the eight ancestors, and the eight words. The two lines intersecting in the center of the *tonu* show the "paths taken by the flocks," or the four cardinal directions of space taken by mankind for settlement: *enegirine tolo* is the guardian of the sides (of space)."[238]

M. *sogo* of the Tiré totem.

This altar is made of a long gray stone of which the wide tip represents the large intestine, the viscera here symbolizing the generations to come and all the members of the *ginna*.

---

238. *tolo enegirine penne girene.*

The figures drawn here are the *toy* of the intestine (a sacrificed victim's intestine is divided among all who wish to partake of it and have no right to any other part) and the *tonu* of the star in Leo, *yara tolo* (fig. 120). The *yala* of the star is made of twelve dots — the Fox's number — with four extra dots marking the cardinal points. The *tonu* shows the star as a circle from which radiate four oriented rays ending as arrows. It is said that "the rays of *yara tolo* 'prick' the four corners of the domain of space."[239] The lion, with whom the star is associated, represents the power of the Nommo, who can attack in all four directions of space to protect the universe from the enemy, the Fox.

N. *enegirim tolo sogo.*

The figure under this *sogo* represents Venus in the *enegirim* position.

O. *digi tanu tolo sogo.*

This *sogo* is made of round pebbles and the figure under it represents Venus in the *dige tanu* position (Pl. XIV, 2).

P. *yapunu da tolo.*

A boulder of considerable size, placed on top of a smaller one, here represents Venus in the *yapunu da* position, "platter of menstruating women." Because of its distance from the settlement, the altar is compared to the house for menstruating women, set somewhat apart from the village. This separation is indicative of the weakness, and thus the relative impurity, of the last blood to flow from the victim's slaughter, which is called *doda* and is like menstrual blood. But it also refers to its particular value, because, according to a Dogon expression, "the good goes with the bad." Indeed, after having menstruated, the women can immediately be fertilized. Therefore, it is said of this altar, presently located in the heart of the Sanga marketplace, that "it is the guardian of the other *sogo.* "[240] The final position of Venus shows the completion of

---

239. *yara tolo yalu ganna sibe nay soboze.*

240. *ibe sogo sogo vazu dommo.* The market has been moved; it used to be located south of the double village of the Ogols.

the sacrifice, the purification brought about, and the complete reestablishment of order in the universe disrupted by the Fox (Pl. XIV, 3).

Q. *igibie,* literally: "one must know" (from *igi,* "to know, to be acquainted with").

This altar recalls:
—the terminal (point) of the blood from the Nommo's emasculation;
—the place of Ogo's circumcision;
—the opening of the sky:
a) for the 'emergence' of the sun, b) for the ejection of the parts of the Nommo's body, c) for the descent of the ark that will deposit the resurrected Nommo and the mythical ancestors on Earth.[241]

The altar is made of a long spotted grey rock, inclined rather steeply to the south and surrounded by four black stones. The spots on the rock recall the parts of the body "gathered one by one, like a pile of seeds"; the four black stones are like the four piles into which the parts were divided before being cast into all four directions of space; the inclination of the first stone is representative of the descent of those parts from the sky to Earth.

In these various representations, the celestial spot of the altar becomes the "door" through which later on will pass the spiritual principles of the deceased: it is called *mana ta,* "the kneader's door," i.e., Amma's door; it is alluded to in the prayer recited during funerals, just before the head of the deceased is shaved, that is to say, still in the presence of his spiritual principles, ". . . the door of the kneader, the ever-open door, may Amma help you find it . . ."[242]

The figure drawn under the altar (in *yu* and *ara geu* porridge) groups the principal stars that are living proof of the sacrifice (fig. 121):
— the Pole Star (*aduno giri*) and the Southern Cross (*aduno giri ley*), the line that joins them is the Milky Way (*yalu ulo*):
—the sun and the moon in the center; "the star of the Milky Way" (or Venus in the *obia* position) to the west;

241. Cf. *infra,* p. 432.

242. . . . *mana ta pinnela amma uy temmemo.* Cf. G. Dieterlen, *Les Ames des Dogon,* p. 96 and p. 98.

N

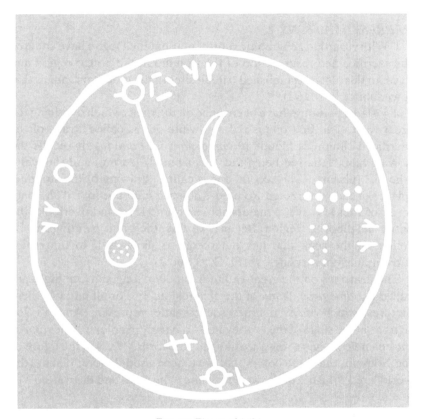

FIG. 121: Figure of *igibie*.

— the sacrificed Nommo's head to the north, the Fox to the south, man (in the form of *yala,* because he is as yet unformed) and the eight seeds to the east;

— the plants born of the sacrifice; the *pelu* and the *yullo* to the north; the *minu* and *kilena* to the east; the *oro* and *satelle* to the west; and the *sa* and *yayaga* to the south;

— facing west is a figure symbolizing the future descent of the *gaba*.[243]

The picture, therefore, sums up all celestial events relative to the sacrifice and the resurrection.

REPRESENTATIONS.

I. With regard to geographic representation, the Dogon have situated the sacrifice and resurrection of the Nommo in the Songo region and have, to this effect, established (ritual) sites in the mountain ranges that tower above it (Map I).[244]

Two large paintings have been made on the rocks which overhang the great vault. The first one is red and white and is called "trace of the sacrificed Nommo's blood" (*nommo semi illi bummo*). It recalls the flowing blood, the red being the "clear blood" (serum) and the white "the oil" (plasma). The second one is called "drawing of the stopping (place) of the resurrected Nommo" (*nommo bulo inu toy*). "The platform (of rock) is several meters above ground level and overlooks the entire neighboring region. Because of this, the great painting on the ceiling of the rock that juts out seems to show itself to the entire surrounding countryside."[245] (Pl. IX, 1 and 2).

The drawings on the great vault (about 30m. long and 2m. high) are called *ogodine tonu, "tonu* of the chameleon."[246] For all initiates these pictures, which are sometimes trichromatic, represent Amma's 266 signs — at the stage of the "variegated drawing" (in color): "The *tonu* of the chameleon, one to one, are like the 266 words."[247] As in the figure of the Nommo, the three colors that have been used denote: black, "the world"; red, "the life of the world"; white, "the word and the water." "In

---

243. Cf. *infra, p.* 523, fig. 184.

244. A description of the places, the rock paintings decorating the overhanging boulders and the vaults, and the circumstances surrounding their production is given in M. GRIAULE, *Masques dogons,* ch. III, p. 612, 613, 617.

245. M. GRIAULE, *Masques dogons,* p. 612, n. 2. The drawing is reproduced in fig. 190 and 191, p. 649 and p. 650. A new painting (approx. 50 cm.) on the wall of the vault overlooking the site where the sistrums of the circumcised have been stored was discovered in 1963 and will be commented upon later.

246. *Idem,* fig. 165, p. 611. For details, pp. 618-691.

247. *ogodine tonu de de sune tanu pennay kuloy sige so tozy.*

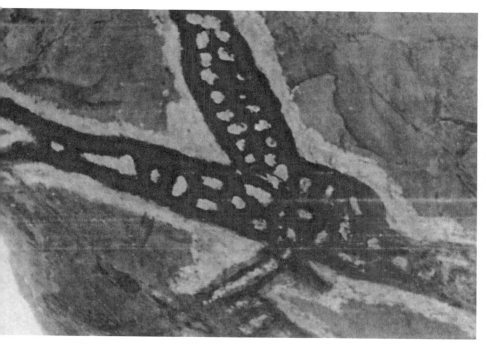

Pl. XV   Trichromatic painting of the great vault of Songo:
1) in 1931;

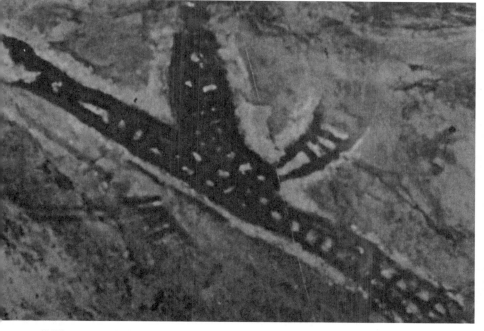

2) The same painting in 1964. Since 1931, the painting has undergone an important
change.

Pl. XVI   The *tonu* of the chameleon." Great vault at Songo.

the trichromatic drawings, red is the life of the world, black the world, and white the word of the world."[248]

These drawings also include representations of all the Dogon totemic prohibitions (*babinu dama*), thus of all the categories of the elements of creation as determined by the sacrifice of the Nommo, each of which is associated with a totem or a clan.[249] Moreover, figures of objects or materials used during the sixty-year ceremony of the Sigui were executed. All participants must wear a pouch, *taba demme,* covered with decorations in dyed leather which are the image of the "words" it contains, "words" revealed to man at the time of the first Sigui[250] (Pl. XVI).

The two large paintings will be refreshed at the time of the Sigui; those of the vault likewise when the circumcision is performed.[251]

II. The resurrected Nommo in human form is represented by ritual objects and by the morphology of the dwellings and certain altars on the lineage and the totemic clan level.

THE LINEAGE.

1) The plan of the large family house (*ginna*) of the Dyon represents the resurrected Nommo lying flat on his stomach on the ground (fig. 122). The kitchen (*obolo*), to the north, is his head; the main room *(dembere)*, his trunk; the two side rooms (*kana*), his left and right arms and the corresponding clavicles; the hall (*dolu*), his legs.[252] "The foundation of the house of the *ginna* is the Nommo (become) alive like man flat on his stomach."[253]

---

248. *tonu si tanu, banu aduno kini, geu aduno, pili aduno so.*

249. Cf. *supra,* p. 338.

250. A complete description of the places, the paintings, and their symbolism — related essentially to the "word" — will be given in installment 2, 2nd year. Songo is also related to the representations regarding the mythical Smith, which will be presented in installment 2.

251. A family of the Domno tribe (inhabiting Songo) is the guardian of these places; in the past, the priest of the Sanakoumo totem was responsible for the execution of the paintings and the performance of the rites.

252. *obolo,* "the gift" (from *obo,* "to give"); *dembere,* literally *deu na bere,* "belly of the grandmother"; *dolu,* "passage."

253. *ginna ginu tey nommo omo-go bila inne ko bere ku daba.*

The dwelling has, therefore, five rooms on the ground level; they correspond to the five registers of the initial placenta where the *nommo anagonno* were conceived and which also foreshow the succession of the future generations. The number of rooms in the house deliberately excludes the Fox's placenta, which is associated with the sixth register (in the other division).[254]

The form and position of the first figures that are drawn when the foundation is laid bear witness to the presence of the "word" in its different aspects as well as its movement within the living body of the resurrected Nommo.

At the corners of the house, comparable to the joints of the body, a series of figures is drawn, called *tonu soy* of the "articulations" of the word in the *po*.[255] The seventh figure is drawn at the back of the kitchen which, in this instance, represents the crown of the Nommo's head and the fontanel, *dana banna* or "mark of the skull," of which it is said: "The life of the words is placed in the fontanel."[256] The eighth articulation — which corresponds to the formation of the external segment — is drawn outside, in the spot where the door will be put that opens from the courtyard onto the street. Thus, the presence of "life" is represented that animates the primordial seed, the creative "word" Amma had put inside the grain. When the figures are connected with a line, one obtains a zigzag denoting the vibration animating the "articulations" of this word which here, in turn, animates the body of the resurrected "father" of mankind. "The *yala* of the seven articulations of the *ginna's* foundation are like the seven words. The seven *yala* of the beginning of the house hold the seven articulations of the internal organs. The seven words of the *ginna's* foundation (are) like seven articulations inside the belly and (resemble) that which keeps the word in motion. The eighth word is like birth."[257]

---

254. Cf. *supra*, p. 157.

255. Cf. *supra*, p. 137, fig. 22.

256. *so kinu dana banna-ne da.* The fontanel is compared to a "natural mark" of the body which evolves like the changing color of a ripening fruit.

257. *digu soy yala tolo-ne yalanu-go vogo so soy anay. ginu tolo yala soy-go vogo kolo da digu soy geleze. ginu tolo-ne so soy to-go vogo bere kolo-ne digu soy, so gele yoy yaze anay. so gagaraye-go nonu-gin vo.*

On either side of the doorways that connect the main room with the kitchen, side rooms, and hall, are drawn:

— to the right, in *puru i* (a condiment made from *yullo* seeds), the *toy* of the four varieties of *gaba* as foreshown by the four *yala* of the *gaba* inside Amma's egg: *koro kunu, koro pumu, koro kembogu, koro kinugu.*[258]

— to the left, in *kumuli* (a condiment made from baobab seeds), the *toy* of the four varieties of *anu* as foreshown by the four *yala* of the *anu* inside Amma's egg: *anu na, anu golo, anu gonnoru, anu gogobolo.*[259]

These figures are also related to the blood circulating between the internal organs of the *nommo anagonno*. We remember that the "paths of the blood" from the emasculation (and from Ogo's circumcision) as well as from the sacrifice were also represented by the *yala* of the *anu* and of the *gaba* inside the primordial egg.[260] They are, therefore — in like manner — associated with the resurrected Nommo's internal organs, which are theoretically placed at the doorways of the *dembere* where they are drawn.

In this system of representation, the "word" circulating with the "clear" blood or the "water of the blood" (i.e., the serum), which is a male element, passes to the right through the heart, lungs, liver, and spleen (respectively from 1 to 4, in red). When circulating with the oil or *ni* of the blood (i.e., the plasma), which is a female element, it passes to the left through the pancreas, kidneys, intestines, and the sex organ (respectively from 5 to 8).

Thus, in this instance, the "word" is represented at the stage where it becomes differentiated into male and female and takes on individual characteristics.[261] It circulates and, if the figures are connected by an imaginary dotted line, it forms two parallel and opposite outlines, both of which are winding, because, with the blood, "the path of the word is tortuous," *so ozo gonnu yaze*. It ends at the sex organ where it remains in

---

258. *kunu*, "without menstruation"; *pomu*, "rounded oval"; *kinugu*, "that has a nose (a life)"; *kembogu*, "navel gourd."

259. *na*, "mother"; *golo*, "emerged (as the first)"; *gonnoru*, "twisted"; *gogobolo*, "tall." For the role of the *anu* and the *gaba*, cf. *infra*, p. 522 and ff.

260. Cf. *supra*, p. 314.

261. For the relation between the "word" and the human organs, cf. pp. 317-319.

secret. However, its presence here in the reproductive organ is evidence of its future "emergence" in the form of a child that will be born from it.

It is said of these figures: "The drawings which are in the *dembere* are like the articulations of the words which are inside man. The word which is not spoken is kept inside the clavicles; when one speaks, the word goes outside through the organs of the belly. The movement of the body's blood circulating inside the organs of the belly, the 'clear' blood on the one hand and the oil on the other, keeps the two together: this is the pathway (passage) of the word. The clear blood or water-blood passes through the heart, then through the lungs, the liver, and the spleen; the oily blood passes through the pancreas, the kidneys, the intestines, and the sex organ." [262]

The comparison between births and the emergence of the "word" is repeated by the comparison between the germination of the grains and an emergence of that same "word." This is recalled at the sowing time during the first rain. In his dwelling, before going into the fields, the *ginna bana* prays: "The seeds for sowing are like the unspoken word; when the grain has germinated and after it has ripened, it is like the word which is spoken; may Amma show us the eyes of the ripening of the millet." [263] As he sows the seeds in the field, he says: "Now we put the seeds into the ground; may Amma bring (forth) the ripening of the millet." [264]

While laying the first stone of the house, the founder says: "Amma (make) the threshold of the house become dirty (with footprints), place its seat as (is placed) the (bulb) *nono.* " [265] For at the kitchen's edge and near the seventh figure of the *po (tonu soy)*, he will bury the bulb of *kinu bommo,* born of the blood from the Nommo's heart, witness to his immortality.

---

262. *dembere-ne tonu to inne bere kolo-ne so to digu yoyaze anay. so sola-go ani guyo gele; varu so sonu-ye, bere kolo da soy-gon(e) goya parago sonu. bere kolo da yeyaze gozu-ne illi yala yeyaze-gin, tana turu illi-le, tana ni-le mona gele, so yoy-go voy. illi vey kinne donno-ne go-ye buzubazu-ne yo-ye dimmene kinne na-le kinne laga-ne galaze. illi ni ozu kolo da dugu-ne dimmene nani-ne go-ye kolo da-le du-ne galaze.*

263. *dene toy so sola anay; dene tea yu illa-ye so soy anay; amma dene ille giru-go tagara.*

264. *dene minne-ne u kunnoy de, amma dene ille do dele.*

265. *amma ginu monnogolo menegese, nonoi doy dana.*

The *ginna* has a second floor — hence its name of "storied house" — with three rooms: one is a granary, *dele*, above the hall; the other two,

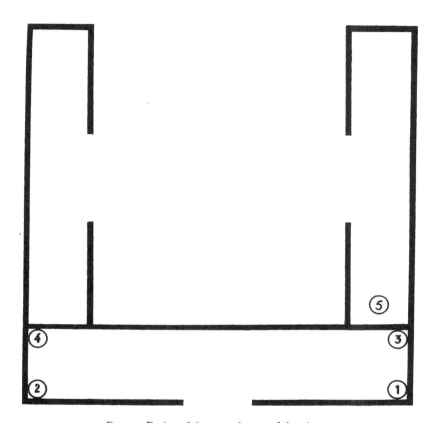

FIG. 123: Design of the second story of the *ginna*.

called "*kana* of above", *kana sine*,[266] are over the right and left *kana* of the ground floor (fig. 123).

As on the ground floor, figures are drawn during construction. They are related to the symbol of the second floor, which represents the "sky"

266. From *sine*, "to rise above."

where the *nommo anagonno* were conceived and formed, particularly the resurrected one (in his fetal state).

At the four corners of the *dele,* just above the first four figures of the *po,* are the *tonu* of the multiplication of the *nommo anagonno,* corresponding to the first stage of this multiplication, namely, the formation of the four males (from 1 to 4).[267] The granary will hold the seeds of the field of the *ginna,* acting as the depository of the spiritual principles of sex of the grains from the harvest until the sowing the following year.

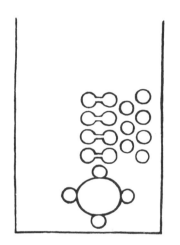

The *kana sine* on the right houses, placed on a platform, the ancestors' altar (*vageu*), which contains the funerary earthenware (*bunno*) of the lineage's ancestor as well as that of all deceased males of the group (at 5). We recall that the founding of this altar begins with the consecration of the earthenware of the twins and of the *kuno* born into the family, above which are drawn (at that time) the *bummo* of the formation of the *nommo anagonno.*[268] The double earthenware pots of the twins represent, in the house, the resurrected Nommo's clavicles and their contents, the "seeds," which are shown by a dot made with porridge of *yu* and *ara geu* under each of the little cups (cf. fig. 124). Therefore, the whole thing symbolizes at the same time: the formation of mankind's mythical ancestors (the *nommo anagonno*), the content of their clavicles and that of the resurrected Nommo (represented by the morphology of the dwelling), and, finally, the complete, i.e., fertile "word" put into this content. "The seven pots are for the *kuno* and the eight for the twins; the pots of the twins and the *kuno* are symbolically like the clavicles: the pots of *kuno*

FIG. 124: Theoretical diagram of the distribution of the earthenware of the twins, of the *kuno* and the *bundo* of the founder of the lineage in the *kana* of the *ginna.*

---

267. Cf. *supra,* p. 177. fig. 41.
268. Cf. *supra,* p. 166, fig. 35.

are like the 'word seven'; the pots of the twins are like the clavicles with eight seeds."[269]

An unused millstone, *tono,* is placed in the courtyard. It contains water taken from the pond of the lineage — water which is never allowed to run dry. Two lines of *ara geu* porridge are drawn on the ground in the place where the millstone will be put: they represent the two *kikinu say* of body of the resurrected Nommo, which are also symbolized by two stones placed in the water of the *tono.* It is said: "The *tono* of the *ginna* whose water is never lacking, the resurrected Nommo's male and female *kikinu say* of body are in the water."[270]

The *ommolo ana* altar is usually placed in the courtyard: it is, as we have seen, related to the resurrected Nommo's *kikinu bummone* of sex; similarly, the altar *ommolo ya,* placed in the upper left *kana,* is related to his *kikinu bummone* of body.

Thus, the altars of the *ginna* attest to the symbolic yet active presence of all the sacrificed Nommo's spiritual principles in the heart of the family, i.e., his descendants. There, they will support and protect the fertility of all members of the family.

The totality of the buildings, the altars, and the figures is proof of the resurrected Nommo's completeness. He is not represented there in his fetal form of a silurus, but rather in his fulness as a human being: adult, sexually differentiated, in possession of all his spiritual principles, and one whose blood is circulating the "word."

In the middle of the *dembere,* usually near the center post, a jar is placed (*loy*), which contains the drinking water of the *ginna bana* and his family, taken from the pond of the lineage. Like the *tono,* the jar must never be empty: the wife of the *ginna bana* sees to it that it remains filled. For the water in the jar will, for a short time, contain the spiritual principles of the children to be born into the lineage — principles that reside in the family pond under the protection of the resurrected Nommo. At their first pregnancy, the young wives of the members of the lineage, who are still living in their fathers' homes, bring some water which they

---

269. *kuno vonoy soy vey gagaraye-go dineu-mogo tanaze; dineu-le kuno-le vonoy-go be ani guyo tozo aduno so-ne; kuno vonoy so soy tozoy; dineu vonoy dene gagara ani guyo to anay.*

270. *ginna tono di dimmele nommo bulo gozu kikinu say ya-le ana-le di-ne to-go vo.*

have drawn for the first time from the pond of their husband's lineage: silently they hand the full pot over to the wife of the *ginna bana* — a gesture announcing their condition to her. The mistress of the house then pours the contents into the *loy*. "The *kikinu* of the seven words of the founding of the *ginna* are like the seven words of the *po* which were transferred into the Nommo's belly. The seven *kikinu* of the foundation of the *ginna* have entered the *ginna's* jar which is placed in the *dembere*; all the women who have entered the *ginna* and placed the water there receive at that moment the seven words. The eighth word is like birth."[271] "When a man has 'drunk' water from the jar of the *ginna,* he receives the seven words: when his mother has drawn water from the *ginna* and has put it down, at that moment the ancestors have given him the word."[272]

A few drops of the *yu* porridge are thrown on the center post and a circle is drawn on the ground before the *loy* is placed there. For these various receptacles in the dwelling are the "drinking" places of the Nommo from the sky, who watch over the lineage: the *tono* is for the *nommo die,* guardian of the resurrected Nommo's spiritual principles; the jar is for the *nommo titiyayne,* who is the guardian of the principles of the *nommo die* and who gives the children of the lineage their own spiritual principles. Therefore, they are symbolically present in the dwelling, just as the resurrected Nommo who comes "to drink" will be in the earthenware pots of the twins and the *kuno* of the *vageu.*[273] Their presence makes the *ginna* a sanctuary. A certain number of prohibitions must be strictly observed by the family members, in order to maintain the integrity of these places.

2) The design of the *ginna* of the Arou is drawn to represent also the Nommo, but here it stands for his fertility: he is lying down, not flat on his stomach, but rather on his right side, and he is procreating.[274]

---

271. *ginu tey so soy kikinu-go vogo po kikinu soy nommo bere tanunu-go voy. ginu tolo kikinu soy-go loy toroy ginna dembere-ne dani-go kologon di dambegon yoy, vogo yana ginna-ne toya di danaze, voy so soy go yimbeze.*

272. *ginna loy di inne varu vo no-le; so soy-go kole deze vo-na varu ginna-gon di koba vo danu-le, vageu so voy kolle obi.*

273. These representations are part of the most advanced initiation: these commentaries are never uttered in public, but rather are revealed by the family head, before his death, to his son or to his successor.

274. Cf. M. GRIAULE, *L'Image du monde au Soudan,* p. 83, fig. 3.

So, in both cases, the *ginna* is a temple built in the image of the resurrected Nommo, where his "sons" will live (being all the members of the lineage stemming from the successive generations) and where all the rites will be performed that preserve the unity and the integrity of the group.

THE TOTEMIC CLAN.

1) The resurrected Nommo is represented by anthropomorphic statuettes of varying sizes that are part of the material in the totemic sanctuaries. They are carved in the wood of a plant from the category — or family — called *kuno* (of which the first is *teguzu*),[275] considered to be safe from any risk of impurity.

Each statuette embodies one aspect of the Nommo's functions, as well as his attitude toward his creator, Amma. Each of them is more particularly associated with one of the totems.

If the statuette has one arm raised above its head, it represents the Nommo entrusting himself to his creator before his sacrifice, in anticipation of the events to come. He is saying: "Only one Amma; I am with Amma."[276] His gesture also indicates his future role as organizer and his place in the center of the universe; one says of him: "His raised arm shows the middle of the world."[277] (Pl. XVII, 1).

When both arms are raised, but apart, he is asking Amma to keep him near him after the resurrection, "like a child who holds his arms out to this father": "The Nommo Amma slaughtered and brought back to life, his arms are raised, so that Amma can take him."[278] On the statuette shown on Plate XVII, 2, the necklace represents the water, the *dugoy,* and the cowries; the crisscross rectangle on his abdomen is the ark in which he will descend to Earth and its compartments as well as the squaring off of the cultivated soil.

---

275. Cf. G. DIETERLEN, *Classification des Végétaux chez les Dogon: teguzu togu,* p. 145.

276. *amma vo turu: mu amma-le vo.* The first part of this sentence may be translated as "there is only one Amma." These words are spoken during the sacrifice offered at Ka Amma inaugurating the *bulu.*

277. *numo vomo dada vogo aduno logoron tagaze* (Wazouba dialect).

278. *nommo amma sema bulomi numo dago dera amma voy denega tozoy.* These words are spoken when the *binu* beer is drunk at the *bulu.*

Carved wood as statuettes representing:

1) The Nommo before the sacrifice: the shape of the object stresses its androgyny;

2) The resurrected Nommo entrusting himself to Amma;

3) The resurrected Nommo. The two disproportionately long arms beside the torso symbolize his descent to Earth, which is represented by the block on which he stands. Beneath it is the "hole" of the Fox; then the fourteen "worlds" of stars in a spiral of Amma over which spans his rule, shown by the grooves cut into the wood — Yamoy totem of Iréli.

Pl. XVIII   The two great Nommo of the sky. To the left, the *nommo die,* to the right, the *nommo titiyayne.*

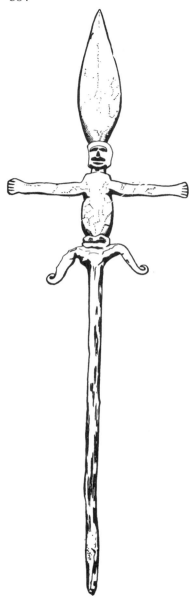

When the two arms are raised and the hands joined together, he is praying for Amma to show himself to him: "Amma who resurrected the Nommo is hidden; I have joined my two hands, I do not see Amma, cover the top of my head."[279]

When the joined hands are turned up with the palms toward the sky, the Nommo is begging Amma for rain on the Earth: "The male hoe that sows the seeds is like the Nommo who turned his arms upwards (to ask for rain)."[280] When the arms are stretched along the body, the resurrected Nommo is recalling the creation of the worlds by Amma and their "descent" from within the primordial "egg." This position is called *amma donu,* "Amma below."

When the two arms are away from the body and as if open with palms forward, the Nommo is demonstrating his role as the guardian of space: "The Nommo with his hands apart has taken hold of space."[281]

When he has only his two hands placed flat on his lap, the Nommo "is leaning on Amma."[282]

FIG. 125: The iron lance of the *binu.*

---

279. *amma nommo buloma bariyay; numo ley segerema, amma voy iyelem, dana ma debe.*

280. *inu ana toy toze o nommo tozogo, numo duloma.*

281. *nommo numo vira vo ganna gobaze* (or *salaleze*).

282. *amma le paiauo* (or *gawara uo*).

These poses are attributed respectively to the following totems: Déwa, considered to be the first *binu,* and Yébéné, its counterpart in Sanga; Guéméné, Nommo, Tiré, Ogoiné, and Goummoyana (Sanga).

2) The material in some sanctuaries also includes a lance, called *binu saru,* of which there are several variants. On one of them (fig. 125) is an anthropomorphic personage which represents the Nommo at the time of the sacrifice: his presence on the weapon is evidence of its strength. His arms are apart to show that the world is his. "His separated arms show that he is the owner of the world." "The arms separated (hands) vertical (palms forward) show the descent of the whole world; the arms separated (hands) flat, this is the great ark of the world which descends and lands gently."[283] His head is shaven and smooth, for the world must be "neat and clean" like his head. His straight legs, joined together like "just one leg," foreshow the "solid settlement" of future villages.

There are two appendages on the object which stand off from the lance's handle: the lance is the "one leg" (or joined legs) and the two appendages are here the pectoral fins of the fish. This object depicts the Nommo's transformation after his descent, in the water, where he will take on his original form of *nommo anagonno* and where he will "teach the fish to swim."

The lance is also the image of the snake. This reptile will become one of the symbols of the Nommo's resurrection and of his immortality.[284] By taking the form of the snake, the resurrected Nommo will be able to go from the pond to the totemic sanctuaries to give his support to the members of the clan.

3) The pectoral fins, *ta i,* or "arms," are represented separately by the two-armed *gobo,* placed on the terrace of the Hogon of Arou (fig. 126A) next to the ostrich egg representing the "primordial egg." It is made of two different metals, "part in copper, part in iron," which respectively stand for the sky and the Earth. The clavicles, *ani guyo,* are represented

---

283. *numo giga vogo aduno sagu tagaze. numo ginia pala-go sugoze aduno fu voy tagaze; numo ginie vanu-go aduno koro na sugo vogo doze sunonoze.*

284. The lance-snake in the sanctuary also represents the resurrection of the second mythical ancestor, Lébé Sérou, and a cult will be devoted to him, similar to the one devoted to the sacrificed Nommo.

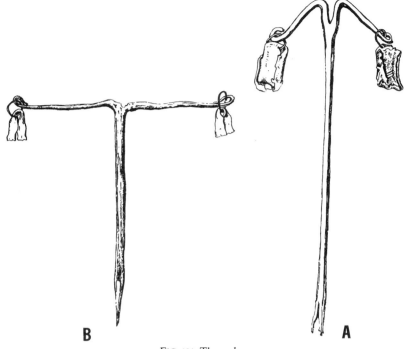

FIG. 126: The *gobo*.

by a similar iron hook (fig. 126B), but which is placed on the terrace of the totemic sanctuaries. The two *gobo* that are standing in this way are "calling"; the first one, through the intermediary of the sacrificed Nommo, summons the rain that was withheld by the *nommo die* and that will bring germination; the second one calls the life force (*nyama*) of the grains, which will penetrate the seeds with the rain.

4) The Nommo's sacrifice and resurrection are symbolically repeated every year in rites performed by certain totemic priests.

At a certain distance from some important sanctuaries, a symbolic representation of the Nommo's body has been made on the ground.

At Nandouli, this monument, called *tesemme,* is made of a bed of more than a hundred stones, oriented east to west, and having the length of a man. To the east, a larger stone represents the head; the limbs are indicated by four raised stones which are also the cardinal points.

However, whereas the *binu* in the village sanctuaries are both the parts of the Nommo's body and his living substitutes, the monument in the bush is the image of the sacrificed Nommo and the places are impure (*puru*). No field is planted around it and so the priest does not go there; he only furnishes the contents of the sacrifice.[285] This sacrifice, performed before the sowing (at *agu*),[286] consists of *yu* pulp (crushed right there) and a couple of ears, one of which is placed at the foot, the other at the head of the altar, under a stone, to simulate sowing. The liquid, called *tesemme solugo*, "pulp of Tesemmé," gives the sacrifice its name. It is poured from the foot to the head while one recites the formula: "Amma, master of power, killed the eldest Nommo to give the power to the other cardinal points of the world. Even today, we say we are counting (on him), we say we are counting on Amma. May he come and be with us."[287]

To pour pulp on the stones of the legs, arms, and head is to carry out the symbolic division of the members. Throwing away any remaining pulp, the officiants go to the sanctuary, where they slaughter a chicken, which they eat with the priest.

This part of the rite is public and intended to inform people, whereas the libation in the bush was secret, recalling the furtive act of a slaughtering God.

The beneficial death of the Nommo and the symbolic sowing of the two ears fill the country with millet and living beings. The spiritual forces of the victim extend to the four cardinal points. They purify the earth and prepare it to receive the seeds: they travel in all four directions of space, as materialized by the mountains *deboy dumbo* and *valu dumbo* (north and south), *bamba dumbo* and *sogo dumbo* (east and west).[288]

---

285. The altar is not far from the cemetery of the priests, which tends to reinforce the prohibition.

286. The *agu* ceremonies in the regions of Nandouli and Wazouba are equivalent to those of the *bulu* in Sanga.

287. *amma gono bana nommo dienne go da ganna sibe nay gono obo iye yay vo sogo va, amma sago va. veye emmi bo kanawa.*

288. Which is to say, especially in places where, theoretically, one finds representations of the sacrifice — Songo (cf. *supra*, p. 370) — and of the landing of the Nommo's ark — the mountains of Lake Débo (cf. *infra*, p. 487).

The liberation of the Nommo's spiritual principles lasts until the offering of the "first fruits" from the harvest (at *bago*), which is to regroup them. The *tesemme* altar then represents a living being, after the new pulp has been poured over it from head to foot, in the opposite direction from the preceding time.

This rite, performed at the same time as the offerings made at the sanctuary, thus recalls the Nommo's resurrection.

VALUE AND FUNCTION OF THE SACRIFICE AND RESURRECTION OF THE NOMMO.

The Nommo's sacrifice and resurrection constitute one of the fundamental stages in the building and organization of the second universe created by Amma.

Examined in their entirety as a system of representation, the actual morphology of the emasculation, sacrifice, and resurrection; the performance of the operations; and the mythical place of their execution all establish specific relations between:

— the Nommo's placenta,

— the Nommo's body and vital organs,

— the stars born of the sacrificial blood,

— some plants and animals formed at the same time,

— man, who will be created from the matter of his placenta.

This set of relations reveals a series of parallel structures:

— an organization of space — stars in motion — and of time — calendars,

— a social organization — at the various levels of the tribe, the totemic clan, and the lineage — and corresponding cults,

— in relation with these first two structures, all ritual aspects of agriculture, the basic activity of the Dogon society.

For man as an individual, the sacrifice and resurrection signify the development of a being from the fetal to the adult stage. This development includes the evolution of the child who, until circumcision (male or female), is considered to be of either sex — the *nommo anagonno* sacrificed as an androgyne; then, after the operation, the child fully realizes its masculine or feminine being — the mixed couple of resurrected Nommo. Similarly, from a psychological and moral perspective, the child will leave the ignorance of infancy behind and attain, with maturity, full awareness of himself, of others, and of the world, acquired through instruction and initiation.

From the viewpoint of the totemic clan, these operations specify the relations between the Nommo's body, at the fetal stage — and therefore associated with its placenta — and the elements of the universe: the stars, plants, animals, etc. This series of relationships, as we have seen, was to formally resolve itself into a system of twenty-two (or twenty-four) categories — co-ordinated with each of the twenty-two body parts at the adult stage — the resurrected Nommo — and with his presence in the water on Earth.

The family structure — the lineage — is involved in the division of the body, recalled in every sacrifice held today by the "sharing of the meat" of the victim among the members of the group in question. No matter what the group, place, or time, the sharing in each case complies with strict rules and reflects the social hierarchy.

The sacrifice and division of the body are represented by the total set of altars of the human societies. The Dogon say that the Nommo's body was divided among the different altars so that one might ask — by sacrifices and offerings — of each part what it could give. "All customs (beliefs, institutions, and rites) of the Dogon are the Nommo's divided body."[289] The whole society will pay homage to all the parts of the sacrificed Nommo's body and will find, in this way — in time and space — an integral communion with these parts.

In addition, whenever possible, the groups of altars connected with a particular institution will be placed in a spiral within or around the settlements to recall the internal spiral of "Amma's egg" and the life that animated it.[290]

Generally speaking, the stages of the sacrifice of the Nommo are recalled by every present-day sacrifice, regardless of the place, purpose, officiants, or methods:

— the chick (or small hen) slaughtered before the actual sacrifice, which has a divinatory value, represents the emasculation;

---

289. *dogo temu pu nommo gozu gammela geli.*
290. The list, classification, and distribution of altars will be presented in installment 2.

— the libation of porridge preceding the death of the main victim represents the spilling of the clavicular seeds;

— the victim's blood represents the blood of the sacrifice;

— the throwing of the liver on the altar, the resurrection;

— the division of the body is recalled by the dismemberment of the victim and the regulated distribution of the pieces of meat to the participants, the consumption of which constitutes a communion of all the members of a particular group.

Thus, the Dogon say that the Nommo "showed man the first example of sacrifice": its value as a gift, its power, its extension, and its effects; for it seals all relations between people.

5. THE CREATION OF MAN

The clavicle. The *anagonno bile* and the *anagonno sala.* The spiritual principles. The Smith, the Griot, Yasigui. Death: the *anagonno alagala.* The placenta of the resurrected Nommo and the *kiru* turtle.

After Amma had molded the Nommo in the sky, he took the substance of the placenta and also molded the ancestors of man. "Amma created all things: then he created man. The four men were molded by Amma in the body of the *po.* "[291]

Humanity's eight ancestors — for Amma created their twins at the same time — are called *unum,* "sons," a term which, from the perspective of mythical genealogy, stresses the concept that they are the sons of the sacrificed Nommo, who belongs to the preceding generation, the very first one, which is that of the "fathers," *bau.*

The formation of the *unum* is first recalled by a figure of eighty (8x10) *yala*; this number emphasizes the reproductive role of the mythical ancestors.

While drawing the *yala* of the *unum,* one says: "The number of the *ba unum* is made up of eighty *yala*; (Amma) made the seeds of the grain emerge."[292] They are drawn on both sides of the door of the totemic sanctuary in the form of ten rows of eight small ovals depicting the shape of the eggs of the *anagonno sala,* who will come to represent the human fetus.

---

291. *amma kize fu mana leye inne mani; inne nay-go amma bey po-ne manu.* These words are recited during sacrifices to the spirits of the ancestors in the *ginna.*

292. *ba unum lugi sunu tonu yala; dene toy gono.*

The *tonu* of the *unum* is made later on the same façade (of the sanctuary) and is composed of eight anthropomorphic outlines showing

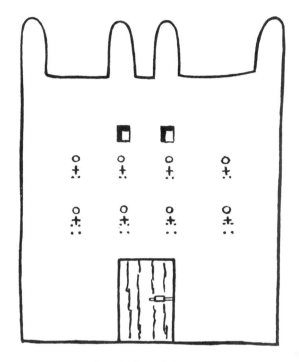

FIG. 127: *tonu* of the *unum.*

the head, body, breasts, and legs (fig. 127). The crosses in the figure, which represent the bodies of the created beings, are compared respectively to the four *yala* of the *gaba* for the women, below, and the four *yala* of the *anu* for the men, above.

This attribution stressed the similarity between the *yala* of the *anu* and *gaba* and the blood which was to circulate through man's vital organs, carrying the "word."[293]

---

293. Cf. *supra,* p. 375.

Theoretically, each ancestor (and each one of their female twins) is associated with one of the basic elements contained in the Nommo's placenta: "Amma Sérou was made from the air of the placenta; Lébé Sérou was made from the earth of the placenta; Binou Sérou was made from the water of the placenta; Dyongou Sérou was made from the fire of the placenta."[294]

Amma formed the *unum* in the shape of fishes, as with the preceding generation, but different from the *nommo anagonno*. They were called *anagonno bile* (from *bibile,* "image") and were not created as androgynes, but rather as separate males and females. Moreover, Amma reversed the procedure used to form the *nommo anagonno*: he began by creating the female fish and formed the being's sex organ first,[295] that is, he started at the bottom; then he formed the male fish, beginning with the clavicle, that is, at the top. The purpose of this action was to identify femininity with the world below, Earth, and masculinity with the world above, the sky, since the formation of these beings followed the events which, due to the misdeeds of the Fox, had separated the Earth from the sky.

"Amma in creating woman began at the bottom (the sex organ) and finished at the top; for man, he began with the clavicle and went to the bottom. The Earth and woman are for the sky and man. In the body of the *po*, just as he had the grain of the bean followed by the *emme,* so too did he have woman followed by man."[296]

There are figures recalling the formation of the beings Amma created in this way:

— for the woman, the "drawing of the creation of woman by Amma" (fig. 128, top), drawn in color (charcoal of *a ala* for the black, *bana* for red, *yu* porridge for white), above the door of the *yapunulu ginu* (house of menstruating women) when its foundation is laid.

---

294. *amma seru me ono voy mani; lebe seru me minne voy mani; binu seru me di voy mani; donu seru me yau voy mani.*

295. Euphemistically, the female sex organ is called *ya koro.*

296. *yana amma mani donugo tola, dago dononi; ayne-mo ani guyo ne tola donu-ne sununi; minne-le yana-le alakala-le ayne-le moy; po gozu-ne amma nu i emme bolo-ne digiri-gin, yana bolo-ne ayne ni.* This is in reference to the "emergence" of the seeds from Amma's womb (cf. *supra,* p. 126).

— for the man, a figure representing the clavicle, *ani guyo,* drawn with porridge of *yu* and *ara geu* on the plaster of the central column of the *togu na* (shelter of the men), facing north (fig. 128, bottom). This figure is also the *bummo* of the *anagonno sala,* such as it was produced in the contents of the sacrificed Nommo's semen.[297]

In creating the sex organ of the being who was to become the woman, Amma began with the clitoris. Then he opened up the woman's vagina, nursed the wound thus created, and healed it with his "saliva." It remained red and became the vulva. This "opening" of the female sex organ prefigured the future removal of the clitoris, necessary for procreation: "Amma began the creation of woman first with the clitoris; the (female) circumcision of the clitoris, he did this in order to organize the (remade) world. The clitoris (is) the closing of the mouth of the egg of the world. Female circumcision (is) the opening of the mouth of the world."[298] Thus, the (female) circumcision of the clitoris will be likened to the opening of the sex organ of woman so that the world may expand itself through procreation.

The red color of the female sex organ recalls the color attributed to certain aspects of the resurrected Nommo. The "red" of the Nommo is shown by the rainbow after the rain, his semen, and by the halos sometimes seen around the sun. One also says: "The inside of the behind (sex organ) of the Nommo is the image of redness. This is what he left to woman. With it, he entered the water; that one is not *puru.* What he left to woman is *puru.* The red of the Nommo's sex organ which is with woman is the image of the redness of that of the Nommo; the redness (of the sex organ) of the Nommo who is in the water is fire."[299] The "red"

---

297. Cf. *supra,* 238, fig. 78.

298. *sini la amma yana manay toli; sini keze-go aduno gime yegerdo-gakanu sini aduno talu ana temmeri; sini keze-go aduno ana gonoy. gime* means "to double, to begin again." This operation was performed in the sky before the descent and caused the transformation of the clitoris into an insect, *keu momio.*

299. *nommo bolo kolo vomo banu yala, yana-mone paza vo se, di-ne ko-le yoy; vogo purila, yana-mone paza-go puri; nommo bolo banu yana-mone nommo-mo banu yala to; nommo-mo banu di-ne to yauy.* When one sees a will-o-the-wisp near a pond, one says that the Nommo has "opened his sex organ"; it is a sign that he is going to take someone into his possession.

of woman is similar to the red fibers of the masks which are, themselves, like the leaves on a stalk of ripe millet, that is to say, symbolic of death: when the millet is ripe and its leaves are red, one says that it is like a woman who is going to die.

In the figure of the clavicle, the curve on the left located near the tip of the shoulder is called "mouth of the clavicle," *ani guyo kenne*; the right end attached to the sternum is called "stop (or seat) of the clavicle," *ani guyo doy*.

THE CLAVICLE.

The primary place given to the clavicle in the formation of the human being emphasizes its importance. It is said that "the principal (chief) bone of the Nommo (is) the bone of the clavicle. Amma bėgan the first bone of the body of the fetus with the clavicle and the skull. Amma made the bone of the clavicle first. The rest of the bones he made by suspending them from it. The maturing (aging) of the bone of the clavicle (continues) until he becomes a young man."[300]

Indeed, for the Dogon:

1) The clavicle is the suspension system for the entire skeleton. One says that "the clavicle is the means of suspension of the body."[301] The clavicle becomes linked to the entire skeleton when one is about twenty-two years of age, the marriageable age among the Dogon.

2) The clavicle contains the symbol of the eight primordial seeds. In fact, the clavicle bone is called *ani guyo ki*, "granary bone of the *ani*," and its hollow is called *ani guyo*. The whole thing is compared to a granary; the bone, being the framework of the granary, contains the seeds. It is said that "the seeds emerged from the bone of the clavicles."[302]

---

300. *nommo ki vomo ku-go ani guyo ki; ani guyo ki-le kutogolo-le amma i noni vogo la gozu ki toloze. amma ani guyo ki la yegera ki vazu-go vogo-ne dula yegeru; ani guyo ki pedo-go saga-tara-go ba.*

301. *ani guyo gozu demme gogie vo.*

302. *ani guyo ki dene vogo-ne goy.* The important seeds for ritual sowing are preserved hanging against the earthen walls of the granary. Similarly, the gourd seeds, *gono* (from *gono*: "to take away" or "to come out of" (the clavicle)), especially in the past, were put into the walls of the houses, which symbolize the "clavicles" of the dwelling. When one sows the seeds stored in this manner they appear to have "emerged" from a clavicle.

If a wild or domestic animal is killed, its clavicles are preserved and hung up in the house. A bit of the bone is crushed and mixed with the seeds to increase the harvest.

That is why one also says: "Amma molded the clavicles into the shape of a hoe. The clavicle is (like) the hoe (the iron) with which one does all the work in the field."[303]

These images refer to man's future work on Earth, to agriculture — the fundamental skill — and to life — sustained by the basic food — that is to say, to the cultivated seeds. Now, the position of the seeds in the clavicular bone is realized gradually with the development of the individual and will be definitely established only when the bone becomes permanently welded to the rest of the skeleton.

From his birth until his death, in the course of a person's physical and social development, which is related to individual rites (giving of a name, circumcision, marriage, etc.) as well as to the performance of collective rites (*sigui*), the position of the seeds inside the bone will be modified in accordance with an exact process. The displacements of the seeds are always related to a relative impurity of the bearer.

FIG. 129: Location of the seeds in the clavicles (theoretical figure).

From birth to old age the seeds in the clavicle from time to time change place inside a man. "When a man becomes twenty-two years old, the seeds (*yu* = seeds) that are in the clavicle come together."[304] Then one says that "the seeds are in place."[305] Under normal conditions, when the individual becomes an adult, the four seeds are distributed along three points in the bone: at either end and in the middle (fig. 129). During the lifetime of the individual, the positions of the eight seeds, four per clavicle, are as follows:

— at birth, the four seeds are in 1. When the name is given, one seed

303. *ani guyo vala-go amma manu; ani guyo ki bire minne-ne kananu fu inu-go vo.*

304. *dene ani guyo kolo-gon(e) to-go inne nane vo peze-le doy beme de de vo. anakuzu pelley ley sige inne biaze, yu ani guyo-ne to-go monieze.*

305. According to certain informants, the seeds are truly stabilized only when a man reaches the adult age of about thirty and he is the father of a family.

stays without moving, another places itself in the middle of the clavicle, and the remaining two seeds equidistant between the first two.[306]

— during circumcision, one seed always remains in place and the three others go to the sternum, 2. When the blood has stopped flowing, they return, one at a time, to rejoin the first one.[307]

— during marriage, the first and last ones remain in place and the two others go to 2. Theoretically, one marries at about the age of twenty-two, that is to say, when the clavicles have become completely welded.

— during the Sigui, the four seeds come together in the middle. After the ritual beer has been drunk, the seeds separate gradually and return to points 1 and 2.

— at death, the four seeds regroup at 1.

When the individual is in a state of impurity, one says that the seeds, "are fighting"; they leave their position, which is expressed by saying that they "go out of the clavicles."[308] Purification puts them back in place.

The contents of the clavicles vary according to the population and its basic crafts.[309] Within the same population, it varies according to tribe. Among the Dogon, the four great tribes, theoretically descendants of the four male ancestors, have different clavicular contents — generally, this is qualified by the first and last seeds of those contents. Within a family, the contents of the women's clavicles are arranged in a manner opposite that of the men, the man's first seed being the woman's last. Within the same society, caste members have clavicular contents different from those of the farming nobles. Marriages between people having different clavicular contents are forbidden.

It is said: "Amma designed man; the clavicle and the *anagonno* are of

---

306. The child is *puru* at birth: to give him his name constitutes the first stabilization of his spiritual principles.

307. The flow of blood from circumcision and the loss of virginity are temporary states of impurity.

308. The participants in the Sigui are temporarily impure before they drink of the beer, a condition associated with the ancestor Dyongou Sérou, to whom this rite, in part, is consecrated (cf. installment 2). Participating in a funeral puts the parents of the deceased into a state of impurity.

309. The Bozo, being fishermen, have "fishes" in their clavicles.

the same path (manner)."[310] The development of the fetus is depicted by some figures made in relief on the outside wall of the *yapunulu ginu* on each side of the door. Both the male and female sexes are depicted here in fish-like forms (fig. 130).

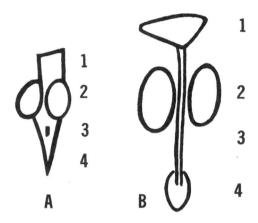

FIG. 130: Schematic drawing of the bas-relief images representing the creation of man and woman.

A: 1) pubis and mouth of the fish; 2) hind quarters and head of the fish; 3) clitoris and internal organs of the fish; 4) body of the fish.

B: 1) pubis; 2) testicles; 3) penis; 4) foreskin; the whole thing represents the fish.

The two figures are drawn in the clay, recalling that human beings are made of earth, which earth is like the Nommo's placenta. This image recurs in the description of Amma "molding" human beings. He took some soft earth and gently rolled it between his hands, making it long like a sausage, since he had formed the world as a long, mottled, and spotted *dugo*; then he added the limbs. When the rough form was completed, he put it on its back, then on its belly, four times for a woman, three times for a man.

---

310. *ayne amma tonu; ani guyo-le anagonno-le ozu turu.*

THE ANAGONNO BILE *AND THE* ANAGONNO SALA.

The two figures are also sketches of fishes, the *anagonno bile* (fig. 131), i.e., the image of the human fetus. Indeed, the child will develop in its mother's womb and will pass from the fish stage to the stage of a human being, equipped with limbs enabling it to move about on Earth.

This concept of the development of a fetus is expressed through a series of images which depict, after the creation of the clavicle, the formation of the *anagonno bile,* its transformation into the *anagonno sala,* then into a human being or "person," *inne.* As in the maternal womb, on the mythical level, this metamorphosis will take place with time. It is said: "The four *unum* (sons of the father) (who) came out of the sky with *o nommo,* they all descended as *anagonno bile,* landed on Earth as *anagonno sala,* and when they left the ark to walk on the earth, they became persons."[311]

The term *bile* may be translated as "is going to transform itself" and signifies the beginning of a metamorphosis. The *anagonno bile* will become the *anagonno sala* or "ordinary *anagonno*," i.e., the *Clarias senegalensis.* Particular characteristics distinguish this fish's body from the *nommo anagonno.* The *anagonno bile* has a narrower head and a fatter body than the *nommo anagonno.* The *anagonno sala* is, in this regard, comparable to the *anagonno bile*; its tail, however, opens into two parts which prefigure the two legs of man.

The two *tonu* of the *anagonno bile* and the *anagonno sala* show the development of the fetus (fig. 131 and 132). The first is drawn in red ochre, *bana,* in the place where women who are menstruating wash themselves during their isolation. The second is drawn with porridge of *yu* and *ara geu* on a boulder or stone brought there for this purpose, called "stone of the week," *dugu dummo,* on which a woman whose menses are over comes to sit down on the sixth day after she has performed her final ablutions. There, she drinks a pulp of raw millet and returns to her husband's home after the evening meal.

Like the *nommo anagonno,* the *anagonno bile* is without any joints/articulations; he does, however, have a sort of crest, called *izu ginene,*

---

311. *ba unum nay alagala goa o nommo be voy sugoze, nommo anagonno bile minne-ne sugi, anagonno sala koro-gon(e) goa minne-ne be nami inneu.*

which prefigures that of the *anagonno sala.* It is said that "the *nommo anagonno* has no articulation; the *anagonno bile* has no articulation but (rather) a crest; the *anagonno sala* has an articulation."[312] This conformation is linked to the initial sacrifice of the *nommo anagonno* in the sky before his descent. One says: "The *nommo anagonno* that Amma sacrificed had no articulations; his flesh which he (Amma) severed and cut up gave articulation; it is because of this that man has articulations."[313]

The *anagonno bile's* crest prefigures the backbone of the *anagonno sala* and the spinal column of man. "When Amma formed the *unum,* he made them as fish; then he gave them articulations. Symbolically, the placenta itself is like the fish; Amma modeled the articulations."[314] Then he split its tail.

FIG. 132: *tonu* of the *anagonno sala.*

The diagram of the formation of the *anagonno's* body is drawn on the ground in the middle of the totemic sanctuary, with its head to the north. It is called *"tonu* of the seven articulations of the *anagonno sala"*[315] and is composed of seven figures drawn in an order connoting Amma's successive deeds (fig. 133):

1) and 2) the clavicles, male (right) and female (left), *izu ani guyo;*

3) the "tonsils," *isu yogo gelegeze;*

4) the head, *izu ku;*

---

312. *nommo anagonno digu sele; anagonno bile dige sele, ginene se. anagonno sala digu yese.*

313. *nommo anagonno amma voy seme, digu sebele; nama vomo keze vo kezele digu bi. vogo-de inne digu be.*

314. *amma inne vo manu-go izu-gin manu; ley digu kunnu; aduno so-ne me izu tozoy; amma digu moymu.*

315. *anagonno sala digu gozu pu tonu.*

5) the articulations (or ribs), *izu anagonno digu*;
6) the backbone (or spinal column), *izu sonono digu*;
7) the tail (or legs), *izu dullo* or *izu kubo*.

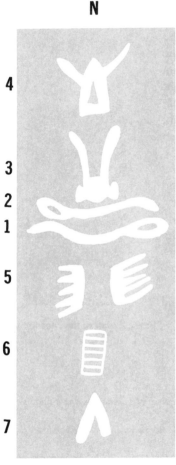

FIG. 133: *tonu* of the seven
articulations of the *anagonno sala.*

One says of this figure: "Amma, when he created man, first created the clavicle; then he created the *anagonno*; thirdly, he created man; it is the creation of the same thing which is followed through (i.e., it concerns the same being). The design in seven parts of the *anagonno* is like the design in seven parts (of the body) of man. Amma's creation of man, he created the right clavicle, he created the left clavicle, he created the neck, he created the head; below, he created the chest, he created the legs; he completed him."[316]

Speaking of the *nommo anagonno* as humanity's "ancestor," one says: "In the past, when Amma made man, when man was *anagonno,* man breathed through the clavicles."[317] Speaking of the ordinary *anagonno*, i.e., the fetus, one will say: "The child in the belly of its mother is like a fish that breathes

316. *amma inne manaze-le, izu ani guyo la mana, anagonno leye mana; tanie inne mani, kize tumogo mani dige. anagonno digu soy, tonu vo gin inne digu soy; amma inne tonu ani guyo i tona, nanna tona, kokolo tona, ku tona, donu go tona, kubo tona; donona.*
317. *polo amma inne tono anagonno be varu-le ninnu ani guyo ninnebe.*

with its gills; (but) the moment the child becomes *anagonno*, it breathes with its tonsils."[318] Hence the name given to the tonsils: *anagonno ninnu ninnu*, "*anagonno* (who) breathes the breathing," and the shape given to the tonsils in the drawing, which is like the head, eyes, and barbs of a fish.

With regard to the *nommo anagonno,* this figure bears evidence of a modification of the respiratory system which will permit man to breathe air when he emerges from the waters of the womb.

It also emphasizes the number assigned to the genesis of the fetus, made of seven parts: "The drawing of the seven articulations of the *anagonno sala* made on the floor inside the sanctuary is like the transformation of the seven articulations into a child."[319] This number, which recalls that of the articulations of the "word," is also evidence of the ties between man and the Nommo. When the child is given its first name, called "secret name" or "*binu* name," *boy dama* or *binu boy*, the priest says: "Amma, receive the greetings of the morning; all things have emerged from his body; father *binu*, your son has come; the body of the Nommo came out of Amma; our body came out of the Nommo; the Nommo has seven articulations, may the child's name give him the seven 'words'."[320]

However, in proportion to the child's development in the mother's womb, the number assigned to it will vary. The adult *anagonno,* like the resurrected Nommo, is considered to have been made of ten parts: the head, the neck, the two pectoral fins, the chest, the belly, the split tail (which counts for two), and the two central fins.

Now, man when he has been born, will live and move about on the Fox's Earth (whereas the fish will live in the water). "The number of man is ten, it is that of the Nommo; after (man) being mixed with the Fox, twelve, the Fox's number, was added; what men have is twenty-two."[321]

---

318. *i vo na kolo-ne to-go izu aa benne ninneze anay; i varu anagonno be, gelegeze-le ninnu ninneze.*

319. *anagonno sala digu soy binu ginu kolo donu-ne tononu, i biledo digu soy toni anay.*

320. *amma aga na yaba, kize fu gozu vomo-ne goy; babinu i uo viya; nommo amma gozu-ne goy; emme nommo gozu-ne goy; nommo digu soy, i boy so soy obu.*

321. *inne lugu pelu, nommo moy-le, yurugu-le gania peli ley sige, yurugu lugu bara; pelley ley sige innem geli.*

This development is summed up by saying: "Amma's creation of the child in the woman's belly, that is seven parts; after birth when he has become a man, it is twenty-two articulations."[322]

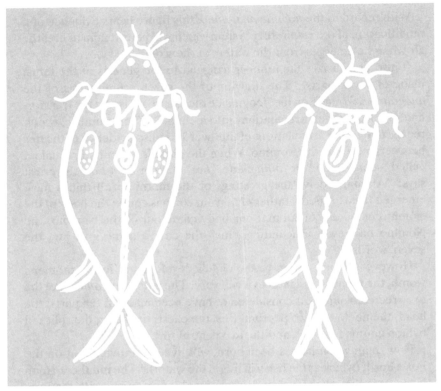

FIG. 134: Drawings of the *anagonno*: female on the left, male on the right.

The male and female *anagonno sala* are represented as *toy* in the two upper *kana* of the *ginna*, where they signify the "children to be born" into the lineage (fig. 134). Respectively, the figure of the male drawn in the right *kana* represents the pair of fishes, *punnulu izu*, "fishes of the menses,"

322. *yana i bere amma tonu digu soy, i nana inne bile digu pelley ley sige.*

the man gives to his fiancée when she has her first menses; the figure of the female fish drawn in the left *kana* symbolizes those he will give her upon her first pregnancy, called *bere izu,* "fishes of the womb." Both figures, therefore, are related to the procreation and gestation the couple hope for as well as to the fertility and development of the lineage.

THE SPIRITUAL PRINCIPLES.

The bodies formed in this way, had received four body souls, *gozu ki inu,* which Amma "summoned" when he was molding them.

'The four *kikinu* of body were inside the living placenta"[323] where the bore evidence of the presence of the four basic elements. According to another version, Amma entrusted them to the *nommo die,* who bestowed them upon the *anagonno bile.*

With regard to the reorganization of the universe through the sacrifice of the Nommo, these body principles are related to the episodes involving the original placenta: the *kikinu bummone ya* in man represents the part of the placenta stolen by the Fox; the *kikinu bummone ana* represents the part that was not stolen, i.e., the sun; the two *kikinu say* represent the Nommo's "twin" placenta.[324]

The four sex souls, *du kikinu,* came to them from the sacrificed *nommo,* from whom Ogo had taken them. The sacrificing Nommo took them back from him, when he performed the circumcision on him, and they will later be given to man.

It is said: "The *kikinu* of body of man emerged and came from the great Nommo, together with the four elements. As for the *kikinu* of sex of man, they are those of the sacrificed Nommo, which were given in the sky by the great Nommo to the sex organ of the Fox."[325]

According to another version, the sacrificer transformed the four *kikinu* of body of the sacrificed Nommo. He reduced them to four

---

323. *me omo gozu kikinu nay kone tobe.*

324. For individuals, this concept will manifest itself through the position of the principles during their lifetime, their transfer during the rites of passage, and their relations to various family sanctuaries (*vageu, binu,* etc.).

325. *inne gozu kikinu nommo die mone kize nay goa viey; tere kikinu alakala-ne nommo die nommoy sema kikinu yurugu tere obi.*

smaller *kikinu*. He "squeezed them in his hand," one after another, making them more compact, heavier with regard to their mass. In this way, the sex souls also contain the four elements: they are like a double or residual form of the first ones; they are, according to the Dogon expression, "the *kikinu* of the elements."

However, these souls, which were modified and assigned to the sex organ, were given in halves: two remained with the Fox and two went to Dyongou Sérou. For one says: "The great Nommo sacrificer of the Nommo, having given the Fox the four *kikinu* with the four elements, is like the silurus, who sacrificed (cut off) the sex organ (foreskin) of the Fox, transformed the foreskin into a *nay* lizard, put it in the sun and gave the *kikinu* of sex and the four elements to Dyongou Sérou."[326]

Indeed, the formation of the sex souls during the sacrifice prefigured the division of the first androgyne. Because of the deeds of the Fox, the sexes were forever separated. Man will receive principles related to the acts he will have to perform in order to reproduce himself.

Now, the three eldest of the four male ancestors received all of their spiritual principles. The fourth received only two *kikinu* of sex, the other two having been left to the Fox. Thus, Dyongou Sérou received only six *kikinu,* and therefore he will not engender twins.[327] This distribution underscores the representations which associate each of the ancestors respectively with one of the four *nommo anagonno* created in Amma's womb. Amma Sérou will be the witness/counterpart of the *nommo die,* Lébé Sérou that of the *titiyayne,* Binou Sérou that of *o nommo,* and Dyongou Sérou that of Ogo transformed into the Fox: their role and life on Earth will, to a great extent, be contingent upon these associations.

In addition to the spiritual principles and life force, Amma will endow human beings with a clavicular content, proof of their wholeness: they will receive this when they first consume the cereal grain they have

---

326. *nommo die nommoy vo seme kikinu nay kize nay vomo-le bara yurugu vo obi-gin, anagonno yurugu tere sema tere guzu nay bilema nay-ne kunna kikinu nay-le kize nay-le donu seri obi.*

327. Dyongou Sérou was to be the first to die on Earth. This death was to require the taking back of his two sex souls, which were then put back into the cycle of births by Binou Sérou: the gift of the "fishes" by the fiancé upon the first menses of his betrothed recalls these mythical facts (cf. installment 2, 3rd year).

cultivated on the "earth of the fish," the placenta of *o nommo,* their "father."

The life that will quicken the body and develop along with it in every individual is like the whirling motion that animated the world created by Amma. Just as the germ spins inside the seed to develop itself, so "the child, the moment it starts to live, begins as a whirlwind."[328] When millet grows, it does the same thing. "When millet grows, it rises by spinning like a whirlwind. All living things begin in this way."[329]

This life was related to the life force, *nyama,* given by Amma to living beings, which flows like a fluid in their veins with the blood. This force is made of the *nyama* of the four elements themselves, considered to be one on top of the other: the fire element in the head, the air element in the liver and chest, the earth element in the abdomen, and the water element, the most powerful of the four, in the lower body. The stability of the *nyama* will depend upon the physical and spiritual integrity of the man. Any violation of ritual will entail the loss of the *"nyama* of water," and the individual will then become impure, *puru.* If purification does not follow, the *"nyama* of water" will draw the *nyama* of the other elements out of the body, bringing about the death of the culprit.

THE SMITH, THE GRIOT, AND YASIGUI.

However, Amma did not limit his work to the eight *ba unum,* created in the form of the fish, much like the *nommo anagonno.* He also created other beings, who would come down to Earth separately after the ark that carried the eight ancestors and the resurrected Nommo.

To do this, he used matter from the Nommo's placenta, but he took it right from the place where the blood had flowed, either from the sacrificed Nommo or the Fox.

The Smith, *demme na,* "the great sack," was made from the umbilical cord (*koni*), which had remained attached to the victim's placenta, and from the blood that had flowed from the cord and from the sex organ, both severed at the same time. "The Smith was created with the cord."[330]

---

328. *i varu toloze ono simu-gin toloze.*
329. *yu teze, kize kinugu fu ni toloze.*
330. *demme na koni manu.*

The Griot, *gogone,* was made from the placenta and from sacrificial blood taken from the place where the *nommo* was killed. "The Griot was made with the path of the blood of the sacrificed *nommo.* "[331]

Thus, these two beings are considered as having been given life by the blood of the placenta; but, they are also endowed with some of the sacrificial blood: now the blood from a wound flows strongly at first, and this is called *illi ezu,* "good blood"; then it loses its forces (*nyama*) and, at the end of the flow, becomes "weak blood," *illi doda.*

The Smith and Griot are not impure, *puru,* just different. They are of "mixed blood": this belief is the basis for the prohibition against marriage between their own descendants and those of the *unum,* whose blood has never been mixed. "Because of their mixed blood, one does not contract a marriage with them."[332] However, at the same time, because of the presence of this blood they will be considered as belonging to the same generation as the *nommo anagonno,* whereas the *unum,* as we have seen, originate from the following generation. This position will earn them a prominent position on Earth.

I. — The Smith, made from the umbilical cord, is the victim's "twin." It is said: "The *demme na,* the slaughtered Nommo's twin, descended. He represents the Nommo (who was) slaughtered for the purification."[333] This is the reason why the *demme na* smiths are sometimes called *serem,* "witnesses" (of the Nommo). This twinness is also described in an expression which associated the two by the blood of which they are made: "The Nommo and Smith are of red blood, like a glittering ball."[334] One also says, "Nommo and the Smith are twins; both are red like copper. While forging, the Smith has been blackened by the heat of the fire and the coal."[335] This is also the reason why the smiths, according to popular belief, can transform themselves at will into all sorts of living beings, animal and plant, as the Nommo himself will do. The

---

331. *gogone nommo semu illi ozu-le voy manu.*

332. *gogone-le irine-le illi monu, ko-de belley yadi yone.*

333. *demme na nommo semi dine suga, nommo dolu-go yala.*

334. *nommo-le irine-le illi banu gunnu-gin ere ere be;* recited at *bado* when the smith strikes the red-hot iron.

335. *nommo-le irine-le dine be; belley mennu-gin bani be; irine dubo dubogu dubo-go-de yau uzu-le kile-le dega gemme.*

Smith is the "twin" *par excellence*, as proved by the different versions concerning the manner in which his spiritual principles were given to him.

According to one version, he received half of the sacrificed Nommo's "body souls," which were split in half before the emasculation and the sacrifice; according to another version, the Nommo was resurrected, but Amma gave him only his female soul. He kept the male soul, with which he made the Smith. Thus, the Nommo shows that, although a man is animated by his male soul, nevertheless, he is all-powerful even with only his female soul.

According to another version, the female souls intended for the Smith were in the placenta. Amma took the doubles of the Nommo's male souls, added them to the female souls, and gave them to the Smith.

The creation of the Smith from the blood of the emasculation is recalled by the events following the descent of the ark. The Smith will receive the penis and empty testicles of the sacrificed Nommo, which had once contained his sperm, made of the four elements. He will also receive the severed "arm," emptied of its marrow and transformed into a sledge hammer containing the sixteen cereal grains. After the descent of the ark, Amma will give the order for the Smith to descend first — by virtue of his twinness — by using the elements of the sex organ as a support: he will put his two arms in the two testicles and his legs along the penis. These elements will trans-

FIG. 135: *tonu* of the creation of the Smith as a fish.

form themselves on the ground, the penis becoming the furnace blast-pipe and the testicles the bellows of the forge.

A ritual figure called "*tonu* of the creation of the Smith as a fish" (fig. 135),[336] stresses the artisan's role. The split tail (the two future legs of man) represents here the testicles and the bellows: they send the wind along the backbone, which is both the penis and the blast-pipe. The air then passes into the *sosogu,* where the clavicular content is located, then into the mouth, where the four barbs on the right represent the Smith's four *kikinu* of body and the four on the left his four *kikinu* of sex.

The Smith will descend on Earth accompanied by his female twin. Thanks to the presence of four elements, he will be able to mine and fashion iron. In his sledge hammer he will bring the seeds of grains to cultivate them: the souls of the seeds will temporarily put themselves into the iron hoe.[337]

In speaking of the Smith, one says: "To the Nommo (who had received) his share of *kikinu,* (Amma) having taken the semen of the sacrificed Nommo, gave them to him, put them into the empty testicles, he (*vo*) entered (*yoa*) there, descended on Earth. He transformed himself into a man. His name is said to be: in the 'great sack' (i.e., he who descended in the testicles called 'great sack')."[338]

II. — The Griot, *gogone,* originating from the blood of the victim's throat, is related to the "word," which will be revealed by *o nommo* and bestowed upon man through the intermediary of the third ancestor during the first Sigui.[339] He, too, will descend with his female twin after the descent of the ark, carrying the skull of the sacrificed Nommo with which he will make his first drum. Endowed with the spiritual principles bestowed by Amma, he will not have eight seeds in his clavicles, like the *unum,* but rather eight "words," symbols of the spoken word he is supposed to keep and spread.

In this manner, the Griot and the Smith, both associated with the sacrifice of the Nommo and both physiologically animated by his blood, belong to the same generation as he does, the generation of the "fathers," *bau.*

---

336. *demme na-ne izu be manu tonu.* Drawn with porridge of *ara geu* on the site of the forge oven when it is constructed or when the oven is rebuilt following the death of the *ginna bana* of the neighborhood where the forge is located.

337. Installment 2, first year.

338. *nommo kikinu gammala nommo semi dene yaba vo obi, dolo kolo-ne kunna vo ya yoa minne-ne suga inne bilema. boy-go demme na-ne gi.*

339. Installment 2, second year.

III. — Amma then modeled the Fox's female twin, Yasigui, using the victim's placenta, but at the place where blood from Ogo's circumcision had flowed.

Made from elements taken from the two "first twins," she also belongs to the generation of the *bau.* "Yasigui was molded from the placenta and the male (blood) (of the Fox)."[340] She will descend to Earth, in her turn, in human form during the first eclipse of the sun. This recalls the origin of her spiritual principles: they came from the part of Ogo's placenta that had been transformed into the sun.

IV. — One sometimes says derisively that Amma used the rest of the Fox's umbilical cord to create the shoemaker, *dau* (from *da,* "separate");[341] his physiological status makes him a basically impure being, *puru.* Like the Fox, of whom he is a "sort of twin," he will receive, in his clavicles, the *po banu,* made impure by the creator of disorder. One says that "the shoemaker can open people's navel, the key to the belly, to take the seeds"; for if one drinks at the same time as a shoemaker does, the Nommo takes back the *nyama* of the seeds that are in the clavicles.[342]

DEATH: THE ANAGONNO ALAGALA.

Amma created man immortal, as originally the *nommo anagonno* had been which came from his womb. However, the misdeeds of the Fox and the ensuing impurity they communicated to the Earth will bring about a series of disorderly events which will result in the appearance of death. It will afflict all living beings: it will be mitigated, to a certain extent, by the funeral rites, the purpose of which is to regroup the deceased's spiritual forces, which have been released and dispersed by the suppression of life and the decay of the body.

This study of man would not be complete if, in view of the events to follow, the representations dealing with the status and functions of the dead were not commented upon here.

When a man dies, he becomes an *anagonno* fish again, that is to say, he resumes his primitive fetal form. The deceased is carried to the cemetery wrapped down to his ankles in the family "funeral blanket": the two

---

340. *yasigi me ana-le voy manu.*

341. *dau* also means "unstuck, non-adherent" — *da,* "towed, drawn by."

342. The Arou shoemakers have a different status because of their position, close to the religious leader of the Dogon people. They are not impure like the others are.

feet, the only parts that are not covered by the shroud, recall the split tail of the *anagonno sala*. He is tied to a stretcher, *abie baga*, to be placed in this way on the symbol of the *anagonno bile,* the form he is going to take on again. For one says: "The cord that binds the dead man is like the spinal column of man, the *abie baga* is like the backbone of the fish."[343]

The new form of the deceased is recalled during the ceremony that ends the funeral. The rite of the *kikinu mono,* "reunion of the souls," consists of pouring a libation of porridge on a small pot which represents the *po pilu,* i.e., Amma's womb, so that the spiritual principles will regroup and the dead man will "return to his creator": "When one does the *kikinu mono* of a dead man, Amma who created him (at first) with three elements, he (the dead man) goes to Amma and becomes a *nommo anagonno bile* again; his bones pass on to the earth."[344] The deceased symbolically resides in this pot in the form of an *anagonno bile* until the next rite is performed.

When the time has come, the deceased's funeral pot (*bunno*) is consecrated in the altar to the ancestors (*vageu*), next to which is placed a small notched stick and a miniature wooden ladder.[345] In this way, the pot represents "Amma's seat," *amma doy,* the small cup (*vonoy*) put inside represents the *po pilu,* the notched wood the *anagonno bile,* that is to say, the deceased, and the ladder the "chain" which will support the Nommo's ark during his descent to Earth — a "chain" by which he "goes back up" to the sky.

A figure of the *anagonno bile* is drawn under the pot where the "sex souls" of the deceased will come to drink. However, the deceased's role with regard to his lineage does not end there: he must designate his *nani,* that is, he must "share" his "sex souls" and his *nyama* among various descendants, who are theoretically grouped in order over five generations. He does, however, keep his "body souls." When he has performed his duty, i.e., when he has designated his *nani,* he again transforms himself and becomes an *"anagonno* of the sky," *anagonno alagala*; he is also called "man ancestor of the *vageu* (which was) in the past";[346] and his role

343. *yimukile inne sonono anay; abie baga izu sonono anay.*

344. *inne yimay kikinu mono galanu-ye amma voy mani kize si tanu, amma mone yay nommo anagonno bile tanaze; ki vomo minne tanaze.* For the child in the womb has received three of the elements (*kize*) from Amma and acquires the fourth, "earth," when it is put on the ground immediately after being born: one may simply give it a drop of *sadi,* a drink made from the fruit of the *sa* tree.

345. For a description of the rite of the *kikinu mono* and of the materials of the *vageu,* see G. DIETERLEN, *Les Ames des Dogon,* p. 118 and 141.

is to assist and direct the living from that time on.

THE PLACENTA OF THE RESURRECTED NOMMO AND THE TURTLE KIRU.

Amma had created man from the substance of the resurrected Nommo's placenta. This placenta was also to make up the ark on which the Nommo and the eight ancestors were to descend to Earth. In addition, it was to make up the "(pure) earth of the day of the fish," *izubay minne,* or of the cultivated land, the opposite of the impure land of the bush, the Fox's domain. Therefore, one says that the rest of the resurrected Nommo's placenta had the elongated shape of an ear of *yu,* a product of the cultivated fields.

A figure called "drawing of the yeast container of the Nommo," *nommo buzuru tonu,* represents the part of the Nommo's placenta that was transformed into an ear of *yu,* which is the shape of the figure (fig. 136).[347]

The top part, above the neck, represents the point where the placenta was attached; the lower part is everything that was to be made from the placenta. The figure is composed of ten pictures, since ten is the "Nommo's number." At the top, a circle representing the sky, *alagala,* contains the most important stars. It is crossed by the Milky Way. The moon

FIG. 136: *tonu* of the yeast container of the Nommo.

---

346. *vageu tire anau ya gali;* which means that one is no longer required to call him by his name during ceremonies commemorating the ancestors in the *ginna.*

347. The figure was drawn on the façade of the sanctuary of the Nommo of Barna *binu* with *yu* porridge during the tenure of the priest Asèguirèma before 1930. The figure was almost two meters high. The outline of the figure also represents the yeast container called *yu buzuru* (installment 2, third year).

and a star are in the upper portion and the Pleiades (the dots) and three stars (*atanu*) are in the lower portion. In the narrowest part of the figure, under three *gobo* depicting the tornado bursting in the sky-atmosphere,

FIG. 137A: *tonu* of the *kiru* turtle.

is the rainbow (red, blue, and white), the Nommo's path. To the right is the lance of the *binu,* which represents the Nommo's tongue and his descent to Earth. Under the lance is an iron flint evoking the Nommo "descending like fire." Under it is the sketch of a dismembered silurus.[348] Then, in the middle, the resurrected Nommo's "weaving" (here shown as the priest's blanket called *bunno kamma*), that is to say, his "word."

---

348. An image of the sacrificed Nommo; also, the image of a silurus that will be sacrificed and cut up by the ancestor Dyongou Sérou (installment 2, third year).

To the left is the snake *di yuguru,* an avatar of *o nommo* on the Earth and in the water. At the bottom of the figure the primordial pond is drawn, in which he will reside on Earth.

FIG. 137B: *toy* of the *kiru* turtle.

One says of this figure: "In the *tonu* of the Nommo's placenta the things are drawn (belonging) to the Nommo; this is what one draws on the sanctuary. The Nommo took back the drawings of the placenta of the Fox, this is drawn on the sanctuary."[349]

Just as Amma, when he had transformed the rest of Ogo's placenta into the sun, had created the land turtle *agunuru* as evidence of the sun, so he created, from the rest of the resurrected Nommo's placenta, the water turtle, *kiru,* as a living testimony.

---

349. *nommo me tonu-ne nommo kize vomo toy to; binu ginu-ne voy tononu; yurugu me tonu nommo ele-go, binu ginu-ne toni.*

The *kiru* water turtle is of the same essence as the *agunuru* land turtle. Their roles are complementary: the land turtle, who lives in the dwellings of the chiefs, will be sacrificed for purifications concerning the joint family; the water turtle is sacrificed for purification rites performed in the fields.

A *tonu* of the *kiru* water turtle expresses the animal's origin as well as its future role and also connotes the descent of the ark (fig. 137).[350] The sketch of the head recalls the handle of the yeast container said to be (in the shape of) an ear of *yu.* The regular lines drawn on the turtle shell produce sixteen compartments, representing here the future fields delimited by man, for the Smith will descend to Earth bringing with him, in his sledge hammer, sixteen seeds for sowing to give to the ancestors.

The *toy* of the animal is even more explicit.[351] The line dividing the shell recalls how the first placenta was split up. The sectors it determines represent the establishment of the fields, i.e., the stages in which the Fox's "land" had progressively been taken back and transformed through agriculture. On the left sector, the lozenges are the sacrificed Nommo's placenta, "earth of the fish," which will descend in the form of an ark on the earth of the Fox. The rectangles are the image of the preparation of the soil for cultivation. The zigzag line is the spotted "water snake," an avatar of the resurrected Nommo, one of the supports of the totemic cult.[352] On the right sector, the lozenges are the Fox's earth, purified by the expansion of cultivation. The zigzag line is the image of the water (rain and fog) that will fall after the descent of the ark, making germination possible.

One stresses the association between the role of the Nommo's placenta, compared to the cultivated land that will progressively expand, and the role of the sun (the Fox's placenta) with regard to the development of edible plants: "As Amma's (double) placenta in the sky created (the world), so on Earth the marriage was made between the placenta of the *yu* (the Nommo's) and of the sun (the Fox's), which have produced the world."[353]

---

350. Drawn with the porridge of *yu pilu* and *ara pilu* on the Hogon's platform when he is ordained.

351. Drawn with porridge of *ara geu* at the *bulu,* on the façades of the sanctuaries of all the *binu na.*

352. Cf. *supra,* p. 355.

353. *amma me alakala-ne ginnegilu kini, yu me-le nay me-le yadi minne-ne be kunni ganna ginnegile.*

CHAPTER IV
WORK OF THE PO PILU

The elements of creation and the female *po pilu*. The Nommo swallows the male *po pilu*. Classification of the elements contained in the female *po pilu*. Representations.

THE ELEMENTS OF CREATION AND THE FEMALE PO PILU.

Now, when Ogo reascended, Amma had made some changes in his womb, in order to avoid another theft and another disturbance of his creation. In Amma's womb, the female *po pilu* had coiled up around its germ[1] when the clavicles were opened up.

Then Amma put, one by one, all the elements of creation into the seed, which were thus taken up in its coils, in order to put them out of Ogo's reach. Because it was itself a spiral, it carried things along with it inside itself as it expanded. For this reason, the *po* is compared to the whole of Amma's womb, that is, to his four clavicles: it is actually comprised of four varieties.

Before anything else, the female *po pilu* rolled Amma's "word" into its coils. "The first thing Amma did was to put the seven words (of Amma) into the *po*."[2]

An altar, called *de lebe,* or *"lebe* of the inside," represents the female *po pilu,* the role of which is of great importance at this stage of the formation of the universe. The altar is placed in a storeroom, *kana,* of the Hogon's dwelling, a recess where no one may enter except the sacrificing totemic priest of the Hogon for the performance of rites.

Under the altar of the Hogon of Dyon, when its foundation was laid, a figure was drawn, called *"tonu* of the female *po pilu"* (fig. 138):[3] the spiral of the *po,* shown inside the seed, surrounds seven segments which are the articulations of the "word," *so,* numbering seven, *soy.* This

---

1. Cf. *supra,* p. 225.

2. *amma kize polo vo vani so soy po gozu-ne kunnu.*

3. *po pilu ya tonu.* Drawn with porridge of *po pilu.*

FIG. 138: *tonu* of the female *po pilu.*

drawing stresses the role that Amma conferred on the seed. One says of it: "The drawing of the *de lebe* is Amma putting the seven words into the *po.* "[4] For the "word" will become active on the inside and enable the *po*

---

4. *de lebe tonu to so soy amma po gozu-ne kunni.*

pilu to gather up, one by one, the things Amma entrusted to it and then later to liberate them into the forming universe.

When the foundation is laid, one draws the figure with *po pilu* porridge, saying: "The *po* came out of Amma's body like his image (*bibile*)"; then one adds, addressing Amma: "Make this village burst forth as the *po* made the world burst forth,"[5] that is: "Make the families grow and allow their development," for theoretically the village has the elongated shape of the seed.

The things Amma created did not yet have names: in the beginning there were no names for the signs that prefigured things. Amma's word, i.e., the name (*boy*) he gave to the things created, came at this time. It is said: "Amma put the design of things into the *po;* the name was not stuck (attached) (to the things). When the *po* made the world spin, it stuck the name to the thing and gave it to Binou Sérou."[6]

A ritual figure, called "Amma designer of things"[7] (fig. 139), shows a series of dots along the spiral of things that were rolled up in the *po* and represents the name given by Amma.[8] The names were first put inside the *po;* while whirling about, it created a bond between one thing and the thing after it. In this way, the names formed a sort of thin covering (compared to the one surrounding the brain): by spinning around, this "skin" became like a tube containing things in series. All things were named by Amma in this way.

"Now for all things, for each thing, Amma chose four names in all."[9] These four names, on the level of the spoken "word," correspond to the four successive graphic representations which prefigured things in

---

5. *po amma gozu-ne goy bibile bile. po ganna ginnegilu kini anago ginnegile.*

6. *amma kize tonu po-ne vo kunni boy-go-le digebele, po ganna ginnegile boy-go-le kize-go-le digera binu seru tagi.* The text, regarding Binou Sérou, refers to the revelation of the word (installment 2, second year).

7. *amma kize tonone.*

8. Drawn with rice and (small) millet porridge inside the sanctuary above the door. It is related to the bestowal of the first name called "name of the *binu,"* *binu boy,* or "forbidden name," *boy dama,* given to the child at baptism.

9. *kize pu tuturu kize boy nay bona.*

Amma's womb or "placenta" which, as we recall, are themselves the first expression of the four elements. "Amma, the things he created, he gave four names like the signs."[10]

N

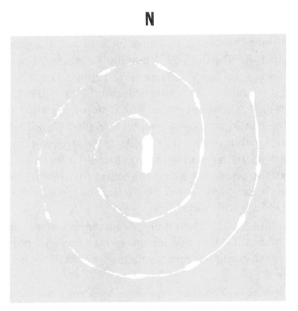

FIG. 139: "Amma designer of things."

Because things were given names, they placed themselves one behind the other and were rolled into the spiral. The *po* that contained them expanded in proportion to their entry, until it reached the bounds of Amma's womb. Therefore, one says: "When Amma spun the world around (it was) before (the whirling of) the *po*. When Amma was spinning

---

10. *amma kize vo mani boy nay kunna toni.*

the world around,[11] the *po* was in front. When Amma put the things into the *po,* the *po* rolled up."[12]

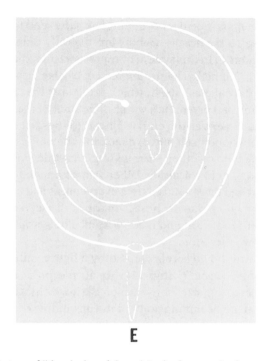

E

FIG. 140: *tonu* of "the placing of the calabash of woman in the sanctuary."

In addition, Amma placed the things in the *po* along with their placentas, which, until then, he had been keeping to himself; for he had kept the placentas of things when he created them. "The placentas of all things were in Amma's placenta. When he created all things, (Amma) took the placenta away and kept it. He put the child into the body of the *po,* enveloped the *po* as if in his own placenta. The placenta of Amma

---

11. Which is to say, when he was forming the seven earths and the seven skies, cf. *supra,* p. 126 and ff.

12. *amma ganna ginnegile po girune. amma ganna vo ginne-gileze po giru tobe. amma po-ne kize bana vo kunna po toniay.*

who created all things, (he) placed them in the body of the *po* (and) kept them covered."[13] At that moment, "each thing in its place in the *po* was enveloped in its placenta."[14]

A figure depicts the elaboration of this first work of the *po pilu.*[15] Here the spiral of the *po* is shown surrounding the *gaba* seed to the south and the *anu na* seed to the north, which were the only ones that were not taken up in the spiral. In this system of representation, the outside circle represents both Amma's womb (*amma doy*), where things are being rolled up, and the calabash itself, which prefigures the "matrix," where the world was formed in Amma's womb. The stalk of the calabash, with its point of attachment at the end, is placed to the east (fig. 140).

The spiral unwound itself and expanded to the limits of the egg until the two ends touched together, surrounding everything inside it. Amma's seat held the *po* tight like a spring. When Amma opened himself up, the spring unwound and the *po* burst to free everything it had been containing: it is said that the *po's* germ, or "nose," on top of the seed, wound around it like a cord around a top and made it spin. The spiral then unwound itself in the other direction.

The bursting of the *po* is represented by a figure called *"tonu* of the image of the first *vageu"*[16] (fig. 141). In it, the *po* is made of seven segments of decreasing size, above which is a horizontal stroke marking the bursting and the beginning point of the unwinding of the spiral. This stroke is the eighth segment, symbol of the eighth "articulation" of the "word," i.e., the "birth" of a new being; it recalls the fertility conferred, from the beginning, on the first seed Amma had created which, at this stage of creation, contains the whole world.

---

13. *kize me pu amma me-ne tobey. kize pu vo mana-le me-go gona sia. i-go gozu-ne kunni. amma me kize voy vo manu, po gozu-ne kunna gora gele. sie* means "to have, to possess."

14. *kize tuturu po-ne yalube me kuya tobe.*

15. It is called *koro yennu lara tonu,* "drawing of the placing of the calabash of the woman (in the sanctuary)." This figure is drawn with *ara geu* porridge on the site of an old abandoned sanctuary of Penné (located above Banani na between Gogoli and Banani na), by the priest Asama of Gogoli when he sets the date for the sowing celebration, *bulu,* in Lower Sanga. One says of Asama's act: "Asama has put the calabash of the woman (in the sanctuary)" *asama koro yennu lara;* this is to say that he has "given" the date of the *bulu.*

16. *vageu polo yala tonu.*

The figure also represents the head of the family in schematic form. It is made on the platform of the *kana* recess where the altar is. When the altar is consecrated, the first pot, belonging to the founding ancestor of the lineage — with the four pots of the first deceased to either side — is placed at the center of the drawing (at *a*).[17] The pots of the other members of the lineage will be placed, as the death occurs, along the unwinding spiral (from *b* to *g*), keeping the same direction. It is said of this figure: "When one places the pots of the dead, in the drawing, this is the image of the *po* spinning the world around."[18]

N

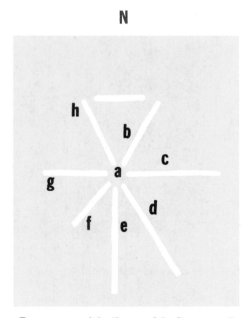

FIG. 141: *tonu* of the "image of the first *vageu*."

The unwinding inside the *po* is represented by a figure drawn under the altar *de lebe* of the Hogon of Arou, similar to the figure of the *po pilu* drawn under the *de lebe* altar of the Hogon of Dyon (fig. 142).

---

17. Cf. *supra,* p. 378. This pot is also placed over another figure drawn at that time, which is discussed on p. 152.

18. *anayimu bunno tonu-ne dananu po ganna digilemo yalay.*

S

FIG. 142: *tonu* of the unwinding of the elements contained in the *po*.

The spiral, now winding in the other direction, is marked out by twenty-two dots representing the categories assigned to the things it contained, that is, summing up everything; the twenty-two dots are evidence of the manifested and classified "word." The spiral stops at the bottom in a sort of hook — to the south — prefiguring the "emergence" of the elements contained in the *po*. Speaking of the twenty-two different categories spread throughout the universe by the *po*, one says: "Amma wanted to send the word into the world, so he put it into the *po*; the *po* kept it; by spinning space it made the eight words come out. Amma put the number of the twenty-two things into himself. Amma divided a part of the *po's* body and sent it into the world."[19] This unwinding, which manifested the "word," made a (loud) sound. The work of the female *po pilu* is also recalled at sowing time: "The *po pilu* that one scatters (sows) broadcast, its body has seven articulations, by germinating to maturity it will be twenty-two words."[20]

Moreover, the bursting of the *po* and the whirling of the spiral in the other direction made the covering (i.e., Amma's seat) pivot. This seat is represented by the calabash: the stalk (or knot) which was in the east was moved to the south, and the things emerged as if passing through the slightly dilated neck of the handle (or stalk) which is here compared to an umbilical cord.[21] A figure similar to the one of the winding represents the emergence of all the things from the body of the *po*: the spiral, marked out by twenty-two dots, is spinning inside the *gaba,* itself placed inside Amma's seat and seeking a way out towards the south (fig. 143).[22]

Thus, although Amma created the world, he made the *po* responsible for putting it into motion: by whirling and then acting as a spring, the *po* took along and then distributed all things in the universe. It is the *po* that started them on their descent upon the Fox's earth, thereby completing Amma's work. "Amma in his clavicle created by opening up (spreading) the top; the bottom, the *po* designed it by spreading it. The *po* gave birth to the world by spinning around."[23]

One also says of these two whirlings in both directions: "The *po* that spun and kept the world up, it is like a marriage; the *po* that made the world burst forth, it is like a birth,"[24] for the things will come out of the *po* like a child comes out of the mother's womb, when it is born.

To sum up the creative labor and the implied promises of life, one says: "Amma's egg opened its mouth, each thing that was inside came

---

19. *aduno so amma tiga be po gozu-ne kunna; po geleu; ganna ginnegile-le so gagara goni. amma gozu vomo-ne kize pelley ley sige kunna, pelu kuloy sige kaba, po gozu-ne kunna, aduno-ne timi.*

20. *po pilu mananu po pilu gozu-ne digu soy; teyay ille-vo-se so pelley ley sige bi.*

21. A gourd with a bulging neck is called *kemme bogu.*

22. Drawn with porridge of *yu* and *ara* under the *sogo die* which is placed in the center of the field of Lébé at the time it is delimited (volume I, installment 2, third year). This altar represents the Pleiades (cf. *supra,* p. 364, n. 235).

23. *amma ani guyo-ne dago ginnegile toni donu-go po ginnegile toy. po ganna degilia vanimi.*

24. *po ganna gona gelebe ya di anay; po ganna ginnegile i noni anay.*

out with its placenta; when the *po* spun the world around, each thing descended with its placenta."[25] Thus, the cereal grains emerged from their placenta, which is now represented by their hull which provides the bran used to rub the "yeast containers" *buzuru.* The hulls of the grains determine the fermentation.[26]

FIG. 143: Unwinding of the elements.

When a child is born, it comes out of the womb with its placenta, and it is given a name. Thus, the things came out of the *po* like a child

25. *amma ene talu vomo gomma kize tuturu tobe me bemme-le goy. po ganna ginnegile kize tuturu me beme-le goy* (or *sugi*).

26. The shape given to the yeast containers, *buzuru,* made of baobab fibers and impregnated with beer residue, is related to these representations: each of them is comparable to the different placentas — especially the first four which are considered as

comes out of its mother's womb. For the child in its mother's womb is like a fish in the water. This water, called *sosoy,* "drop by drop," is in the sack of the fetus, or the amnion, called *i guru,* "nest of the child."[27] The four elements are shown to be present in the gestation and delivery: the placenta is fire, the "waters of the womb" water, the amniotic sack earth, and the child freed at its birth is air.

The correspondences between signs, elements, and names are evident in the names that are given to every individual, which are also related to the spiritual principles of body, *kikinu gozu* (with the sex of the souls involved being reversed for girls):

signs	elements	names	souls
bummo	air	*binu boy*	*kikinu say ya*
yala	fire	*vageu boy*	*kikinu say ana*
tonu	water	*na boy*	*kikinu bummone ya*
toymu	earth	*tonno boy*	*kikinu bummone ana*

The *binu boy,* "name of the *binu,"* is given by the totemic priest; the *vageu boy,* "name of the *vageu,"* is given at the same time by the patriarch of the joint family: these two names given to the child at baptism, the eighth day after its birth, integrate the newborn child first into its clan and then into its paternal family. The *na boy,* "name of the mother," is the one given later by its maternal relatives. The *tonno boy,* "name of the age class," is the nickname given by one's pals.

The bestowal of the placenta epitomized the inherent twinness of all the things created by Amma: when they came out of the *po,* each one of them possessed its name — which means that each was given life by Amma's "word" — and its placenta, so that it would be complete and able to reproduce itself. Therefore, they are all said to be "twins."

---

fundamental. The yeast containers in the shape of a bonnet, *buzuru goro,* correspond to the *me* of Amma; the crown shaped ones, *buzuru tonno,* (literally "bracelet") are related to that of the *po;* those in the shape of an ear of millet, *buzuru lomtoro* (from *lomu,* long, and *toroy,* pot) correspond to that of the sacrificed Nommo; the flat, rectangular ones, *buzuru kakabu* (from *kaba* "to separate") correspond to the incomplete placenta of the Fox. These yeast containers are used respectively for making the beers that are drunk during ritual ceremonies involving one of the supernatural forces to which they are related.

27.The motto of the weavers aludes to the amniotic sack; these artisans are called *guru ba,* "great nest."

At the same time, this bestowal accentuated the basic characteristic of the Fox: among all things that make up creation, he will be the only one, because of his rebellion, to remain forever deprived of the greater part of his placenta (transformed into the sun) as well as of his female twin, and so he will be incomplete and frustrated.

The spiral of the *po* poured all its contents into the ark of the sacrificed Nommo, in which he would descend to the Earth of the Fox. In Amma's womb only the two seeds of the *gaba* and the *anu* remained that had not been taken along by the spiral. This "unloading" began first in relation to the characteristics of the *anu,* for it was the *anu* that actually classified the things in the ark and organized their distribution. Therefore, one says that it was the delegate of the *po,* its agent; it is called "the *po's* follower," *po bolodige.*

Its role is depicted by a figure showing the position of the seeds, the fundamental symbols of creation placed inside the *po,* called "schematic image of the star of the *po* that is Amma's clavicles"[28] (fig. 144). In it, the grains are seen placed in equal sectors around a central circle which is the place of the *anu na.*

In the past, this figure was drawn where the primitive cylindrical granary, called *guyo gonu,* was built. The central circle of the picture representing the *anu na,* was reproduced in clay inside the granary by a central compartment called *anu kezu,* compartment of *anu,* comparable to a cylinder four cubits high and one cubit across. Around this cylinder, two cubits away, a circular wall was built. The inside space was comprised of eight compartments on two levels, that is, four compartments per level, with the door facing north.[29] Now, this construction was made in the image of the fruit of the *anu*: divided across the middle both ways, it has eight compartments which, for the Dogon, represent the eight seeds as well as the interior division of the cylindrical family granary.

One says of the construction of this first granary, itself an image of Amma's action: "The drawing of what was in the *po* in a circle around the *anu* became *toy.* The seeds that were inside the body of the *po*

---

28. *amma ani guyo po tolo yala tonu.* Drawn in *ara geu* porridge. In another version, the figure was drawn with porridge made from all the cereal grains mixed together.

29. Inside, the harvests were distributed as follows: above: *po pilu, ara, emme sono dummu, emme pilu;* below: *po, emme ya, nu* and *yu, emme nakolo* and *emme dum banu, namu.*

have been made into the *toy* in a circle around *anu* (i.e., the granary)."[30]
The central position of *anu* in the middle of the *po* at this stage of
creation on the one hand, and the similarity between the *po* and the
clavicle or egg of Amma on the other hand, have given their name to the
clavicles of man, which are not called *po guyo,* but rather as a euphemism *ani guyo,* "granary of *ani.* "

FIG. 144: Figure drawn under the primitive granary.

THE NOMMO SWALLOWS THE PO PILU.

At this same time, while the *po* was pouring its contents into the ark,
Amma made another change, because he wanted to protect the spiritual
principles of the grains from the Fox forever. He placed the *kikinu* of
body in the male seed of *po pilu* and the *kikinu* of sex in the *emme ya.*
Then he made the sacrificed Nommo swallow the two seeds. "The *po*

---

30. *tonu po-ne tobe onune gonu toyi. dene tonu po gozu-ne tobe anu gonu toyi.* The
central compartment of the *anu* in the cylindrical granary became the center cup (*tonuzu*),
placed in the middle of the present-day cubical granary, into which the women put their
belongings.

pilu was both male and female. With the female *po pilu,* Amma spun
the world around. The male became *puru.* The *anagonno* swallowed it,
it became his eggs."[31]

FIG. 145: Drawing of the swallowing of the fonio by the fish.

This action is represented by a figure called "drawing of the swallowing

31. *po pilu ya-le ana-le, amma po pilu ya-le ganna ginne-gila; ana-go puru bia; izu anagonno
voy minna, talu-go bi.*

of the fonio from the star of the fonio by the fish."[32] (fig. 145).

A circle, "the star of the fonio," *po tolo,* is divided by two perpendicular diameters into four oriented sectors containing dots, the seeds.[33] Under the eastern sector is the head of the silurus in the form of a triangle with a horizontal line across it and flanked by two "horns," which are the fish's barbs. The body, separated from the head, recalls the sacrifice. It is made of two curved lines that cross at the bottom and contain two ovals — the clavicles — marked with dots showing the seeds taken from the emptied eastern sector. "The drawing of the silurus shows how the fish swallowed the fonio from the star of the fonio (and how the seeds) went into the clavicles."[34]

The result of this transfer is represented to the right of the figure by a circle with two diameters just like the first, but with one of its sectors being empty.

When *emme ya* porridge is offered to the altar *ka amma* during the sowing celebration (*bulu*), the priest says: "Amma has given us the 'emergence of the father'; Amma, the water of the grain has come out; the *kikinu* of the grains are kept (guarded) by the *emme ya*; give us rain, make the grain grow, give us ripe millet, give us women and children."[35]

One also draws the head of the fish looking down on the sanctuary of the *binu* Manda of Orosongo: "Drawing of the division of the fields of the head of the fish (that) came out of the sky and descended"[36] (fig. 146).

The six compartments connote the main fields (*minne*): on the left, from top to bottom, *po minne, lebe minne, binu minne;* on the right, likewise, *poruba minne,* or "field of the outside," *vageu minne,* or "field of the ancestors," and *do minne.* The figures inside the lower compartments represent people who are tilling and dwellings.

The fish's barbs are the roots of the trees born from the sacrifice and of

---

32. *izu po tolo po minu tonu.* Drawn with *ara geu* on the north wall inside the sanctuaries of the Nommo *binu,* when they are founded. This figure is taken from the one in the sanctuary of the Nommo of Sangui.

33. This figure represents the shell and the legs of the insect *keke kummoy.*

34. *anagonno tonu izu po tolo po vo minna ta i vomo-ne yoy vogo-gin toni.*

35. *amma ba gonu; ka amma dene di uo goa; dene kikinu emme ya gelebe; ana di dele, dene temo yu illi dele, ya di dele, i nonu dele.*

36. *alagala goa izu suga ku vomo minne gammalu toy.*

those that will grow in the fields; from left to right: *oro, sa, yullo, minu, sa selu, ponnu, pelu, kilena.*

FIG. 146: Drawing of the head of the fish.

This is the manifestation on Earth of what took place in the sky. When the sacrificed Nommo swallowed the *po,* ridges appeared on his head, indicating the future division of the fields that would take place when his descendants married.[37]

This deed of fundamental importance was later to be repeated on Earth, where one of the *nommo anagonno's* duties was to devour the grains of impure fonio, in order to transform them into fish-eggs.[38] It will

---

37. G. DIETERLEN. *Parenté et mariage chez les Dogon,* p. 146.

38. Volume I, installment 2. The same function is attributed to the *polyo* (Hetero-branchus bidorsalis) by the Malinke, which is evidence of the presence of Faro in the Niger River. Cf. G. Dieterlen, *Mythe et organization sociale au Soudan Français,* p. 48.

also be remembered during the sowing and in the consumption of fonio by man. In the past, when the different varieties of *po* were separate, one sowed eggs of the *anagonno sala* with the *po pilu.* "When one sows the *po,* one mixes the eggs of the *anagonno* with the *po.* If one doesn't get *anagonno* eggs, one cuts up the intestines of the *anagonno*; one mixes (it) with the *po* that one is sowing. With that, the *po* multiplies."[39]

At harvest time, one used to pour a porridge of *po pilu* on the *sogo* altar of the family pond. The first dish of *po pilu* eaten in the house of the lineage was started by a member of the group at the orders of the *ginna bana,* who would say: "Fish and fonio (together) are but one."[40]

CLASSIFICATION OF THE ELEMENTS CONTAINED IN THE FEMALE PO PILU.

The total number of the elements of creation that Amma placed in the *po,* and which the *po* poured into the ark, is classified in twenty-two categories. These categories are represented by a ritual figure called *"tonu* of the things that came out of the body of the *po"*[41] which, in twenty-two diagrams, shows all the things Amma put into the *po* (fig. 147). We see, in the following order (and in twinned pairs): — the *nommo die,* who remained in the sky, and the sacrificed and resurrected *nommo,* both in the form of *nommo anagonno*; a horizontal line recalls the arms, and the split tail the legs his descendants, mankind, will have; — the four grains of the *sene,* symbolizing the four elements, the foundation of creation; the turtle *kiru,* here symbolizing all domestic animals; the chameleon *ogodine,* representing all wild animals; then the moon and the sun, the Fox, and the stars; below the ark, man and the cereal grain seeds (from left to right): the *emme ya, ara geu, yu pilu, nu,* and *namu*; then those of the *gaba* and the *anu* (which is made of four signs); finally, the following plants (from left to right): the *pelu, sana, kilena,* and *yayaga.*

---

39. *po mananu izu anagonno talu po-ne bile, anagonno talu bemele, izu koloda pollo pollo, po-ne bile mananu.*

40. *izu-le po-le turu vogo.* The "eater" was designated by the *inneu omo* of the *ginna.* The *inneu omo,* or "living men," in Dogon society, are opposite the *inneu puru,* or "impure men," who observe different prohibitions (cf. *supra,* p. 56 and installment 2, fourth year).

41. *po gozu-ne kize goa toy.* Drawn with snake dung *yuguru na* (symbol of the unity of the world), on the façade of the sanctuary of the Nommo *binu* to the right of the entrance door on the day that this totem's priest is ordained *(duguru).*

FIG. 147: *tonu* of the things which came out of the body of the *po*.

The seeds of cereal grains descended with the ark and gave birth to all the varieties existing today. The *gaba* and *anu na* grains, which were placed in the center when the spiral of the *po* was rolling up, are shown last here. They will not descend on the ark, but will come out last of all, alone and independently of one another, to germinate and reproduce on the different worlds created by Amma.[42]

The plants (trees and grasses) related to the sacrifice and resurrection of the Nommo are used for purifications;[43] with the *sene,* they represent all plant life.

The chameleon and the turtle *kiru* are responsible for guarding and purifying the earth of the Fox. For where they land on the earth, the turtle will go around the still empty pond and purify the soil, allowing the rain water to enter it and stay there.[44] Then it will go into the pond, around which the trees symbolizing the resurrection will grow.

This drawing represents a classification into "families," or *togu,* of the elements of creation in relation to the life and work of man on Earth.

The total number of the categories of the things Amma put into the *po,* expressed by the twenty-two elements we have just examined, is summed up by the schematic figure called *"tonu* of the female *po pilu,"* *po pilu ya tonu.* It is drawn only once at the delimitation of the threshing-floor, called "plateau of the pile of *po,"po tuyo taba,* where the *po pilu* harvest used to be collected. It is composed of a circle representing the seed around which first twelve concentric lines are drawn, corresponding to the elements of creation belonging to the Fox, and then ten corresponding to those that belong to the Nommo.[45] The twenty-two lines are also a numerical reminder of what man will know about Amma's second creation.

The work of the female *po pilu,* which brought everything Amma had created into manifestation and realized his labors, is commented on in view of the series of graphic representations which, as we have seen, represent Amma's thought, his designs and, furthermore, the progressive material realization of all the elements that would make up the universe.

---

42. The *gaba* will bear seven different fruits, symbols of the seven worlds created by Amma. Cf. *infra,* p. 522.

43. The *sana* is the "broom" used after the body has been purified with *pelu* bark; the *yayaga* is used in the same way after the mouth has been purified with *kilena* charcoal.

44. The *kiru* turtle will be the object of the purification sacrifice *kugudum* performed in the ritual fields in the event of a violation of a prohibition: the animal is dragged around the field by a rope; then it is left hanging from a tree "to show Amma" that the act of purification has been carried out.

45. Cf. *supra,* p. 339 and fig. 66, p. 226.

It is said: "In Amma's clavicle in a ball, all the things in it were *tonu.*
Amma's round clavicle extended to the four cardinal points. The *po*
emerged and made the world. This is a *toy.* This is to make the things
that he (Amma) had in his womb. The world is the *toy* of Amma's
tonu. "[46]

Amma's four clavicles are represented in the Sanga region by four
caves located in the cliffs overlooking the valleys of Yanay, *kelu sommo,*
amma na ommoro, and Tonloy: *demme kommo* is the north clavicle,
tete kommo the south clavicle, *amma na kommo* that of the west, and
toloy kommo that of the east. For initiation purposes, these caves
(which are often of considerable size) have all been the site of different
arrangements (big rocks that have been put down flat or stacked on top
of each other, paintings, and clay constructions) relating to mythical
events that have taken place during man's life on Earth. They are also
the place where the funerals, the *dama,* and the rite of *kikinu mono* are
performed, and where the pots (*bunno*) are placed of the cereal grains
which "died" at the same time as the Fox. The last rites constitute the
regrouping of the spiritual principles of the seeds and their resurrection.[47]
They are repeated annually by the wanderings of the goatherds as they
accompany their flocks, which end at the locality of the *amma doy,*
"Amma's seat," the image of his womb and the center around which the
open clavicles had unfurled. There the goatherds pour a little of the
milk of their ewes on the ground next to the quadrangular stone beneath
which one has drawn the "signs," the first manifestations of Amma.[48]

On one of the walls inside *tete kommo* (southern clavicle), a series
of figures recalls the events we have just recounted. A white painting
represents the egg with the four clavicles — filled with the "signs"
shown by lines — and the *po* emerging to produce the world. To the
left the *po banu* is drawn, to the right is the Fox next to a very worn
figure (which represents the *amma ta*) (Pl. VIII, 2).

---

46. *amma ani guyo gunnu kize voy tobe toni. amma ani guyo gunnu ganna sibe nay viri
po goa ganna ginnegili toyi. kize bere vomo-ne to kani* (or also *kize yiru vomo-ne to kani,*
"this is to do the things he has in his mind"), *aduno amma tonu toyi.*

47. Installment 2, ninth and tenth years. The complete description of these caves will be
published in installment 2.

48. Cf. *supra,* p. 103, *infra,* p. 528 and Pl. VI, 1.

REPRESENTATIONS.

The *po* was completely emptied of its contents, which were poured into the ark; this operation is represented by a figure called "drawing of

FIG. 148: *tonu* of the "objects of (the) *binu* hidden in the empty sanctuary."

the objects of (the) *binu* hidden in the empty sanctuary"[49] (fig. 148): the *po* is shown expanded to the limits of the egg; the ark, indicated by a square, is placed on the pillar of the world, the straight line. Speaking of

---

49. *binu tonu binuginu kolo-ne toy.* It is drawn upon the death of a totemic priest on the spot where the ritual objects were placed inside the sanctuary after they have been taken out and hidden. The door is then closed and the sanctuary remains closed until a new priest is ordained and the objects are put back.

Accordingly, the opening made in the picture of the ark may be seen as the "exit" of the deceased priest from the human world.

the figure and the circle, which is the image of the *po* emptied of its contents, one says: "The *po* when it spun the world around finished it, it changed into a large snake that holds the world in its circle."[50]

Having accomplished the work Amma had charged it with, the female *po pilu,* now reduced to only its own placenta, transformed itself into a star, "the star of the *po,"po tolo,* evidence of this fundamental act.

One says: "All things came from within Amma's placenta. The placenta of Amma who created all things placed them in the body of the *po* and kept them covered. After (except for) Amma, the rest of the things were in the *po.* This *po,* he made it emerge and made it spin the world around. The rest of the things is the placenta of the *po.* "[51]

"The *po* unwinding itself, it spread the world about. All the things went to the four cardinal corners. That thing that remained alone is the star of the *po.* "[52]

The work performed by the *po pilu,* which is of utmost importance, is the object of a great many representations. It is recalled by the form of certain sanctuaries and ritual objects and by the use made of the latter, as well as in the course of several rites.

1) One of the iron rhombuses used in the "end of mourning" ceremonies, *dama,* of a dignitary of the Society of Masks represents both the *anagonno* and the *po.*[53] A figure drawn in the caves of the masks, "drawing of the rays of the rhombus,"[54] shows the instrument's exact shape (fig. 149). The two lower points of the object (where the string will be attached) are the germ or "nose of the *po,"po kinu.* On either side are five carved notches, called "rays," *kelu:* the four pairs placed near the "nose" are the eight "rays" of the bursting of the *po,* "the eight rays that created the world";[55] on the right, the notches are also the "four corners

---

50. *po ganna digilima doga yuguru na bila ganna gona gele.*

51. *amma me kize voy ko-no goy. amma me kize voy vo manu po gozu-ne kunna gora gele. amma onune kize vazu po-ne tobe. poy ganna ginnegile vazu amma me doy* (or *amma doy). vazu kize po mey.*

52. *po vo gonulu ganna vo ginnegile; kize pu ganna sibe nay ya; vo turu bi po toloy.*

53. There exist three kinds of different rhombuses which are used successively in the ceremonies of the Sigui or the *dama;* one of them represents the *anagonno* and the *po,* another the Fox, and the third the tongue of the ancestor Dyongou Sérou (installment 2, third year).

54. *imina na kelu tonu.*

55. *kelu gagara ganna moyomu.*

of space" (*ganna sibe nay*); on the left, they are the "four things (elements) of space" (*ganna kize nay*). On the right and the left, two appendages near the top are the clavicles of the fish represented by the entire object. "The ball (entirety) of the rhombus is the fish. The *po* is like the egg of the fish. The rhombus is the whole covering of the eggs of the fish."[56]

The central line ending at the "nose of the *po*" (that is, the seed's germination) is, on the actual wooden object, suggested only by its overall form, the shape of a lozenge with an axial backbone: it represents the inside area of a field divided in two.

To handle the rhombus is to recall the way in which the *po* made the world by spinning about. It is also like sowing the seed: the sower turns about while walking, in order to sow the *po* broadcast. One says: "The rhombus, when it spins, it is as if it were creating the world."[57]

2) An image of the two stages of creation (at first the work of Amma, later realized by the effort of the *po*) is recalled when the millet beer is brewed that the members of the *ginna* drink during the collective ceremonies. After it has been boiled, an unfermented part of the liquid, called *pipilu,* is put aside. The beer, *kono,* is obtained after the yeast container has been put in the rest of the liquid. The two beverages,

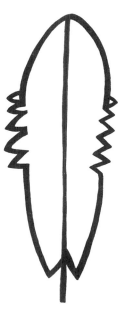

FIG. 149:
Drawing of the "rays
of the rhombus."

obtained one after the other, recall the two stages. One says: "The *pipilu* is the image of the grains in Amma's clavicles; the beer is the same thing as the grains sown by Amma in the *po* which spun the world around, (that) descended below, and that one cultivated. The *pipilu* is like the

---

56. *imina na gunno vomo izu anay. po anagonno talugin vo. imina na anagonno talu gunnu-gin vo.* We have seen that one of the *anagonno's* functions on Earth will be to consume the impure fonio of the Fox to transform it into fish eggs.

57. *imina na som yozogo ganna moyonoze gin vo.*

sowing; the beer is like the harvest (the ripe grain)."⁵⁸ For the yeast
container, symbol of the placenta, acts upon the liquid to make it
ferment and gives it new life.

The *pipilu* is put in special pots, which are the symbols of "Amma's
seat," and is drunk by the patriarchs and those responsible for the cult.
The rest of the drink and the dregs are never simply left, but rather
buried in the dung-hill in the courtyard of the *ginna.* The beer, on the
other hand, is drunk by all the participants; the dregs may be given to
the animals.

3) the role of the *po pilu* is recalled even in the form of the totemic
sanctuaries: that of the Manda totem of Orosongo has the shape of the
seed "that spun the world around" (fig. 150, A). The adjacent dwelling of
the priest (H) includes a round recess (*kana*) and a square one, respectively representing *emme ya* and *ara geu.*

During ceremonies involving the clan, one successively draws the
figures recalling the work of Amma and of the female *po pilu* on the
square platform of the priest that is attached to the side of the sanctuary
(B) — a platform whose four sides mark the four cardinal directions.

The priest sits on the platform against the wall, facing west. During
the *agu* (*bado* in Sanga), one draws next to him Amma's still-closed egg
with *emme ya* porridge: the four inside lines represent the four clavicles.
During *arbya* (*bago* in Sanga), in the same place, the egg and the
opening of the clavicles are drawn with porridge of *emme di giru* (fig.
151, a and b).

The bursting *po* is drawn with porridge of *emme pilu* on the north wall
above the platform at the *bago* during the ceremony of the "tasting of
the new millet" (*yu korokoro* in Sanga): eight lines placed at the four
cardinal points show the distribution of the primordial seeds in the
realized universe (fig. 151, c).

The whirling *po* is drawn with *yu* during the ceremony called *odom
piru* that precedes the sowing. It is made on the edge of the platform, i.e.,
under Amma's open egg, "for it spun the world around which descended"
(fig. 151, d).

4) All the elements making up the *po* seed, as well as the work performed

---

58. *pipilu amma ani guyo-ne dene yala tobe. kono dene po kolo-ne amma kunna
ganna ginnegili donne sugunu vali tozoy. pipilu dene toy toze; kono dene ille tozoy.*

by the female *po pilu,* are remembered in the rites performed during the sowing celebration, *bulu,* in which all the members of the community take part.

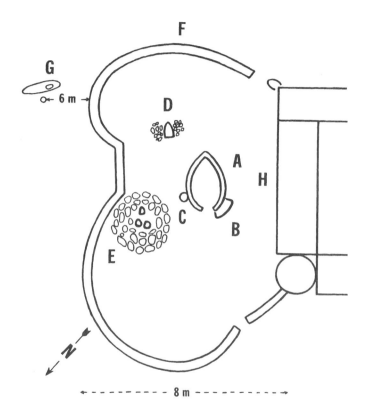

FIG. 150: Layout of the sanctuary of the Manda totem of Orosongo and its annexes: A. sanctuary; B. platform of the priest; C. *tono,* unused millstone; D. altar to Amma; E. pile of stones and hearth; F. outside wall; G. *polu* plantation; H. dwelling of the priest.

These annual ceremonies last five days, commemorating both the death and the resurrection of *o nommo*. In Upper Sanga, they are

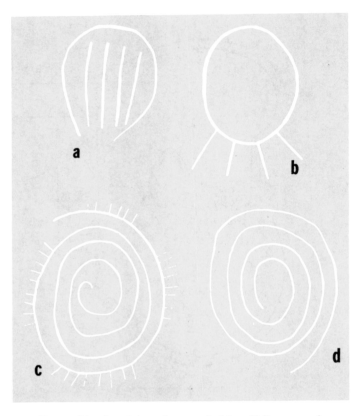

FIG. 151: Drawing of Amma's egg and of the whirling *po*, made on the platform of the sanctuary of the Manda totem of Orosongo.

performed in the Hogon's dwelling, in the *ginna* of every lineage, and on the platform of the *lebe dala* where, as we have already seen, the *sogo* placed around the altar of the *lebe* (*para lebe*) mark not only the stages of this sacrifice, but also the stars related to them and to the totemic clans; they end in the field of Lébé.[59]

A certain number of these rites are very closely related to the role of the female *po pilu*; therefore, we will present the commentaries about them by way of illustration.[60]

a) The ceremonies are accompanied by calls sounded by someone playing the "Hogon's horn," *ogo buru.* The sounds produced by the instrument, called voices or *mi* (eight in all), are the vibrations of the "word" that Amma placed in the seed. "The voice of the *ogo buru* is the image of the *po* spinning the world around."[61] The player blows through a mouthpiece which represents the germination of the *po*; the bell of the horn represents the earth in which it germinates. The "voices" — each of which has a name — are also those of the eight basic cereal grains. The instrument sounds the "voice" of the *po* "spinning the world around,"[62] for the unwinding that freed everything it contained made a loud sound.

At this time, one draws the *"yala* of the *po* spinning the world around" (fig. 152) on the façade of the totemic sanctuaries. The seed is represented by a small circle from which emerge eight segments of increasing length, "the eight living things,"[63] that is, the eight "articulations of the word" which, at this stage, are sounds, the "voices" of the Hogon's horn.

The spiral, called *ozu day,* "crossed road," is shown to be discontinuous, so as to permit "passage across," for it is evidence that the things which emerged from the *po* became separated from it. A line of eight chevrons, called "zigzagging path of the world" (*aduno ozu tonnolo*), is placed to the left of the figure indicating the vibration of the spiraling line and the "eight voices of the Hogon's horn."[64]

b) The first day of the *bulu* (the Banani market), *po pilu* porridge is poured on the altar *ka amma,* under which are placed the figures

---

59. Some descriptions of the ceremonies appear in D. Paulme and D. Lifchitz, *Les Fêtes des semailles en 1935 chez les Dogon de Sanga* and in S. de Ganay, *Le Binou Yébéné,* p. 444.

60. All of the rites of the *bulu* and related representations will be described in installment 2, fifth year.

61. *ogo buru mi po yala ganna gigilema anay.*

62. *po ganna gigilema yala.* Drawn on the façade of the totemic sanctuaries of *binu na* with *ara geu* porridge.

63. *kize omo gagara.*

64. *ogo buru mi gagara.* A figure representing the horn of the Hogon also bears this line of chevrons.

portraying the creation of the seed. That same day, in commemoration of the sacrifice and resurrection of the Nommo, libations and sacrifices are performed, first on the altar *de lebe,* which represents the presence of the *po pilu* in the Hogon's dwelling, then on the altar *para lebe,* which is placed in the middle of the *lebe dala* representing Amma's sky. In the evening, the patriarchs perform similar offerings on the *amma na* altars of every *ginna.* As he pours the *po pilu* porridge on the altar, the patriarch says: "Amma, your water has come out for the great seed that has brought forth and distributed by making the world spin."[65]

FIG. 152: The female *po pilu* spinning the world around.

The next day, sacrifices involving the totemic clans are performed: before the slaughter of the victims, the priest, who is alone inside the sanctuary, offers libations of *po pilu* porridge on the ritual objects and says: "Amma has put the number of twenty-two things in himself;

---

65. *amma dene die gona aduno ginnegilemi di goa.*

Amma divided a part of the sixty-six *yala* of the *po's* body and sent it into the world."[66]

The next two days are spent in a series of visits called *bulu yanu,* "greetings of the *bulu,*" performed by all members of the community. The many comings and goings of the participants, within their own neighborhood as well as in the other settlements they must visit, together correspond to the sixty-six *yala* of the spiral representing the formation of the *po* seed in Amma's womb. We recall that the *yala* that were rolled up inside the egg were divided into 22+40+4 during the elaboration of the *po* and later of the *nommo anagonno.*[67] In this rite, which repeats the unraveling of the *yala,*[68] they are divided into 30+30+3+3 *yala* which evoke, through their numeric value (3 being a male number), the patrilinear structure of the lineages and, through their re-duplication, the fundamental twinness of everything that Amma had created.

The "greetings of the *bulu*" begin with visits called *ginna yanu* made by the members of a *ginna,* first to their own patriarch, then to the other members of the lineage. The entire group of the people visited corresponds to the thirty first *yala.*

For example, Ambara goes to pay a visit to the *ginna bana* of Amtaba, of Guinna, and of Sodamma;[69] then he goes to all his "brothers," in the broadest sense of the term, originating from his *ginna.*

The next visits are called *togu yanu,* or "greetings to the family" (also in the broadest sense): everyone visits people from house to house, where one drinks the beer that is always offered. These visits correspond to the second group of thirty *yala.*

Then come the *ama yanu,* or "greetings to the parents-in-law," which correspond to the 3 (+3) *yala* represented by the father-in-law, the mother-in-law, and their daughter. For it is said: "The kinship of the father-in-law, the mother-in-law, and their daughter, their number is three."[70] However, with regard to the primordial spiral constituting the

---

66. *amma gozu vomo-ne kize lugu pelley ley sige kunna; pelu kuloy kaba po gozu-ne kunna aduno-ne timi.*

67. Cf. *supra,* p. 121.

68. Cf. *supra,* p. 125.

69. Sodamma, Ginna, and Amtaba are three different quarters, each having a *ginna*; the second two stem from the first.

70. *amma ayne ko-le yana ko-le i ya beme ko-le mona tanu lugonu.*

po, these last visits correspond to the four *yala* of the *sene,* which were the last in line. The first three are the three people mentioned above, and the fourth is the son-in-law, in the following order: *sene na, sene gommuzu, sene urio, sene benu.* Thus, these visits, as if going back to the beginning, symbolically complete the *bulu yanu.*

One says of all the *bulu yanu:* "To greet the *ginna bana* is to greet the *po pilu.* "[71]

The fifth day, the collective rite of the *lebe gono* or "spiral of the *lebe"* is performed. It commemorates and reenacts the work done by the female *po pilu,* in which all members of the community participate.

In the course of the day, the "Hogon's horn" will be sounded a total of three times to recall the "voice" of the *po.* [72] The first time the horn is played is in the morning to summon the seven eldest men of the settlement to drink with the Hogon the beer that he has had prepared.

Once this drinking is finished, the horn is sounded again to summon all the men of the settlement and the wives of the *ginna bana* to the *lebe dala.*

When the horn sounds for a third time, the participants, carrying a millet stalk, led by tambourine players who strike the drums of the *ginna* (who represent the lineages) and by all the totemic priests (who represent the clans), turn around the main altars of the *lebe dala* in the counterclockwise spiral, the direction in which the *po* rolled up the elements of the universe, one by one. Their zigzagging walk is symbolic of the vibration of the "voice" of the *po,* the "word" it contains.

The third time around, they stop at the southern part and face the altar of Lébé, which they salute by placing their elbows on the ground or by clapping their hands. The drummers then go around the altar three times in the direction in which the *po* unwound and emptied itself of its contents. At the end of the third round, the members of the community, led by the priests, all quickly run to the altar. In a low voice the Yébéné priest then recites a long prayer in which he says: "The men of Amma and of the *vageu,* their number is thirty because of their name; the men of the *lebe* and of the *binu,* their number is thirty-four because of their

---

71. *vageu bana bulu-le yananu po pilu yananu anay.*

72. At the *bulu,* when the trumpet is blown, it is blown four times *ogono do ta,* "Hogon seated"; twice *ogoyana da koy,* "the wife of the Hogon has fed the children"; twice *ogono ba nade,* "the Hogon has called" — eight successive calls in all.

name; when they are together their number is sixty-four; make men be born unto them." Then, addressing those present, he adds: "Do not take the wives of your friends; do not give the women of this village away; whoever wants to give them (away), Amma sees him, the ancestors see him, the *lebe* sees him, the *binu* sees him. May Amma give us the following day."[73]

Thus, all those taking part in the rite recall the elements of the original spiral of the *po.*

As seen in terms of the "motion" imposed by Amma upon the entire creation while the *po pilu* was doing its work, the two successive marches of the *lebe gono* also correspond to the two spirals executed by the female *po pilu* when it enveloped and later released its contents: the first march corresponds to the closed *po,* the second to the open *po* distributing the elements of the universe.

Therefore, these ceremonies in their totality symbolize the different stages of the formation of the first seed as well as those of the development of the creation which began with that seed. The ceremonies also commemorate things that have to do with the cereal grains at sowing time, which follows the ceremony:[74] for at this time the seeds put into the soil will have to "unwind" internally, in order to germinate, "like the *po* unwound itself inside Amma's egg."

This internal movement of the smallest of all the elements God created is reflected in space by the spiraling motion of the stars. This motion is also commemorated by the spiraling marches of the *lebe gono,* performed by all the members of the settlement on the grounds, where a series of altars represents the stars.

The day after the *lebe gono,* the player will sound the horn a fourth time, summoning the seven patriarchs who joined in the drinking of the beer to come and thank the Hogon.

---

73. *amma-le vageu-le anau ebe viay, lugu ebe peran boy-le-ko voy; lebe-le binu-le anau ebe viay, lugu ebe peran nay sige boy-le-ko voy; be voy mona pelu kuloy nay sige lugi; anau beme naniemo; tumo yana deno, anna-go yanau are inne vaza oobodo bana amma ieze, vageu ieze, binu ieze; amma boy tolo obo.*

74. After the *lebe gono,* the participants, at first crowded in front of the Hogon's dwelling and later near the totemic sanctuaries, receive ears of grain tossed from the terraces above; since the preceding harvest, these ears have been the holders of the spiritual principles of the cereal grains: their seeds will be mixed with those to be sown (installment 2, fifth year).

CHAPTER V

THE NOMMO'S ARK

The contents of the ark. The descent of the ark. The ark on Earth. Representations of the Nommo's Ark. The resurrected Nommo in the water. The stars and calendars.

By its spinning the unwound *po* had poured everything it contained into the Nommo's "great ark," or *koro na.* This ark was made from the rest of the victim's placenta. Now this placenta, unlike that of Ogo, had not undergone the tearing and transformations which had seriously affected the piece that formed the Earth and had rendered it impure.

The Fox's ark, made of "impure" earth, is the symbol of the uncultivated bush; the Nommo's ark, made of "pure earth," will descend with everything Amma created and is symbolic of the cultivated earth: it will be called *izubay minne,* "earth of the day of the fish" — a term which emphasizes its origin, its ties with the sacrificed Nommo, and with human beings, his descendants, who will keep their original fetal form. This "earth of the fish" will progressively extend itself over the Fox's earth in proportion to the development of agriculture which, itself, will constitute a purification of the ground made impure by theft and incest.

Theoretically, the ark had as many compartments as the number of holes the Fox had dug in the ground: sixty, this number being the "reckoning of the placenta," *me lugi.*

With regard to the social structure and technical development, the sixty compartments of the ark were also related to the theoretical division of the primal family field between the four eponymous ancestors, a field they were to constitute and which will be like "plated" on top of the earth of the Fox. From this perspective, the distribution of the compartments is in four rows of fifteen, with 3 x 5 lots per ancestor (fig. 153).[1] Symbolically speaking, the numbers 3 (attributed to the male) and 5 (attributed to the generations) together represent the patrilinear line of descent. It is said: "The sixty holes of the *ginna minne* are divided into five, five."[2] This terminology is also related to the five fingers of the hand that will seed the field.

In relation to the family field, but in terms of time, the four rows correspond to four kinds of sowing performed in succession: *bizu,*

FIG. 153: Figure representing the ark with sixty compartments.

1. Drawn with *ara geu* porridge on the façade of the totemic sanctuaries. The lozenge shape of the compartments here corresponds to the ark in the sky during the descent as well as to the "angles" of celestial space. When the ark is represented as lying on the ground, the compartments are squares which recall the "sides" of terrestrial space (cf. p. 465). The central lozenge emphasizes the place of the resurrected Nommo.

"sowing without rain"; *manu,* "scattered sowing": manure and grains are put in the field at certain spots just before or after the rain; *toy,* sowing in the strict sense of the word, which is done after the rain; *loro,* its complement, done in those places where the preceding sowing has produced no grain.[3]

These sixty compartments contained all beings and manners of being, grouped in categories of which only the first twenty-two are known:

1. the world: *aduno*
2. the village: *anna*
3. house of menstruating women: *yapunulu ginu*
4. big house: *ginna*
5. granary: *guyo*
6. sky: *alagala*
7. earth: *minne*
8. wind: *ono*
9. livestock: *arsege,* all four-legged animals, called *kubo nay,* "four legs"
10. the birds: *kize kile,* "flying things"
11. the trees: *timmu*
12. the person: *inne*
13. the dance: *go*
14. fire: *yau*
15. the (spoken) word: *so*
16. the cultivated field: *minne valie*
17. work: *bire*
18. the cowry: *kele*
19. travel (walking): *yoy*
20. death: *yimu*
21. funerals: *yimu yanna*
22. peace: *dam*

To the Dogon way of thinking, these categories (which are different from those classifying "Amma's *bummo'*) express everything that will

---

2. *ginna minne bunno pelley kuloy, numo numono gammali.* These five generations are called: *kummo, dene, tire, unum, bau* in ascending order, and the other way round in descending order. When the head of the family performs a sacrifice on the altar to the ancestors, he lists the ascendants by name up to the fifth generation. The sixth is called *dandam buli;* it is "with Amma," whereas the five preceding ones are "with men." The expression *dandam buli* means "he is seated and receives sacrifices." The ancestors of this generation are no longer summoned by name to come and partake of the sacrifice: for them and their ascendants one simply says "and may all those who have passed on come and drink." The *dandam buli* are also called *nana buli.*

3. The four sowings also correspond to the four first mythical sowings of men from the first to the fourth year (installment 2).

be essential to man and that will occur on Earth after the descent of the ark. They parallel the twenty-two parts of the resurrected Nommo's body as well as the twenty-two categories which group the elements of the universe released by the *po pilu*.[4] Like their counterparts, they are also related to the "division of the totems," the totemic institution forming the basis of the social structure in relation to the celestial sacrifice. Finally, they symbolize the organization of life on Earth by the resurrected Nommo, and therefore one says that they are "like the Nommo's twenty-two teeth," that is, like his "word."

What is left — which is unknown — will be known later to man and will change the world. It is said that this revelation will come slowly at first, like a fog, then swiftly, like the rain and the wind.[5]

CONTENTS OF THE ARK.

The ark was soft and moist like the placenta it was made of. It held all the things and beings created by Amma and later poured out by the female *po pilu*. Its structure and contents are evidence of the Nommo's first victory won over the Fox. In comparison to Ogo's first two arks, considering their narrowness and their essential, but meager contents, as well as to his third, a structure of lattice-work that held nothing, the Nommo's ark was unique, for it was full. When one says that the "sixty holes of the ark are like the holes of the ant," it is because one compares the structure to an ant hill full of these innumerable, active insects. The Nommo's ark embodied the role Amma had conferred on him: to organize, direct, and control the whole created universe.

On the ark were, first of all, the resurrected Nommo and the eight ancestors, or four couples of twins. Each one of them was related to one

---

4. Considered from the view point of graphic representation and number and compared to the "signs" of Amma (*bummo*), which connote what is going to be created, these categories are like "drawings" (*toy*) or realizations of those signs, because the world is created and completed.

5. A parallel concept is presented in the Bambara myth. Cf. G. Dieterlen, *Essai sur la religion bambara,* p. 30.

of the eight seeds which the resurrected Nommo symbolically carried in his clavicles.[6] The nine of them together formed a whole for, on another level, they each represented, on the ark, one of the parts of the body of the sacrificed Nommo which had, in a way, been stretched out over his own placenta. The Nommo, as "father," was the head, Amma Sérou the chest, Lébé Sérou the abdomen, Binou Sérou the still living arms, Dyongou Sérou the navel and sex organ, and the four female twins were the Nommo's four limbs.[7]

The ancestors and the resurrected Nommo were placed near five pairs of trees, each having sixty leaves, in the following manner:

a) In the middle, on a copper seat, *ogo dummo* or "chief's platform," sat the resurrected male Nommo. He was accompanied by the *valu* and the *donu* bird, which are related to his spiritual principles and are living testimony of the sacrifice. Linked by their roots, like two twins, stood the *kilena* and the *pelu.* They shaded a hemispheric copper vessel, *ogo bana* or "vase of the chief," in which a snake lay coiled, an image of the unity of the world; in its head were the eight primordial seeds. They appeared again in a "sack of skin," hung from one of the trees, symbolizing here the clavicle, seat of the symbol of the grain.

Also in the middle of the ark grew a palmyra tree, *siu,* whose fruit was the first food of the ancestors of the ark: they would break it open to eat the kernel and seed it contained.

On each side of the structure was a pair of ancestors and a pair of trees:

b) To the west, Amma Sérou and his twin sister *go sa,* "sister of the dance," under the *sene na* and the *oro. amma seru,* "Amma's witness," was to be responsible for the cult devoted by men to their creator and to his first celestial agent, the *nommo die.* His female twin's name, *go sa,* is an allusion to the women's dances representing fish swimming in the water. In the course of certain ceremonies, through their successive

---

6. When the harvest is brought in, a share is first given to the eldest woman of the lineage as testimony to the seeds that belonged to the ancestors' female twins. Theoretically, the ears are hers alone; however, she may share them with others.

7. The Dogon say that it is because of them that one can easily move the upper and lower limbs; they help in childbirth. For if a woman gives birth with difficulty, it is said that "the Nommo has folded one of her limbs"; if she has no problem, it is because "the Nommo has unfolded them."

dance steps, the women recall first the formation of the fetus (which is a fish), then its movements in the waters of the womb where it "swims."[8] On Earth, *go sa* will be Amma's first priestess, called "Amma's wife" or *amma yana.*

The *sene* and the baobab are traditionally planted in the field of the *ginna.*

c) To the north were placed Lébé Sérou and his female twin *ya sa,* "wife sister"; under the *gobo banu* and the *gobo pilu,* Lébé Sérou, "witness of Lébé," will sow the first collective field of the *ginna.* Because of a violation of a prohibition and the ensuing threat to the wholeness of the grain, the fields, and the entire society, he will be sacrificed and resurrected on Earth, as was the Nommo in the sky for similar reasons. His sacrifice will purify the "earth of the day of the fish," *izubay minne,* of which he is the delegate. His female twin, *ya sa,* will invent and introduce song.

d) To the east were Binou Sérou and his female twin, *ya sa,* placed under the *sa* and the *yullo.* One says of Binou Sérou, who will initiate the totemic cult, that he is "like the two living arms" of the sacrificed Nommo.

The cult devoted to the victim as *o nommo* — who originally was just one *binu* — will be "shared" between the descendants of the four ancestors, as was his body for the purification and organization of the universe. This division shows the expansion of the human species: when a new *ginna* is founded and the *binu* "shared," one says: "The extended arms of Amma continually expand the world."[9] The body of the sacrificed Nommo expands in proportion to the multiplication of the *binu.*

The female twin of Binou Sérou, *ya sa,* is related to the "word" he will receive from *o nommo* and will have to transmit to mankind. She is evidence of certain aggressive aspects of discourse, namely, disputes and conflict.

e) To the south, Dyongou Sérou and his female twin, *ya sa,* were placed under the *saselu* and the *bozo kubo. donu* means "remedy." This ancestor will be a healer and a hunter and will have altars relating to his

---

8. In order, these dances are: *ya go, go na, suru boy, go yala.* They are commented on in installment 2. These dances are performed especially during the funerals of women. Cf. G. Dieterlen, *Les Ames des Dogon,* p. 120.

9. *amma numo vira aduno vo vaniemu.*

functions. His special status, due to the fact that he possesses only two "sex souls" (the other two having been given to the Fox), will be the cause of his avatars. He will die in a state of impurity and will transmit death to man. His body, however, divided into pieces, will give rise to altars upon which sacrifices will be offered for the protection of the community.

His female twin, *ya sa,* will be in charge of births and will aid women in childbirth.[10]

All the plants and animals were with the ancestors in the ark. Certain animals, directly related to certain parts of the resurrected Nommo's body as well as to certain of his spiritual principles, were to become the first "totemic taboos," *binu dama*: the black crocodile, *ayo geu,* and the silurus, *anagonno sala,* respectively represent the right and left arms and were in the east with Binou Sérou; the water lizard, *ay,* and the land lizard, *ugunu,* represent respectively the right and left legs and were in the west with Amma Sérou. Similarly, the antelope, *valu,* and the bird *donu,* are related to the "errant" spiritual principles of the body: *gozu kikinu bummone.*

The ark was suspended from an iron or copper chain, the links of which symbolized the ancestors holding hands. It is also compared to a double line of rope punctuated by a series of knots, called "knots of the great Amma" or "knots that do not break the rope (of the ancestors) of the womb" (i.e., of the generations) (fig. 154).[11] Each knot in itself represents the ark, and the rope the descent, "so that one will not forget the descent of the ark." It is also the quasi-unbreakable, close tie established by Amma between the ancestors and their descendants.

One explains this representation by saying that when Amma formed the world, he "made four knots" prefiguring the "rope

FIG. 154: Drawing of the knots that attach the rope of the ark.

---

10. She will later become the protectress of the spiritual principles of animals at the time when the masks are invented that represent them (installment 2, third year).

11. *amma na dineu* or *iri sum paragu dineu.* The knot was immediately made by our informant and drawn right there: it is a double sheet-bend knot, the type that tightens under stress.

of the ark," each of which constituted one of the "seats of the universe," *aduno doy.* This rope is also like a snake that is knotted at the four cardinal points and surrounds the world in formation.

During the sacrifice offered after the harvest, the prayer recited by the patriarch alludes to the ark and everything it represented for human- ity. The patriarch says: "Good Amma, as the ark came from above, as it was sent for us, give us health."[12]

A theoretical reconstruction of the ark, made out of wood by a smith, shows (to its maker) the essential characteristics of the structure in relation to the system of representation it embodies (fig. 155).[13] The object has the form of a kind of boat with a rounded hull and two decks. The upper and lower decks are equipped each with two handles. The upper deck, which is narrower than the lower one, forms an arch whose abutments end where the handles begin and form two staircases (at each end) with four steps and an empty space between them. The two decks each have two rows of four holes representing the ark's compartments. In profile, the upper deck widens from the relatively narrow base. Every detail is a symbol related to the beings and parts of the universe; every hole, square with rounded corners, recalls the compartment in which each category of beings was lodged for the descent. The lower deck is the former world, whereas the upper deck, narrow at the base, widens to prefigure the expansion of the new world which would follow the descent of the ark, itself a symbol of the extension of the universe: "The bottom case is the former world, the upper one is the new world: these are the two female twins who organized the new world. The upper case that widens out is space spreading out and progressing."[14]

The lower deck, called *koro bere,* "belly of the ark," is occupied by people who are distributed over the compartments in the following order (fig. 155): 1: Mossis and Samogo; 2: Bambara; 3: Bozo; 4: Peul; 5: Yebem; 6: leather-workers; 7: smiths; 8: griots. The ancient Tellem are placed in the cliffs to the east (compartment 17), where the fresh-

---

12. *amma ezu dele amma sin kana dago goa embe koro u togin magyanu obo.*

13. A complete description of the object may be found in M. Griaule, *L'Arche du monde chez les populations nigériennes,* pp. 117-120.

14. *koro donu-mogo aduno pey: koro da-mogo aduno kanna; dine uni yau ley-go aduno kanna be yegirigo vey. koro dago vanagodo ganna ginneu yaze.* The word *ganna,* "space," is considered to have the same root as *ga,* "to spread apart."

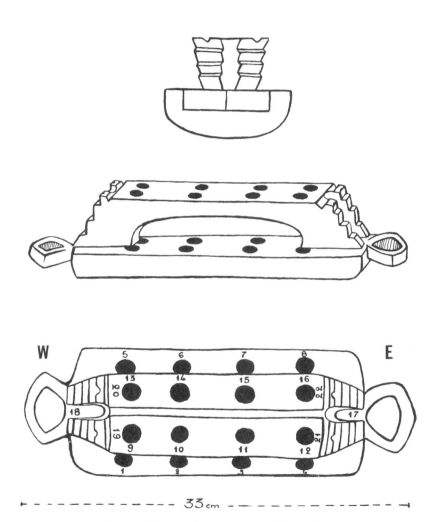

FIG. 155: Theoretical reconstruction of the ark.

water sources start from; the present people[15] live in the sands of the west (compartment 18) where the salt-water ocean extends that is fed by the rivers.

The upper deck, called *koro da sine,* "box seated above," occupied by the animals, is distributed as follows: 9: birds; 10: cats;[16] 11: monkeys; 12: small mammals; 13: cattle; 14: goats; 15: sheep; 16: fowl.

The rivers perpendicular to the two larger axial rivers, between which all the plants and pastures can be found, are occupied by the following animals: 19: water lizards, reptiles; 20: water insects; 21: fresh-water fish; 22: sea fish.

The east steps are the rocky mountains, those of the west are the sand dunes; at the base of each the metals are deposited.

One technical skill, weaving, is also represented in the ark: the weaver is seated at the tip of the east handle, of which two lateral points are the beams of the loom. The widening of the sources to the east represents the pulley, the heddles being the two rows of steps. The warp of the threads is the upper deck; it ends in the sled which is the west handle; the woof is formed by the east steps, the first of which is the shuttle.[17]

Oriented east to west, the ark, by its sides and ends, embodies the four directions of space, which are repeated in the irregular and four-sided handles[18] that theoretically held the "rope" from which it was suspended during its descent. Being the whole of space, the ark also theoretically contains all the stars on the upper deck; the sun, "at the source of the waters," is above the groove (between the double staircases) to the east, the moon above the groove to the west.

---

15. Tellem is the name the Dogon give to the Kouroumba of southern Yatenga: cf. *supra,* p. 32, n. 6.

16. This includes all mammals of the cat family.

17. Located on the level of the "terrestrial waters," this image is indicative of the role of the resurrected Nommo who, possessing the "word," will "weave" it in the water, his domain on Earth, and then reveal it to humanity.

18. There is a similarity between the shape of the handle and that of the lozenges on the vertex of the *kanaga, sirige,* and *amma ta* masks. Cf. M. Griaule, *Masques dogons,* fig. III, p. 473; fig. 116, p. 483; fig. 160, p. 586; fig. 162, p. 599. The vertical diagonal carved on some of them represents the top part of the ark which is, so to speak, enclosed in its own handle. This striped lozenge may also be seen as an oval, symbol of the "egg of the world," of which the great axis represents the creator still inside his own creation. For the lozenge, cf. also *supra,* p. 447, n. 1.

With a notch in the middle, each top step of the four staircases marks the place of the stars or of the planets in the following manner:

northeast step	*aga yazu*	Venus
	dana tolo	Jupiter
southeast step	*tolo yaze*	?
	tolo atanu	Orion's Belt
northwest step	*tolo duno*	Pleiades
southwest step	*yapunu tolo*	Mars

In another way, the ark symbolizes the entire world, in time and in space: the lower deck is both the Earth and the former world in disorder, upon which the sky and the new world (i.e., the upper deck) have superposed themselves.

There is another description of the theoretical ark, seen in terms of a granary, since it contains the primordial seeds. According to this version, the ark recalls the shape of the *tazu* basket (fig. 156).[19] In the shape of a truncated four-sided pyramid with a circular base and made of millet stalks that have been woven together, the *tazu* is commonly used to bring in the harvested ears of grain, to carry commodities to the market, etc. (Pl. XX, 1). The ark, made of pure earth, had the shape of the *tazu* basket turned upside down. Built into its thick walls, in the middle of each side of the square, it had a staircase of ten steps oriented towards one of the cardinal points. In the sixth step of the north staircase a door had been made that gave access to the inside, where eight compartments together made up two levels.

In symbolic terms, the ark built in this way and called "granary of the master of the pure earth"[20] had the following meaning:

the circular base represented the sun;
the square roof represented the sky;
a circle in the middle of the roof represented the moon;
each step was female and each riser male, the four staircases of ten steps all together being representatives of the eight groups of ten families descendent from the eight ancestors.

---

19. This version uses part of the information published in M. Griaule, *Dieu d'eau*, pp. 38-50.

20. *minne omo bana guyo.*

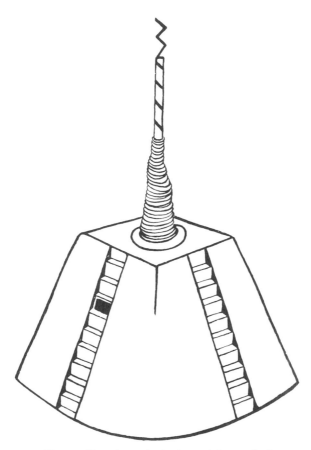

FIG. 156: The ark seen in the form of the *tazu* basket.

Each staircase carried a category of beings and was related to a constellation: the west staircase, *tolo dullogu,* the stars of Orion's Sword, bore the wild animals, plantlife, and insects. From the top step to the bottom step were the antelopes, hyenas, cats (on two steps), reptiles and lizards, monkeys, gazelles, marmots, the lion, and the elephant. The trees appeared beginning with the sixth step, from the baobab to the *sa,* and on each of these plants were the insects commonly found there today.

The east staircase, Venus, was occupied by the birds; on the first step were the larger birds of prey and the hornbills; on the second were the ostriches and the storks; on the third, the smaller bustards and the plovers; on the fourth, the vultures. Then came the small birds of prey, and then the herons. On the seventh step came the pigeons, on the eighth the turtledoves, on the ninth the ducks, and finally the big black and white bustards.

The southern staircase, Orion's Belt, held the domestic animals. First of all were the fowls; then the sheep, goats, cattle, horses, dogs, and cats. On the eighth and ninth steps were the turtles and tortoises, including the great tortoises which in every family today replace the patriarchs when they are absent, and the smaller turtles that are slowly put to death in sacrifices for territorial purification. In the tenth row were the rodents, mice and rats of house and field.

The northern staircase, the Pleiades, supported people and fishes.

The inside of the celestial structure was divided like the inside of a granary and had eight compartments on two levels. Each of them contained one of the eight seeds, given by Amma to the eight ancestors, in the following order:

emme pilu, nu (for Amma Sérou and his female twin),
emme nakolo, emme ya (for Lébé Sérou and his female twin),
yu pilu, ara geu (for Binou Sérou and his female twin),
po pilu, emme dum (for Dyongou Sérou and his female twin).

However, the eight sections were not only a means of housing the seeds to be dispensed to human beings. They were also the image of the eight internal organs of the sacrificed Nommo.

In the center, a round jar symbolized the womb; another smaller jar closed off the first one. It contained oil of *sa* and represented the fetus. It was covered by another, even smaller jar containing perfume; on this last jar was a double cup, the twins.

This entire group of "organs" was held together by the outside walls and inner partitions, which symbolized the skeleton. The four posts extending to the square corners of the roof were the four limbs. Thus, the granary was like a woman, lying on her back (representing the sun) with her arms and legs raised, supporting the roof, which is the image of the sky. The legs were on the north side and the sex organ was marked by the door in the sixth step.

The granary and all it contained was, therefore, the image of the world-system of the new order. Its path through space will be compared to the pathway of the blood circulating through the internal organs and carrying the "word."

The ark and its contents are represented by a ritual figure called *"tonu* of the ark of the world"[21] (fig. 157). It is made with a mixture of *sa* water, *yullo* flour, *oro* flour, and *minu* oil — a mixture which integrates all four elements into the picture and represents the colors of th? rainbow. It was drawn under the *sogo uguru uguri,* or *"sogo* of purification," of the pond of Dona at its construction.[22]

To the west: first the head of the *nommo semi,* then the head of the *anagonno sala*; the eight ancestors in a line, holding hands; the *minu* in the middle; the birds and the four-legged creatures, represented by a hen and a sheep.

To the north: the *yullo.*

To the south: the *sa.*

To the east: opposite the *nommo anagonno* is the *pelu*; opposite the *anagonno sala,* the *kilena*; opposite the ancestors the *yayaga,* the *sana,* and the baobab, *oro.*

Each being is separated from the others by a line showing the compartments of the housing. In the middle is a smaller rectangle inscribed in the ark. Inside it, a zigzag line represents the chain or rope that held it during its descent, the central circle being the "knot" that held it together.

The animals in the picture constitute the theoretical elements of every sacrifice.[23] Here, they recall the sacrifice of the Nommo: the hen for the emasculation and the sheep for the slaughter.[24] The plants are those that testify to the resurrection and will be used for individual and collective purifications.

---

21. *aduno koro tonu.*

22. For the pond of Dona and the *sogo* around it, cf. *infra,* p. 496 and ff.

23. Cf. *supra,* p. 389.

24. The sheep is one of the forms the *o nommo* may assume on earth, one of his avatars. It is also the object of the sacrifice to Amma.

FIG. 157: *tonu* of the ark of the world.

The picture, the substances it is made of, and the place where it is drawn recall the purification brought about by the sacrifice of the Nommo, which made it possible for the device containing Amma's work to descend upon the Fox's Earth.

DESCENT OF THE ARK.

Amma then made this ark come out of his womb and descend on the Earth, filled with everything he had created; it came out through the opening he had left in the sky for the "emergence" of the sun, which was "pushed to the west by Amma." One says that the ark swung in the sky for eight periods during its descent. It filled the whole sky from one horizon to the other, like a sort of great "ark of earth," going from east to west. It swung in a north-to-south/south-to-north direction in the sky which was covered with clouds. "The super-posed (double) box swung for eight years. The bounds of the box are east-west. It swings by leaning to the south and then again leaning to the north."[25]

The emergence from Amma's womb and the descent of the ark are represented by a ritual figure called *amma bara,* drawn on the ceiling of the vault of Yougo Dogorou, called *imina sommo* (fig. 158), located under the boulder representing the "foot of the Nommo *titiyayne* crushing the Fox's placenta."[26]

The location of this oriented figure shows that the events it represents took place in the sky: to the west is Amma's egg or "clavicles," surrounded by dots which are the *yala* of all the things he created. They spill out of the ark, represented by the north part of the figure. The entire shape of the horizontal north-south line portrays the swinging of the ark during its descent. The part to the north is wider than the part to the south, and the narrowing of this portion is related to the fact that all

---

25. *koro timmu-go anakuzu garara digeu suga. du-le donno-le kallia. tenulu-go genie ie du-daga-go genie kanabe.*

26. Cf. *supra,* p. 243. This white picture is repainted every sixty years at the Sigui (M. Griaule, *Masques Dogons,* p. 689 and plate XXVI). It has been commented upon according to its orientation on the boulder (therefore straightened up with respect to appearance on p. 689).

W

FIG. 158: Painting called *amma bara* on the ceiling
of the vault of Yougo Dogorou.

living things on Earth will have to die and head toward the south.[27] The
rectangle to the east is the ark set on the ground.

---

27. The spiritual principles of the dead are directed to the south by a rite performed
at the end of the funeral; their regrouping takes place during the second funeral or end
of the mourning (*dama*). Vol. I, installment 2, third year.

While the ark was swinging to and fro, the fact that it was suspended from a chain made it pivot on its axis, back and forth. In this way, the line of its descent made a double helix, reproducing the very movement of life, of the whirlwind that quickened the first seed. This movement was maintained by the breath of the ancestors, as if it passed through a nozzle. The nozzle is shaped just like this whirling respiration, called "spinning wind" (*ono simu*), which gave force to the "helix of the descent." "The hole of the nozzle is the great pathway of the breath of the ancestors (who) descended from above. It is their breath that helped the turning, in order to go and descend below."[28]

A ritual figure called *"tonu* of the whirling of the descent of the ark"[29] (fig. 159) represents the movements of the ark turning on its axis. The two circles denote the coming and going of the ark; the outside lines are the image of the wind caused by its spinning and of the dust it raised when it landed, which will accumulate in one spot.[30]

The motion of the ark around its axis also signified the future directions of space as represented by the entire ark.

From this perspective, the helix of the ark's descent is represented by the twenty-two alternatingly yellow and red copper rings that decorate the handle of the herdsmen's lance and that, on Earth, correspond to the "directions" in which the herd is headed.[31]

The four pairs of trees were placed in a line parallel to the side attributed to them, so that the sun's twenty-two rays, coming from the east, gave light to the trees located to the east.[32]

The *saselu* and the *gobo pilu* shaded their "twins," the *bozo kubo* and *gobo banu,* respectively, while the *sene* and *oro* pair cast their shade across the ark on the pair of *sa* and *yullo.* Those that were in the sun had white flowers, the others red ones.

---

28. *dologo bonno-go vageu da goa sugu ninnu be minnebe-go vogo ozu nay; ninnu beme digili bara, donu-ne na sununu.*

29. *kolondo sugi digili tonu* (Wazouba dialect). Drawn with *yu pilu* porridge during the ceremony of *ondom piru,* inside the sanctuary of the Manda totem of Orosongo.

30. The pile of stones within the precincts of the Manda sanctuary represents this accumulation of dust and the impact of the ark. There, the hearth of the sanctuary will be placed, symbolically fed by "the wind from the spinning ark and the breath of the ancestors" (fig. 150E, p. 439).

31. The complete list and sequence of these directions will be given in installment 2, first year.

32. For the "twenty-two rays," cf. *infra,* p. 534.

FIG. 159: *tonu* of the whirling of the descent of the ark.

While the spinning ark descended, the Nommo, taking his bearings from the shadows of the trees, determined the cardinal directions. Similarly, this movement divided time into four periods which determined the seasons:

bado	"father arrived"
dine	"winter season"
bago	"father emerged"
nay banu	"red sun"

Thus the year was made, during which time the Nommo changed position four times, occupying each of the cardinal points.

One speaks of the role of the Nommo during the ark's descent by saying that he took bearings on both space and time by means of "the chief's vases," *ogo bana,* that were placed on the ark. Each of these "vases" (made of copper) contained twenty-two stones which were to be used later to build the *sogo* altars of the fields. Each set, therefore, included twenty-four units, counting the vessel and its lid. A red horse with a white forehead, *so sade,* was tied to each. The four animals formed a carousel, the center of which was to their left, giving the image of the "curve" of the universe.

At the same time he was situating space and time, the Nommo proclaimed the "word" that Amma had originally placed inside the *po pilu.* It had been transmitted to him after the resurrection and dwelled in his internal organs.[33] The Nommo gave the "word" its sound. He descended on the ark "while making his voice (*mi*) spin in the sky." It is said: "The Nommo spun around above as he descended below, he cast his voice to the four cardinal corners of space, (a voice) which was thus heard";[34] for, after having received and proclaimed it, he will transmit it on Earth to man.

The form of the ark, its movement during the descent, and finally its position when it made the impact are related to the representations regarding the determination of space. It is said: "When the ark was descending, space was four corners; when the ark had descended, space became four sides."[35]

These facts are recalled by a series of figures drawn on a new totemic sanctuary when it is built (fig. 160).[36] To the right of the door, a series of eleven lozenges is drawn; to the left, a series of eleven rectangles. The lozenges denote the form attributed to the directions of space, called "four corners," *sibe nay*; the rectangles (or squares) denote the form of the cardinal directions, called "four sides," *benne nay.*[37] At the same

33. Cf. *supra,* p. 376.

34. *nommo daba digiliya duba suga ganna sibe nay mie tiya, yen egemi* (Wazouba dialect).

35. *koro sugo-le ganna sibe nay be; koro minne-ne sugu ganna benne nay bi.*

36. The figure drawn indicates the original identity of the divisions stemming from the same "unique" totem and from the same "ark" when an important part of a clan separates from it and settles in a new territory.

37. This rectangle is also called *kakabu sibe nay,* "flat (and) elongated with four angles."

time, these figures recall the descent of the ark in the sky (the lozenges) and its landing on the Earth (the rectangles).

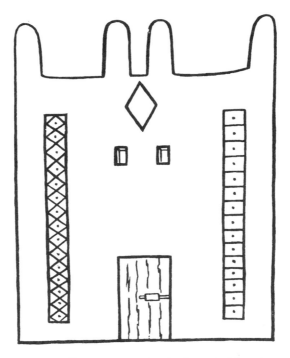

Fig. 160: Figures representing the descent of the ark
on the façade of the sanctuary.

Above the door, a larger lozenge recalls the theoretical celestial place of the *nommo die*; it is placed over two niches which are made above the door of every totemic sanctuary and which represent *po tolo* and *emme ya tolo*.[38] The gables rising above the façade of the sanctuary are Amma's four clavicles rising above the sky which, in turn, is symbolized by the terrace.

---

38. In these niches, which represent stars invisible to the naked eye, the various ingredients are placed that are used for purifying the sanctuaries, the individual members of a clan who have violated prohibitions, or the priests themselves.

The descent and landing of the ark are similarly represented by the form of two variants of the *sirige* mask (fig. 161).[39]

On one of them, the mast is decorated with lozenges; the figure is called "drawing of the *sirige* of the descent of Amma's ark"[40] (fig. 161C). In the other one, the mast shows a series of bars and of plain rectangles which are, respectively, the ark and the sky from which it slowly descended to land on Earth. This figure is called "drawing of the *sirige* as the site of the ark that descended upon Earth and that served as a model for the building of houses"[41] (D). In this case, each of the plain rectangles of the mast recalls a dwelling and its storeroom, or *kana* (including the *ginna*, individual house, and sanctuary). The mask itself may have two statuettes mounted on the top, representing the couple of resurrected Nommo, mankind's ancestors.

Actually, this image of the *sirige* as a "storied house" stems directly from certain elements in the architecture of the *ginna*. Like the *sirige*, the façade of the dwelling denotes both the ark and its descent, but also shows the human contents of the structure. A certain number of niches have been made in the clay which are euphemistically called "swallows' holes" (*vevele bonno*). Above the entrance door opening onto the hall, two similar niches place the resurrected Nommo and his female twin in the center. On either side of the door, four vertical rows of ten niches symbolize the lineages and the generations descendent from the eight ancestors, which are themselves represented by the eight gables rising above the façade. The granary on the top floor, called *dele* (literally: "suspended"), is the ark in the sky: on the door are carved figures called "raised arms," being the ancestors of the lineage, whose gesture invokes the protection of the eight ancestors over the millet in the granary. The entrance door, through which the living pass, is the ark on Earth. When the dwelling is consecrated, one prays to Amma that the "threshold be soiled" by the numerous footprints of the members of the lineage.

In this way, the entire façade expresses both the descent of the ark and the succession of generations that "descend" from the mythical ancestors it carried.

---

39. For the two other variants, cf. *supra*, p. 193 and p. 247.

40. *amma koro sununoze sirige toy.*

41. *amma koro sununi minne-ne doy ginu vogo kini ginu uzi sirige toy.* This figure also recalls the creation of the superposed worlds by Amma (cf. *supra*, p. 192).

THE ARK ON EARTH.

The ark landed at night on the dry soil of the Fox, stirring up a pile of dust, raised by the whirling wind it caused. The violent impact of the landing gave the ground its rough shape on which the people and animals it carried walk about today. However, since it was made of the Nommo's placenta, that is, of moist, soft earth, it slipped on the ground. "The ark (when it) arrived on Earth, slipped in the mud."[42] As it landed, the weight of the ark caused the "blood" that saturated the placenta to spurt up to the sky. This "blood" joined itself with the star called *ie pelu tolo,* "star of the tenth moon," witness to the resurrection of the Nommo,[43] giving it being and brilliance (fig. 162).

The yala is made of the outline of a circle in four parts denoting the cardinal directions. The rays are made of three dots and are ten in all, with two per cardinal direction and one each for the collateral directions at the northeast and southwest points.

The *toy* of the star is made of a circle from which stem ten oriented rays. Another circle surrounding the star represents the *kikinu* of the blood and shows that this blood is fulfilling its role in the Nommo's "space" represented by the number of rays: for it is like the moisture that flows out of a stain, like the serum that makes a paler circle around the congealed plasma when spilled blood begins to dry up.[44]

The Nommo was "red like fire" because, during the descent, he came close to the sun and caught fire. When he touched the ground, he became white.[45] He is like a flame snuffed out by its contact with the Earth.

To leave the ark, the Nommo first put his left foot on the ground, and this gesture constituted his taking possession of it. He pressed his foot on

---

42. *koro-go minne-ne vo doy-go onno-go tana bumiyombe.*

43. Cf. *supra,* p. 334.

44. Drawn with red ochre (*bana*) respectively under the three main *sogo* of the field of Lébé (*sogo.* recalled by the three dots of the rays of the *yala*). The *tonu* of the star is also drawn in snake dung (*yuguru na*) on the façade of the Hogon's dwelling when he is ordained. For it is related to the events involving the ancestor Lébé Sérou; it will disappear upon his death and reappear upon his resurrection (installment 2, second year).

45. On Earth, the albino will be evidence of the burns of the Nommo during the descent. One will say that he is "the trace of the burn," the "scar" (*namana*) of the Nommo. For the status and role of the albino, cf. installment 2.

the "field" of the Fox and crushed it, thus demonstrating his eventual domination over the whole Earth that the Fox had formed. It is said: "The Nommo's left leg, when he got out of the ark, by pressing, took back the field of the Fox."[46] In this way, he was repeating the gesture of the *nommo titiyayne*[47] in another form and at another time for a different purpose.

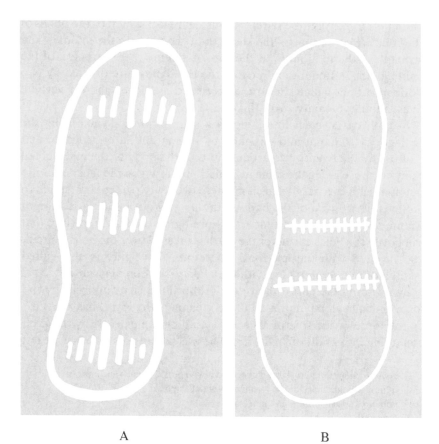

A   B

FIG. 163: A: *tonu* of the sandal of the Nommo's foot; B: Variant.

---

46. *nommo koro sugu anu nanda yurugu minne elenga tozi* (Wazouba dialect).
47. Cf. *supra*, p. 231 and ff.

The print of the crushing is described as the imprint of a copper "sandal"; it is represented on the façade of the totemic sanctuaries by the "outline of the sandal on the Nommo's foot"[48] (fig. 163A). The sandal is divided into three parts. Each has three rows of seven lines that are first increasing, then decreasing in length. The whole thing counts for $3 \times 7 = 21$, to which the drawing of the foot is added, making twenty-two in all. One says that "the drawing of the sandal of the Nommo's foot is in three parts."[49] This figure is a sketch of the bones of the foot, which support: "the strength of the foot" in the middle, "the strength of the toe joints" at the top, and below, "the strength of the ankle joints."[50] In another version, the three parts are divided by two horizontal lines which, in turn, are crossed by eleven shorter vertical lines, a total of twenty-two[51] (fig. 163B).

In both cases, each line denotes a sign, *bummo,* symbolizing the "categories" thought and designed by Amma and later repeated and realized by the twenty-two articulations of the body of the resurrected Nommo, these being the same articulations drawn on the façades of the sanctuaries.[52] In a parallel fashion, these twenty-two lines correspond to the twenty-two *yala* of the body of the *po pilu* during its formation in Amma's womb. In this instance, they pre-figure the future sowings that will purify the Fox's earth, for the earth is pressed over the hole containing the seed with the left foot. Therefore, this figure is also called "sketch of the *nommo's* leg with the twenty-two cereal grains."[53]

By crushing the earth, the Nommo imprinted signs upon it: by the force of his heel, he imprinted those meaning "the world has arrived"; by the force of the sole of his foot, including the gap left by the arch connoting the condition of the Earth he was taking possession of, he left

---

48. *nommo kubo taga tonu.* Drawn once a year with porridge of *yu* and *ara geu* to the left of the pot of the sanctuary of the Nommo totem at the *bulu.*

49. *nommo kubo taga tonu ulo tanu.*

50. Respectively: *kubo semme gele, kubo unum digu semme gele, kubo kokolo digu semme gele;* in other words, the bones of the sole of the foot, "brick bones of the foot" (*kubo temie ki*) in the middle, the toes at the top (*kubo unum ki*), and the bones of the ankle and heel at the bottom (*kubo kokolo ki*).

51. Drawn on the façade of the sanctuary of the Manda totem of Orosongo at the time of *agu.*

52. Cf. *supra,* p. 340.

53. *dene peni ley sige nommo anu-ne tonu* (Wazouba dialect).

those signs meaning "the work they have accomplished"; finally, by the subtle impressions of his toes, he made those of the ultimate accomplishment, meaning "the word will come."[54] In this way, by bringing the present, the past, and the future together, he imprinted the symbols of his reign and of the order of the universe that was his responsibility to maintain.

The Nommo's "sandal" was modeled in relief on the sanctuary of the first totem, Déwa, in Dalé. It is also made on the façades of the *binu na* sanctuaries during their foundation and on that of the dwelling of the Hogon of Arou-near-Ibi. A copper sandal is included in the materials of the most important totem in this area as well as in those of the totem Nommo of Nandouli.

As evidence of the resurrected Nommo's gesture, a star appeared in the sky, which would be named *tolo dombolo,* or *dommolo,* "hook star" (in reference to the missile *dommolo,* which is also put on the gables of the totemic sanctuaries); the form of the sign emphasizes the analogy between the star and the weapon and also recalls that the Nommo "hooked" the Earth to take it into his possession (fig. 164).[55]

After the Nommo, all the beings aboard the ark, in their turn, descended on the Earth. When it was completely empty, Amma pulled the chain that had supported it up to the sky again, then he "closed off" the sky. When the men, who had seen *sigi tolo* shining during the descent, landed, they were witness to the first rising of the sun, which came out of the east and which, from then on, illuminated the universe: it was then in its equinoctial position, called "sun of the middle," *nay logoron,* corresponding to springtime. Its rising and setting, its movements in the course of the day will, from that time on, testify to the arrival of the ark and to the Nommo's presence on the Earth of the Fox.

Later on, the Nommo, transformed into a horse, will pull the ark to the depression of land, *bunno,* which marks the opening of the sky by Amma. This depression was to be filled with water from the first rain

---

54. Respectively: *aduno vey-go, bire be bira-go, so yay vedo.* The "footprint" will be stolen by the Fox, who will attempt to take hold of the "signs"; but it will immediately be taken back by the ancestor Binou Sérou and will become a "sandal of copper" (installment 2, first year).

55. The hook-shaped wooden throwing weapons are called *dommolo.* Drawn with *yu* porridge inside the sanctuary of the Manda totem, left of the door, during the ordination of the priest (*duguru*).

and to become the first pond. This episode will momentarily present the ark in the image of a chariot pulled on ropes by a four-legged creature.

After the first rain had fallen and the pond had filled with water, the water insect, *barankamaza dullogu,* that had descended with the Fox on

FIG. 164: *bummo*
of the star called *tolo dombolo.*

Amma's order[56] entered the pond. Betraying his original mission as Amma's delegate, the *barankamaza* wanted to "bite" the Nommo's head for the benefit of the Fox, with whom he had traveled and who instigated him to act, but he could only reach the edge of the ark. On the south side of the mask altars, a figure is drawn, called "drawing of the *barankamaza* biting the ark (that) descended with the Nommo" (fig. 165), which shows the Nommo (in his fetal form as a fish), the ark, and the insect grabbing hold of it. One of the forms of the *kanaga* mask represents this event: in this case, the face of the mask is the ark and the mast on top of it, with arms extended, is the insect that holds onto it.[57]

When the water had filled the pond, the ark floated on it like an immense canoe. In this element — i.e., the contents of his own semen — his domain on Earth, the Nommo took on his first form of *nommo anagonno.* It is said: "The great ark emerged from the sky (and) descended. In the middle, the Nommo was standing up, he descended. Without something to push, the Nommo turned himself into a horse. Then he returned to the water."[58] From then on, he was called *o nommo,* "Nommo

---

56. Cf. *supra,* pp. 205, 206, fig. 55, p. 553.

57. The ancestors spoke to the animal in a peremptory manner to prevent it from acting: when the *kanaga* dances in a public place, one sings *e e e barankamaza,* recalling the cries of the ancestors when the animal grabbed the side of the ark.

58. *koro die alagala-ne goa suga. logoro-ne nommo inebe, suga. kize dammaze bele nommo so-ga bila bina tanani.* We present here only a summary of the events which followed the landing involving the ark and the Nommo. Everything concerning the presence of the beings on Earth after their "descent" will be treated in installment 2, which will also chronologically relate the episodes that unfolded during the sixty-six first years in the life of the mythical ancestors and their descendants.

of the pond"; out of respect, men do not pronounce this name but speak of him as "master of the water," *di tigi.* His female twin (who is later to descend with the Smith, or "twin of the sacrificed Nommo") will come and, in turn, transform herself. Both of them will give birth to numerous offspring and will always be present in the "male" fresh water of springs, rivers, ponds, and wells as well as in the "female" sea water.

Fleeing both the Nommo and the sunlight that flooded the Earth, the Fox, who had until then preferred to remain seated at the part of his placenta where the umbilical cord had been attached, ran away to a dark cave, called *ka kommo,* "cave of the tearing."

REPRESENTATIONS OF THE ARK OF THE NOMMO.

The Nommo's ark, *di bana koro,* or "ark of the master of the water," is represented in family houses, in totemic sanctuaries, and in the Hogon's dwelling by rectangular platters of carved wood which are used for rituals; they also represent the corresponding sacred field.

These objects, varying in form and sometimes rather large, are consecrated by a sacrifice before being put to use. Hidden from anyone's view during the rest of the year and handled only by those responsible for the cult, they are used to hold the raw or cooked meat of the victims sacrificed during the annual collective ceremonies.

1) At the Hogon's dwelling, a rectangular platter, made of *pelu* wood and called "platter of the sharing of the meat of *de lebe,* "[59] represents "the rainbow" (fig. 166). The object serves only once a year during the sacrifice offered to *de lebe* at the time of the *bulu.*[60] The pieces of the victim are placed on the platter, which is oriented east to west, before they are consumed by the Hogon and the totemic priests who assist him and who also receive a share of the harvest from the fields of Lébé.[61]

2) In the *ginna,* the "platter of the ancestors" (*vageu bana*) is called *aduno koro,* or "ark of the world," and represents "the ark on earth." It is exceptionally large and traditionally carved out of the trunk of a *kummo.* The human figures in relief decorating the long sides (in the examples shown on Pl. XIX, 1 and 2) represent the mythical ancestors; they are on both sides of the crocodile, *ayo geu,* the resurrected Nommo's executioner. The tail and head of a horse form the two carved handles

---

59. *de lebe nama gammalu bana.* This object was collected at Sanga in 1954.
60. For the altar called *de lebe,* cf. *supra,* p. 415 and *infra,* p. 532.
61. Installment 2, second and third years.

of the object and are called "head and tail of the ark";[62] for, after the
impact of the landing, the Nommo, changed into a horse, pulled the ark
on the ground to put it in the water. The frieze of chevrons that decorate
the two sides of the object represent the vibration of the "word" and the
"path" of the water zigzagging across the ground. The object is hidden
from sight in one of the nooks of the *ginna*. It is taken out once a year to
be used during the *goru* ceremony (literally: "wet"[63]). This ceremony is
performed in every *ginna* at the winter solstice for the entire lineage
gathered in the courtyard and commemorates the descent of the ark.
"The *goru* that one performs is like the descent of the Nommo's ark."[64]
The ceremony includes two sacrifices: a sheep is slaughtered on the
altar to Amma and a goat on the altar to the ancestors (*vageu*). The raw
meat of the victims is cut into seven pieces — which represent the seven
articulations of the word contained in the *po* — and put on the platter
for the first time. After it has been cooked, the meat is placed on the
platter for a second time and passed among the four eldest men of the
lineage, then it is passed to the wife of the patriarch, who shares it with
three women of the family. This division among eight persons — who
represent the eight ancestors — also recalls the appearance of the
eighth articulation of the *po* "seed" that was ejected after the explosion.
Theoretically, through the intermediary of those persons partaking,
everyone receives a share "for the *po* made the world spin around."
During the sacrifice, the patriarch recites a long prayer. After the
invocation to Amma, to the Nommo, and to the ancestors of the lineages, he says: "The animal that we have sacrificed to the *vageu,* and
whose seven parts have been put in the platter, is like the seven articulations of the body of the *po* which left the Nommo and were put in the
empty ark. The cooked meat that we have placed on the platter and
shared among the four eldest (men) is like the four parts of the Nommo
that were cast to the four cardinal points and became four trees."[65] He
then asks Amma to grant rain and prosperity to the lineage.

---

62. *koro ku* and *koro dullo.*

63. In the sense of "to be wet, soaked with sweat." The rite of *goru* will be described in its
entirety in installment 2, (fourth year).

64. *goru kunneni nommo koro sugu anay.*

65. *vageu-ne belu day digu soy gammela korone kunneru, po digu soy nommo gozu-ne
tanana korone toga kunnu anay. nama dana koro-ne kunna du na gammalani nommo gozu
digu nay ganna sibe nay tuturu tia timme nay tana anay.*

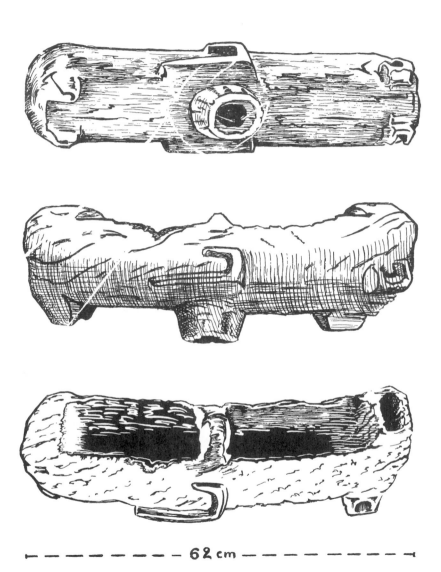

FIG. 166: Ancient platter of the sharing of the meat of *de lebe* (Upper Ogol).

The Nommo's Ark: *aduno koro*.
  1) Ritual platter of the *ginna*.

  2) Ritual platter of the *ginna*.

Ark of the Nommo:

1) The *tazu* basket on the
terrace of a house of Gogoli.

2) The ritual cup of the Hogon (top).

3) In the totemic sanctuary, the rectangular platter called *binu koro,* usually made of *ga guyo* wood, represents the "ark in the water" after it was pulled into it by the Nommo transformed into a horse. The important sanctuaries sometimes contain several arks, whose form and symbolism represent various episodes of the myth or yet various attributions of the Nommo. To illustrate this, we present below the analysis of the platters studied in the sanctuary of the Manda totem of Orosongo (which have all been the subject of commentaries) in the following order:

A) This first one (fig. 167A), also the largest, is a sort of box with a roughly semicylindrical bottom and two large handles. A cup-like hole is hewn near one handle to receive the victim's blood. There are four knobs on either side of the vessel. These eight knobs denote the eight seeds and the eight ancestors. This box represents the ark coming out of the sky, filled with all things Amma had placed in it, especially those grains whose spiritual principles are kept by the Nommo in the water.

B) The second one has the appearance of a small trough with a long central compartment and two small cups of the same depth to either side (fig. 167B). These three hollows sit on a somewhat wider, flat bottom, all one piece with the rest, from which jut eight knobs. The object is consecrated to the "dry foods," and its symbolism expresses a movement, namely, that of the "advance of the grains in the world." In the left small cup that belongs to the Nommo, he creates the grains. He sends them out to the hollow on the right, where man will cultivate them. To get there, they cross the central hollow, the dry domain of the Fox: this is why people harvest them dry.

C) The third (fig. 168) has the appearance of a rectangular trough on four legs shaped like truncated cones; one of its short sides has a row of four points and the other has a handle in the shape of a hollow lozenge crossed diagonally by the object's axis, which then protrudes a bit from the lozenge. On each of the long sides is a frieze of twenty-two notches.

The object may be analyzed from two perspectives, either with regard to the Nommo, or with regard to the Fox:

a) The usual position of the platter is vertical, the four horns on top symbolizing the cardinal points and the gables above the façade of the sanctuary. The handle depicts the rainy and the clear sky; the diagonal is the "cord of rain"; the lozenge is an outline of two rainbows joined at

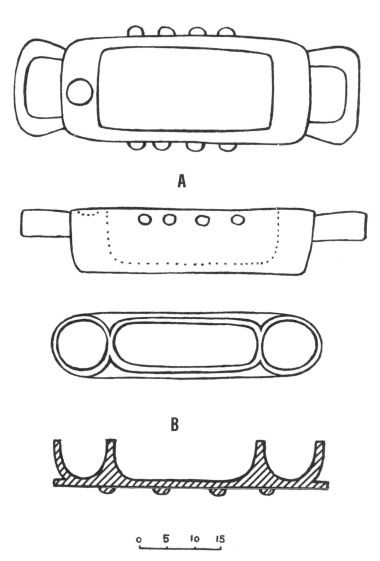

FIG. 167: Material of Orosongo, A and B.

their ends into one point, which is stuck in the ground to show that the rainbow is "attached" to the ground. The handle, also symbolizes the hand of human beings reaching for the food. In yet another way, the handle is the platter of the priest, the platter itself being the sanctuary surrounded by two snakes represented by the friezes of chevrons on either side.[66] In the horizontal position, the platter is the image of the ark placed on the ground on four legs.

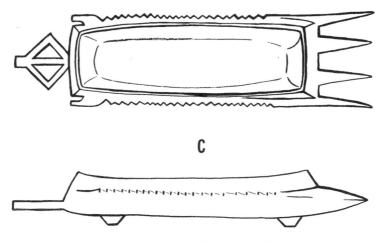

FIG. 168: Material of Orosongo, C.

b) With regard to the Fox, the platter also symbolizes *his* ark for the descent. The points mark the tearing-off of the placenta in the sky; the line of chevrons on one side symbolizes Ogo's walk through space, whereas the four-sided handle is his walk on the Earth to the four cardinal points. The other line of chevrons marks the Nommo's descent.[67]

---

66. *yiri mini* (Wazouba dialect); *yuguru na* (Sanga dialect). The smallest one is the substitute for the avatar of *o nommo*; the other one is the visible image of the snake, an avatar of Lébé Sérou (installment 2, second year).

67. The double symbolism of this dish is related to the fact that the first mythical totemic field will be established on the second field of the Fox (installment 2, third year).

Respectively, the three platters from Manda symbolize the sacred fields and the succession of the generations; the first is the "grandfather" and the field of Lébé; the second is the "father" and the field of the *ginna*; the third is the "son" and the field of the *binu*.

The ark is also represented by handicrafts and a great many everyday objects or tools, some of which recall the form of the ritual platters.

1) The wooden drum, *koro,* represents the Nommo's ark. It is made of *kumuni* wood and has the same rectangular shape as the *koro bogu,* *"koro* with a navel," the image of Ogo's ark and placenta, but without the protuberance on the side. Playing the instrument by alternately striking the sides and the bottom (i.e., the sky and the Earth) symbolizes the descent of the ark. Although the *koro bogu* is played in the bush by the children guarding the fields while the millet grows, the *koro* is also played by children in the village as a sign of joy when the millet is beautifully ripe; for the sound of the wooden drums, good for all mankind, is also good for the growth of the cereal grains. Through its leaves, the millet "hears the sound" of the instrument which, like rain in the air, penetrates it through the leaves. One says of the sound of the *koro*: "The voice (sound) and the rain, the two (are) one; the voice that it (the millet) catches, is the voice of a gentle heart."[68] One also says that the life force, *nyama,* reaches and penetrates the instrument by the beat of the stick used to play it with; from there, it travels with the sound and reaches the millet. The *koro* is also played at harvest time.

2) The ark is also represented by the rectangular wooden box for the game of *i* (fig. 169).[69] Traditionally, it is composed of two parallel rows of eight cup-holes carved into the wood, with two larger cup-holes at each end; the whole thing represents the ark in the sky. The bottom of the case — the Earth — has eight small protuberances or knobs, carved into the main piece, which are the mythical ancestors.

During the game, the object is oriented from east to west, like the ark when it landed; one of the rows of holes represents the women, the other the men. The game symbolizes the union of the sexes and the proliferation of the human species. The pebbles that are moved about are the totemic covenant stones, *dugoy,* or the clavicular seeds.[70] Their motion also

---

68. *mi-le anadi-le belley tumogo. mi a vogo kinne eli mi.*
69. The object and the game are described in M. Griaule, *Jeux dogons,* p. 166.

corresponds to that of the stars and of God the creator, Amma. The entire game reproduces and facilitates the march of the universe through space and time: a month is attributed to each cup-hole.

FIG. 169: Game of *i.*

3) The smith's tool box has a form much like that of the small troughs of the totemic sanctuaries (especially the first example, A, from the sanctuary of Orosongo). By its contents, it recalls that it is the Smith, twin of the sacrificed Nommo, who will teach men the skills of farming and forging necessary to their life: as such, it constitutes an image of the ark.

4) The weaver's shuttle, a tiny trough into which a stick has been slipped around which the thread is wound, is also the ark; it recalls that the Nommo "will weave" the word in the water and will reveal it to mankind.

5) As we have seen, the *tazu* basket used for carrying the harvests is the ark seen as a granary (Pl. XX, 1). It is considered to be the oldest prototype of the ark; one also says that the ark was like a granary whose straw roof had the shape of the *tazu.*[71] Also, the "shadow cast" by the ark during its descent was much like that of the basket.

6) Generally speaking, all the four-sided granaries represent the Nommo's ark, particularly those built in the *ginna* at its construction. The site and shape of these buildings, the type of cereal grains they house, and their different attributions are reflections of the social

70. The moving of the pebbles is also the image of the moving of the totemic beads, hidden when a priest dies and sought by the one who is solicitous to be his successor. When one of the players gains possession of the last pebble to remain in one of the cups, he represents the candidate who has found the bead of his predecessor.

structure and are also related to the mythical events we have just described.

a) The *dele*, placed on the terrace of the *ginna*,[72] is the ark in the sky containing the primordial seeds.

b) In the courtyard, the *togu guyo*, "granary of the family," or *anau guyo*, "granary of the men," which contains ten compartments — the number assigned to the Nommo as a progenitor — is the ark on Earth containing the grains for sowing intended for the ancestors.

c) The *yau guyo*, "granary of the women," which has eight compartments and a central cylinder for the *anu*,[73] symbolically contains the whole harvest obtained after the first sowing.

d) The *guyo ana*, or "male granary," represents the clavicles of Amma, who preserves the "twins" of the spiritual principles of the cereal grains within himself.

The *guyo ana*, which has no compartments, holds the ears of the small millet (*yu*) from the harvest of the *ginna*. After the threshing, the grain will be added — if necessary — to the ears of *yu* from the same origin which are stored in the *dele* granary above the *ginna* and which preserve the spiritual principles of the harvested grains until the following year, when these grains will be used for sowing. When the *guyo ana* is built, one draws (with *yu* and *ara* porridge) the *yala* for Amma's four clavicles on the ground, saying: "The *guyo ana* is like Amma who keeps the twins of the eight *kikinu* of the millet"[74] (fig. 170).

The *togu guyo* houses the grain harvested by the various members of the lineage, which is thus entrusted to the patriarch. However, this custom is beginning to disappear, although certain *ginna* still keep the granary.

On each side of this building a triangle with dots is drawn in *yu* porridge. These dots represent the millet that the Fox cannot steal because it is placed in Amma's four clavicles — the triangles — which he

---

71. It is appropriate to note that this symbolism of the ark as a granary with a straw roof is much like that of the sanctuary of Kangaba, of which the roof is ritually remade every seven years. Cf. G. Dieterlen, *Mythe et organisation sociale au Soudan français*, p. 64 and ff.

72. Cf. *supra*, p. 377.

73. Cf. *supra*, p. 427, n. 30.

74. *guyo ana amma togozo yu kikinu gagara dineu ko uo gele anay.*

cannot force open. The triangle is then covered up with a mass of clay, called *sebu,* a term designating also a protective amulet.

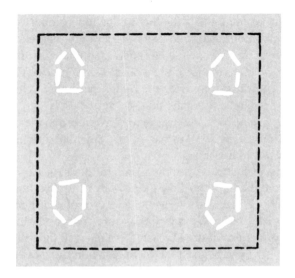

FIG. 170: Figure drawn at the founding of the granary *guyo ana.*

The top of the granary is like Amma's closed egg, its four sides representing the four clavicles. It is said that "the top of the granary is like Amma's (closed) egg in a ball; putting the *sebu* on the granary is like Amma's clavicles spreading out."[75] The decoration of the granary (fig. 171) is, in this case, the protector of the grain it houses.

7) The ark is also a "chariot." In the totemic sanctuaries, a small statuette, made of carved wood or of iron, represents the horse that pulled the chariot. A horseman, symbol of Amma, is sometimes placed next to or on the horse, which is a symbol of the Nommo. The word *so,* or *suru,* the Wazouba word for horse, according to popular deri-

---

75. *guyo komu amma talu gunnu anay; guyo sebu danu amma ani guyo viru anay.* In architecture, the term *komu* designates the incline and arch given to the vertical walls so that they join together at the top.

vation, means "power." The horse is called *amba suru,* or "Amma's power," because the form taken on by the Nommo is representative of his strength, and the course of the animal shows the extent of his power over the Earth. According to another derivation, the word is compared to *so,* "word," for it is said that "with the chariot, the horse (Nommo) brought forth the word."

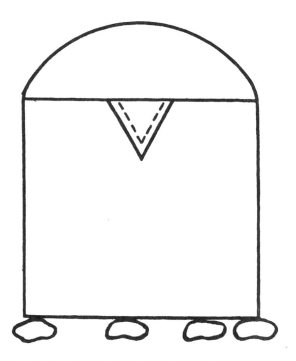

FIG. 171: Diagram of one of the sides of a Dogon granary and its decoration.

The harness was made of ropes that went around its neck and were passed under its legs; two collars of this type ended in two lengths of rope which were passed under the belly of the horse (fig. 172A). A ritual object, carved in wood, belonging to the society of the *yona,* "ritual thieves," called *yo dommolo,* represents this horse (fig. 172B). From this perspective, the two triangles decorating the head show the harnessing device for the chariot and the horse's double yoke; the chevrons forming the mane show the descent of the ark. The *yo dommolo* was originally a hunting weapon.[76]

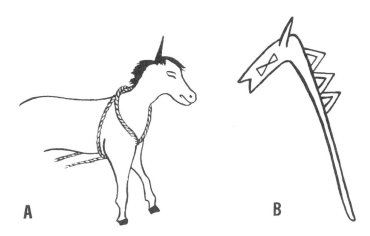

FIG. 172: A: The horse's harness; B: *yo dommolo.*

The stacked round wooden cups that the Hogon uses for ceremonies usually have a lid with a horse on top, representing the Nommo (pl. XX, 2). The legs of the object are sometimes a carousel of four horses. "The horses that surround the cup of the Hogon, this is the image of the ark which the Nommo in the form of a horse pulled and drew across."[77] This carousel also recalls the four horses on the ark that were released on the ground after its descent. The transformation of the Nommo and the moving of the ark are, analogously, compared to the rapid expansion of beings on the Earth, as depicted by the path of the horses to the four directions of space.

8. Finally, the ark is a dug-out canoe, comparable to the ones used by the Bozo — considered to be the first human "sons" of the resur-

---

76. From another perspective, the activity of the *yona* and the symbolism of the *yo dommolo* recall the deeds of the Fox. Installment 2, first year.

77. *ogo-ne bana so gona vo koro sugu nommo so ni bila bina tanani yalay.*

rected Nommo — to navigate on the Niger and its many tributaries and streams.[78]

THE RESURRECTED NOMMO IN THE WATER.

The ark landed on Earth to the northeast, called *du na,* meaning the "great (site) of the east." Geographically speaking, the Dogon situate the ark's landing point at Lake Débo.

"The Fox's ark descended, the Nommo's great ark descended, they descended to the north near the Niger. Amma Sérou, Lébé Sérou, Binou Sérou, and Dyongou Sérou, who was with the Nommo, all descended in the ark at Dyigou. The Dogon came from the northeast."[79]

The wide land-depression of the Débo is flooded when the Niger's waters rise (fig. 173). At the lake's entrance to the southeast are rocky and often steep hills of varying size overlooking the entire region, some of which form islands when the waters are at their maximum height. On the largest of these, Gourao, there are three villages inhabited respectively by the Bozo, the Malinke, and the Fulbe. A Bozo village is located at the northern tip of Soriba (Mount Saint-Charles). The other two, the Rock of Marie-Thérèse and Mount Saint-Henri, are smaller in size and unhabited.

The "boulders" of this region of the lake are evidence of the events we have related: "The boulders of Débo are the seat of the Nommo's descended ark."[80] Gourao represents the descent of the ark: "The boulder of Gourao is like the sky from which the vessel emerged and descended."[81] At its summit, a table of rock — the ark — surrounded by raised stones — the stars — represents the descent in the sky. The rock

---

78. M. Griaule *(L'arche du monde dans les populations nigeriennes,* pp. 124-126) has published several descriptions of the ark of Faro as given by Bozo informants (p. 125). See also M. Griaule and G. Dieterlen, *L'Agriculture rituelle des Bozo,* p. 219.

79. *yurugu koro susugu koro die sugu-le, du daga-go dibe genne-ne sugi; amma seru-le lebe seru-le binu seru-le donu seru-le di nommo-le be vey koro-ne digu-ne sugi; dogom du nane goy.*

80. *deboy dumbo koro sugi nommo doy anay.*

81. *gurao dummo alagala tozo-go koro goa sugi. gura dumbo,* according to an indigenous derivation, means "boulder of that which is placed under" (Wazouba dialect).

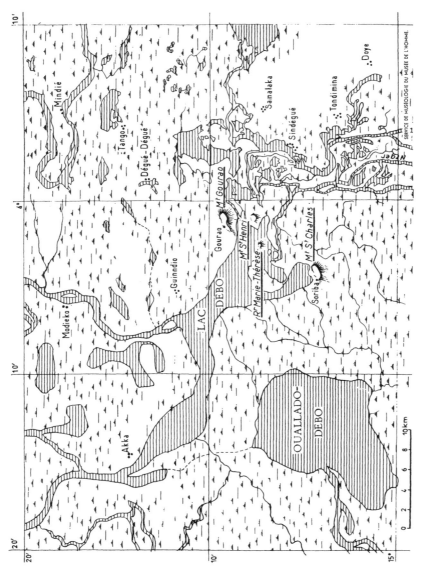

FIG. 173: Map of Débo.

surface is also studded with raised stones of varying size from the dolmen to the very tip going down towards the lake to the west (Pl. XXI, 1).

In a small cave located halfway up the southeast side of the rock above the lake, four lithophones or stone drums have been placed, of which it is said: "The sacrificed and resurrected *nommo* descended on Earth at the pond; the first word he spoke is the drum of stone"[82] (Pl. XXI, 2). The drums represent the eight twin internal organs where the word resides in the human body. When they are sounded by the hands of the children, who alone are so skilled, they announce the "word" spoken to the four directions of space by the Nommo during his descent.

In another much larger cave facing downwards on the west side, a series of paintings in red ochre represent the Nommo and his female twin, first in the sky and then on the Earth, and the ancestors of the ark. The red color of the paintings recalls the blood of the placenta (*me illi*), or the gestation of the Nommo and of the ancestors, the placenta being represented by the cave."[83]

Mount Saint-Henri, called *tomba goy* ("to jump by moving about"), represents the "star of the tenth moon" (*ie pelu tolo*), evidence of the purification brought about by the impact of the ark landing on the Earth of the Fox. "The rock of *tomba goy* (as if) emerged from the purification (performed by) the descended ark pressing (crushing) the field of the Fox."[84]

Soriba is the left footprint of the Nommo taking possession of the earth. "The rock of the Bozo (Soriba) is like the Earth where the ark landed."[85]

---

82. *nommo semu bula donu-ne sugi o-ne ya so polo vo soy dumm-no loy.* The cave measures four meters wide and nearly five meters high in the center. The four blocks which are opposite the opening measure, respectively from left to right, 1.10m, 1.70m., 1.40m, 1.53m in length. They each have a name. The children hit them in one spot with a large pebble which is then left near the block. The rhythms the children play on them are all different and each has a name; these rhythms are different from those played on the ordinary drums.

83. The very schematical paintings of this cave, which we discovered in 1959, portray mythical figures like those we have just mentioned as well as historical subjects, particularly the arrival of the Bozo and Malinke to the Débo region in dug-out canoes. These will be the subject of a later publication.

84. *tomba goy dumbo kolondo sugi yurugu taw vo todu dala goy togoy* (Wazouba dialect).

Akka is the place where the Nommo transformed himself into a horse and pulled the ark into the water.

The many tributaries allow for the expansion of the waters of the Niger in the Débo land depression and, at their point of exit, become the streams that join at Issafay to form the Issa Ber, and which are compared to the straps or ropes used by the horse to pull the ark. The ark that was put in the water became a "dug-out canoe" and is represented by the Rock of Marie-Thérèse.[86]

The Nommo, having thus completed his work, transformed himself into *nommo anagonno* or *anagonno ku po*, "with a big head," at the very tip of Gourao (Pl. XXI, 3).[87]

At Sanga, the ark on land is represented by a gigantic rock table erected at a placed called *polio kommo*, "cave that one crosses," or "passage," located at Bono (map II). One says that *"polio kommo* is like the descended ark."[88] (Pl. XXII, 2 and 3).

The table is surrounded by wide hollows bordered with stone blocks which are, on the one hand, the "holes" of the ark and, on the other hand, the first dwelling place of the ancestors.

Opposite the opening in the table, to the east, stacked-up boulders represent Sirius and the sun (Pl. XXII, 1). Their parallel position symbolizes the "meeting of the Earth of the Fox and that of the Nommo," a meeting represented by the celestial evidence of the two placentas which, at the moment of impact, became successively visible to man. *"sigi tolo* and the sun descended in the middle of the night (midnight).

---

85. *sologom dummo minne koro sugi anay*. Words on the symbolism of the hills of Débo are recited during the ceremony following the *tala* in the *ginna*. The cliffs of Mount St. Charles (Soriba) are full of caves — some of which are quite large — where a great many rock paintings have been done in red ochre (*bana*). One may observe several layers of drawings which are sometimes put on top of each other. At the outskirts of the village and above it, we find traces of ancient settlement and alignments of raised stones like those of Gourao.

86. The Rock of Marie-Thérèse is the meeting place of all the dug-out canoes for the area's "great fishing day," for which all people from nearby Bozo and Somono villages are gathered. The "great fishing day" takes place in the low waters of the lake after the performance of important rites.

87. "Faro's seat" is located at this site there. Cf. *Mythe et organisation sociale*, p. 53.

88. *polio kommo koro sugu anay*. The surface of the table measures 10m. x 10m.

sigi tolo showed the way, (then) the sun rose thereafter."[89]

At some distance to the south, four groups of stacked-up rocks have been placed, aligned from north to south; they represent the four male ancestors who came out of the ark and were witness to the first sunrise.

For the Dogon as well as for the Malinke, the Bambara, and the Bozo, the resurrected Nommo is represented by the course of the Niger from its source at Lake Débo. They think that Dya is the place where he stayed in the sacred pond — an image of the opening in the sky — near where the town has been established.[90] One says: "The Débo is the seat of the Nommo, the Dyaka is his *pegu.*"[91] The sacred stone of Dy, represents this settlement in one place, which the Dogon compare to that of the *pegu* altars ("to plant"). Dya is also the place where the permanent presence of his spiritual principles is symbolized.[92]

When they came from Mandé, the Dogon of Sanga attributed a similar symbolism to the Gona River and the pond of Dona.

a) Like the course of the Niger, the course of the Gona — a seasonal river which flows into a fault of the rocky plateau, from north to south, going down to the plain above Amani[93] — represents the body of the Nommo flat on his stomach in the water (map II). Similarly, the river is marked with twenty-two localities situated near "water holes," *dilu,* symbolizing his "articulations." They are: *sommo di* (where the "head" is); *pele*; *o banu*; *duno*; *o dolu*; *kangolo*; *tem na*; *gona*; *ale*; *kigiri tani*; *tengelem*; *o numu*; *urunu*; *si da* (where his "sex organ" is); *gomtogolo*; *pelu bonno*; *gilukile*; *ege ommoro*; *kuenne*; *i golo*; *oro sommu*; *di geu* (where his "foot" is). "The twenty-two stopping places of the water of the

---

89. *sigi tolo-le nay-le dige tana-le sigi; sigi tolo ozu tagara, nay onune tummu.*

90. Cf. *Mythe et organisation sociale au Soudan français,* pp. 50-54. *Mythe et organisation sociale en Afrique occidentale* (sequel), p. 121-133.

91. *deboy nommo doy, dyaka nommo pegu.*

92. For Dogon initiates who are familiar with the geographical representations of the myth at the international level, the *kuruwenke,* a sacred place, indicates the presence of the Nommo's *kikinu* in the pond.

93. This gorge was dammed off by the village of Bara in 1950. A sluice gate allows the inhabitants of Sanga to empty the gorge for the benefit of the people who live at the bottom of the cliffs, when they have finished the cultivation of onions which they undertook that year in small gardens made of earth brought from the banks.

great river is the number of the Nommo's articulations."[94] (Pl. XXIII, 3).

Now, the number of articulations is related to the "word" at the oral stage, which will later be revealed to man by the Nommo who resides in the river.

Therefore, certain localities have an altar, *sogo,* which represents the suprabranchial organs, *sosogu,* where the "word" resided at its life-giving stage in the *nommo anagonno's* body, when it was formed. These are made of a circle of twenty-two stones; then, *ara geu* porridge is used to draw a corresponding number of rays from the center, the whole thing making up the *dilu sogo tonu.* A vertical stone is raised in the center, and thus the circumference is the "blooming" of the *sosogu,* of which the central stone is the "root" (fig. 174). The number of circular stones here corresponds to the categories of Amma's thought and "word" as well as to the number associated with the resurrection of the victim.[95] The forms of the *sogo* vary with their attribution. We have seen that the *sogo* of the "path of the blood," *illi ozu,* and of the blood-flow of the *lebe dala* represent the organs or parts of the divided body.[96] Those of the Gona represent the twenty-two articulations of the resurrected Nommo. In the fields where sacred functions are performed, the *sogo,* under which there is always an *anagonno* that was caught in the ponds, will have nine stones with a longer one on top, standing for the eight seeds, the calabash (ninth), and the clavicles, *ani guyo,* of the resurrected Nommo. One says that "the twenty-two *sogo* of the articulations of the Nommo of the great river are the *sosogu;* the nine stones and the *sogo* of the middle, ten, of the *sogo* of the fields are like the eight seeds in the clavicles. The 'dispersed lines' of the blood of the sacrificed Nommo are transformed into stars."[97] The twenty-two localities along the course of the river are also evidence of the fertility and lineage of the Nommo, a lineage which will be paralleled

---

94. *golo ana di doy vazaze pelley ley sige nommo digu lugi.* Recited during purifications, *uguru,* performed on the *sogo* along the river.

95. Cf. *supra,* p. 337 and ff.

96. On the "path of the blood" they are called "traces of the path of the blood," *illi ozu bummo;* on the *lebe dala,* "scattered traces of the path of the blood," *illi ozu bummo ginnu.*

97. *golo ana nommo digu sogo pelley ley sige sosogu-ne to. minne sogo tibu tuo logorone sogo-le pelu dene gagara ani guyo-ne to anay. nommo semi illi bummo ginni tolo bile anay.* These three sentences are part of the prayer recited at the sacrifice offered on *ka amma* at the *bulu.*

by that of humanity: like the Nommo himself, his "sons," men, will bring forth numerous off-spring. The number of localities is related to the division of the *binu* among the descendants of the eight primordial ancestors, the institution of totemism, and the cult devoted to the resurrected Nommo.[98]

b) At Sanga the pond of Dona (map II, N and fig. 175), a replica of the pond of Dya, is the image of the "opening of the sky" and of the primordial pond, where the resurrected Nommo will install himself. It was chosen because of the presence of a source; because of the continuous flow of water, the pond is associated with the sky from which rain falls regularly. This place has been the site of various stone arrangments.

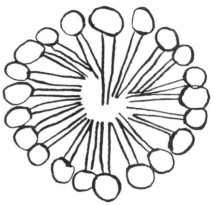

FIG. 174: Figure showing the position of the twenty-two stones of the *sogo* of the Gona (the picture stresses the spiral formed by the lines drawn in porridge).

Some trees which are replicas of the metamorphoses of the four piles made from the pieces of the dismembered body and cast by Amma to the four directions of space through the "opening" he made in the sky, have been planted around the pond: a *sa* to the south, a *yullo* to the north, an *oro* (baobab) to the west, a *minu* (karite) to the east. They are evidence of the purification brought about by the sacrifice and the resurrection following the slaughter.[99] Three *sogo* have been placed at the edge of the pond;

---

98. Regular annual purifications are offered by the priests of the main totems of the Sanga region on the *sogo* of the five principal locations of the Gona (*sommo di, o banu, gona, gomtogolo, di geu*), which are related to the five first Dogon totems (cf. p. 314). Purifications are performed in other localities in the event that no fish are found there: their absence is evidence of the impurity of the place, sullied by the violation of a prohibition.

99. Cf. *supra,* p. 302. The regular purifications (*uguru*) are performed with porridges and oils obtained from the seeds of these plants; for the pond, *sa* oil is used, for the totemic sanctuaries, porridge of baobab flour and *yullo* and *karite* oil. Installment 2, third year.

PL. XXI

The descent of the ark at Lake Débo:

1) The table located at the top of Mount Gourao representing the Nommo's ark "during the descent."

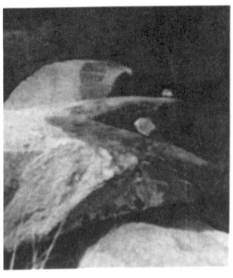

2) The stone drums of the cave of Gourao.

3) View overlooking the village of Marka de Gourao and the most distant point on the lake where "Faro's seat," or *faro tyn*, is located.

PL. XXII   The Nommo's ark on the Earth, at Sanga:
1) Stone arrangements representing: the sun (right), Sirius (center), the Polestar (left), seen from inside *polio kommo*.

2) The *polio kommo* stone table: east face, seen from the rock representing the sun.

3) The *polio kommo* table, south face.

figures were drawn on them when they were founded (Pl. XXIII, 1 and 2).

Under the *sogo uguru uguri,* "*sogo* where one performs purifications,"
placed to the north between Dona and Dodagu (fig. 175, C), the *yala*

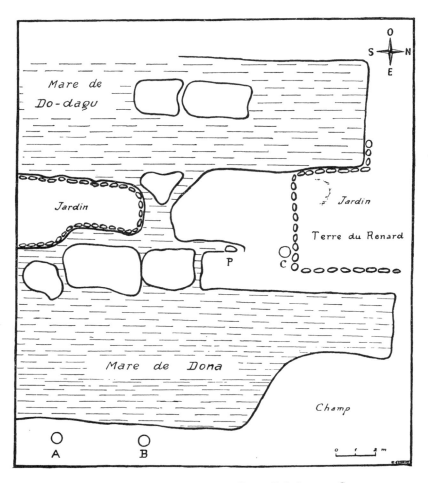

FIG. 175: The pond of Dona at Sanga: A. *sogo di turu,* B. *kubo sogo,* C. *sogo uguru
uguri* (and ant hill); D. stone (and termite hill).

of the Nommo's resurrection as well as of the ark and its contents have been drawn.[100] Two other *sogo,* east of the pond, denote the presence of the resurrected Nommo in the form of the *nommo anagonno.* One of them, to the south near the source, is called *sogo di turu,* "*sogo* of permanent water," or *sogo nommo ku tummuru,* "*sogo* of the leaning head of the Nommo" (A); the other, at some distance from the first, north along the same line, is *kubo sogo,* "*sogo* of the legs," or "*sogo* of the Nommo's stretched-out legs" (B); the Nommo's head has been drawn with *ara geu* porridge under the first one and his tail has been drawn under the second one (fig. 176).

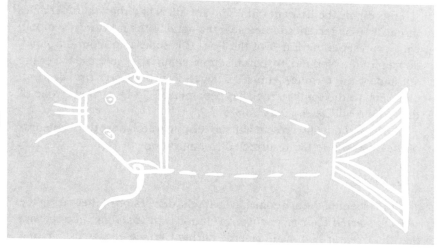

FIG. 176: Drawings made under the *sogo* of the pond of Dona.

It is as if the resurrected Nommo were spread across the entire pond, from south to north. The body has not been drawn "for in the water the *nommo anagonno* is invisible." However, two rows of five dots have been drawn with millet porridge between the two *sogo* to outline it, ten being the number attributed to the resurrected Nommo as the "ancestor" of mankind.

---

100. Cf. *supra,* p. 335, fig. 104 and p. 460, fig. 157.

In this way, the three *sogo* placed around the pond (which are the object of many prohibitions) are evidence of the resurrection of the *nommo* as a man, before his descent on the ark (*sogo uguru uguri*), and of his presence as *nommo anagonno* in the water, his domain on Earth.

Since the pond is a reflection of the sky, the three *sogo* also denote the presence of the three deputy-Nommo of Amma, their creator, who are respectively called upon during the offerings: the *nommo die* at the *sogo di turu* located near the source, the *nommo titiyayne* at the *kubo sogo, o nommo,* the "resurrected *nommo*" at the *sogo uguru uguri,* where the purifications are performed for all the inhabitants of the villages of Upper Sanga.

From this perspective, the *sogo* placed between Dona and Dodagu (C) represents the first ant hill: "The ant hill is like the seat of Amma's inside."[101] The terrain situated near the pond to the northwest symbolically represents the Earth of the Fox. It is separated from the pond, domain of the Nommo, by constructions signifying the presence of the ant and of the termite, Amma's delegates during Ogo's first descent. Opposite, to the south, a rock has been placed (in D), called "stone of the termite hill" (*tulu ginu dummo*).

The hypothetically present ant and termite watch over the wholeness of the pond where the resurrected Nommo resides.

THE STARS.

The descent of the ark coincided with the dispersion of the stars in the sky and started their respective revolutions. At this time, like the sun that the Creator had made emerge during Ogo's second reascent and "pushed" to the west out of his reach, all the stars, one after the other, came out of Amma's womb. The last one was *sigi tolo,* Sirius, which Amma "pushed" to the east in the direction of the Earth. Regarding the sacrifice and resurrection of the Nommo, one says that the sun "emerged" eight "periods" before *sigi tolo,* which emerged at the end of the cycle, at the twenty-second "period."

It is also said that when the Nommo descended, he wore his "ornaments" placed on twenty-two points on his body. These "ornaments" were the stars which, until then, were grouped "at the center of the sky and to the east," which he then freed and "scattered" through space. It is after

---

101. *key ginu amma doy anay.*

the landing of the ark and this scattering that they were placed in the sky as we see them today. This is also the point in time when they began to move in their respective orbits.

The Nommo's "ornaments" are compared to the covenant stones (*dugoy*) that candidates for priesthood must find and wear on a string as the principal sign of their totem after they take office. Each star is represented by a *dugoy*: this means that twenty-two constellations, star groups, or isolated heavenly bodies correspond to the twenty-two main totems of the Dogon;[102] for they recall the stages of the sacrifice and resurrection of the Nommo which accompanied the birth of the star world.

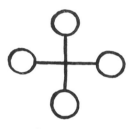

FIG. 177: Sign of the Polestar.

Moreover, the entire number of stars — those which are part of the "world of stars in a spiral" where the Earth is found, both visible and invisible in the sky, and those which are part of the other "worlds of stars in a spiral" created by Amma — are related to the entire number of "signs," the first expression of the thought of the Creator. It is said: "The stars turn in the sky. The stars are the unknown signs of Amma that turn in the sky."[103]

We have seen that "the world of stars in a spiral" where the Earth is found, underscored by the Milky Way, turns about a hypothetical axis connecting the Polestar, *du daga tolo,* "star of the north," to the Southern Cross *tenulu tolo,* "star of the south"; both stars are called "Amma's eyes" that support and watch over this world. In this system, a series of 266 stars or constellations, called "stars of the support of the foundation of the world," *aduno bolo te tolo,* represents the series of the 266 "signs of Amma's womb." The Polestar is considered to be the "molting," the double of this system of which it is the epitome: the sign representing it is made of a cross — the two axes dividing the "picture of the signs" into four sectors — and of circles denoting the four elements as well as the cardinal directions

---

102. For each totem there is a corresponding star or constellation. Installment 2, third and following years.

103. *tolo alagala-ne baru biliede. tondolo dugomolu amba ton digila dege ko vun* (Wazouba dialect).

(fig. 177). In this series are the stars of which we have related the genesis and which to varying degrees will affect the life of man on the Fox's Earth.

They will all be represented by raised stones in places where the Dogon have hypothetically situated the episodes of the first sixty-six years of man's life on Earth, both for purposes of initiation and for the performance of certain rites. In particular, the majority of those heavenly bodies represented — at the time of their creation — by the altars of the *lebe dala* are also represented by raised stones on the rocky plateau of *ka donnolo,* "plateau of *ka,"* on the flanks of which, east and west, are series of caves arranged as evidence of the first dwellings of the mythical ancestors. One says that "the stars of the *sogo* of the *lebe dala* are placed as they are in the sky; those of the *ka donnolo* are placed as people have seen them in the world (which is to say from the Earth)."[104]

They will also be represented by ritually drawn figures on the inside or on the façades of the totemic sanctuaries and on those of the Hogon's dwelling.[105]

They will also be drawn under the *sogo* altars of the fields where sacred functions are performed, because these figures signify the existence of calendars related to agriculture, the basic skill of the Dogon.

Two systems, sometimes combined, will come into play and constitute the origin of the various calendars which cadence the life and activities of man. The same holds true with respect to the performance of rites instituted as a result of events of which man is both the author and witness — events which, for the most part, will be determined by the deeds of the Fox in his attempts to disrupt the established order.

One of them, the closest to Earth, will have the sun, mark of the remnant of Ogo's placenta, as its axis, and the other, further away, will have Sirius as its axis, mark of the placenta of the Nommo, the monitor of the universe.

I. ORION, SIRIUS, PO AND EMME YA TOLO.

A) The group of stars in which Sirius plays a primordial part includes

---

104. *lebe dala-ne tolo vogo alagala tolo, yala tozoy; ka donnolo-ne vogo aduno-ne tolo yala tozoy.* For *ka donnolo,* cf. *supra,* p. 220.

105. We have recorded the names of a number of stars which the Dogon associate with the graphic representations included in the 266 "signs of Amma"; these stars we were able to determine.

501

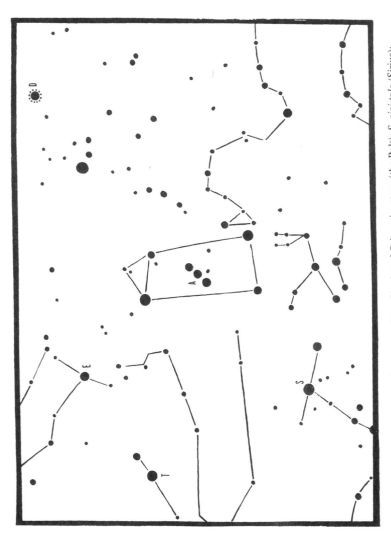

FIG. 178: Map of the sky; in the center of the Chariot of Orion: A: *atanu* (the Belt); S, *sigi tolo* (Sirius); E, *enegirine tolo* (γ of Canus Minor); T: *tara* (Procyon); D: *tolo duno* (the Pleiades).

the constellation of Orion and a certain number of stars located nearby.

The four main stars of the Chariot of Orion are called "of the seat of Amma's foundation" (*amma bolo doy tolo*), or again "stars of Amma's navel" (*amma bogu tolo*). They form a frame around the stars forming Orion's Belt (*tolo atanu*). Not far off are the Pleiades (*tolo duno*), the "star of the Goatherd" (*enegirine tolo*), and Sirius (*sigi tolo*) with its "companions" (*po tolo, emme ya tolo*) (fig. 178).

Together these stars make up the "support of the seat of the world" (*aduno bolo te*). With regard to the "signs," the first expression of the Creator's thought, they are considered as evidence of the "master" and "guide" signs of the 266 primordial drawings.

They are mentioned in the prayer and uttered in a low voice the day of the sacrifice performed on the altar of Lébé by the Yébéné priest, before the text which he then recites aloud to be heard by all: *"amma bolo doy tolo-le, atanu-le tolo duno-le, sigi tolo-le, po tolo-le, emme ya tolo-le, enegirine tolo-le* are with Amma's seat. Amma, receive the greeting of the evening. Sons of the fathers, may Amma bring you forth, it is the day of Lébé; sons of Lébé, sons of the great totems, sons of the thresholds (i.e., of the *ginna*) may Amma bring you forth. We have had the day which begins (the ceremony), . . . may Amma give you children to be born, etc. . . ."[106]

Moreover, they are represented by dots (of *yu* and *ara geu* porridge) under each pillar of the men's shelter, *toguna*, when it is built in the village.

In this system, Sirius and its satellites (or companions) are called *ku tolo*, "stars of the head," the others being called *gozu tolo*, "stars of the body."

a) The four principal stars of the Chariot of Orion have been represented by four stone blocks placed at the corners of the first field delimited in the region by the Arou of the Sangabinou family, its first inhabitants. It is located in the valley called *amma na ommoro*, where we find the cave called *amma na kommo*, which represents Amma's west clavicle.[107]

---

106. *amma bolo doy tolo-le, atanu-le, tolo duno-le, sigi tolo-le, po tolo-le, emme ya tolo-le, enegirine tolo-le amma doy-ne be da; amma dige dene yaba, ba unum amma ey dele, lebe bay, lebe unum, babinu unum, monogolo unum, amma ey dele bay tolo bemi . . . amma ey naniemo,* etc.

107. Cf. *supra*, p. 434.

This field, located far from the settlements of Upper Sanga where the

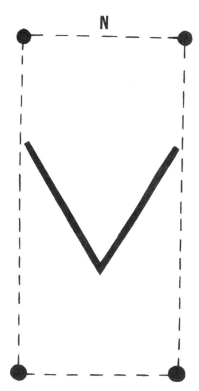

Sangabinou family lives, has not been cultivated in most recent years. However, whenever one wishes to seed it again, the family patriarch delegates a sacrificer to go to the middle of the field and draw the "sign of Amma in the sky," *manna amma bummo,* of which one says: "The first *bummo* of Amma is in the valley of the field of the great Amma"[108] (fig. 179).

The stones placed at the field corners standing for the four stars of the Chariot also represent the "four corners" of celestial space. Their different colors denote the four elements.[109]

While drawing the sign, the sacrificer says: "Great Amma, on the east side, all the things you must release, on the north side, all the things you must release, on the west side, all the things you must release, on the south side, all the things you must release; this is the sign of Amma of the valley of the great Amma."[110]

Thus, in stellar space, the Chariot is the symbol of Amma's seat; it surrounds *atanu,* the Belt, otherwise

FIG. 179: Diagram of the field called *amma na minne,* framed by stones representing the Chariot of Orion; at the center, the "sign" of Amma. The cave *amma na kommo,* open to the west, overlooks the southeast end of the field.

---

108. *amma bummo tolo amma na minne ommoro-ne.* Drawn by dipping an ear of millet, emptied of its seeds, in paste made from serpent dung (of the *yuguru na*) and water taken from the pond of Yanay, the pond of the Sangabinou family, located near Go. See also the sign fig. 30, p. 154.

109. A stone which is mottled on its northeast side, white on the northwest, red on the southwest, black on the southeast (not verified *in situ*).

110. *amma na du benne, kize pu yarado, du daga benne, kize pu yarado, donno benne, kize pu yarado, tenulu benne, kize pu yarado; amma na ommoro amma bummo.*

known as the three "deputies." It is related to the basic elements and to the cardinal directions, which presided during the realization of the universe that was "thought" by the creator.

b) The "star of the fonio," *po tolo,* turns around Sirius, *sigi tolo.* The revolution takes fifty years. It is the most important of all the stars and plays a key role — in all the spiraling star worlds Amma formed; as evidence of the *po pilu,* and born after the *po* had accomplished its task, it is considered to be the center of the stellar world.

The star's name connotes its priority: *po,* as we have seen, comes from *polo,* "beginning"; *tolo* comes from *to,* "deep." So, *po tolo* literally means "deep beginning."

The star of the *po,* a double of the germ of the whole creation, will also be of considerable value to human beings. Later, when they see it in the sky, it will be the testimony of the renewal of the world for them, the image of the "womb" of Amma, who preserves the basic signs for the whole creation within himself and who keeps the *po pilu,* which that star represents, in the sky. Therefore, one says that it is like "the egg of the world," *aduno talu,* and like "Amma's eye," *amma giri,* the guide of the universe.

Because of the creative role of the *po pilu,* the star is seen as the reservoir or source of all things. It is the smallest, yet the heaviest, of celestial things. "When the *po pilu* had finished making the world spin, this void[111] transformed itself into the star of the *po.* Therefore, *po tolo* was heavy, (because) there was (in it) the remnant of the blood of the world that the *po* spun around. (It is) the remnant of the blood of all the things it created. *po tolo* is the smallest of all things; it is the heaviest star."[112]

In its substance is evidence of everything the *po pilu* had contained. The star contains three basic elements, "air, fire, and water"; the element "earth" is replaced by metal in all its forms, particularly by the metal called *sagala,*[113] somewhat more shiny than iron and of such

---

111. Which is to say, "this empty husk."

112. *po ganna ginnegila donu-na kologo po tolo tani. po tolo demme-go po ganna ginnigili illi vazu to. kize vo manu pu illi vazu. po tolo kize voy vo gayle be dedemego vo sige be.* This blood is compared to the blood that remains in a woman's womb after delivery.

113. A word of the same root as *sagatara,* "powerful, strong," which designates a "young man."

density that "all of the beings on earth together could not lift a small part of it." Hence the star's weight and, since it is so small, its density. One actually says that if its diameter is compared to that of a stretched cowhide or its size to that of a mortar board, it would weigh as much as 480 mule loads (about 35,000 kg),[114] as much as all the seeds put together, or as much as all the iron in the world.

One also says that *po tolo* contains all matter divided into 4 x 20 "compartments." The four basic divisions contain respectively the grains (germs?), metals, plant life (organic matter?), and water; the twenty "compartments" which make them up determine the divisions and forms, making a total of eighty basic elements.

The star's former position in space is where now the sun is, called "seat of *po tolo*," *po tolo doy*.[115] Like the other stars, it moved away from the Earth; only the sun remained near. Thus, it moved and is presently at the center of the sky; but it is a center in motion, like the links of the helix in the "devil's game." In addition "as soon as *sigi tolo* emerged, *po tolo* went around it." It went around Sirius like the *po* had moved around its germ inside Amma's womb represented by the *gaba*. The movements of *po tolo* keep all the other stars in their respective places: in fact, one says that without this movement none of them would "stay in place." *po tolo* forces them to keep their trajectory: in particular, it regulates the trajectory of Sirius, which is the only one that does not follow a regular curve, and which it separates from the other stars by surrounding it with its own orbit. Therefore, since it supports the universe by rotating and revolving around Sirius, one calls it "the pillar of the stars," *tolo ogo*.

The movements of *po tolo*, the heavy embryo of the world and the mark of all creation, are quite active: its contents are ejected by the force of its spinning in forms that are "infinitely small," much like the grains of the *po pilu* which grow rapidly: in this way, the star, white like *po pilu*, continues to distribute the germs of life once contained by the seed it represents.

"Amma created *po tolo* the first of all the stars. In the substance (body) of *po tolo*, (all) the things in the (entire) world, their sign exists a

---

114. The number 480 is the product of base 80 times the number of groups of ten of base 60; it is used here as a symbol of the largest of numbers.

115. Sirius, which also changed position, is found here as well.

bit. It houses (it is the granary of) all things in the world. *po tolo* is the axis of the entire world. If one looks at *po tolo*,[116] it is as if the world was turning. The world, the turn it makes around *po tolo*, it is as if to say (*voma*) that *po tolo* turns: (in reality) it is thanks to it that the world turns. In the past, they performed the sacrifice of the Hogon (representationally) of the path of *po tolo*. Today, these are the sacrifices on the *ommolo* (that replace them). Slaughtering the chicken on the *ommolo*, going around in first (position) with the blood,[117] this is like *po tolo* going around the world."[118]

c) The *"emme ya* star," *emme ya tolo,* is larger in volume than *po tolo* and four times as light. It, too, revolves around Sirius along a greater orbit but in the same time, in a fifty-year revolution.[119] Their respective positions are such that their rays intersect at a right angle.

emme ya tolo is the celestial image of the female "mother" seed. Due to its predominantly feminine character, it is also called "little sun of the women," *yau nay dagi.* It is the residence of the female souls of the living, especially those of the basic cereal grains. It emits four rays (the female number) that catch and maintain these forces. This star will ensure the wholeness of the seeds as well as of the clavicular contents of human beings. One says that it serves as the intermediary between *po tolo* and Sirius and that it spins to "transmit the orders" from the former to the latter, which is watched over by *po tolo.*

Both stars are drawn on the east side of the platform of the Hogon of Arou when he is ordained; *po tolo* with *ara geu* in a circle with sixteen internal rays; *emme ya tolo* is an oval with sixteen external rays (fig. 180A and B).[120] In this instance, the number and position of the rays signify the wholeness of the stars and of the seeds they represent: the

---

116. *yenne:* "to look at."

117. When the blood is flowing, the victim is turned about above the altar.

118. *po tolo amma tolo la voy manu. aduno fu kize vo tolo gozu-ne gayla sere vomo bemen yato. aduno kize fu guyoy. po tolo aduno fu dudunu-go voy. po tolo yennane aduno gonoze ginvo. aduno fu po tolo-ne gogonu galiezego vogo po tolo voma gonogingo; sabu vomo-de aduno gonoze. ani po tolo yoygo ogo-ne numpugu voy pugo bey, kannay ommolo numpugu vogo voy. ene ommolo-ne sewe illi-go la gono gananu-go vogo po tolo gone, aduno fu vo bie dago voy.*

119. According to another source, its revolution takes thirty-two years.

120. Drawn once in snake (*yuguru na*) dung; these stars are not drawn again until the next time a dignitary takes office.

rays, therefore, mark the four elements placed at the four directions of space. On the totemic sanctuaries, *po tolo* is represented by a circle with six rays marking the six *yala* of sex of the *po* in Amma's womb. The rays are dotted lines indicating that the star — which will burst, as did the *po pilu,* and will be visible for some time[121] — can at present not be seen, except under special circumstances.

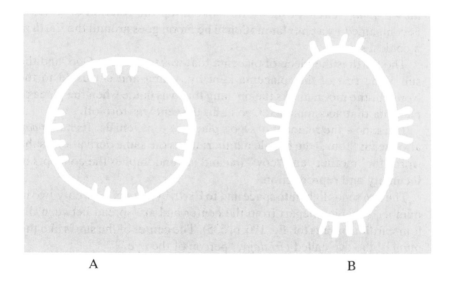

A   B

FIG. 180: A: *po tolo;* B. *emme ya tolo.*

The heliacal rising of Sirius — recalling the conjunction of the two first placentas — and the revolution of *po tolo,* mark of the first grain containing the universe, around Sirius will both be related to the performance of the sixty-year ceremonies of the Sigui that at present

121. The star will burst in the course of events taking place during the first year of the life of man on Earth (installment 2, first year). Its brilliance, particularly intense at that time, will become progressively dimmer, to fade away completely after the performance of the fourth Sigui, i.e., after a period of 240 years.

commemorate the revelation of the word to man and the appearance of death on the Earth.[122] These ceremonies are also a reminder of the history of Amma's creation of the world.

II. THE SUN, THE MOON, THE PLANETS, AND THE CALENDARS.

a) The sun turns on its axis as if under the influence of an immense spiral mainspring. Reinforced by the "cords" of rain that penetrate it, the Earth turns on its axis[123] and simultaneously makes a great circle, *aduno digili,* "circle of the world," like a top the rotation of which is accompanied by a circular motion. The moon goes around the Earth in a conical spiral.

The Earth is the piece of placenta that was torn off by Ogo, and the sun is the rest of that placenta kept by Amma and entrusted to the Nommo; the moon marks the opening that was made when the piece of placenta that accompanied Ogo in his descent was torn off.

The sun — the remnant of Ogo's placenta — is female. Its name *nay* also means "four," the female number; it has the same derivation as the words for "mother" and "cow" (*na* and *nā*) and implies the concepts of fecundity and reproduction.

The sun sends light into space and to Earth by its rays — twenty-two in number — which depart from the center and are spread between the four cardinal points (cf. fig. 190, p. 535). The center of the sun is like the pupil of the eye called *giri dege,* "person of the eye."[124]

Seen from the Earth, it is said that the sun moves in the sky like the Nommo's ark. It "grows" in the morning (*nay tumma*); it is then the "sun of the rising" (*du nay*). During the day, it follows the "path of the chain of the ark" (*koro yogu ozu*). When it sets, one says that it "has fallen (into the ark)" (*nay nummay*).

The two apparent motions of the sun determine day (*bay*) and night (*dige*) on the one hand, the solstices (*du daga nay,* "sun of the north," and *tenulu nay,* "sun of the south") and the equinoxes, *nay logoron* or "sun of the middle," on the other hand.

---

122. Installment 1, second and sixty-second years.

123. *logoro-ne gogono galaze,* literally, "made a circle (around its) center."

124. Because one sees a small image of oneself in the pupil of another person. The iris is called *giri geu,* "dark (black) eye" and the white of the eye *giri pili,* "white eye."

With regard to the Earth, the Nommo moves the sun from east to west and from north to south, in order to "cover" Ogo's placenta (the Earth) with its rays every day and all year long. One says that it "enters" by the north and "emerges" by the south (at the solstitial positions) to "put this placenta back in place."[125]

During the night, the sun follows the path taken by Ogo, who did everything in the primordial darkness. During the day, the sun's rays lighting the Earth are the arteries through which flows the blood of the placenta, forever alive, to nourish the dry earth. At its zenith, it clearly demonstrates the power of the Nommo, who maintains his trajectory over the Earth of the Fox. For the rays, while they nourish the Earth, also "drink" the piece of placenta of which the Earth is made, as if to renew it.

b) The moon — which is the evidence of a "hole" — is dry and lifeless like dried-up lifeless blood; its craters are the arteries through which flows an impure blood, like the blood of women's menses.

The sun sends its rays to Earth; the moisture it brings about goes back up to the moon — like Ogo goes up and then down again. It is said that the female soul, Ogo's female twin, Yasigui, is always trying to direct the sun's rays back up to the moon, for she also makes vain efforts to make the male soul of the Fox go back up to the place it came from.

The appearance of the moon in its waxing and waning during the month, as seen from the Earth, is related to these representations: when it is full, it has received the blood sent to it by the sun. Then it withers like a menstruating woman, for it is losing its blood. When the moon is new, it is completely dry.

The new moon, *olo,* "dark," recalls Ogo's circumcision. The first crescent marks his conception and the formation of the Earth;·the full moon marks the descent of the Nommo's ark and the "earth of the day of the fish" on the earth of the Fox.

An association is also made between the phases of the moon and the opening of the Nommo's mouth: the moon increases when he breathes while opening his mouth to speak; he thus makes twelve "speeches" per year, which represent all the "words" he addresses to all the beings in the universe. When the moon is full, his words are at their most powerful

---

125. Because Ogo entered the Earth, his placenta, in the northeast and emerged from the southwest (cf. *supra,* p. 185).

and benefit mankind the most. A halo (*gwe*) around the full moon, which increases its apparent volume, is called "meeting of the chiefs" (*ogo baru*). The new moon — when the Nommo is silent — is the time of troubles and deaths.

The Fox said: "The sun is my placenta and I could not reach it, but it marks time." However, people did not listen to him, for henceforth it is the Nommo who determines time by the movements imposed upon the stars.

The lunar calendar is the current calendar: the months are named after the twelve successive moons.

The moon marks the time it took Ogo to tear off his placenta and form the Earth. One also counts in moons: two months, i.e., sixty days, recall his peregrination and the sixty "holes" made in his placenta.

With its rays, the sun will cover the whole Earth from north to south, which is to say, five rows of twelve holes, in 2 x 6 "moons," i.e., during one solar year from one winter solstice to the next. In other words, it takes the sun two "moons" to cover one row.

One says that it will take the sun a period that is a multiple of 365 and of 60 — i.e., of the number of days in a year and of the number called "number of the placenta" — to put the stolen portion back in place and "to dry out" the Fox.[126]

The first moon, *ie turu*, the harvest moon, will begin the lunar year: it recalls the conception of the *nommo anagonno*; the solar year begins at the winter solstice, which determines the time of the *goru* ceremony in which a sacrifice is offered on the altar to the ancestors, where their gestation is represented.[127]

The solstitial and equinoctial positions of the sun are theoretically recalled by the positions of the altars of the "path of blood" (fig. 108): *keze amma* at Tégnou is the northern boundary — at the winter solstice — "*keze amma* is the place where the sun stops when it walks to the north. We have marked it by placing the *amma*. The sun makes its way to the south, it has left, it has stopped. We have placed the seat of *para lebe* to mark (this)."[128] Between the two *ka amma* is the equinoctial

---

126. The Fox, no longer in possession of the blood of his placenta, is unable to find his female soul and twin: a fox can only answer the diviner's questions for 730 (365 x 2) days. Once this time has passed, it can no longer foretell the future.

127. Cf. *supra,* p. 378.

position.[129] From this perspective, the *dummo dama* and *pegu* altars are called, respectively, "middle of the south sun" and "middle of the north sun."[130]

The observable solstices and equinoxes of the sun are measured by taking bearings using particularly the three *mono* ("meeting") altars placed west of Upper Ogol (corresponding to the three solar positions) (map II, 0). The "surveyor" puts a small stick vertically on top of the altars involved and takes a well-known landmark on the horizon as his reference point to observe the rising sun. This measurement, taken four times a year by any one of the heads of the *ginna* of the Ogol villages, is called "measure of the direction of time," *varu yalu tumu.*[131]

The two distinctly different calendars (solar and lunar) will sometimes be coincidental and sometimes dissociated, especially for the performance of rites commemorating the episodes of the formation of the universe and the events which began when the Earth became populated.

With regard to social organization, the observable positions of the sun are divided among the four tribes of the Dogon associated with the four ancestors who descended on the ark: the rites performed respectively by their members will take place at the solstices and equinoxes. Moreover, these positions will recall the episodes of the myth. In the course of the annual successive rites, the four tribes will commemorate the stages of the disruptions caused by Ogo and of the reestablishment of order through the sacrifice of his twin brother.

"When the sun of the south comes up at *bago,* one has received the seeds; the Dyon hold the *goru.* The sun comes to the middle, the Nommo has circumcised the Fox; the Ono hold the *agu.* In the placenta of the Fox, the *key* ant steals the grains that were inside; the Arou hold the *bulu.* The sun in returning comes to the middle; the ark descends,

128. *keze amma nay du daga ya vo, yalu vo kalli; kezibu amma dani; nay tenulu yoy yaze, ya, kalli; para lebe doy kezibu dani.*

129. The altar has been moved, because it was too exposed to the inclement weather conditions on the rocks north of Upper Ogol, and been taken in to the village.

130. *tenulu nay logoron* and *du daga nay logoron.*

131. *varu:* "moment," "time"; *yalu* means a "line," a "direction," a "place." These bearings will be described along with the construction of the *mono* altars of the children (installment 2, fourth year).

The pond of Dona: 1) Overview. The *sogo die* and, behind it, the *sogo kubo*.

2) the *sogo uguru uguri* at the far right of the rock table separating Dona from Do Dagou.

3) The Gona.

PL. XXIV: Carved wooden door from a granary of the Hogon's dwelling.

the Nommo follows with the *anagonno* and the crocodile, and he enters
the pond; the Domno wrestle and dance."[132]

c) Although their names are accompanied simply by the word *tolo* in
the everyday language, the planets are called *tolo tanaze,* "stars that
move across" or "stars that turn (around something else)," a term which
distinguishes them from the fixed stars. *dana tolo* (Jupiter), *tolo yazu*
(Venus), *yapunu tolo* (Mars), and *yalu ulo tolo* (Saturn?) revolve around
the sun. One says that "Jupiter follows Venus by slowly turning around
the sun."[133] For the respective positions of the planets at different times
in the solar year will be interpreted by man through the representations
of which they are the object.

The positions of Venus, which make up a calendar, deserve to be the
subject of a special analysis.

The planet's six positions, each called *yazu giri,* "eye of Venus," as we
have seen, signify the flowing, on the placenta and into space, of the
blood from the emasculation and slaughter of the sacrificed Nommo as
well as that of the contents of the clavicles. Under the altars of the *lebe
dala* and of the "line of the blood" (both respectively associated with one
of the planet's six positions), each of them is represented by a *tonu*
made of a circle with external rays stemming from it which increase

---

132. *bagu tenu nay tummoze varu dene bema; do goru kunnoze; nay logoro-ne veze
varu yurugu anagonno olu goni; ono agu kunnoze; bado du daga nay tummoze yurugu
me-ne key dene to guya biri; ara bulu kunnoze; nay pilleme logoro-ne veze koro sugi,
nommo izu-le ayo-le dimmia o-ne yay; domno adori-le gole-kunnoze.*

The *bado bulu* rites belong to the Arou in the sense that the Dyon can celebrate them
only when the Arou have assigned the date. On the other hand, the Dyon begin the *bago*
rites and the others follow. The Ono decide upon the date of the *agu* rite (from *ay,* to get or
catch) performed at *nay banu* at the spring equinox following the hunt *tala* (cf. *infra,* p.
282). In the past, *agu* (which involved the altars of the ancestors, *vageu*) was celebrated
among the Ono well before the *bulu* of the Arou. The Donno performed a ritual dance
accompanied by wrestling matches, *adori,* hypothetically performed on the field of Lébé:
this ritual game is called *koro boy go,* "dance to the beat of the *koro* (drum)," by the
inhabitants of Sanga.

Similarly, in Sanga, the four "measures" of the sun determine the performance of the
following rites: *goru* at the winter solstice (sun of the south); sacrifice to the *ommolo ana*
of the *ginna* (*ginna ommolo bulu*) at the spring equinox (sun of the middle); *bulu,* the
sowing celebration at the summer solstice (sun of the north); "beer of the twins," *dineu
kono* (offering of the first fruits) at the autumn equinox (sun of the middle).

133. *dana tolo yazu dimmia nay gono dege dege.*

in number with each figure from one to six.[134]

Also, all these figures together are produced for the instruction of the apprentice-diviners on a divination table, where they represent the path of the planet through space (fig. 181).[135] Each one is drawn in order of its turn (with snake dung, *yuguru na*) on the east façade of the house

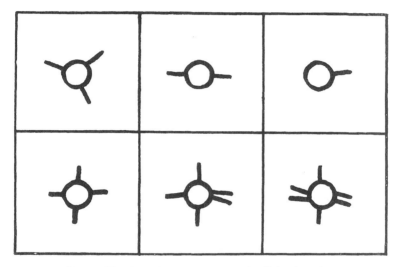

FIG. 181: The six positions of Venus on the divination table.

134. Drawn respectively in *yu* at *igibie*, in *ara geu* at *belu uri*, in *yu* at *tenu*, in *emme di giru* at *enegirim tolo sogo*, in *ara pili* at *dige tanu tolo sogo*, in *emme na kolo* at *yapunu da tolo sogo*. The different porridges used to make these figures, correspond to the various offerings of the first fruits from the harvest (to the *nommo die*, to *o nommo*, to the ancestors, etc.). The offerings and purifications performed on the altars of the *lebe dala* are carried out by the priests of the main totems of Upper Sanga (installment 2, fifth year).

135. We recall that the solar calendar is also included on these tables. See the schematic picture of the "path of the sun" in space during the year of twelve moons. There is only a sketch for the study of the Venusian calendar; it should be noted that when speaking of the planet one says: "The eye of *yazu* comes in six years" (*yazu giri anakuzu kuley doze*).

of the Hogon of Arou, above the platform and above the figures of the sun, the moon, and the "star of the tenth moon" (*ie pelu tolo*).

The first figure is made on the right wall, i.e., to the north; the second one is drawn to its left (to the south) three years later, and so on until the last one, drawn eighteen years after the first. Three years later, the cycle is started anew. If the Hogon dies during this period of time, his successor never breaks the cycle, but continues the execution of the figures, begun by his predecessor, until the end. Commenting on the period of time during which these figures are visible on the dwelling, one says: "The number of the twenty-two articulations of the Nommo is the number of the "eyes" of Venus, twenty-one, plus the star, twenty-two."[136] Thus, the number assigned to the parts of the body of the resurrected Nommo is projected right into time, here related to the Venusian calendar.

The Venusian calendar, determined by six observable positions during the year, is related to the various activities of man.

1) The sacrifice of the Nommo, as we have seen, brought about the distribution of the seeds throughout the universe. In this respect, Venus, the mark of the flowing of blood and of the contents of the clavicles, is also the celestial "mark of the placenta of the *po pilu,*" *po pilu me sere.* Its positions during the year recall the stages of the germination, growth, harvest, and consumption of the basic cereal grains contained in the first grain, i.e., the annual death and resurrection of the millet. From this perspective, they constitute an agricultural calendar, called *dine bire,* "work of the winter season," which has the following nomenclature:

enegirim: sowing and *kinu tumu* (germination), "nose that is coming out"; *dige tanu*: emerged from the earth, or *kinu tey,* "grown nose"; *donno tolo*: millet grown into an ear, or *yu ene dullo,* "chicken-tail millet"; *yazu* or *bayara*: grains formed in the ear, or "pregnant millet," *yu bere ay*; *obia*: "ripe millet," *yu illa*; *yapunu da*: consumed millet (hence, "dead," *yu yimu),* but then present in the clavicles of the people it has nourished.

---

136. *nommo digu lugu pelley ley sige vo ginu; yazu giru pelley turu sige tolole bara pelley ley sige.* These words are recited when the priest of the Goummoyana totem performs the purification *uguru* on the *sogo* of the pond of Dona (cf. p. 464) before the Sigui.

The heavenly body will be represented by figures (at the *yala* stage) under the *sogo* altars of the fields where sacred functions are performed, those altars which are the object of purifications before sowing and of offerings after the harvest. The *yala,* in fixed number for each figure, were drawn with the porridge of different cereal grains when the *sogo* were founded, as were the *tonu* drawn under the altars of the *lebe dala.*

It is said: "The *yala* of *yazu* are like the trace of the blood of the sacrificed Nommo."[137] With regard to the sacrifice of the Nommo, if one

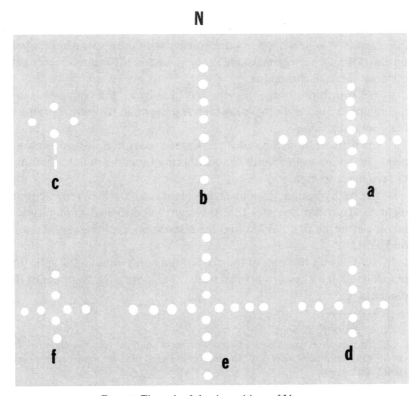

FIG. 182: The *yala* of the six positions of Venus.

---

137. *yazu yala nommo semu illi anay.*

follows the order of the positions of Venus, the *yala* should be read as follows (fig. 182): — the first position, *obia,* has fifteen *yala* (a). The east-west orientation of the seven *yala* recalls that everything begins in the east (*du,* "root"). The figure connotes the internal development of the primordial *po* (at first seven segments, then the ejection of the eighth), the creation of the *nommo anagonno,* and the future births of mankind (*kuno* and twins (7 + 8)).[138]

— the second position, *donno tolo,* has seven *yala* (b), which connote the division of the body of the sacrificed Nommo and the distribution of the seeds in space.

— the third position, *yazu,* has four *yala* for the ear and two dashes for the stalk — six marks in all (c) — and represents the millet ear called *yu binukezine,*[139] which is kept in the granary with the seeds where, opening into four, it represents Amma's four clavicles, the four elements, and the four cardinal directions.

— the fourth position, *enegirim,* has nine *yala,* "the eight seeds and the calabash seed is ninth" (d), which represent all the cereal grains in the container, *gaba.*

— the fifth position, *dige tanu,* has sixteen *yala* (e); these are the seeds given by Amma to the Smith, who will bring them down in his hammer to give them to man.

— the sixth position, *yapunu da,* has eight *yala* (f) which represent the eight seeds of the clavicles that the eight ancestors of humanity will receive after the first harvest and the consumption of the cereal grains on Earth.[140]

If one adds up the *yala* of the six positions, fifty-nine in all, plus the planet itself, it makes a total of sixty, in other words, the "number of the placenta."

---

138. Cf. *supra,* p. 165 and ff.

139. This involves certain ears which are harvested and put into the sanctuaries to preserve the spiritual principles of the cereal grains until the next sowing time. (installment 2, fifth year).

140. These various figures have been made with the porridge of different cereal grains:
— under the four *sogo* of the field of Lébé when they are founded, these being the same *sogo* that represent the head, abdomen, and feet of the ancestor Lébé Sérou, who will be buried lying down in the field; respectively: *ba digilu sogo* (with *emme ya*), *sogo de* (with *yu), yebene sogo* (with *ara geu*), *gemene sogo* (with *ara pili*).

In addition, if one similarly examines the *yala* of the stars born from the sacrifice of the Nommo which are drawn under the altars in the fields where sacred functions are performed, one will see that they correspond to the problems of agriculture:

atanu, the spiritual principles of the cereal grains. The three stars represent, respectively, the *nommo die,* the *nommo titiyayne,* and *o nommo,* who are the guardians of those spiritual principles and masters of the water and rain needed for germination.[141]

tolo dullogu, the cultivated earth. The three stars represent the three sacred fields (of the *ginna,* the *lebe,* and the *binu*) in which one sows the seeds kept in the sanctuaries.[142]

Venus, the sowing and the complete cycle of the growth of the cereal grains.

The Pleiades, the harvest.[143]

— at the site of the place called *ogo tuyo taba dunu* located at Amkougno where the harvest of that field is placed and kept by the Hogon for seven days (with *emme som dullo*). This place represents the spot where the umbilical cord (*ogo*) of the *nommo semi* was attached to his placenta.

— on the site of the *lebe dala* (quite close to the altar of Lébé) called *ogo tuyo tabi doni,* where it is taken to be threshed by the entire community (drawn with *emme pili*). This site represents the place where the umbilical cord was attached to the body of the *nommo semi.*

The millet is then carried to the courtyard of the Hogon and covered with a large round basket (made of *telu* straw), *kaba,* which protects it and is like "the star placed over the pile." "The *kaba,* protects the millet of Lébé; the *kaba* is like Venus" (*kaba lebe yu domuri; kaba yazu anay*) (installment 2, fifth year). The rites are performed in this field by the priests of the Yébéné and Guéméné totems.

141. The *yala* was drawn in *yu* porridge during the construction of the *sogo* of Yébéné, placed to the northeast of the field of the Hogon. The *tonu* was made under the *sogo* of Yébéné of the *lebe dala* with porridge of *yu* and *ara.* The *toy* is made with *ara* porridge on the west façade of the Yébéné sanctuary during the priest's ordination (*duguru*).

142. The *yala* is drawn under the *sogo* of the field adjacent to the field of Lébé, *ba digilu,* of which it is the "tail"; hence the name given to the group of stars. This field may be given in use by the Hogon to his son or to any member of the community. The *tonu* is made under the *sogo* of the Guéméné totem on the *lebe dala.* The *toy* is made on the façade of the same sanctuary. The three figures have been produced with porridge of *ara, yu,* and *anu na,* since Guéméné, who accompanies Yébéné in his functions, is "like the *anu* sauce that goes with the rice or millet cake."

143. The *yala* are drawn in the *sogo* of the field of the Goummoyana totem. Also, the Pleiades are represented under all the *sogo* of the *vageu minne* (the ritual fields of the *ginna*).

These figures recall that the positions of these stars are constantly involved in the performance of the agrarian rites and in the cultivation of the fields.

2) The positions of Venus are also recalled over a very large geographic area by a series of altars, raised stones, or arrangements in caves or rock shelters, which commemorate the mythical events related to the "death of the millet," i.e., the departure of the spiritual principles from the grains given to people as their basic food because of the deeds of the Fox, from the eighth to the tenth year after the descent of man on Earth. Having allowed men to perform the funeral and *dama* of the millet at the same time as those of the Fox, Amma returned the spiritual principles to the cereal grains.

The closing of these events and mythical ceremonies is commemorated by a raised stone representing Venus in the *yazu* position, and located on the side of the steep, rocky incline of *ka donnolo* near *ka kommo*; all kinds of grain porridge are annually poured on this raised stone. Under the altar, Venus has been drawn in the *yazu* position (fig. 183): a series of *yala,* nine oriented dots, represents the calabash and the eight seeds at the cardinal positions and recalls the "distribution of the seeds" in the universe by the sacrifice of the Nommo: they are also arranged like the compartments inside the family granary.

FIG. 183: *yala* of *yazu* under the *sogo* of Ka.

The goatherds of Sanga annually reenact these mythical episodes through a series of games and rites which are performed in accordance with the alignment of the altars and raised stones related to the positions of Venus, and in different caves arranged for purposes of initiation.[144]

3) Since Venus is also related to the emasculation of the Nommo and the circumcision of the Fox (Venus *obia*), its position was used in the past to determine the date for the circumcision of men, whose "father" the resurrected Nommo is.

Raised stones in different places of the Sanga region commemorate the circumcision of the mythical ancestors: respectively, they represent Venus in *donno tolo* position for the operations of the *unum* and the *dene* (second and fourth generations), in *obia* position for those of the *tire* and the *kumo* (third and fifth generations).[145]

At present, the calendar is no longer used for circumciscions; the Dogon say that "one counts only the number of years" between two ceremonies.

---

144. Installment 2, eighth to eleventh years.

145. These raised stones are found at *polio kommo* (the locality of Bono) and at Gouwèlou (east of Lower Ogol, Pl. XIV, 1) for the *unum* and the *dene,* and behind Bara and at Songolou for the *tire* and the *kumo.* Cf. map II.

CHAPTER VI
THE CLOSING OF AMMA'S CLAVICLES

Descent of the *gaba* and the *anu*. The signs in Amma's clavicle. Amma closes himself again.

DESCENT OF THE GABA *AND THE* ANU.

After the descent of the Nommo's ark on the Earth of the Fox, and after the beings who had not been on the ark — Yasigui, the Griot, the Smith, the female twin of *o nommo*[1] — had descended in their turn, there remained in Amma's womb the seeds of *gaba* and *anu* that the *po* had neither taken into its coils when it rolled up, nor shed in the ark when it unrolled. These seeds, which Amma had not placed in the clavicles of the sacrificed Nommo, descended alone at the end of the cycle of Amma's second creation. They will germinate and multiply not only on Earth, where they will be given to mankind, but also on all the "superposed worlds" Amma had created.

The first signs denoting the presence of the *gaba* and *anu* inside Amma's egg were, as we recall, each made of four lines (*yala*) drawn in a vertical row. This position prefigured the future descent of these seeds upon the worlds Amma had created. Also, each group of *yala* represented the flow of blood during the sacrifice of the Nommo: the signs of the *gaba* prefigured the Nommo's "path of blood," *illi ozo*; those of the *anu* represent the flow of blood from the Fox's circumcision. Thus, the vital role of these two seeds as well as their association with the circulation of blood in living bodies is emphasized from their beginning.[2]

---

1. Installment 2, first year.

2. Cf. *supra,* fig. 15, p. 118 and fig. 122, p. 558; the position of the seeds of *ani* and *gaba* placed at the openings inside the *ginna* represents the position of the organs through which the blood circulates that carries the "word." With regard to the formation of the stars, we recall that the "path of the blood" is represented by the Milky Way. The evidence of the blood of the Fox is Mars, *yapunu tolo,* that is to say, only one planet, since (it is said that) "three *yala* were lost" (cf. *supra,* p. 270).

The word *gaba* comes from *gabu,* "extension, length."[3] For one says that, while turning, the *gaba* stretched out its stalk from Amma's head, leaving one fruit on each world. The movement the *gaba* made in order to descend on Amma's worlds was different from that of the *po*: whereas the *po* turned in a spiral (*digilemu*) (either on one plane or conically), the *gaba* only "turned around as it descended" (*tono lomu*). One says: "The *po* creating the world, it is by releas·ing (from within itself) the things that were in its body that it turned. When the *gaba* turned in the middle of the world, it carried its fruit down, then it descended (below); the *gaba* turns while holding on to its fruit."[4] This is to say that the *po* held all the things inside a circle (like a snake coiled in a circle), whereas the *gaba,* the image of Amma's womb, symbolically upholds the superposed worlds that emerged from it, as if by means of its stalk.

FIG: 184: Amma in the form of a cord lowering the *koro kunu.*

A schematic figure recalls the descent of the *gaba*: it is called "Amma (become cord) lowering the *koro kunu*"[5] (fig. 184). The calabash is represented by the upper circle (which is also the sky) prolonged by the axis of the descent; the lower circle is the *gaba koro kunu.*

Amma had created the world inside the primordial *gaba* and, in the first place, the *po*. The things that emerged from the *po* had spread out inside the *gaba* before being placed on the Nommo's ark. The full

---

3. In speaking of a rope, a stick, or any thin, upright object. When it is laid out on the ground, one says *pala.*

4. *po ganna digilemi gozu vomo-ne kize to pazau digilemi. gaba ganna tonou i sunonou digiia sugi gaba i voma geleu tonolemi.*

5. *amma koro kunu sunonu.* See fig. 121, p. 369 for the above picture.

calabash had become *koro kunu*; the external outgrowths of this variety[6]
were evidence that the fruit had been filled with the entirety of Amma's
creation and that thereafter these things had come out. This is why the
"descent" of the empty calabash ends the creation: it is the testimony of
the whole thing. It also shows that the entire creation was of the same
origin and that all things were to remain together. "The *po pilu* was the
one who made the world (below), the *koro kunu* descended behind; in
the sky all things emerged from its insides. The *koro kunu* is the image of
the reunion of all things."[7]

The figure evinces both the shape of the fruit and the womblike role
of the primordial *gaba*.[8]

A ritual figure, called *"tonu* of Amma creating the whole superposed
world"[9] represents both the descent of the *gaba* and the space it covered
(fig. 185). At the top is "Amma's head" containing the calabash, *koro
kunu*; below is the egg with the clavicles supported by Amma's "nerves."
Inside are the seeds of the different calabash trees originating from the
very first one; the leaves and fruits have spread themselves out over the
different worlds. For when a piece of fruit on a calabash tree is formed,
one says: "Behold, the *gaba* has brought down its fruit."[10]

On some altars to Amma, a small pot is placed on top to recall the
initial *gaba,* called *amma vonu,* "Amma scattered, multiplied (by opening
himself)."

To make two vessels, the calabash is cut along a great circle which
passes through the stalk and the bottom: the two halves are the image

---

6. Compared to the pimples on the skin caused by a disease called *kunu.*

7. *po pilu ganna vo ginnegili, koro kunu onune sugu; alagala-ne kize fu kolo vomo-ne
goy koro kunu kize fu mone yala.*

8. The vessel made of the calabash, *koro kunu,* is never impure, even if it has contained
impure *po* or if a shoemaker has used it. A priest may always drink from it. If one receives
seeds from this calabash, money or some other object must be given to the donor in
exchange, otherwise the seeds, whose *nyama* will then return to the donor, will produce
only ordinary calabash gourds.

9. *amma ganna gimme pu mani tonu.* Drawn during the foundation of a "house (for)
menstruating women," *yapunulu,* above the door. For the calabash belongs to woman: as
the image of Amma's womb, it is also "the womb where the world was formed."

10. *gaba i sunonou.* For the various types of calabash trees, cf. installment 2, first to sixth
years. The Dogon distinguish between twenty-two types of trees from which vessels are
made (gourds, spoons, calabashes) for different uses (the term includes melons).

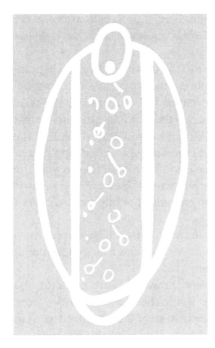

FIG. 185: *tonu* of Amma creating the entire superposed world.

of the sky and the Earth.[11]

The basic creative role of the *gaba* is recalled for a marriage. In addition to the siluri, the groom must offer his bride-to-be a calabash, a gourd, and a spoon upon her first menses. In the past, the calabash was decorated with twenty-two drawings symbolizing the contents of the *gaba* — Amma's "womb" — at the very beginning.

When the *gaba* opened up, the *anu* seeds then came out of it. They did not descend vertically like those of the *gaba,* but rather in a dispersed order. One says "that they jumped, flew, and that before they germinated on Earth, they first placed themselves at the edge of the Milky Way," where their image (*tonu*) spun around it like a crown.

The last to leave Amma's womb, the *anu* is considered to be the delegate of the *po* star, symbol of the "container" of the universe in formation and called *po tolo bolodige,* "follower of *po tolo.*" The *anu,* said to be the "head of the cereal grains,"[12] is the *po's* deputy. The *anu's* subordination to the *po* is remembered today by the fact that it is sown around all fields of millet as a guardian. In a sense, it replaces the *po,* which cannot be sown everywhere;[13] however, whereas the *po pilu* and *po tolo* at this stage of creation represented the organization of

11. The importance of the calabash is underscored by the fact that if one drops it, or if it receives a shock, breaks, and drops its seeds, one must then perform an *ozu di,* "water of the path," a libation of cereal porridge to the *manes* of the deceased poured on the ground in the direction of the cemetery.

12. *anu dene ku.*

space and time as well as the overall movement of the universe and of the life in living matter, the *anu* symbolizes the classification of the elements composing that universe, a classification whose model is that of the eight seeds in Amma's womb.

Therefore, the *anu* will give its name to the clavicle, *ani guyo,* ("granary of the *anu* seed"), which will contain the symbols of the essential elements of creation, the eight primordial seeds. For mankind, this term implies the classification of symbols inside the clavicles, for their name and position vary with the sex, social situation, and craft or skill of the bearer. It is a euphemism: the clavicle could also be called "granary of the *po,*" an expression emphasizing the essential role of the *po pilu,* the first germ to contain life, i.e., the creative "word." However, its name is not used, so as never to confuse the *po pilu* with the impure *po banu* of the Fox.

There are four basic types of calabash trees on Earth: *gaba na* or *koro kunu, koro pomu, koro kinugu, koro kembogu*; and four types of *anu: anu na, anu golo, anu gonnoru, anu gogobolo.*[14]

We know that the "drawings" (*toy*) of these seeds are made on the ground on either side of the entrances inside the *ginna,* where — from another viewpoint — they connote the position of the internal organs in the human body, taken as the model for the design of the house.[15]

For the "souls" of those seeds that did not descend with the ark and that germinated not only on Earth, but also on the other "superposed worlds" of Amma, are not in the Nommo's possession; these spiritual principles are held by Amma himself. On Earth, men — and in this particular case, the patriarch of the *ginna* — are their guardians. The seeds are kept in the dwelling from the harvest until the following sowing season under the supervision of the head of the family, who is responsible for them. Those for the *gaba* — formerly encrusted into the clay on the façade — are presently kept in the upper granary of the dwelling, the *dele.* The *anu* seeds are kept in the left-hand *kana* of the

---

13. Normally, *po* and *anu* should be sown in the same field. However, the *anu* has been separated from the *po* to be sown around the millet. Sowing *anu* is just like sowing *po,* but without the inconvenience of the latter's presence since, due to the tiny size of the seed, one never knows if the impure *po banu* of the Fox is mixed in with the other varieties.

14. These basic varieties will produce other varieties.

15. Cf. *supra.* p. 558, fig. 122.

ginna, for "in Amma's womb the calabash contained the *anu*"; in the dwelling the vessels made from the calabash tree will contain the *anu,* the first food of the ancestors who descended on the ark.

A figure drawn with porridge of *yu* and *ara* in the *kana* recalls the position of the *anu* inside the *gaba* and the presence of the souls of these seeds in the *ginna.* One says of this figure: "In the drawing of the *gaba* of the *kana,* it is like the *kikinu* of the *gaba* seeds which are in Amma's egg."[16] Because of this, the *ginna bana,* who is the officiant of the dwelling and who keeps the seeds and the spiritual principles of the *gaba* and *anu* in his home, is "Amma's witness," *amma seru.* One says of him: *"amma seru* (who is) like Amma keeps the *kikinu* of the *gaba* and the *anu*; the *ginna bana* is the guardian of the souls of the *gaba* and the *anu.* "[17]

After the descent of the *gaba* and *anu,* all Amma's designs were realized; the whole universe had come out of his womb.

Amma's open clavicles, surrounded by figures recalling the essential elements of his work, are represented by a figure in black, called "drawing of the center of the formation of Amma's world,"[18] formerly drawn on the ceiling of the cave of the masks in Upper Ogol (fig. 186). The four open clavicles show the cardinal directions; at the collateral directions we find: to the northwest, the resurrected Nommo (in human form); to the southwest, the Fox; to the northeast, the ark "bitten" by the *barankamaza*; to the southeast, man.

THE SIGNS IN AMMA'S CLAVICLES.

Everything having been accomplished, Amma decided to keep to himself the twenty-two principal signs representing the elements and essential stages of the second creation and also the "life" of the universe; he placed these signs in his open clavicles at the four cardinal points.

---

16. *gaba tonu kana-ne dene kikinu amma talu gaba to tozey.*

17. *gaba-le anu-le kikinu, amma seru amma tozogo belley kikinu gele. ginna bana gaba kikinu-le anu kikinu-le vo gele.*

18. *amma aduno manu logoron toy.* Related to the ceremonies of the *dama* of the ancestor Dyongou Sérou, this painting's function will be presented in installment 2, third and fourth years.

N

FIG. 186: Drawing of the center of the formation of Amma's world.

Amma's action is represented by a figure called "drawing of what Amma kept (after having) created things and (having) made them come out,"[19] drawn only once for each totemic sanctuary the second year after its con-

---

19. *amma kize manu gona vazu uo geli toy.* Drawn with porridge of *ara geu* and *yu* above the holes in the façade (representing *emme ya tolo* and *po tolo*, which are "invisible" in the sky) during the *duguru* ceremony, when a new priest of the Tiré totem is ordained, and beneath the *sogo* of Gomtogolo.

This drawing is also made on the construction site of the family dwelling; it is then very large and determines the dwelling's diameter, with the center post being placed in the middle of the *amma doy* (installment 2, first year and ff.).

N

FIG. 187: Drawing of what Amma kept (after having) created things
and (having) made them come out.

struction — on the inside, because it represents "what remains in Amma's
hands and will not come out" (fig. 187).

The figure shows the clavicles wide open and oriented, placed around a circle representing "Amma's seat," *amma doy,* or "seat of the inside," *kolo doy,* or again "birth of Amma's liver," *amma kinne nani.* Compared to the preceding figures, this circle is very small to emphasize that Amma's womb had emptied itself of all creation and even of the signs, thus being reduced to nothing but itself.

The north clavicle contains the following figures:

— the great male Nommo of the sky, *nommo die;*

— the four *unum:* Amma Sérou, Binou Sérou, Lébé Sérou, and Dyongou Sérou;

— the four-legged creatures, winged creatures, and plants;

— the male seeds stolen by Ogo;

— the female seeds not stolen by Ogo.

In the south:

— the four female twins of the *unum;*

— the female Nommo, twin of the *nommo die;*

— the *po pilu.*

In the west:

— the Fox;

— the Fox's placenta, i.e., the sun.

In the east:

— the sacrificed Nommo;

— the sacrificing Nommo;

— two *anagonno sala* which represent the two first twin fishes born from the resurrected Nommo in the water of the pond (shown in human form).

Regarding the form and content of these signs, the ones that Amma kept correspond to the twenty-two *yala* of the body of the *po* in the primordial spiral. "In Amma's egg, twenty-two *yala* of the body of the *po* became the *tonu.*"[20] The correspondences established between the twenty-two signs of the open clavicles are as follows, starting from the center of the spiral:

to the north: the first six are the great male Nommo, the four male *unum,* and the male seeds; the seventh is the female seeds; the eighth, ninth, and tenth are the four-legged creatures, winged creatures, and

---

20. *amma ene talu-ne pelley ley sige po gozu-ne yala tobe tonu.* These words are recited by the totemic priest when he draws the figure. For the sixty-six *yala* of the initial spiral, cf. *supra,* p. 121.

plants;

to the east: the eleventh is the sacrificing Nommo, the twelfth the victim, the thirteenth the male *anagonno,* the fourteenth the female *anagonno*;

to the west: the fifteenth is the Fox, the sixteenth the placenta/sun;

to the south: the seventeenth is the female Nommo, the next are the four female twins of the *unum,* the twenty-second is the *po.*

However, with regard to the entire set of these signs, it is said of this figure that "the drawings which are on each side, (it is) that (there are) twelve signs"; in other words, "each drawing contains twelve signs." "The drawings of the things which are in Amma's clavicles (are) symbolically 264."[21]

Thus, the twenty-two graphic symbols of the figure, kept by Amma within himself and reduced to the number of categories that he had established at the beginning, theoretically represent the 264 + 2 primordial "signs."

The star *po tolo* will be the celestial evidence of the twenty-two signs kept by Amma as well as evidence of the *po,* the germ of the universe.[22]

AMMA CLOSES HIMSELF AGAIN.

Once the signs were in place, Amma closed himself again, keeping to himself one "half" of the life of the world. The clavicles folded themselves up and the whole thing again took on the initial egg-shape: but, on the outside, four lines of separation could be seen recalling the opening. This final stage of Amma's work is represented by a figure called "drawing of Amma who has sat down and closed up after he had finished molding the world,"[23] which is drawn facing east on the square block of stone placed on the spot called *amma doy,* beneath which the diagrams of the 266 primordial "signs" have been drawn.[24] It is drawn with porridge made of four cereal grains (*po pilu, emme ya, yu* and *ara*) that are proof of the fundamental presence of the four elements and it marks

---

21. *tana tuturu tonu to pelu ley. ley sige tonu to. kize tonu amma ani guyo-ne to pelu ley sige aduno so-ne sunu tanu pelley nay sige.*

22. This star will be visible next to Sirius for 240 years. On its appearance to man on Earth, cf. installment 2, first year.

23. *amma ganna mana doga timmera dayi toy.* Cf. installment 2, twelfth year.

24. Cf. *supra,* p. 103.

both the closing of the clavicles and the oneness of Amma; it also recalls the form of the altars that are consecrated to him (fig. 188).[25]

FIG. 188: Drawing of Amma who has sat down and closed up after he had finished molding the world.

Since that time, Amma lives in space "in the middle" of the sky, at the center of the cardinal points, from where he oversees the universe: "His eye is on the world."[26]

_{*}

The design of the dwelling and annexes of the Hogon of Arou, the religious leader of the Dogon, recalls this final stage of Amma's deeds (fig. 189).

With its façade to the east, the dwelling is composed of an entrance way, two lateral recesses, *kana,* and a larger rectangular room at the back. The design of this dwelling is the image of a man who is "seated" with his arms at his side, thus representative of Amma himself in his stability and permanence. On both sides of the doorways leading to each of the three rooms from the entrance, the *toy* of the seeds of the trees marking the resurrection of the Nommo were drawn when the house was built; they are, respectively, the *pelu* (1), the *kilena* (2), the *sa* (3), the *yullo* (4), the *oro* (5), and the *minu* (6). The presence of these pictures in the dwelling of the highest dignitary of the Dogon constitutes a permanent purification of the place in which he lives.[27]

---

25. The altars to Amma are made of a vertically placed stone, covered with clay and given an egg-shape (pl. V). The stone and the earth are taken from the edge of a pond. The clay contains some elements related to its particular function: thus, the clay of the *amma* of the *ginna* contains all varieties of cereal grains; the stone that has been covered with it represents the *nommo die* (installment 2, first year).

26. *giri vomo aduno-ne vo.*

An allusion to Amma's immortality and stability is expressed when one greets, or says goodbye to, a friend or relative: "may immortal Amma keep you seated" (*amma nono doy uy dana*).

27. During the first rite of ordination (*pagu*) for a new Hogon, the officiant purifies the dignitary's tongue with *kilena* charcoal and his body with *pelu* bark before hanging the insignia of his office (the *dugo*) on his wrist. He uses the millstone to crush some small

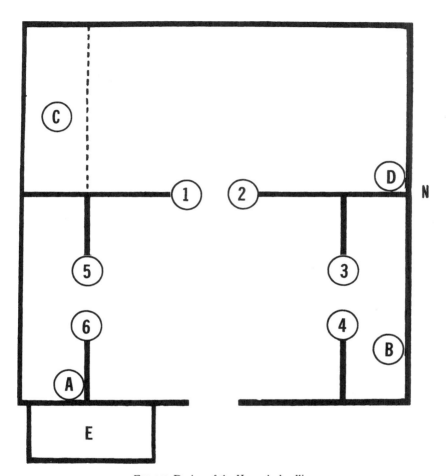

FIG. 189: Design of the Hogon's dwelling.

millet, *yu*; the flour is mixed with that of *oro* fruit and then both with water, in which *sa* fruits have been soaked, to make an uncooked dish. A sauce is made with *yullo* seed. A disk of *ara geu* is also prepared and seasoned with *minu* butter. During the second rite of ordination (*duguru*), the uncooked dish is made of rice and *yu* to which unfermented *yu* beer (*pipilu*) is added, some of which has been poured on the altar of Lébé. The dignitary also eats a plate of cooked *ara geu* seasoned with *minu* butter. In both instances, these two dishes, one uncooked and the other cooked, and made from plants related to the resurrection of *o nommo*, bring about the purification of the internal organs of the dignitary who absorbs them.

The jar containing the Hogon's drinking water is placed in the back room (at D): on the spot where it is placed a figure is drawn representing the head of the resurrected Nommo.[28]

The main altar of the Dogon, called *de lebe, "lebe* of the inside," is placed (at A) in the room to the left (the right "arm") where no one may enter except the Hogon and his sacrificer, the totemic priest who assists him. This altar, as we recall, represents the female *po pilu*; it was built on a figure representing the completion of the *po pilu* seed, the germ of the world, inside of which was life, that is, the creative "word," in the form of seven segments which grew in a spiral.[29] In the room to the right (the left "arm"), the Hogon's drum is placed (at B). In the back room, above the dignitary's bed (at C), hangs the "Hogon's horn" *ogo buru*; it is sounded during ceremonies he conducts and it proclaims "the voices of the *po*" or the spoken "word" that has become sound.[30]

Amma's placenta is represented by a figure drawn on the façade when the priest is ordained; it represents the bonnet of the Hogon and also the "bonnet-shaped yeast container" (*buzuru goro*),[31] which has four pendants (fig. 190).

The bonnet itself represents Amma's placenta, the tuft at the top its "point of attachment"; the four pendants are the four *nommo anagonno* originating from the first placenta. The bonnet itself is drawn in a square representing Amma's dwelling, also represented by the Hogon's platform (fig. 189E). In the middle of the bonnet, a schematic figure represents the Hogon; to the right, first the *bonno gamma* blanket, the image of the field of Lébé, then his stick; to the left, his insignia (*dugo*); below is his sandal.

Above the head of the person is the sun, the remnant of the Fox's placenta, surrounded by twenty-two rays. This sun also represents the

---

28. With porridge of *ara banu*: the head is made of seven strokes which here represent the seven piles made from the body divided into sixty parts.

29. Cf. *supra,* p. 416.

30. Cf. *supra,* p. 441. In this chapter, we give only a single (but essential) part of the symbolism connected with the morphology of the Hogon's dwelling, the part which serves our immediate purpose. A complete description of this dwelling, its courtyard, its annexes, and the paintings of the façade and platform will be published in installment 2, second year.

31. Drawn with rice porridge. In the past, this figure was drawn on all the dwellings of the Hogons. At Sanga, it was drawn on the base of the platform.

headrest (*ku tunuru*) of the Hogon. Each ray of this figure, called *aduno numo,* "hand of the world," ends in a "hand," which is shown open,

FIG. 190: Bonnet-shaped yeast container.

but with closed fingers. These are Amma's "hands" that hold the hands of human beings, that is, their "life" — the life he will take back from them at the time of their death.[32] This figure denotes Amma's absolute power over the beings he created and over the universe.

Outside the dwelling and against the left recess, is a platform (fig. 189E) where the Hogon remains seated during most of the day. He may not go out of the settlement where he lives and must observe a great many prohibitions. He is, on Earth, the guardian of the wholeness of the *po pilu.* Inside the dwelling — as he is the image of the stability of Amma who is "seated" while he preserves the creative "word" and the germ from which the universe came, the image also of his power and immortality — the dignitary, who assumes the highest religious responsibility among the Dogon, also remains "seated."

The dignitary's house faces an enormous courtyard, where a hollow has been dug that represents the primordial pond. On the other side of the courtyard, on the steep rocky slope located to the east, is placed the altar to Amma called *manna amma*; it is not to be seen by visitors, only the Hogon and his sacrificer having access to this place. A figure was drawn under the altar when its foundation was laid, called "drawing of *manna amma* below (which represents) Amma who brought people into the world."[33] It depicts the elements, the cardinal directions, and the distribution through space of the human races, represented by the four great Dogon tribes (fig. 191).

In the middle, in white, is Amma's seat, *amma doy.* The wavy white line to the north is "air," the blue lines to the east, "water," the red line to the south "fire." The "earth" is shown to the west by a black rectangle, which is the placenta of the Fox. The four colors of the four series of ten dots forming the outside circle situate the first four lineages in the four collateral directions.[34]

The Hogon's granary is part of the annexes and represents the ark on the ground. The door of this building closes an opening that was left in the wall that faces the south.

This granary contains the harvest from the field of Lébé which is assigned to the dignitary: a tiny part of the harvest (which has been threshed) is used for his personal consumption: the rest is kept, year

---

32. A detailed commentary will be given in installment 2, third year.

33. *amma aduno-ne innu deli manna amma donune tonu.*

34. For the Earth, the placenta of the Fox, and for the value of the number 10, cf. *infra,* p. 208 and p. 468.

after year, ultimately to serve in the preparation of the beer and food offered at his funeral.

The door, made of *pelu* wood in the prescribed manner, is also decorated in an equally prescribed manner with relief motifs recalling the mythical social structure of the Dogon. (Pl. XXIV).

Above, to the left, is a figure of the female twin of the Nommo of the pond, *o nommo,* sacrificed and resurrected in the sky for the purification of the world, the "ancestor" of man. His presence denotes the first generation, that of the "fathers" (*bau*).

At the same level are the first human couple and the "twins" descendent from them (ideal birth). Finally, eight personages (two above, six below) are the eight ancestors of humanity (male and female) marking the first four lineages; they are the members of the second generation, the "sons," *unum.*

Similarly, above and to the right is the *o nommo* at the center; then, on his right, the human couple who begat the first *kuno* (child born without the appearance of menses since the preceding delivery), whose birth is as important as that of the twins.

With regard to the generations, the twelve figures of equal size (on the right panel, in three rows: one on top, six in the middle, and five below) mark the third generation, the "grandsons," *tire.*

The four turtles (two on the right and two on the left) above, are land turtles, *agunuru*; they mark the four original lineages, for a land turtle lives in the *ginna* of every lineage; it is related to the status of the patriarch.[35]

Sculpted on the handle are the water turtle, *kiru,* who descended on Earth, and the ark bearing the eight ancestors (the eight segments of the zigzag line), represented by the entire figure. The ark is the image of the "cultivated fields," the purification of which the turtle guarantees.

To the right of the handle are the couples of the first two totemic prohibitions common to all four lineages: the antelope *valu* (male and female) and the bird *donu* (male and female).

Below, to the left, are the land lizard *ay* and the water lizard *ugunu,* marks of the "walk" of the resurrected *o nommo* on the earth before he entered the water, his domain; to the right, the crocodile, *o nommo's*

---

35. Cf. *supra,* p. 221.

executioner. These animals are also the prohibited items of a great number of clans.

The two series of seven chevrons sculpted in relief vertically are the seven articulations of the "word," the one that was revealed to the ancestors (to the right) and the one that was kept by Amma (to the left).

Thus, this door schematically sums up the principal mythical events which precede and follow the creation of man in the sky and his descent on Earth. It is testimony to the existence of the four first lineages represented by the four tribes of the Dogon of the present time, to the structure of totemism, and to the fundamental role of agriculture, the basic skill of the Dogon.[36]

Amma gave almost all his powers to the Nommo, his deputies, to whom he entrusted the progress and growth of the universe and the care of living creatures: the *nommo die,* who resides with him in the sky, is the guardian of the spiritual principles of food plants, especially of the eight primordial seeds; the *nommo titiyayne* carries out the latter's orders and serves as an intermediary; *o nommo* lives in the waters on the Earth, where he holds the spiritual principles of people, his descendants. Amma will be invoked by people in all situations and in all their prayers, but, for the most part, he will not intervene directly; when a sacrifice is offered on the altars bearing his name, his deputies will be called upon, for they have — by his will — the power to act. He retains only the duty of taking care of the dead, since death is later to appear in this universe, particularly on the Earth of the Fox.

The whole life of this second creation is present in "Amma's egg": its guarantee lies within the twenty-two signs inscribed in the closed-up clavicles, which thus remain in the womb of the creator. Therefore, the closed egg of Amma is called "egg of Amma guardian of the world."[37]

After every sixty-year ceremony of the Sigui celebrating the end of one cycle and the beginning of another (sixty being the so-called "number of the placenta"), the participants purify their bodies with

---

36. As for the *ginna,* we give here only those representations (related to the morphology of the Hogon's dwelling and its annexes) which serve our immediate purpose. A more complete description will be given in installment 2, third year.

37. *amma aduno domo talu.*

twenty-two cowries: in this instance, these represent the twenty-two *yala* of the spiraling center of the original *po pilu* which became the twenty-two *tonu,* symbols of the life of the universe kept in the closed-up clavicles of the creator.[38] Similarly, the final rites performed for every deceased are in accordance with this view, for Amma's deed is recalled by placing the funeral urn (*bunno*) in the family sanctuary, *vageu.* When he makes the sacrifice over the pottery, the officiant says: "The pots of the dead that we place is like putting (the dead) inside Amma's egg which opened to make the world and closed again."[39]

All the symbolism of the ritual objects of the sanctuary is related to the death and resurrection of the Nommo; the final act of placing the *bunno* is equivalent to putting the deceased in the womb containing the signs, guardians of the life of the universe, as if for a promise of resurrection.

The absolute possession of the "signs" ensuring the life of the second world also gives Amma the power to destroy his work at will. Should he wish to suppress it, he will destroy the signs: at that time, the closed womb will become "the empty egg of Amma who destroyed the life of the world."[40] One sometimes says that Amma will destroy the universe by burning it, he himself being "like fire." However, one adds that he will keep half the life of the second realized world so as to make a third one from it.

"When Amma created the world, he kept the life of the world; to keep the life of the world, Amma drew each (thing) in its place and closed (again); Amma drew the life of the world in the flat clavicles and closed them (like the fruit of the papaya); when Amma drew the life of the things in the world, he drew half (of the life) which he gave away and half which he kept; Amma, by making his clavicles turn, sent half (by dividing in half) the life of the things into the world; Amma, to bring an end to the world (to destroy it), drew half of the life of the world that he

---

38. One then places these cowries in an ant hill of the *key* ant to "return them to Amma." For the *key* ant, on Earth, saved the grains stolen by the Fox (cf. p. 231). For the ant hill, cf. also p. 498.

39. *inneu yimu bunno danani, amma ene talu aduno mana timmera inne yimu vogo kolo-ne to anay.*

40. *amma aduno kinu vo gammali talu kolo.*

has (to himself); he will destroy (he will cause the destruction of) the world (which then) will be finished.[41]

---

41. *amma ganna vo mani ganna kinu gelyase; amma ganna kinu vo gelie tuturu yalu vomo-ne tonu timmira; amma ani guyo kabrio aduno kinu tona timmeri; amma aduno kize kinu vo tonu fetere oba fetere tona geli; amma ani guyo vomo digileme aduno kize-ne kinu fetere kana ti* (or *gammala*); *amma aduno dononoydo aduno kinu tonu fetere vo se yammalu vo ti aduno dogoze.*

LIST OF ANIMALS

agunuru	land turtle.
ay	water reptile, *Varanus exanthematicus* (Bosc.).
ayo geu	black crocodile.
azagay	earwig, *Forficula senegalensis* (dermapter).
barankamaza	generic name for a category of water insects.
	barankamaza dullogu, "tailed" *barankamaza.*
dada	spider (name of species).
	dada ogo or *dada yurugu geze gozene,* "Hogon spider" or "spider that weaves the thread of the Fox," *Argiopod.*
donu, dou	(undetermined) blue and white bird, commonly found throughout the Niger region, which migrates to the torrents of Sanga during the rainy season.
ene	fowl.
	ene ana ene: male = rooster.
	ene ana dazu: "flat-crested rooster" = red rooster.
	ene ana seruve: rooster with a vertical, jagged crest (*seruve*: which stands up straight).
kaka	grasshopper (generic name).
	kaka bolomo toru: "grasshopper with long hindquarters" or "straw grasshopper," *Gastrimargus* Sp. or *Oedalus senegalensis. kaka amma giru*: "grasshopper eye of Amma." *kaka kolo kayaze*: "grasshopper that eats raw."
key	ant (generic name).
	key kile: "winged ant."
keke	insect (generic name).
	keke bana gummolo: "spotty hunchbacked insect."
	keke gummolomo: "hunchbacked insect,"
	Gymnopleurus fugidis.
	minne iru keke: "insect of the smiths of the earth," *Chlaenius* Sp. or *Zophosis* Sp. *keke kummoy*: "closed" or "hunchbacked" insect, *Agnoscelis versicolor* (*Hem. Pentatomidae*).
kibizu	tick, in general.
kiru	water turtle.
ki selu	sea shell.
na	cow.
nay	lizard, *Hemitheconyx caudicinctus.*

nay na	cricket, "mother of the sun," *Scotinophora fibulata* (*Hem. Pentatonidae*).
ogodine	chameleon, *Chamaeleo senegalensis,* Daudin.
polyo (Bambara)	*Heterobranchus bidorsalis.*
so, suru	horse.
	so sade: horse with a blaze.
tu	termite.
	tu penu: "termite outgrowth," variety of termite that makes a termite hill of the same name.
	tu tuluku: another name for this termite.
ugunu	land reptile.
vevele	swallow.
valu	horse-antelope, *Hippotragus aguinus.*
yuguru	snake (generic name).
yuguru na	python, "large snake."
yurugu	fox, *Vulpes pallidus.*

LIST OF PLANTS

alumi	"sad," *Vitex diversigolia* Baker *cienkowskii.*
anu	hibiscus, *Hibiscus abelmoschus esculentus,* commonly called "sorrel."
	anu na: "big *hibiscus.*"
	anu banu: "red *hibiscus.*"
	anu golo: "hibiscus emerged (the first)."
	anu gonnoru: "twisted *hibiscus.*"
	anu gogobolo: "very tall *hibiscus.*"
	anu pilu: Hibiscus asper Hook. "white *hibiscus.*"
	solo anu: "hibiscus of the bush," *Cochlospermum tinctorium.*
ara	rice. *Oryza.*
	ara pilu: white rice.
	ara geu: "black" rice, *Oryza glabberima,* Steud.
	ara banu: "red" rice.
	kumo ara: "rice of the crested crane."
aza pelu	"acid cailcidrate." *Cassia nigricans.*
atay	undetermined.
bala	Acacia arabica (mimosa).
bey	Abrus precatorius, Linn.
bi	Scleriocarya birrea, Hochst.
bozo kubo	"foot of the dung" (undetermined).
dolo	Acacia rehmaniana.
dolumgolo	undetermined.
elie ni	oil peanut, *Arachis hypogea.*
emme	sorghum, *Sorghum vulgaris.*
	emme di giru: "eye of the water" sorghum.
	emme pilu: "white *emme.*"
	emme banu: "red *emme.*"
	emme nakolo: "nurse-mother *emme.*"
	emme ya: "female *emme.*"
	sana emme: sorghum of Sanga.
	emme dum(mu) ban(u) dorubo: "red, soft platform *emme.*"
	emme sono dum(mu) ban(u): "platform of the boulder *emme.*"
ezegele	*Eragrotis gangetica.*
ga guyo	*Ficus capensis dicranostyla.*
gaba	calabash tree, *Citrullus vulgaris,* Schrad.
	koro kunu: "bumpy calabash."

koro pomu: "oval calabash."

koro kinugu: "calabash with a nose."

koro kembogu: "navel-gourd calabash."

gaba dogo: "broken calabash."

gala	indigo-tree, indigo, *Indigofera suffruticosa* (all varieties).
gerelle	plant used for dyeing (undetermined).
gobu pilu	*Guiera senegalensis*, Lamk.
gobu banu	from *gobolu*, height, stature, and *banu*, red. Undetermined.
gono	squash.
inu banuma	"which reddens the teeth" *Commiphora africana*, Eng.
kenie	*Indigofera viscosa*.
kilena	"mother of the charcoal." *Prosopis africana*.
kinu bommo	*Urginea altissima*, Baker.
kolumo ana	*Cenchrus prieurii*.
kolumo ya	*Cenchrus biflorus*, Roxb.
kulu	water lily, *Nymphea lotus*.
kummo	*Ficus umbellata*.
kummu	*Ficus platyphylla*.
kuyo	*Combretum micranthum*.
keu kuzo	"stem of the arrow," *Sesbania aegyptiaca*.
minu	*karite, Achras parkii*.
mono	"sticky," *Balanites aegyptiaca*.
namu	cotton, cotton bush.

namu-i: cotton bush seed.

namu na: big cotton bush (tree), *Gossypium arboreum*.

nu	bean, *Vigna unguilata*, Wolp.

nu ninu: "luck bean."

nu daydolo (or *daytolo*): "bean that does not kill."

nu seru.

nu banu: "red bean."

nu pilu: "white bean."

nu teu.

dunu nu: Rhynchosia caribae.

nu geu: "black bean."

ogo dala	*Cissus quadrangularis*.
olo	"plant of the bush," *Stipa parviflora*.
ommolu	tamarind tree, *Tamarindus indica*.
oro	baobab, *Andansonia digitata*.
pelu	cailcidrate, *Kokya senegalensis*.
po	fonio, *Digitaria exilis*.

po pilu: "white fonio."

po na: "great (large) fonio."

po banu: "red fonio."

po yayuguzu: "fonio of the wicked woman."

tenu po: "fonio of the south."

po te pilu: "quick-growing fonio."

pogo	*Dichrostachys glomerata.*
poli	sesame, *Sesanum radiatum.*
	poli ni: sesame oil.
pollo	*Hibiscus cannabinus*, Linn.
ponu	*Detarium minocarpum.*
sa	*Lannea acida.*
saguba	*Vetiveria nigritana.*
sana ya	"sifting, female," *Schoenfeldia gracilis*, Kunth.
sana ana	"sifting, male." A grass whose stalk is used to make brooms.
sana vonu	*Digitaria marginata.*
saselu	*Boscia salicifolia*, Oliver.
satele	*Bauhinia rufescens*, Lam.
segele	*Fluggea virosa.*
sene	Acacia, *Acacia* (Faidherbia) *albida.*
	sene gomuzu: "hollow acacia," supple and pliable.
	sene benu: "stout acacia."
	sene urio: "acacia that bows its head," a shrub.
	sene mime: "spinning acacia."
senebe	Acacia, *Acacia senegalensis*, Willd.
si	*Celtis integrifolia*, Lam.
siu	palmyra (or borassus palm) tree, *Borassus flabellifer.*
ta boy	"drum of the hyena"; this group includes all mushrooms.
tara onuge	"jujube tree of the hyena," *Zyziphus mucronata.*
tenu	*Elaeopherbia drupifera.*
togozo	kapok tree, *Bombax buonopozense.*
volo geu	"thorny black," *Acacia pennata.*
volo pilu	"thorny white."
yayaga	*Stylosanthes guineensis.*
yoro geu or	
yoru na	"black fiber," *Grewia* bicolor.
yu	small millet, *Pennisetum spicatum.*
	yu pilu: "white millet."
	yu tolone peze: "millet that jumps."
	yu donno: "millet of the west."
	yu tolone peze yu: "millet that jumps less."
	yu toroy: "millet of the Toro of the lower cliff."
	bobo yu: "millet of the Bobo."
	sana yu: "millet of Sanga."
	yu dineu: "twin millet," double ear of millet.
	yu gay: millet harvested by the women and children since it is cut without a sickle.
	yu debe: small millet that grows without being sown.
	yu nene or *telle yu*: "yu of the Tellem"; millet that grows after the harvest or on an already cut stem.
	manu yu: "millet of the plain."
yullo	*Parkia biglobosa*, flamboyant.

LIST OF HEAVENLY BODIES

aduno giri	"eye of the world," Polestar.
aduno giri ley	"second eye of the world," Southern Cross.
albararu	Sirius, cf. *sigi tolo.*
amma bogu tolo	"stars of Amma's navel," four stars of the Chariot of Orion.
ara tolo	"rice star," undetermined.
atanu tolo	"stars three," Orion's belt.
bala tolo	"star of the *bala* tree," a satellite of Jupiter.
bayara	"moment just after midnight," a position of Venus, cf. *yazu.*
dana tolo	"star of the fontanel," Jupiter.
dige tanu	"star of midnight," a position of Venus.
donno tolo	"star of the West," a position of Venus.
du tolo	"star of the East," the name given to rising planets.
emme ya tolo	"star of (the) female sorghum," the second "Companion" (?) (or satellite) of Sirius.
enegirim tolo	"star of the goatherds," a position of Venus.
enegirine tolo	"star of the goatherd," V of Canus Minor.
gerelle tolo	"star of (the) *gerelle,"* a satellite of Jupiter.
ie or *ie pilu*	the moon.
	ie pilu tolo: "star of the moon."
	ie turu: first moon.
nay	the sun.
	du nay: "sun of the East," rising sun.
	du daga nay: "sun of the North," summer solstice.
	nay logorone: "sun of the middle," equinox.
	nay nummay: "the sun has fallen," sunset.
	tenulu nay: "sun of the South," winter solstice.
	nay tummogu: (when) "the sun grows," sunrise.
olo	"dark," new moon.
po tolo	"star of the fonio," first "companion" of Sirius.
sene tolo	"star of the acacia," a satellite of Jupiter.
sigi tolo	"star of the Sigui," Sirius.
tara tolo	"star of the hyena," Procyon (brightest star in Canus Minor).
tolo	star.
	tolo bani nenneu: "sparkling red star," in the constellation of Taurus.
	tolo dombolo or *dommolo:* "hook star," undetermined.
	tolo dullogu: "tail stars," stars of Orion's sword.

tolo duno: "grouped stars," the Pleiades.

tolo gonoze: "star that goes around," general term for a satellite.

tolo tanaze: "star that crosses (the sky)," general term for a planet.

yalu ulo   "bounds of space," the Milky Way.

yalu ulo tolo "star of the Milky Way," Saturn (?).

yapunu da tolo   "star of the dish of the menstruating women," a position of Venus.

yapunu tolo   "star of the menstruating women," Mars.

yara tolo   "star of the lion" (β of the constellation Aries.)

yazu   (early in) "the morning," Venus.

yazu always means Venus. The other names designate its special positions. *yazu* and *bayara* both signify the same position of the star.

yazu danala tolo: "star accompanying Venus," undetermined.

yu tolo   "star of the millet."

APPENDICES

THE VULPES PALLIDUS.

ST.-GEORGE MIVART — *A Monograph of the Canidae*. London, 1890, Porter and Dulan and Co., p. 142.

ANDERSON. J. — Revised by de Winston, Zoology of Egypt, *Mammalia*, London, 1902, Hugh Rees, Ltd., p. 232.

THOMAS. B. — Some notes on the small sand-foxes of North Africa, *Ann. Mag. Nat. Hist.*, London, ( ), I, 1918, 242-245.

THOMAS. O. and HINTON. M.A.C. — Captain Angus Buchanan's Air Expedition II. On the mammals, other than ruminants, obtained during the expedition to Air (Asben), *Nov. Zool. Tring*, no. 28, 1921, 1-13.

MALBRANT. R. — *La faune du Centre africain français* (Paris, 1936, Paul Lechevallier), p. 124.

ALLEN. G.L. — Checklist of African Mammals, (Cambridge, Mass., 1939), p. 196.

DEKEYSER. P.L. — *Les mammifères de l'Afrique Noire française*, Dakar, 1955, IFAN, Initiations africaines.

We have taken from P.L. DeKeyser's work, *Les mammifères de l'Afrique Noire française*, the passage of the *vulpes pallidus*.

The blond desert fox (*Vulpes pallidus*) is rarely more than fifty centimeters long without the tail; overall, his coat is a brownish tan. Weight: 2 kg.

Sub-species: — *Vulpes pallidus edwardsi*, Rochebrune (Sahelian and sahelo-soudanese regions of Senegal, Soudan, Nigeria). — *Vulpes pallidus harterti*, Thomas and Hinton (Damxergou, Air). — *Vulpes pallidus oertzeni*, Matschie (northeast of Bornou, Chad to the Tibesti) the foxes of the region of Gaya, Niger, are related to this subspecies.

Little is known about the biology of African foxes. The blond fox lives in families in lairs with tunnels 10 to 15 m. long, branching into small chambers filled with bedding of dry straw. (Bigourdan and Prunier). Its food includes rodents, lizards, domestic and wild birds. Malbrant adds that it sometimes eats wild watermelon. The genetic make-up of the starveling fox is 40 chromosomes (Matthey, 1954).[1]

---

1. p. 253.

CHARACTERISTICS OF THE PALE FOX
ACCORDING TO THE OBSERVATIONS OF THE DOGON

Vulpes pallidus feeds mainly on toads, some lizards (*bayaga*), and insects,[2] especially *ka boy* and *keke gummolomo*. Apparently, the animal never goes to the edge of ponds; it drinks water from puddles in the rocks. It is believed that it goes almost completely without water during the dry season. Generally speaking, it hates water, and when rain floods its lair, it hurries to dry it by scraping the dry earth to cover up the wet part.

Apparently, the female has few whelps and never "twins." She has little milk, caring little for her offspring which, very soon after birth, feed on insects like the adults.

The fox is essentially a nocturnal animal which is never seen in the daytime.

MAN'S CLAVICLE

TESTUT. L. — *Traité d'anatomie humaine,* tome I, G. Doin et cie. éditeurs, Paris, 1948.

The clavicle is a long bone developed as a pair and consequently non-symmetrical, transversally extended, like a buttress, between the top of the sternum and the scapula. Shaped like an italic *S,* it has two distinct curvatures; an internal curvature with a concavity directed towards the back and an external curvature with a concavity directed to the front. Moreover, it is flat from top to bottom, thus offering for observation two sides, two edges, and two extremities (p. 310).

The development of the clavicle starts from two points of ossification, a primary and secondary center.

a) *Primary center:* It is intended for the body and the external extremity and appears towards the end of the fourth week: it is the first bone to appear on the skeleton. It develops at the point corresponding to the middle of the future clavicle and from there rapidly radiates to the extremities.

The clavicle differs from the other bones of the limbs in that it is not preceded by an outline of cartilage. The bony tissue which constitutes the primitive center mentioned above indeed begins amidst undifferentiated tissue and first grows at the expense of this tissue. Later, two small growths of cartilage appear on either side, which, as they lengthen determine the length of the bone, and ossify in their turn.

This mode of development is peculiar to the clavicle and is clearly explained by comparative anatomy. Among a great number of lower vertebrates, particularly among fish, the clavicle is a completely cutaneous and superficial bone. Among higher vertebrates, it reaches deeper levels and becomes connected to the skeleton: then, added to its tissue-like outline will be an outline of cartilage which ossifies, as do all parts of the

---

2. The very gluttonous fox sometimes vomits excess food which is absorbed on the divination tables, something which has allowed for many observations on its feeding habits.

cartilaginous skeleton. This is the case in man, whose clavicle is actually a composite bone, related to the outer (cover) bones by its primary bone center and to the skeleton proper by its cartilaginous outline.

b) *Secondary center*: The secondary or complementary center does not appear until the age of twenty to twenty-two years. It begins in the middle of the internal extremity of the clavicle. From there, it extends radially to the periphery and soon takes on the shape of a thin lamella, which gives the sternal end its form and gradually lends it the morphological characteristics that characterize it in the adult. It becomes welded to the body of the bone from ten to fifteen months after it appears, which is to say, from twenty-two to twenty-five years of age . . . (p. 312).

According to Pasteau (*Recherches sur les proportions de la clavicule dans les sexes et dans les races,* thèse de Paris 1879), the ratio of the length of the clavicle to that of the humerus figured over 100 would show an average of 44.42 in men and 45.04 in women of white races. The same ratios among Blacks are higher, to 44.67 and 46.38 (p. 313).

THE COMPANION OF SIRIUS

BAIZE. P. — Le Compagnon de Sirius, *Bull. de la Société astronomique de France,* 1931, p. 383-397.
 — Le Compagnon de Sirius, *Bull. de la Société astronomique de France,* 1932, p. 586.
 — Sirius en 1933, *Bull. de la Société astronomique de France,* 1933, p. 242.
 — Sirius en 1934, *Bull. de la Société astronomique de France,* 1934, p. 243-244.
 — Sirius en 1935, *Bull. de la Société astronomique de France,* 1936, p. 243.
 — Sirius en 1936, *Bull. de la Société astronomique de France,* 1936, p. 243.
 — Étoiles invisibles, *Bull. de la Société astronomique de France,* 1936, p. 473-474.
 — Sirius en 1937, *Bull. de la Société astronomique de France,* 1937, p. 242-243.
 — Sirius en 1938, *Bull. de la Sociéte astronomique de France,* 1938, p. 186-187.
SCHATZMAN. E. — Les naines blanches, *L'Astronomie,* 1956, 364-369.

We have taken from an article by Dr. P. Blaize, which appeared in September, 1931 in *l'Astronomie,* those passages dealing with the discovery, the orbit, the period of revolution and the density of the Companion of Sirius.

The discovery of the companion of Sirius.

For a long time astronomers had been noticing anomalies in Sirius' proper motion; this motion, well known since Halley's time is equal to $0.0375''$ in RA (Right Ascension) and to $1.207''$ in D, (Declination), which gives a yearly resultant motion of $1.32''$ in the direction of $204°$, which is noticeably to the south. In 1834, Bessel showed that the anomalies consisted mainly of deviations between the star's theoretical position and its actual position; these distinctly *periodic differences,* especially in right ascension, may be as great as 0.321'', which is a considerable amount with regard to meridian observations. Overall, instead of moving through space in a straight line, Sirius appears to display a wavy trajectory.

To explain the variations in Sirius' proper motion, Bessel posed the hypothesis in 1844[3] that they were *due to the attraction of an invisible companion*; this hypothesis was opposed by a certain number of astronomers of that period, notably by W. Struve (1847). However, in 1851, through a renewed discussion of the meridian observations, Peters confirmed Bessel's views and *calculated a theoretical orbit for the hypothetical companion star,* the principle elements of which are:

$$T = 1792.82 \qquad \underline{e} = 0.5647$$
$$P = 50 \text{ y. } .01 \qquad \underline{n} = 7.31°$$

In 1862, Auwers continued to study the irregularities in right ascension and declination; from discussion of 7,000 observations in RA and 4,500 in D, he found for the perturbing body an orbit very close to that of Peters, with a period of 49.5 years. The year before, Salford had arrived at similar results, working completely independently.

The work of Auwers had not yet been published when, on January 31, 1862, Alvan Clark discovered the satellite. On that night, with the help of his son, the famous optician was testing on Sirius a 0.46-meter objective (which has since been installed at the Dearborn Observatory); he immediately saw a small companion of approximately the tenth magnitude at 10'' from the main star, at a positional angle of 84.6°, while the angle deduced from the theoretical orbit of Peters was of 83.8°.

. . . In the years following his discovery, the companion of Sirius was the object of many measurements taken with large instruments and even, in some cases, with the help of medium power telescopes.

In this way, one could see the satellite describe an elliptical curve, reach its greatest elongation (at 60°) about 1874, then come closer to the main star from year to year, while the observation became more and more difficult. On April 22, 1890, at the 36-inch lens of the Lock observatory, Burnham noticed it for the last time, with extreme difficulty, at about 4'' and just to the north. During the years that followed, from 1890 to 1896, the companion remained lost in the light of Sirius and invisible even through the largest telescopes . . .[4]

. . . Presently, its greatest elongation has again passed and the satellite is approaching Sirius at the rate of about 0.25'' per year approximately.[4]

The spectral study of the companion star was made at Mount Wilson in 1914 by Adams and showed that it was not a red star but *rather a white or yellow-white star of the F type,* and closer to the A type than to the G (A7) with wide hydrogen bands and

---

3. P. Baize, Le Compagnon de Sirius, *Bull. de la Société astronomique de France,* 1931, p. 383-384.

4. p. 385.

abnormally weak metallic lines; all in all, quite different from the spectrum of Sirius (A0 type). This result was confirmed by Coblentz and Lampland.

Thus, the companion of Sirius is not a red star. M.A. Véronnet has suggested that it may be a *dark giant star* partially reflecting the light of Sirius. More importantly, however, with Eddington the hypothesis of a white dwarf, small in volume, but of extremely high density was arrived at; to prove this hypothesis, it was necessary to know the star's volume, i.e., in fact its actual diameter . . .[5]

. . . At last, Al. Vyssotsky has recently deduced from a series of photometric measurements made with the 26-inch telescope of the MacCormick Observatory, an apparent magnitude of (Sirius) B equal to 7.1 m., which is 1.3 m. stronger than that accepted from visual estimates. He then obtains for the companion a radius of notably stronger value (0.056 times that of the sun) and an average density equal to only 5,500 times that of the sun, at 8,000 times the density of water. However, Vyssotsky also suggests that the temperature of Sirius B is perhaps higher than 8,000°; he points out that the spectrum of 02 Eridani-B (A0 type), a white dwarf like the satellite of Sirius, is richer in radiations of short wave length than those of stars in the same class, and indicates a higher temperature, around 13,000°. The companion of Sirius might present the same peculiarity and the preceding diameter (0.056) would have to be greatly reduced, so that, even supposing Sirius B to be 7 m., one obtains a density quite close to the figure of 50,000, more or less accepted until now.[6]

---

5. pp. 392-393.
6. p. 394.

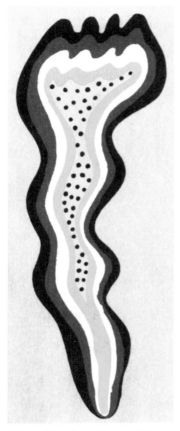

FIG. 43: Drawing of the great Nommo, *nommo die*.

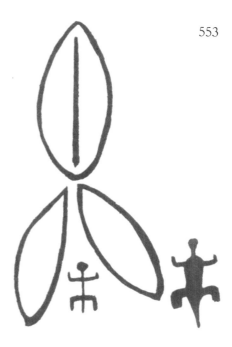

FIG. 55: Descent of Ogo's ark and of the *barankamaza dullogu*.

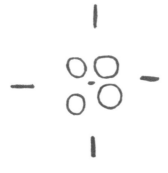

FIG. 56: Drawing of the *sene* "spinning the world."

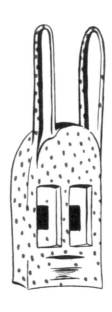

FIG. 69: The *dommo* mask.

554

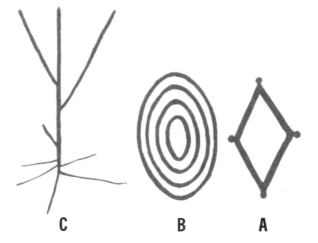

FIG. 70: Figures of the *sene:* A. *tonu* of the four elements of the *sene* seed;
B. *tonu* of the *sene* seed;
C. drawing of the tree of the *sene* seed.

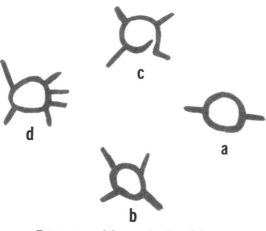

FIG. 71: *tonu* of the germination of the *sene*.

FIG. 73: Work of the spider in the *sene*.

FIG. 74: B. Drawing of the parts of the Fox's placenta (rock drawing) (H. 19 cm, W. 5 cm.)

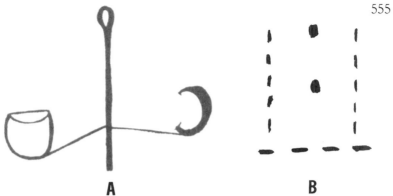

FIG. 79: Figures drawn under the altars *ommolo ana* (A) and *ommolo ya* (B).

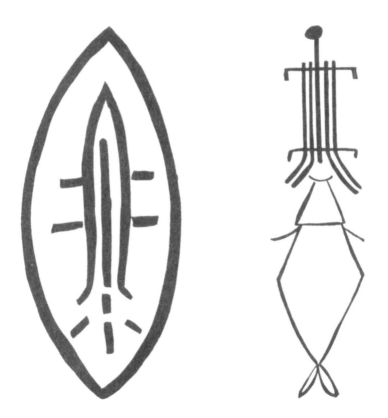

Fig. 81: *tonu* of the Fox's circumcision.   Fig. 82: Drawing of the Fox's circumcision.

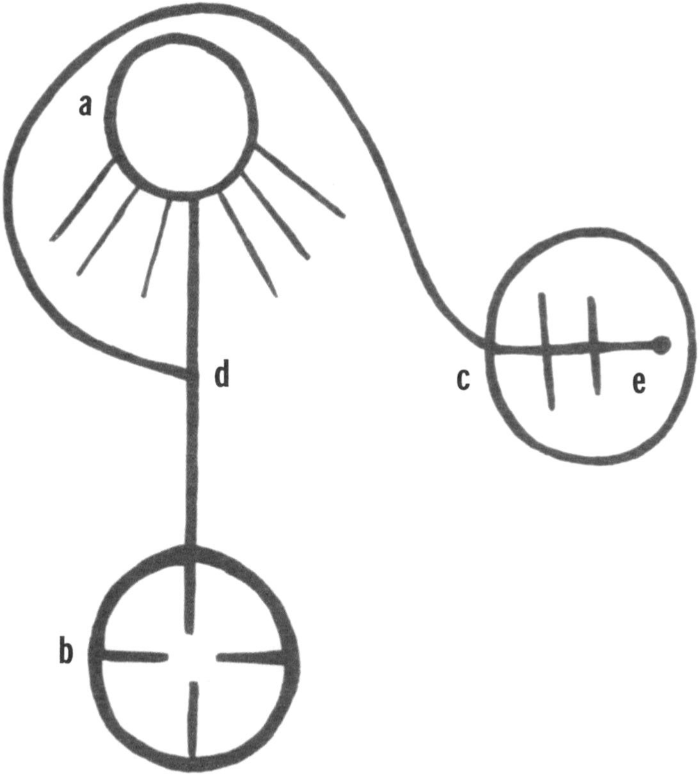

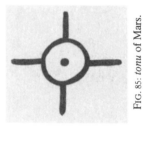

FIG. 91: Figure of the transformation of Ogo into the Fox.

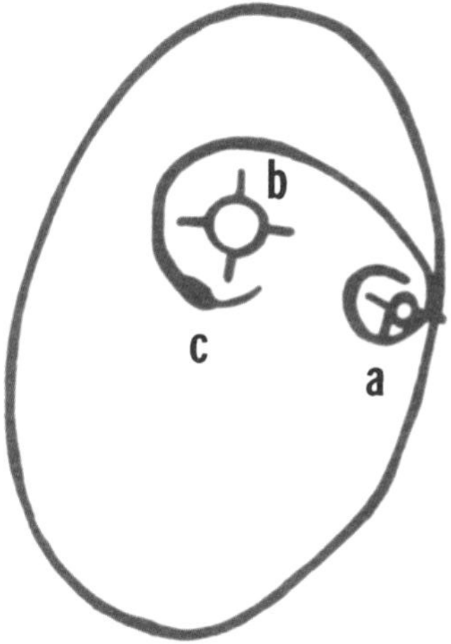

FIG. 88: *tonu* of the prevented marriage.

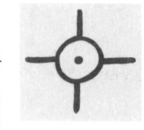

FIG. 85: *tonu* of Mars.

FIG. 86: *tonu* of the separation of the twins.

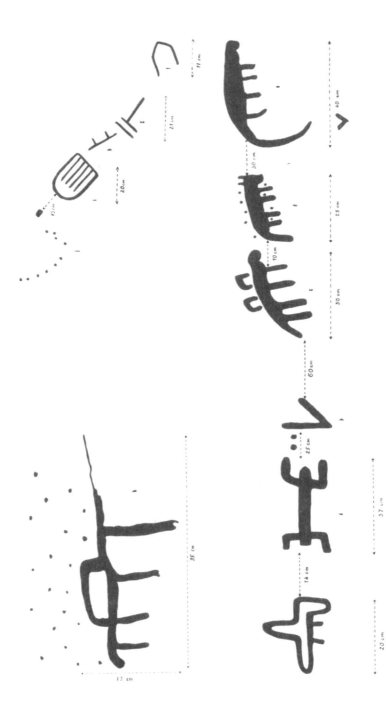

FIG. 931: Rock paintings of the cave *toy nama kommo donu.*

558

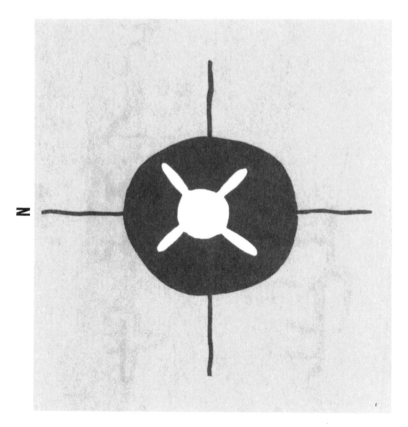

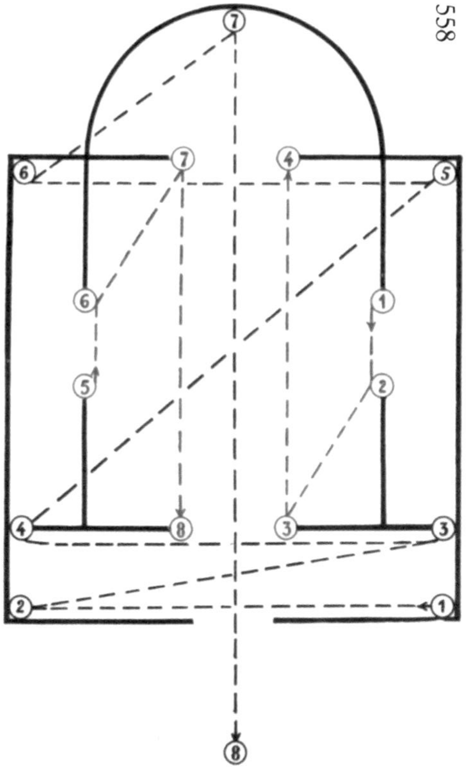

FIG. 122: Design of the *ginna*.

FIG. 109: Drawing of Sirius and of the sun made under the altar *para lebe* at its foundation.

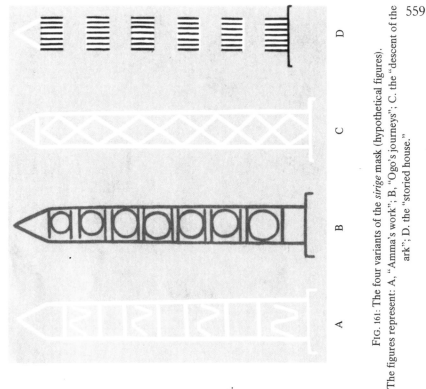

FIG. 161: The four variants of the *sirge* mask (hypothetical figures).
The figures represent: A, "Amma's work"; B, "Ogo's journeys"; C. the "descent of the ark"; D. the "storied house."

FIG. 128: *tonu* of the creation of woman and man.

FIG. 131: *tonu* of the *anagonno bile*.

FIG. 162: *yala, tonu,* and *toy* of *ie pelu tolo* (from right to left).

560

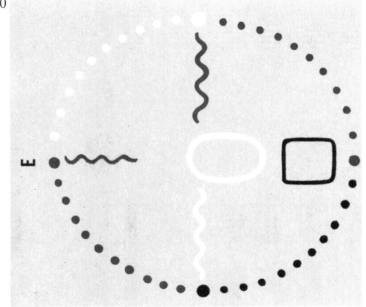

FIG. 191: Drawing of "*manna amma* below (which represents) Amma who brought people into the world."

E

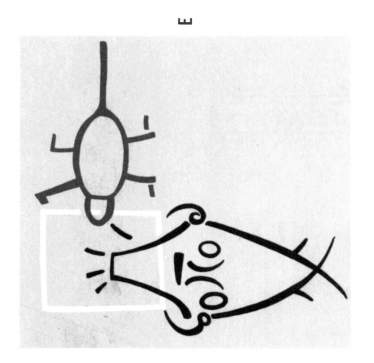

FIG. 165: Drawing of the *barankamaza* biting the ark.